One Foot in the Future

A Woman's Spiritual Journey

Nina Graboi

One Foot in the Future
Third Printing

Copyright ©2022 by Nina Grraboi

Published by
Epigraph Publishing Service
22 East Market Street, Suite 304
Rhinebeck, New York 12572
www.epigraphPS.com

Cover photo by David Jay Brown

Library of Congress Catalog Card Number: 2022904142
ISBN 978-1-954744-67-7

All rights reserved. No part of this publication may be reproduced, stored in a retrieval system, or transmitted in any form or by any means, electronic, mechanical, photocopying, recording, or otherwise without the prior written permission of the publisher.

All the events in this book are real, but some of the people are presented as composite characters in order to protect their privacy. The sequence of events is adapted accordingly.

ONE FOOT IN THE FUTURE

Prologue

There was a crunch as my vehicle scraped through a tunnel that was almost too narrow for passage. Miraculously, I emerged in the light. I was dazed and nearly unconscious. Something slapped against the rear of my vehicle and I cried out in pain. I nearly lost consciousness again while my vehicle passed through a rain storm and then entered a soft white cloud. After that, there was a pause where nothing happened.

My shock was beginning to wear off and I was able to think. I had to remember what brought me here. A habit so old that it was almost instinct made me go backwards to before I lost consciousness, and I suddenly knew. I had been on a spaceship, and now I was in the landing craft that had carried me from the mother ship to my destination. I had been unconscious during the long and boring descent, and now I had apparently arrived.

Anxiously, I checked my vehicle. Had it suffered from the violence of the landing? I knew that I myself was in no danger because I would be beamed up to the mother ship in case of vehicle failure. But to function on the planet, I had to depend on my craft.

I was very tired. I'm an experienced traveler, but there are certain planets where the landing is especially rough, no matter how often you go through it; and this, obviously, was one of them. Forcing myself to stay awake, I let my mind enter every part of my vehicle. Everything seemed to be in order.

Reassured, I fell asleep. I woke with a start. My vehicle was being refuelled. I noticed that it had some difficulty in assimilating the liquid because it gasped and choked. For a moment I panicked, but the native in attendance obviously knew what to do. She made some adjustments on the fuel pump and then lifted my craft to a vertical position while gently pounding on its back. Pretty soon, it emitted a sound that was greeted with delight by the attendant. After that, the fuel was absorbed without further difficulty.

Again, I was left alone. After a while, I noticed that my vehicle spontaneously emptied its waste materials, and that annoyed me. Now I would have to wait until the next time it was serviced to have the mess removed! I made a mental note to point this out to the attendant, who would no doubt know what to do.

My mind was hazy, my eyes unfocused. The drug that had kept me unconscious during the descent had not yet worn off. It was hard to stay awake, but something told me that I had to retrieve some vital information before it was too late. Too late? For what? I knew that my memory of my arrival would soon grow faint, and I had to remember…

I had been here before. There was a certain familiarity about the process of landing, but I couldn't recall the name of this place. Experience told me that my landing craft would supply me with the needed data. I therefore turned my attention to the vehicle and examined it with care.

A clue to its size had already been supplied. The native who had serviced it was much larger. Another clue was her pleasure at the burping sound. This proved that my vehicle was of the 6 type—cute and helpless, a form that appeals to the natives and evokes their desire to cherish and protect. Even the most brutish alien species were known to respond to it, and the Galactic Travel Agency had no doubt advised me to take this form of craft as a precaution against a dangerous and potentially violent native population.

This told me something about the planet on which I found myself, but not enough. I continued to investigate my craft. I took stock of its openings (I counted eight), its inner workings (the plumbing was crowded into a very small space), and its general appearance. It was soft, and responded instantly to my telepathic commands. I was beginning to think of it more as a space suit than a vehicle, and then I suddenly knew: it was a body; and I was on a world where bodies are worn, and where warfare and violence are the rules.

The only safe way to enter such a world was in the shape of a new-born baby, defenseless, helpless, cute.

I still didn't remember the name of the planet, but I knew enough. The prospect was bleak. I went to sleep.

I was awakened by my own crying. The awareness of great discomfort had pierced through the thick layers of my sleep and I suddenly felt helpless and weak. I understood that these feelings originated in the body, and that I would henceforth experience all its experiences as if they were mine.

AS IF they were mine. Here lay the danger and the challenge of my visit to this planet: not to forget the as if. Not to drown in the body's embrace—not to forget who I am.

I was picked up, relieved of the matter my body had discharged, and carried to my mother, whose breasts supplied the fuel that my body craved. After the feeding, I was anxious to be left alone. I managed to keep the drowsiness that threatened to enfold me at bay long enough to pursue my thoughts. Again, I brought myself back to the space ship and remembered how I had inspected my landing craft before the descent. My luggage had included many vehicles of varied forms. I was on an extended tour of the universe. My schedule called for a great number of stops, and it was vitally important to be on time for arrivals and departures. I looked for the alarm system that is built into type 6 vehicles. It was not there. I was about to communicate this negligence to headquarters when I remembered that it had been left out at my request.

The alarm system is almost never left out of type 6 vehicles. The Galactic Travel Agency strongly advises against it. Our history books show that only a handful of travelers have been foolish enough not to take this advice, and almost all of them had unfortunate experiences. Yet I, while going along with the baby shape, had chosen to leave it out. The alarm system is the planned obsolescence factor that humans call death. My schedule was very precise, and a delayed departure would mess things up no end.

As I lay between feedings, diaper changes, spongings and colic attacks, I knew that I had to discover my reason for leaving the death factor out. I strained to remember my previous visits to this planet. My first visit! What fun it had been! I had thrilled to each smell, each touch, each intoxicating sight this new planet offered to me. After the initial difficulties in learning how to navigate a body, I became an expert. For my subsequent visits, I chose increasingly finely tuned and attractive vehicles. This allowed me to explore all the sensual pleasures of the body and all its delights. In those days,

iii

I thought I would never grow tired of the body-body trip; but I did.

There followed a series of unprepossessing bodies, because now I wished to explore the mind. On my next visit, I learned about the rewards and punishments of this lovely, cruel planet. I cried out that I never wanted to return, but I came back again, and again…

Throughout my initial visits, there had been a total absence of memory of my past. This never failed to amaze me when I reviewed my stay upon my return to the mother ship. On later visits, I became increasingly aware of something nagging at me, something lost, something that was just beyond my reach… Gradually, I began to resist the conditioning forced upon me by the natives, and my last series of visits was spent pursuing the goal of self-remembering. It was then that I discovered that the "natives" were all space travelers who had forgotten their true identity.

All these memories came in brief flashes. The break-through was never complete. One day, as I was nibbling my toes to test their resilience, it suddenly came to me: I had decided to leave the alarm system out of my craft because I wanted to try, on this visit, to remember my schedule without its help. I felt sure that I could do this. Headquarters had tried to dissuade me, in vain. When they saw that I was determined to go through with it, they gave me their blessing.

I outlined my ideas and my goals to the Galactic Travel Agency, and they mapped out the exact time and place of my splash-down. The influences that would surround me, the opportunities that would come my way, and the obstacles I would have to surmount were all carefully charted. The whole thing was translated into an astrological blueprint for my body, my personality, and the general outlines of events during my visit; and the building of my body was begun.

Once I had made all the arrangements, the entire matter had slipped from my mind while I directed my attention to the next stop on my schedule, a planet far different from planet Earth.

I arrived at this point in my recollections by slow, laborious stages. My time was taken up with feedings, baths, tiresome and often painful visits to the doctor, and the coochie-cooing of relatives and friends. Most of my efforts were spent trying to orient myself and to relearn to live in a body. I studied the signals my parents gave me and slowly reacquired the necessary skills.

ONE FOOT IN THE FUTURE

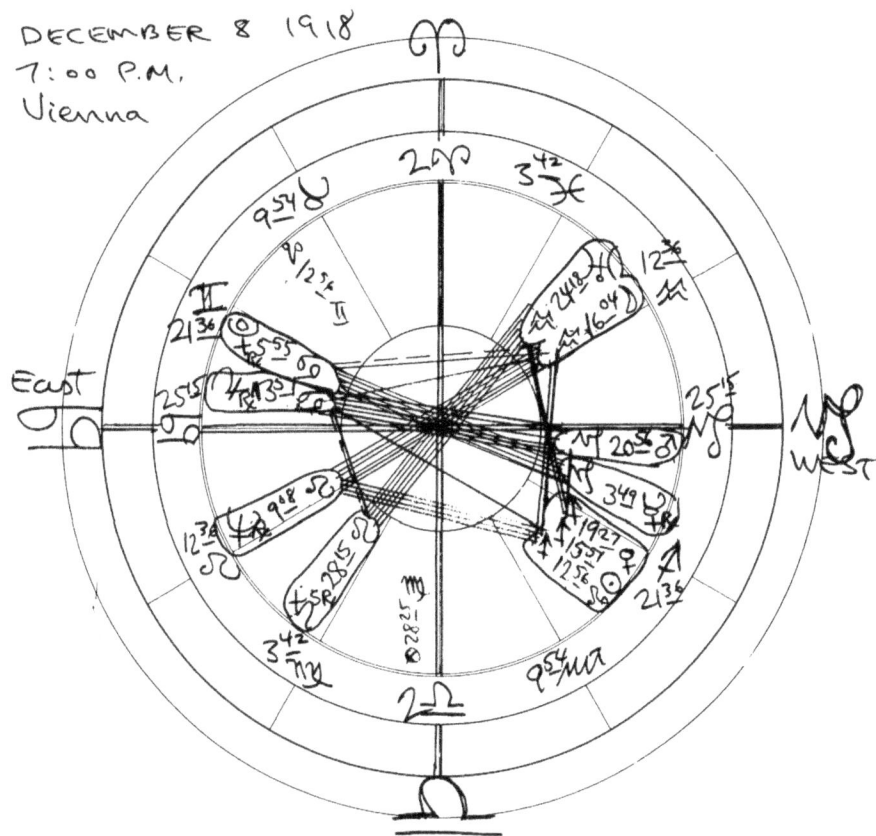

My parents and siblings did not know me as my real self. To them, I was a newborn baby, not the seasoned tourist who had often been here before. The smallness of my body and the fact that I could not yet walk and talk made them treat me like a moron.

Remembering from before that this was inevitable, I made the best of their clumsy but well-meaning attempts to teach me and resigned myself to their ministrations. I did enjoy being picked up and fondled, and I soon discovered that I could bring my mother or elder siblings running to my crib when I cried. Then they would take me in their arms, sing to me, rock me, and entertain me

with a toy.
   I was a girl.
   They called me Gusti.
   The place of my birth was Vienna, Austria, the planet Earth.

Part One

ONE FOOT IN THE FUTURE

One

Throughout my youth, I carried within me a jubilant awareness of my good fortune to have been born on the edge of the modern age. All that lay behind me seemed to have been lived in ignorance. Even the recent 19th century, compared to the glories of the 20th, appeared benighted. I thought of those who had toiled in a world without refrigerators, telephones and vacuum cleaners, and I was happy to be alive at a time when the spirit of democracy was replacing feudal serfdom.

I was also certain that, just as the material aspects of life had been immensely bettered by the new technology, so human nature would be bettered in that future that lay around the edge of tomorrow, when everyone's survival needs would be assured and there would be no more need for fighting.

I was born at the end of World War I. My conception was an accident. It happened while my father was on furlough. I was the youngest of four. My birth took place in Mother's big brass bed, which, twin to my father's, stood in their spacious bedroom that later also held my crib.

We lived in the Leopoldstadt, Vienna's second district, where it borders on the fashionable first. Further away, the Leopoldstadt was the Jewish ghetto. Our street housed mostly prosperous, assimilated Jews who had broken with the old customs. Culturally, my parents inhabited a borderland between ghetto and assimilation. Unlike the Jews whose parents and grandparents had been born in Austria, they kept a kosher home, but we children were allowed to eat non-kosher food as long as we kept it from contaminating Mama's dishes. We were forbidden to ride a vehicle, turn on a light, or write on the Sabbath, and Papa prayed every morning wrapped in his prayer shawl; but he and Mother went to the synagogue only twice a year, on the high holidays.

Both of my parents were born in Polish ghettos. At age thirteen, my father ran away from home and made his way to Germany. After some years of doing odd jobs, he became interested in photography, then in its infancy. He somehow managed to save enough money to buy a bulky camera, a heavy wooden tripod, and a black leather case filled with photographic plates, and proceeded to set himself up as a publisher of picture postcards.

Family myth has it that he kicked off this venture by renting a large field outside of town and persuading a stunt pilot to give an exhibition. He split the admission money with the pilot, and with the balance commissioned the printing of postcards bearing the photos he took of the event. These found a ready market, and Kunstverlag Schreyer was launched.

In her youth, my mother had been a doe-eyed beauty. Her parents moved to Germany when she was in her teens. My father was introduced into her family by a shadchen, the traditional Jewish marriage broker, who brought him there to meet Klara, Mother's elder sister. The story goes that he took one look at Mother and knew that she was for him. After their marriage, they moved to Austria and settled down in Vienna.

By the time I came along, Mama's nerves had been strained by the cares of bringing up my three siblings by herself while Father served in the army. She was sometimes impatient with me, but her nature was warm, generous and gentle, and her sense of humor was easily aroused. Despite her lack of formal education, she was highly intelligent and enjoyed long talks with my brother, who studied law at the University of Vienna. Her looks remained amazingly youthful. The last time I saw her, she was in her late fifties and hardly had a grey hair or a wrinkle.

Pictures of my father in the uniform of the Austrian cavalry show a tall, slender man whose handsome face is crowned by a shock of black hair that sets off his dark, flashing eyes. He was decorated with the Iron Cross of Merit and served as X-ray technician after a thigh wound inflicted by a kick from his horse.

There are romantic tales of a Hungarian countess who fell in love with him, and of my mother confronting her and making a row. But this happened before I was born, and my memory of my parents includes occasionally hearing their raised voices behind closed doors, but no scenes of jealousy.

My arrival was greeted with great affection by my parents and siblings. Papa called me his peace child because my birth came shortly after the end of the war. In my pre-school days, he never came home without a gift for me. There were foil-wrapped bon-bons in gold mesh nets, hand-painted Easter eggs, chocolate Santa Clauses, small dolls, shells. These gifts lent enchantment to my days. What I liked best about them was the element of surprise.

Hearing Papa's key in the lock, I would rush to the door and call excitedly, "Papa, what did you bring me today?" With a secretive smile, he made an elaborate ritual of searching through his briefcase, while I waited in an agony of suspense. Not unexpectedly, I became so spoiled after a while that I had fits of temper if he came home empty-handed, and Mama put a stop to Papa's surprises.

At bedtime, my eldest sister Dolly told me fairy tales. When she ran out of them, I made her shake more out of her sleeve. She often played the piano and sang Schubert songs, and there was one in particular that I both dreaded and adored. It was about an old organ grinder who stood outside the city gate and cranked his hurdy-gurdy with his cold, stiff hands. It seemed to me that I heard the wind howl and saw the snow fall on the bent figure in the threadbare coat.

This image and the sad, beautiful melody never failed to drive me to tears. As soon as Dolly struck the first chord I would run out of the room and stand with my ear pressed to the closed door, sobbing.

Fanny was seven years older than I. She was headstrong, impish, and endless fun. When she grew towards her teens, she often found herself saddled with a kid sister who worshipfully tagged after her. She took it in good grace, teasing me and showering me with affection in the same breath. In a sense, it was she who brought me up, and my childhood memories of her are more vivid than those of my mother. Sometimes she took me to the Hauptallee, one of Vienna's lovely parks where shady walks are flanked by chestnut trees. Dropping me off at the children's playground, she disappeared with her friends after making me swear not to tell Mama about the presence of boys in her crowd. Innocent as her activities were, my parents regarded all contact with boys as sinful before marriage.

My parents were an anachronism in post-World War I in Vienna. It was the era of the vamp. Marlene Dietrich, Jean Harlow and our own Austrian movie stars held up a model of femininity that was a far cry from the virginal maidens of an earlier day. In my teens, the girls I knew spoke of giving themselves to a man; holding out for a wedding band was in poor taste. Most of them probably never went quite that far, for virginity was still highly prized by marriagable males who themselves busily sowed their "wild oats." But the anxious and suspicious eyes my parents kept on their nubile daughters were out of step with the times.

The dining room windows of our apartment faced a courtyard enclosed by three other buildings. I spent endless hours by the window observing the life below. Sometimes street musicians came, singly or in groups. If they played well, heads would appear in the windows, and coins wrapped in newspaper would hit the pavement with a plop.

When the weather was warm, Papa sometimes took me to Vienna's famous amusement park, the Prater. Putting me on a merry-go-round horse, he would wave happily to me each time I spun around, while I, perched miserably on my garishly painted steed, tried to conceal the motion sickness that gripped me whenever I sat in, or on, a moving object. "Well? How did you like it?" he would ask when the ride was over. "It was lovely," I would say, trying to sound enthusiastic. His pleasure at giving me this treat was so great that I could not bear to disappoint him. In the wintertime, when the Prater was closed, he pulled my sled through the soft, powdery snow. How proud I was of that tall, strong man! No matter what happened to me, I was certain that he would protect me and keep me from all harm.

The floor below ours was occupied by Helga's family. She was a slow, stolid child the same age as I. Her large, languorous mother was generally seated at her dressing table. Powder puff in hand, she was surrounded by a cloud of Coty. The sight of a Coty box, whose distinctive white and gold design has not changed in all these years, is inextricably linked in my memory with buxom blondes whose dressing gowns open to expose large, white breasts. I loved looking inside the wardrobes and chests in Helga's immaculate apartment, where clothes hung in fragrant rows, shoes stood flawlessly aligned, and lavender-scented linen was ranged in dazzling white piles. Even at that tender age I was aware of the contrast this formed to the more haphazard arrangements in my home. Four children of assorted ages and genders are not conducive to a flawlessly tidy household, and ours was always in somewhat a state of disarray.

One floor above lived Georgie, a fragile, adenoidal boy who often had to stay home from school. I was as fond of the candies his mother produced for us from the sideboard as of the rocking chair that belonged to Georgie's grandfather. Afternoons, while the old gentleman took his stroll, we turned the chair upside down and it became a ship sailing to far-off places, or Ali Baba's cave, or Rapunzel's tower.

It was a time when even the children of the well-to-do had few toys. We learned to improvise with whatever we had at hand. For hours, I would amuse myself with rows of empty cartons. Standing them on end, I arranged them in a circle and played counting-out games. The cartons became doll's beds lined with silk scraps from Mama's rag bag, or fortresses, or towers. The few toys I possessed were treasures. For years I cherished a doll that had a broken nose and only one arm.

I was six years old when my brother Oscar took his first trip to the Near East. The handsome young law student was a romantic figure as he set out with his rucksack on his back. For protection, he carried a toy pistol that was shaped like the real thing but shot corks instead of bullets. With this, he meant to scare off would-be assailants. When he returned, he set out the exotic objects he brought back in the dining room. Wrapped in a cloud of smoke that issued from a tall water pipe, he sat cross-legged on the red plush couch and told me about his "adventures." The dimly lit room filled with Turks whose white teeth gleamed in the dark. A knife flashes and is ready to strike, but once more Oscar's cork pistol saves his life. Camels cross the desert and take him to a cave where, after a brush with a deadly snake, he finds the ancient potsherds I am reverently fingering. Shivering with delight and terror, I hang on to his every word and beg him to take me to the Near East when I grow up.

Neither of us knew then that the real life adventures awaiting me would put even his make-believe ones to shame. But in the meanwhile, I was still cozily ensconced in a home that provided a rich, nourishing soil for my growth and gave me a strength and security that rarely deserted me in later years.

One of my pastimes was watching the dust motes dance in the sun rays that filtered through the window in the hall. Another was walking, precariously balanced, on a low stone wall in the Stadtpark, another one of Vienna's splendid parks. There was the open-air Christmas market outside the St. Stefans Cathedral, and the solemn yet opulent splendor within. There were Sunday excursions to the Vienna woods, and summers spent in the Austrian Alps where I found secret hiding places in the woods and played with the local peasant children.

My most vivid childhood memories have to do with nature. My brother tells me that my first word was not Mama but "umi," short for the German word Blume (flower). To this day, flowers have remained a passion. I remember the smell of moist leaves in the woods, the rapture of tasting the wild strawberries I picked, the sound of cowbells on hilly pastures.

I can still feel my excitement when the radio arrived in my parents' home. I couldn't have been older than two or three. The presence of that magical box in my life was a source of endless delight; it gave me the assurance that the unseen exists. So did the phonograph, and the telephone, which was installed when I was four. The miracles of technology must have been in wealthier homes well before they came to mine, but for me, the sense of their miraculousness continued for a long time.

Cars were still rare. To own one was a sign of affluence. I was seven when Dolly married a man who owned a car. The memory of the Sundays when the whole family went for an outing in the canvas-topped Mercedes-Benz still lingers. My brother-in-law, who was not built on the heroic model, became a god in my eyes as he steered the clumsy vehicle through the narrow side streets of Vienna.

When I entered first grade, boys and girls were in separate but adjacent buildings. That year, more girls than the class could hold were registered to begin school, and it was decided to place the six whose names came last in the alphabet in the boys' class. I was one of them. At first, this was a heavy blow;

it made me feel odd and different from the 'regular' girls. But the advantages of the arrangement soon became apparent.

Miss Probst, my teacher, was a sunny, attractive young woman whom we all adored. Chivalry was still considered a necessary part of male education, and Miss Probst urged the boys to be little gentlemen. For the next two years, 22 boys fought over who could help me into my coat and carry my school satchel. During recess, Miss Probst often took me to the room where the teachers gathered and asked me to dance, sing, or recite a poem. She obviously enjoyed showing me off to her colleagues.

My progress in school was sadly lacking. There seemed no need to learn such boring things as the three R's. Walter, the best student in class, faithfully filled my slate with his fine, even writing while I played jump rope, diavolo and tag in the park; so why bother? Miss Probst must have been aware of the deception, but if she ever scolded me, it left no impression.

The world was my oyster, I could do no wrong. Grown-ups crooned over me in the street, I was in demand at neighborhood weddings as flower girl, and twice a year I was the star of the student performances in school. There was applause, and from my parents and the boys in class there were flowers and boxes of candy.

My 'leading man' was Herbert, two years my senior. His family name was Engel (angel), and it fit him well. I thought he was the most beautiful boy who ever lived. A romance between us was encouraged by his charming and amused young mother, who called me her daughter-in-law. The wife of a wealthy jeweler, she sometimes picked us up in her chauffeur-driven car and toyed with my curly hair while I contentedly nestled in her lap, inhaling her lovely perfume.

Arrived at my house, Herbert would escort me to the foot of the stairs, click his heels, and bow. Children of that era were taught manners early. Herbert's may appear somewhat excessive in view of our tender years, but I myself never failed to curtsy to adults—a habit so deeply ingrained that I even curtsied while talking on the telephone. My idyll with Herbert provided my siblings much entertainment. They called me "Frau Engel," and I was sure Herbert and I would be married when we grew up.

While most of my memories from that period are happy ones, there were painful moments too. I have a poignant memory of sobbing over a broken doll which involves my mother's laughing voice saying, "I should have your worries!" I can still feel the heartbreak of that moment, and I still believe that my bereavement was as deep and real as that of an adult over the loss of a loved one.

Two

In the years that followed, I was to become familiar with sorrow. When I was eight, an abrupt change took place in my life. I was transferred to the girls' school, and suddenly, without warning, I found myself in a hostile, cruel world.

My new teacher disliked me from the first. My reading and writing skills were woefully inadequate, and she enjoyed calling on me to read aloud. Her sarcasm provoked the happy tittering of my classmates who, with her implicit approval, baited me mercilessly. At first, I tried to win them with the cute tricks that had been so successful with the boys, but that made things only worse.

I discovered that relations between boys and girls were not the pot of honey they had been for me. There was open warfare between the sexes. The girls left the schoolhouse in tight, defensive groups, ready to scream for help or run. Some of the rowdier boys lurked outside the door and tripped the first girl that emerged, yanked the next one's braids, and snatched the school satchel of another while the rest hurriedly passed by. Boys were the enemy, and the fact that I walked home with some of my former classmates did not help my popularity with the girls.

Before long, they added whispering behind my back to their overt teasing. Wild, incomprehensible stories about things I was supposed to be doing with the boys—especially with Herbert, who continued to wait for me every day—were circulated loud enough for me to hear. The source of the anatomical description that embellished these tales was Zillie, a girl who was neither too bright nor too clean, but knew things the sheltered middle-class girls did not know. She enjoyed a sudden popularity, and her graphic, though highly inaccurate description of the sex act was lent hair-raising realism by focusing on Herbert and me.

The next few years are too shrouded in misery for any clear memory. I don't know when I stopped seeing Herbert and the other boys. I couldn't hold out against the girls' taunts. I remember a red beret that I wore jauntily tilted over one eye at the beginning of the school year. It became an instrument of torture. The girls seized it and used it as a ball, while I desperately tried to catch it.

My chief tormenter was Gerda, the class favorite. A neat and efficient girl, her homework was always free of the mysterious blotches that seemed to attach themselves to mine. While not an exemplary student, she was a "good girl" in the teacher's eyes, who allowed her to get away with much that would have been punished had any of the rest of us done it. This, plus her natural boldness, put her in a position of leadership, and she used it to incite the others to the cruel sport they had with me.

Though Mama scolded me when she saw the torn and muddied cap, I told no-one at home about the humiliation I experienced in school. The only bright spot in those years were the summer and winter vacations we spent in the Austrian Alps and at seaside resorts in Italy and Yugoslavia.

Soon after the transfer to the girls' school, my reading skills improved spectacularly. I learned to read with a vengeance. Books became the focal point of my life, a world where I was infinitely more at home than in the real, everyday one. From fairy tales by the Grimm Brothers and by Hans Christian Anderson, I graduated to tales of Greek mythology written for children. I was as thrilled by the gods' exploits as by their ringing names. "Aphrodite!" I would intone. "Hephaestos! Minotaur! Apollo!"

I must have been nine or ten when I first discovered Karl May. It was Georgie who brought him to my attention.

"I'm reading a great book," he told me. "I think you'd like it too."

"What's it about?" I asked, eager as always for new reading material.

"It's called Winnetou," he said. "It's about a redskinned Indian chief. Lots of adventures. You'll like it," he repeated. He was probably remembering our adventures with the inverted rocking chair.

With Winnetou began an obsession that did not stop until I had read all, or most, of Karl May's books. About half of them take place in some unspecified middle-eastern locale, the other half in America. The author, who died in 1912, was said to have written most of his books in prison. He never left his native Germany, but his descriptions of foreign customs and exotic lands conveyed a sense of great authenticity. The adventures he invented held the interest of his readers, mostly adolescent boys, but there was an added dimension, something I can only call nobility, that distinguished his heroes from the cardboard heroes of other adventure books.

It was fifty years later, long after I had forgotten Karl May, that a new book on the science fiction shelf of my favorite bookstore caught my eye. The cover showed a seated man; his hands, palms up and thumb and index finger touching, resting on his wide-spread knees. His eyes are closed, his expression is serene. Two wing-like extensions flank his shoulders, and within each of these, on a background of flames, a human head can be seen. The one on the left seems anguished, while the one on the right looks at peace.

Intrigued by the psychedelic cover, I looked more closely. The author's name was Karl May! The title of the book was Ardistan and Djinnistan, and when I picked it up, I saw comments by Hermann Hesse, Albert Einstein and Albert Schweitzer on the fly leaf. It appeared that Karl May had had a deep impact on them in their youth. "Pretty good company my long-ago me kept!" I thought. The price of the book was more than I could easily afford, but I bought it. To my amazement, it affected me as strongly as it had long ago. I was surprised to find that what made me tick in my youth had not changed nearly as much as I had believed.

It was books like this that shaped my ideals and my aspirations, not what I learned in school. But these same books also got me in trouble. Mama was not pleased to see me turn into a bookworm.

"Why don't you go out and play?" she asked, and "Why don't you do your homework?" she chided when it became obvious that my performance in school was poor.

"I will," I said, without raising my eyes from the book I was reading. How dull school was compared to the worlds the books opened up! To escape Mama's reproaches, I began to read late into the night. But the light in my room did not escape her sharp eyes.

"No more reading at night!" she told me. "It's hard enough to get you out of bed even when you've had a full night's sleep. If you don't turn off your light at nine, I'll have to take your books away!"

"Yes, Mama," I replied. "Don't worry, I'll stop." A little white lie couldn't hurt, I reasoned. I was determined to go on reading, but didn't want to get into an argument that would prove to be a deadlock. From then on, I took a flashlight under the covers and went on reading undisturbed.

"What is it with this Karl May?" Mama asked, picking up a book from my desk. "You read him all the time. So what does he write about, your Karl May?"

I had long waited for this opening and launched into an enthusiastic account.

"So what's so interesting about all these adventures with uncivilized people?" she said. "Why do you waste your time on that nonsense instead of learning something useful? Read the classics! Or history! Or practice the piano! We spend all that money on your lessons and you don't even practice!" Despite her love and the indulgence she usually showed me, she was exasperated by her youngest who was so different from her other children.

The principal of my school was Frau Friedmann, a warm, intelligent, but nervous woman in her mid-forties. Austria had a socialist government at the time. Neither Jews nor women were discriminated against, and since Frau Friedmann was both, her position as school principal shows that the regime was remarkably advanced.

Frau Friedmann often shook her head when she saw me. "A pity," she would say. "You could be an all A student if you tried."

"Oh no, I couldn't!" I replied with conviction. If she knew how much I hate school, I thought, she'd understand that I have no desire to try.

But I could not escape into the world of my books all the time. The teacher and the taunts of my classmates had to be faced. I dreaded their cruelty as much as I desired to be accepted by them, and this put me in a double-bind that made each schoolday a fierce ordeal.

Sometimes, a question addressed to me by the teacher found me in the middle of my favorite fantasy: I grew taller and taller, until my head touched the ceiling. Below, the teacher and my classmates cowered in terror. With a thunderous voice, I roared, "I could crush you all under my heel! But this time I will spare you. In the future, you'd better remember who I am, or I shall squash you like bugs!"

I don't remember the name of the fairy tale that inspired this fantasy, but today I can only smile at the comforting certainty that not only the others but I myself would know who I was once my body grew tall. Not surprisingly, the teacher's question found me mute; it wasn't easy to shrink to my normal size in a matter of seconds. While I stood open-mouthed trying to gather my wits, the others dissolved into gales of laughter, and Gerda, the good girl, smugly replied in my place.

Eventually, my need for approval drove me to become the class clown. Sometimes Gerda and her court consented to be amused, and I was allowed to tag after them to the playground. But the shy, warm feeling of being one of the group often ended in renewed persecution.

For a while, an uneasy balance was maintained. The tolerance the girls showed me emboldened me to tell them about my beloved books. My desire to share this wonderful world with them was as great as my need to belong. But the ridicule and scorn I drew proved nearly too much for me. I had prolonged bouts of illness, could not be roused in the morning to go to school, clammed up, grew sullen, and buried myself in books.

My family was alarmed. One day, my sister Fanny found me sobbing. At her probing, the story of my school life spilled out. She took me in her arms.

"Stop crying," she said, stroking my hair. "I'll tell you how you can beat them at their own game." She exuded self-confidence. I was convinced of her ability to cope with all of life's crises.

"How?" I asked, feeling better already.

"To begin with, don't wear your heart on your sleeve. Toughen up! If the girls make fun of you, go them one better. It's easy, once you learn how. You're smarter than most of them. It won't take you long."

She was right. I began to watch the popular girls and saw that their power lay in their ability to subdue the others with cutting, mocking remarks. Within a year, my quick-witted sarcasm earned me the fear of my former enemies; by and by, I rose to the position of opinion-maker. The persona I was building had excellent survival value in a world where it seemed dangerous to reveal my innermost thoughts, and where the high ideals in my books were ridiculed, while insensitivity and cruelty paid off.

My friendship with Gerda, once my worst tormentor, began when we were twelve years old. At first, my new mask won her respect. With the onset of puberty, she began to read romantic novels. Soon, instead of the taunts we threw at each other, we were talking about books. She was as prosaic as I was fanciful, and as practical-minded as I was idealistic. As we neared adolescence, we grew into the intimacy of shared secrets. She had been mainly responsible for the persona I formed, and it was she with whom I now could be most openly myself.

Gerda's family had lived in Austria for generations. Her numerous aunts, uncles and cousins were assimilated Jews whose lifestyle was typical for the Viennese middle class. They enjoyed frequent visits to the theater, opera, and concerts, and set much more liberal standards for Gerda than my puritanical parents did for me.

Gerda played the piano beautifully, and our friendship gave new impetus to my own playing. I had been taking lessons regularly from the age of six. My teacher was a frail, white-haired lady who had a tendency to drift off into catnaps during lessons. Blessed with a good ear for music, it was easy for me to pretend to be reading the notes when in reality I was playing the simple tunes by ear. This deception became a stumbling block to further progress, until my admiration for Gerda's sight reading forced me to resume my studies.

For the next few years, Gerda and I were inseparable. We shared chocolate bars and intimate secrets. Our friendship was severely tested when Leo, the dashing boy who was "going" with Gerda, confessed that he was really in love with me. For a few days, she avoided me. In the end, we looked deeply into each other's eyes and vowed that no mere boy could come between us. Neither of us ever saw Leo again.

I was twelve years old when I won 1st prize in a competition run by the children's section of Vienna's leading newspaper, Der Tag. The story I wrote was full of flying machines, push-buttons and robots. It was my first attempt at writing science fiction and would remain the last until half a century later, when my excitement with technological miracles had been replaced by excitement over the miracles of human consciousness. For my story, I was awarded a fountain pen with a gold nib. It was my proudest possession, despite the ink blots it spit on my homework.

Compulsory education ended after eight years in the school system of the Vienna of that time. Accordingly, I graduated from High School at the age of fourteen. In the same year, I was confirmed at the Temple where I had gone for religious instructions. I had already decided that a belief in God was a hang-over from the dark ages, and the prayer I was to recite at the ceremony placed me in a moral dilemma over which I agonized for weeks. It was long and dramatic, and I loved the sonorous sound of the words, but the pledge to the God of my fathers which they contained forced me to lie. In the end, vanity won out over truthfulness, but my inner struggle showed in my voice as I intoned the fateful words. This only added to the effectiveness of my performance, and I received much praise from family and friends for the sincerity of my devotion to God.

Three

In my youth, I aspired to culture, elegance, sophistication. Vienna's atmosphere was permeated with these qualities, but they seemed always beyond my grasp. The language school I went to after high school was frequented by the daughters of well-to-do families. Here they marked time before the brilliant match that was expected of them. The social circles that now opened up for me promised the longed-for refinement, but below the surface polish I soon discerned the cynicism and the emptiness that was glossed over by the proverbial Viennese charm. The culture, grown brittle with age, had deteriorated into a facade, an empty form that was propped up by the self-satisfaction and arrogance of a people that considered the world outside Vienna barbaric.

The Vienna of my youth was jaded like an old roué. The beauty of her parks, her palaces and her tree-lined boulevards was rendered more charming to the eye by the patina of age. Intellectually and artistically she was in a constant fervor, but it seemed to produce nothing more than constantly repeated echoes of the past. On her stages, maudlin sentimentality alternated with razor-sharp sarcasm. The Viennese's enjoyment of poking fun at everything seems to be as inbred a characteristic as the womanizing of the Italian, the courtliness of the Japanese, and the verbal delirium of the Irish.

In the cabarets, the comedians poked savage fun at the Hitler regime in neighboring Germany. The Nazis were pictured as clowns, yokels, their ideas sheer nonsense; and the possibility that Austria could join Germany was laughed off. The Jews felt secure. Their role in the intellectual, artistic, and financial life of the city was firmly entrenched. They dominated the theater, the newspapers, literature, and the arts. While anti-semitism was never entirely absent from Vienna, it was held in check by the obvious power the Jews held. What overt anti-semitism I encountered was directed against the ghetto Jews whose kaftans and side-locks set them apart. Even to the assimilated Jews themselves they looked like an alien race.

In general, I was not troubled by my Jewish birth throughout my early youth. I knew that the Nazis hated us, but my aunt and uncle who lived in Germany made no plans to leave, and the rumors of Nazi atrocities did not seem real to me. I was absorbed by different matters.

Like most educated people of that time, I called myself an atheist. Contemporary literature, plays and movies steered clear of questions of faith, and from the time when, as a six-year old, God had failed to punish me for some disobedience, I had been sure that He did not exist. But despite this conviction, the question of the meaning of life occupied me greatly. Great authors who had written before my time clearly believed in a higher power. And then there was Lilo, a girl I was friendly with in school.

Lilo was a tall, long-legged girl with large, grey eyes fringed with long black lashes. An air of mystery surrounded her. It had to do with her parents being divorced. The girls whispered about her in class, and this drew me to her. Not too long ago I, too, had been whispered about.

"Will you come for tea on Sunday?" Lilo asked one day. "I'd like you to meet my mother."

I looked forward to the day with eagerness and apprehension. A divorcee was such a rarity that I half expected to meet a scarlet woman. Within minutes, the dark-haired, slender woman put me at ease. Her clothes were more colorful and less fashionably severe than those of the other mothers, and her manner was warm and friendly.

"Lilo tells me you read a lot," she said as she poured the tea. "Tell me, what kind of books do you like best?"

"Many kinds. I love to read books in the original now that I'm getting more fluent in French and English. I like Dreiser, Sinclair Lewis, Gallsworthy, André Maurois, Somerset Maugham, Colette, H.G. Wells, Hermann Hesse, Thomas Mann, Franz Werfel…"

"That's enough," Lilo's mother smiled. "I can see we have a bookworm here. I love to read too. Perhaps you'd like to take a look at my books after tea."

When we had finished, she told Lilo to take the tea tray to the kitchen and excused herself. Lilo and I went to the living room where an entire wall was occupied by bookshelves. As I browsed through them, I noticed that the works of one author dominated the shelves.

"Who is Rudolf Steiner?" I asked Lilo.

"He is a very great man. My mother is a follower of his. He founded Anthroposophy, you know."

"Anthroposophy? What's that?"

"It's a kind of religion without a church."

"A religion?" I was astonished. Lilo's mother did not strike me as one of those benighted people who worshipped an invisible God. "How do they practice their religion?"

"They study a lot and they meet once a week and talk."

As I leafed through some of the books, the word reincarnation often leaped from the page. I was puzzled. The word was not unfamiliar to me, but I had associated it with the superstitions of the illiterate. That someone as cultured as Lilo's mother could be interested in such matters made me want to learn more.

The next time I came for tea, I made bold to ask her. Mrs. Hauser's eyes shone with pleasure.

"From time immemorial, people have believed that there is an afterlife—that we don't simply die, but are born again time after time in new bodies. Rudolf Steiner teaches about all aspects of life, but the foundation of his teachings is metaphysical and rests on the belief in an immortal soul. If you like, you may borrow one of his books."

I didn't feel quite ready for this and politely declined her offer. Nevertheless, I did not forget her words. From that time on, I began to look for information on this subject that was so foreign to the modern age. Soon I discovered that Hermann Hesse, Jacob Wassermann, Franz Werfel and other authors whom I loved spoke of these things in ways I had seen as imaginative metaphors before. What if they were serious? Was it possible that they, too, believed in an immortal soul?

My body was changing. I was turning into a younger edition of my pretty sister, Fanny. At sixteen, I began to go to balls and 5 o'clock dances where, chaperoned by my mother, I was allowed to mingle with the opposite sex. But this parental sanction was surrounded by taboos. No more than one dance with the same partner. No cheek-to-cheek. A hand's breadth between my body and the man's. And no, positively NO dates; no assignations or rendez-vous, as the Viennese called it.

To me, my parents' old-fashioned morality was a source of embarrassment. How I wished they were more progressive! But it was useless to argue with them. I did not have the temperament of a rebel, but neither was I inclined to go along with what I deemed unreasonable. It was easy to arrange with Gerda to cover for me when I made a date, which, as it happened, was rarely enough.

My readiness to disobey my parents stood in sharp contrast to the reality. The good daughter despite myself, I thought, irritated and amused. It was not that I lacked opportunities. There were more than enough young men eager to date me. But alas, they were not like the witty, masterful heroes I read about in books, or saw in the theaters and movies. They sported corny lines; they postured; they had moist, groping hands. My few clandestine dates were unrewarding. Attempts to get to know the men were always frustrated by their firm determination to keep the talk within the limits of a light-hearted flirt. The carefully prescribed ritual precluded the possibility of an intelligent exchange. The girl was reduced to her biological role by this behavior.

The young women I knew seemed quite satisfied with the way things were. They were flattered by the attention the men showed them and only wanted to have many admirers. My own feelings were out of tune with the tempo of the times. To myself, I seemed like a throw-back to a more romantic time. I was not aware that I had one foot in the future—a time when women would refuse to be viewed merely as sex objects and demand to be treated as persons.

The play Reigen by Arthur Schnitzler (it was made into the movie La Ronde) gives a good picture of the mood that prevailed in Vienna when I was growing up. I felt odd, and tried hard to join in the flirtatious dance. But each of my attempts to play the heartless coquette landed me with the unwelcome attentions of some arrogant squirt who was dying to add me to the list of his conquests.

There were no models for me in the contemporary culture. In the '20s, the

Viennese flapper's hemline went up above her knees; bosom strapped tightly to conceal unmodish bulges, her face painted, a cigarette dangling from her lips. She, like her sisters in the USA, danced the Charleston and was free with her love.

While it was still true in the '30s that most men wanted to marry virgins, virtue was no longer an asset in the dating game. Time was beginning to be money, even in Vienna. Long, soulful courtships were out. Men expected heavy petting from their dates. Girls stalled skillfully and held out for a kiss. They stopped looking like boys and became femmes fatales. Alluringly, they slunk around, teasing, but not putting out. It was a compromise between returning to a stricter code and the freedom won in the '20s.

There were not many opportunities in post W.W.I Vienna for the sexes to mingle. Most schools were not co-educational, and very few girls from middle or upper-class backgrounds worked outside the home. The flapper era had not lessened traditional roles. The basic assumptions about maleness and femaleness were still firmly in place, and the "freedom" gained by women served primarily the men. The girl who did not allow heavy petting was rarely asked out again, and if, as I did, she tried to engage the man in some serious talk, she quickly lost appeal.

It happened once or twice that I developed a crush on a man after the first date. When he did not ask me out again, I felt rejected. On weekends, when my girl friends went out on dates, I took solitary hikes in the Wienerwald or rode the tramway to the Westbahnhof, the train station that smelled of steam engines and far-away lands.

It was during that period that I devised a fantasy that I had been put in the wrong body at birth. I knew that many a plain girl would have given much to have my looks. But for me, my sensuous body was a liability—it seemed to attract the wrong men for the wrong reasons.

Four

The political atmosphere was heating up. In Germany, Hitler blared his message of the super race and of hatred for the Jews into Aryan ears. In Italy, Mussolini dosed dissenters with castor-oil. The Viennese intelligentsia hooted with derision at the two power-mad dictators and were certain it would never happen here. The Christian Democrats, under tiny Chancellor Dollfuss, put down the revolt of the workers that threatened to become a civil war, and Schuschnigg, who took office after Dollfuss, seemed to be able to keep Hitler at bay.

When the Anschluss came in the spring of 1938, nobody was prepared for the masses of swasticas that sprouted from rooftops, windows, and men's lapels overnight. The impoverished Austrian peasants and laborers welcomed the Nazis with joy.

And overnight, the gemuetliche Viennese populace turned into a bloodthirsty mob. Their cruelty made the Germans seem humane by contrast. The Germans obeyed authority. They did what they were told. The Viennese were far less disciplined. The Anschluss gave their brutality free rein. "Pureblooded Aryans" felt free to batter Jews on the street, and to loot their homes and businesses openly.

The radio announcement that Hitler had annexed Austria was followed by music of soul-stirring beauty. For the next few days, the soaring chords of Beethoven, Bach, Hayden and Chopin were rarely interrupted. Except for brief announcements of a general nature, the radio took no notice of the hell that had broken loose outside. In my memory, the first days under the Nazis are inextricably linked to that heavenly music.

In the next months, I became accustomed to crossing the street and quickening my steps whenever I saw a small group of people standing around. The one time I stopped to see what was going on had been enough to make me wish I were blind. Two brown-shirted S.A. men were pushing a small, grey-bearded man in black kaftan and scull-cap back and forth between them like a punching bag. There was blood running down his forehead, he was making harsh, bleating sounds, and his small fragile body was doubled over in pain. But even worse than the spectacle of the poor man was the laughter of the bystanders. They were as pleased and appreciative of the S.A. men's agility in catching and pushing their victim as if they were watching a tennis match.

For a while, I continued to go to school. But the attitude of my former friends had changed.

"I didn't know you were Jewish," Eva Duhan, daughter of the famous opera baritone Hans Duhan, exclaimed. "But it doesn't make any difference to me. I'll always be your friend."

Eva's regal bearing, her aquiline Habsburg nose and tall, slender figure made it hard to guess that she was an imp who loved to engage in childish pranks. We had spent afternoons going from door to door in large, elegant apartment houses and hiding after ringing doorbells. We had laughed so hard together that we both peed in our pants, and Eva, whose pleated skirt hung wet and limp on her statuesque frame, had to call home to have a fresh skirt brought. She taught me how to hold out my hand to a young man so that he would inevitably kiss it, and had taken great pains to demonstrate the proper haughty mien I must assume in the process.

"If all the Jews were like you, there wouldn't be any anti-semitism," she said fondly. From then on, I was to hear these words frequently. They were meant to reassure the "exceptional" Jew to whom they were addressed, but were in fact expressions of a virulent kind of anti-semitism that was willing to make exceptions without denying the validity of Hitlerian racism.

Eva did not continue to be my friend, and the rest of the class pretended that I and the other Jewish girls were invisible. At the end of the month, I stopped going to school.

One day, as I was walking through the Augarten, a lovely park on the edge of the Leopoldstadt, two brown-shirted S.A. men stepped in my way. "How about a little Rassenschande, Miss?" one of them said, accompanying his words with a lascivious gesture. (Rassenschande means race shame, the word Hitler coined for sexual relations between pure Aryans and Jews.) Fortunately, they were just having a little fun and did not mean to follow their words with action. I ran all the way home, badly frightened.

The private gym class I attended was taught by a young Jewish woman. Since all her Aryan students had dropped out, it seemed safe to continue going. It was the only activity outside the home that was available to me, and I was grateful for the twice-weekly hour of strenuous exercise. One day, two S.S. men walked in while the class was in progress.

"You're all Jewish pigs, right?" one of them said. It was a statement, not a question. "Get dressed. We have work for you to do. And make it snappy!"

When we had put on our street clothes, we were shoved into a waiting military van and taken to a soldiers barracks, which we were ordered to clean.

"You two," the taller S.S. man said, "clean the toilets. You, wash the windows. And you," he pointed to the gym teacher and to me, "scrub the floors." He handed each of us a bucket filled with sudsy water, and a brush.

When I rose from my knees to refill my bucket, the tall one followed me to the sink. Standing behind me, he put his arms around me. I pulled away. "Bet you're not so stand-offish with the Jew boys!" he said. "Come on, give me a kiss. Bet you don't know what it's like to be kissed by a pure-blooded Aryan!"

I had let the water run into my bucket and now picked it up. It was half full. With cunning born of desperation I managed to upset it all over him without making it look planned. The S.S. man was too busy drying himself off to pursue me any further, and I got home unharmed. It was late; Mama had been waiting for me with ever-increasing fear.

"Where were you?" she asked. Relief at seeing me flooded her pale face. In answer, I broke into tears. "Thank God you're all right!" she said, taking me into her arms.

When I had finished telling her what had happened, she looked at me gravely. "You must leave Vienna, Gusti," she said.

"By myself? What about you and Papa? What about Oscar, Dolly, Fanny?" I was shocked by the idea of leaving alone.

"We'll all make our way. But you are the youngest and the most vulnerable. You must go now." She looked at me tenderly. All her love and her fear for me were in her eyes.

I was in turmoil. Part of me wanted to strike out on my own, but to be cut off from my family was a thought I had never faced before.

Later that evening, Papa joined Mama's urging. "Go, child," he said. "There is nothing but pain and danger here for you."

The next morning, I wrote to Marcel, a distant cousin who was studying at Oxford. He had managed to get a domestic servants permit for his parents. Faced with a shortage of domestic help, England allowed refugees to enter, provided they had a job waiting. Marcel secured a position for his parents as cook and butler in the home of a wealthy family, and so Auntie Rosa and Uncle Max, whose villa in a fashionable suburb of Vienna had been looked after by a cook and housekeeper, were now to become servants themselves.

Marcel had rather a crush on me and wrote back at once. "Do learn to cook. I'll have to tell your prospective employers that you are an expert cook and housemaid. I'd gladly lie for you, but it would be best if you at least knew the rudiments of cooking. See you in London soon!"

The following weeks were filled with excursions to fabric stores where Mama and I selected materials for the wardrobe our dressmaker was to make for me. We spent hours looking at fashion magazines and going to fittings. In between, we shopped for shoes, lingerie, accessories and hats. By the time the permit from my future employers arrived, I had a trunk full of exquisite clothes.

"This is your dowry, Gusti," Mama said. "It's all we can give you. The Nazis won't let you take any money out of Austria. I hope and pray you'll soon find a good husband who can take care of you." My looks had always been seen as my major asset. The lavish wardrobe seemed a good investment in my chances of making a good match.

Soon after I posted my letter to Marcel, Mama called me to the dining room. The door of the heavy iron safe was open. "Please bring the green box from my night table," she said. When I returned with it, I saw that she had pulled out the trays that held the family's jewelry. How I had loved to look at these trinkets when I was a child! There were silver cuff links, gold rings set with semi-precious stones, enamelled lockets, gold chains and bracelets. There was the small signet ring a friend had given me for my tenth birthday. I had refused to take it off until one day my finger grew too big for it, and it had to be sawed off while I cringed in fear. Oh, and there was the thick gold watch Papa used to wear in his vest pocket. I had a vivid memory of clambering up on his lap and grasping for the watch he teasingly dangled on its gold chain. My reward, when I caught it, was that he opened it, and the sweet tinkling sounds of "Oh Tannenbaum" could be heard.

And there, in their blue velvet box, were the diamond earrings Papa bought for Mama years ago. We children all knew that she hated to wear them. She detested ostentation and thought the small earrings far too opulent. Invariably, she appeared dressed to go out with Papa without them, and invariably he would remind her to put them on. She would obey him, for she never argued with him, but soon, her hair would creep forward until it completely covered her ears.

Mama was gathering the gold chains, signet rings, tie clips and bracelets and putting them in the green box.

"What are you doing?" I asked.

"You'll see!" she said, smiling mysteriously. What she did was to bring the trinkets to our family dentist, who was also a trusted friend.

"Melt it all down," she told him, "and make it into a bracelet for Gusti."

"I'm not a jeweler!" the good doctor protested. But under Mama's instructions he fashioned a crude bracelet that looked deceptively light but was so heavy that it pulled my arm down. He finished it with a dull patina, and nobody could have guessed by looking at it that it was solid gold.

I was sure that cooking would be child's play for me. The cooks I knew were no mental giants. Surely that humble art would pose no problems for one of my intellectual stature! When my departure was only two weeks away, I entered a cooking school. My interest in the details of housekeeping had not extended beyond an occasional excursion to the kitchen for a glass of water, or to rinse out the clandestine ashtray I kept hidden in my room. Mama had never insisted that I do anything in the house beyond keeping my room reasonably neat.

The chef who was supposed to turn me into an experienced cook looked dubious when I told him how little time he had to accomplish this. "Tell you what we can do. I'll try to teach you how to make one complete meal, and after that, you must fake it. Pick out one soup, one main dish, and one dessert. But promise never to mention my name when you get to England.

Agreed?"

I agreed not to dishonor my teacher and selected a spring vegetable soup, Wiener Schnitzl (breaded veal cutlets), potato salad, and Apfel Strudl. "That's a good choice," he said. "A typical Viennese dinner, and easy to make. You'll wow the English with it. What an abomination, that English food!" He shook himself in disgust.

Reassured about my professional future, I continued with the preparations for my departure, which meant endless trips to a variety of government agencies to get an endless number of documents stamped. At last, all was ready.

On July 14, 1938, my family took me to the Westbahnhof to see me off.

Five

I waved through the window until the figures of my parents, my brother and my two sisters with their spouses had receded from my view. Will I ever see them again? I wondered. Sobbing, I huddled in the window seat of the train that was carrying me away from everything I had ever known. When my tears finally subsided, I reached into my purse for a fresh handkerchief and discovered a box of Turkish cigarettes that had not been there before. I broke into renewed sobs.

"Are you all right, miss?" the young man sitting next to me asked anxiously.

"Yes. No! It's the cigarettes!" I wailed.

"The cigarettes?" he asked, puzzled.

"Mama must have put them there," I brought out disconsolately. More than all that had gone before, her gesture brought home to me the finality of the parting. My parents strongly disapproved of women smoking. I and my elder sisters had always carefully refrained from doing it in their presence, but we all smoked behind their backs. I had tried my first cigarette three years earlier, when the departure of a summer romance left me temporarily heartbroken. An older girl friend had given it to me, assuring me it would make me feel better. It did, and from then on I smoked whenever I could.

That Mother had known all along what I so carefully kept from her was quite a surprise. But even more surprising was the fact that she herself had now given me a box of the hated cigarettes, which, in her mind, branded the women who smoked them as loose. Better than any words could have done, her gesture told me that from now on, I was on my own. For a long time, I sat fingering the box and crying.

The train made several stops before I grew calm again. The young man beside me was making comforting sounds, and he displayed a touching concern for my tears. His mother opened a picnic basket that held a roast chicken, some Viennese pastries and a bottle of wine. At her urging, I helped myself to a wedge of Linzer Torte.

"Who knows when we'll taste Viennese pastries again," she sighed. At these words, the tears sprang to my eyes again. The beauty of the city of my birth had been blotted out by the events of the last three months. It was only now that I realized how much I would miss it.

"Where are you going?" I asked.

"To Holland," she replied. "We hope that Joseph will be able to complete his studies there. Won't you, dear?" She smiled affectionately at her son.

"And you?" Joseph asked.

"I'm going to England. As a maid-servant."

"Oh dear! That won't be easy for a girl like you!" the old lady commented.

She was right. I had not given much thought to the fate that awaited me while I was busy preparing for the trip. Now, suddenly, the gravity of my situation stared me in the eye. I was frightened. I was nineteen years old. I was still a child.

And like a child, I begged Joseph to tell me a story.

"A story? But I don't know any stories!" he protested.

"Tell me anything! Something that will make me forget what's happening!" I pleaded.

He thought for a moment, then his sensitive face brightened. "Let's pretend we were just married. We're going to Capri on our honeymoon. I'll take you to the Blue Grotto..."

"Oh yes, let's do that!" I said eagerly.

Reality did not intrude on us for the rest of that night as we stood outside the compartment where his parents slept on the hard benches. We told each other about our childhood and youth, we kissed, and the night was filled with magic as we looked at the stars and the ever-changing shadows of the landscape rushing by.

Towards morning, as we approached the German frontier, I grew fearful. The bracelet on my arm suddenly weighed a ton. If the Germans discovered its value, there would be no hope of escape. People had been shot for less.

The young German who examined my passport while another searched through my trunk gave me a searching look. "Why would such a pretty young lady wish to leave our glorious Fatherland?" he inquired.

"I'm Jewish, as you can see in my passport," I replied defiantly.

"But we Germans don't have anything against good-looking Jews! It's only the ones with the hooked noses and the side locks that we don't like. But you, Fräulein, you look like everybody else—only prettier!" he said as he handed back my passport.

We were jubilant when we had left Germany behind. Joseph's father opened the bottle of rare wine he had saved for the occasion, and we all drank a toast to our escape.

When Joseph and his parents arrived at their destination, we embraced each other and parted. We had agreed that it would be useless to exchange addresses, as none of us knew where we would be a month from now. When I waved to them from the train, I knew that I would never see these good people again; but it was some time before I stopped fantasizing that Joseph would find me and carry me off to Capri.

Six

"Hello, Gusty!" a voice said behind me. Who, me? My name is not Gusty, it's Gusti (as in book)! I turned around and faced the tall, lean woman with the weather-beaten face. Yes, it was Mrs. H., my employer. I recognized her from the photo she had sent. Taking my arm, she shepherded me and my luggage to a waiting chauffeur-driven limousine.

It was early in the afternoon when we arrived at the H.'s cabin on the sea shore. Mrs. H. introduced me to the children: Jerry, 15, Jimmy, 14, and Mona, 12. They eyed me with the frank curiosity of healthy youngsters and I knew we would be friends.

I was surprised to note that Mrs. H. had false teeth. Later, I learned that many English people lost their teeth at a fairly young age.

"My husband will be home in the evening," Mrs. H. said as she showed me to my room. It was as bare as an ascetic's cell, containing only a bed, a chest of drawers, and a rickety chair. In the kitchen, Mrs H. opened some cabinets to show me where things were. One of the door handles stayed in her hand. The rest of the cabin was equally dilapidated.

"Why don't you make yourself at home," my employer said. "I'll take the children to the beach. It would be nice if you had something to eat for us when we get back. We're always hungry after a swim. Make anything you want. Improvise!"

The condition of the cabin amazed me. This was not how I expected the family of a member of parliament to live! Mr. H., a member of the Lower

House of Commons, was up for re-election, and the family's finances were strained. For appearance sake, they had to maintain certain signs of affluence, such as the limousine. But for the rest, the family lived very frugally at that time.

Trying to sort out the impressions that came tumbling into my mind, I would have welcomed the chance to stretch out on my bed and lie quietly for a while. But it was time to think about preparing the meal. I was nervous as I set about my task. Fortunately, I had spotted some potatoes in the vegetable bin, and there were eggs. 'My potato salad will be a hit,' I thought. The first thing to do, Chef Heinrich had taught me, is to boil the potatoes. Confidently, I covered them with water and turned on the gas.

Meanwhile, I began to make the mayonnaise by adding oil to the egg yolks, stirring them diligently. The secret of mayonnaise-making is to add the oil carefully drop by drop. Failure to do so with the utmost precision results in curdling. I was on my second batch when I remembered the potatoes. Quickly, I turned off the gas and poured the boiling water in the sink. Unfortunately, I neglected to use a colander; with a plop, the overcooked potatoes fell in the sink and instantly turned to mush.

Cleaning the mashed potatoes out of the sink presented a problem. They refused to go down the drain, and so I finally scooped them up with towels I collected around the cabin.

I put another potful of potatoes on the stove and returned to the mayonnaise. Unhappily, it had curdled like the first batch. Using the last of the eggs, I started a new batch, determined that nothing would go wrong this time.

I was deeply absorbed in my task when the family returned.

"What are you making, Gusty?" Mrs. H. asked, surveying the kitchen.

"Mayonnaise," I said sheepishly.

Wordlessly, Mrs. H. reached into a cupboard and brought out a jar marked "Mayonnaise." I was speechless. In Vienna, no self-respecting Hausfrau would have brought ready-made mayonnaise into her home. I did not know that it existed.

It became quickly apparent to my employers that they were saddled with an imposter, a cuckoo's egg instead of the experienced cook and parlor maid they had expected. That evening, as Mrs. H. watched me unpack, she oh'd and ah'd at my lovely clothes. She eyed the few books I brought with interest.

"Look what Gusty is reading," she called to her husband when she spotted A Short History of the World by H.G. Wells.

"I say! What do we have here?" he exclaimed. Mr. H., was a tall, distinguished-looking Englishman. I had met him at supper. Now he eyed me curiously. "A bit of a scholar, aren't you? Hm. Not quite what we expected, is she, Mildred?" he said to his wife.

"Not quite." She smiled at me. "But we'll make do. You must tell us all about Vienna."

"Yes, do!" he said. As he went back to his desk, I heard him chuckle.

For the rest of that summer, the H family adopted me. I was treated like one of the children. "If the circumstances were reversed, you'd do the same for my daughter," Mrs. H. wrote to my mother. I performed light tasks under her direction and was encouraged to go to the beach with the children while she stayed home to cook and clean. On several occasions, the H's invited some young people to meet me; in general, they did everything they could to make me feel at ease.

But despite their kindness, I was often sad. I waited impatiently for letters from my family. Oscar and his wife Gretl left Vienna three months after my departure. They were in Paris. Fanny and her husband were in Yugoslavia, and Dolly and her family in Belgium. My parents' fate caused me great anxiety. They refused to leave Vienna. Father's business had been confiscated by the Nazis, but their bank account had not yet been seized, and they could still live on their savings.

"I have no intention to be a burden to my children," Papa told me before I left. "You know that we could not take any money with us, and I'm too old to start all over again. Don't worry, the Nazis won't touch us. They respect this!" he said pointing to the ribbon in his lapel. It was the symbol for his war decoration, the Iron Cross of Merit that lay in the old iron safe.

I was trying to fit myself into the H's life. The children taught me how to hit a baseball and slide into first base, and I taught them some German and French cuss words. It seemed a fair exchange. Some mornings, when I had stayed up late, Mrs H. brought me early morning tea in bed along with my eagerly awaited mail.

At first, the cultural differences between Austria and England caused me discomfort. Some of the things I had been carefully taught now suddenly counted for nothing. My table manners, for instance. In Vienna, well-bred people kept the fork in their left hand and the knife in their right. Here, I watched in dizzy fascination as the H's switched forks and knives back and forth. Since they were obviously well-bred, this behavior puzzled me. Another strange English custom was the early morning tea. In Vienna, we woke up to a fragrant cup of coffee—good, strong coffee with foaming, warm milk. On the other hand, I soon began to appreciate the ubiquitous "cupper" and liked the delicate watercress and cucumber sandwiches they had for afternoon tea.

I learned that the customs of well-bred people in one country can be viewed as rude in another. "Table manners" thus became my metaphor for the differences in people's behavior. One of the daintiest ways of eating is that of the Hindus. They eat with their fingers—a custom that appalled the English colonials.

The summer passed. It was time to return to the H's home in London. It was an old, substantial house, situated in a quiet suburb among other old, substantial houses. It was furnished with understated elegance and managed to be cosy, despite its seeming formality. It was large and required a lot of care. Because of their financial crunch, the H's could not afford the well-trained help the house needed; that's why they had sent for me.

The kind-hearted family had made the best of the situation in the primitive summer cabin, but it was obvious that my lack of experience would not do in the London house. I was aware that my presence prevented them from finding someone more competent, and I knew it was time to leave.

"I cannot impose on you any longer," I told Mrs. H. "I'm no good to you. I can't thank you enough for putting up with me so long—I don't deserve your kindness and I don't deserve to be paid." My wages amounted to a few pounds. I had almost no money and no idea what I would do once I left the H's, but my code of honor prevented me from taking money for services not rendered. Feeling very noble, I refused the notes she held out to me.

"You're a foolish child. I want you to promise to call on me if you're in trouble. You're a good girl, you'll be fine, I believe. Do keep in touch. Take care!"

After a tearful farewell I went to the boarding house where I had rented a room. When I opened my purse, I found a post-office savings booklet with my name on it. The sum listed was that of the wages I had refused.

The room was in the home of the Coles in a respectable lower middle-class neighborhood. The heart of the row house was the kitchen. There was a rarely used front parlor with a shiny linoleum floor, but the family stayed in the kitchen, where a small electric heater provided not only warmth but served as a toaster. Mornings, the family would huddle around it, each holding a slice of bread on a fork close to the heat. I learned about putting pennies in the slot when the lights went out, and how to start the geyser in the one bathroom that was usually occupied when I needed it.

I took a part-time job as a nanny for a two-year old boy and really enjoyed taking care of him. His mother was a trained nurse who worked at the hospital in the afternoons, leaving me in charge. We went to a nearby park where I met other nannies and young mothers, and in the evenings, after giving Johnny his supper, I returned to the Coles. My meager wages barely paid for my room, and I generally went without breakfast or lunch.

One morning, Mrs. Coles knocked at my door. She was carrying a tray laden with ham and eggs, toast, jam, and a pot of tea.

"Margie rushed off without 'er breakfast again! Late as usual. Don't know what I'll do with that girl! It's a shame to waste good food, isn't it? I was wonderin' if you'd do me a favor and eat it, seein' as you 'aven't gone out for your breakfast yet?" Without waiting for my answer, she placed the tray on my dresser and left.

After that, I became more and more another one of her daughters. I called her "Mom," and the place she held in my heart was second only to my own mother's. Her down-to-earth common sense helped me to deal with numerous contingencies; I valued her advice greatly.

Margie was her youngest and the closest to me in age. She was vivacious and fun-loving, and she had many beaux. Babs was married, but didn't much like it and spent most of her time at her parents' home talking about how awful it was having to cook and clean "for a brute like Fred." She confided to me that she had an affair with a married man who was terrific in bed. When I asked if she was thinking of getting a divorce, she giggled.

"Coo, I don't want to be married to him! What would be the fun o' that?"

"But you can't stand Fred!" I exclaimed.

"Old Fred's all right. He just wants to come home to a clean house and a good supper. He lets me take the car when I want it, and most of the time he leaves me alone. I'm pretty lucky, I guess. Got a husband who supports me and a boy friend who keeps me happy in bed. What more can a girl ask?"

Olive was a dark-eyed brunette who bore no resemblance to her fair-haired sisters. She and her husband only came to visit on holidays, as they lived in a different part of the city. They appeared to be quite happy with each other.

The most surprising member of the household was six year old Bubbles. Negroes were a rarity in the England of that time, and the black child stood out like an exotic bird. Considering the attention the family showered on her, she was as spoiled as could be expected. Mom Coles gave in to all her whims, and the girls were always bringing her sweets, toys, and ribbons for her hair. I was naturally curious about how she came to be there, but did not venture to ask. Mom hinted mysteriously that Bubbles' father was a very famous man, but his name was never mentioned, nor that of her mother. I had a suspicion that perhaps Paul Robeson, the great American singer, was the father, and flighty Babs the mother, but I never received any confirmation. Certainly no child, white or black, was ever raised more lovingly than Bubbles.

The English I had learned in school was "the King's English," correct and precise as no language that is in daily use can ever be. At the H's, who spoke the distinctive, clipped English of the upper classes, my stilted phrases had not been too much out of place. Something I said would occasionally make them smile, as when I told the children that I was going to wash my "hairs." (In German, 'hair' is singular only when it refers to one hair.) But in general, our communication had posed no problems.

Not so at the Coles. They dropped their h's and used expressions I had never heard and could find in no dictionary. As I have a good ear for languages, however, I had no trouble imitating them and was soon speaking Cockney with a Viennese accent. The result must have been rather startling.

Mom Coles was anxious to give the impression of good breeding. She was contemptuous of the vulgar habits of the working class stiffs, and her husband's way of pouring his tea into the saucer and sipping it noisily drove her wild.

"''e's a card, that 'arry is. Acts like 'e didn't know any better when I've told 'im and told 'im that no gentleman drinks 'is tea like that!"

After a good meal, Mr Coles was in the habit of farting loudly. His wife would glare at him until he said, "'xcuse me." Satisfied that the proprieties had been observed, she would reward him with a smile.

Pa Coles was a man of few words. He was a gardener, and when he came home from work he sat in the overstuffed armchair by the electric heater and smoked his pipe. Once, on a damp, dreary day, he groaned loudly before collapsing into the chair.

"What's up, 'arry?" his wife asked.

"It's me back," he sighed.

"Your back!" she flung back, spitting out the words like a challenge. "Coo! I can 'ardly lift me fork to me mouth, that's how much me back 'urts! And me feet feel like they's fallin' off!"

She launched into a graphic description of all her ills, and he was silenced. Her strategy for dealing with the ailments of the hard-working husband whom she loved was to go him one better. Once, when a sore shoulder forced him to stay in bed, she lay down beside him and moaned loudly until he got up and brought her a cup of tea, which instantly cured her.

The love she felt for her family was like a tangible presence in the house. And I, lonely, bewildered, and sore at heart about my own parents' fate, felt secure and cherished among these kind, simple people.

When the winter began, Mrs. H. asked me to come back. "I think that you and another girl who is more experienced could do the work together," she said. "Do you happen to know a refugee who would fit the bill?"

As it happened, I did. Gerda had also come to England, and had been driven close to suicide by her job as housemaid in an upper-class English home. I remember the first time I went to visit her. The doorbell was answered by a butler who could have come straight out of a Noel Coward play.

"Good afternoon, Miss," he said gravely. "Who may I say is calling?" His face managed to be haughty and obsequious at the same time. When I told him that I came to visit Gerda, his expression changed to outrage. "Kindly use the servants' entrance, Miss. You don't come to the front door for Gerda!"

Following his accusing finger, I went down to the side entrance that led to the basement. The interior of this nether region was desolate. A huge, old-fashioned kitchen without any modern conveniences occupied most of the space. Gerda's room was a dank, dark cell that smelled of mildew. It was a hellish place to live and work in, and Gerda's once rosy face reflected it.

"You have to get out of here!" I told her.

She shrugged. "Where would I go? I have no money, and I don't know much English. At least here I have a roof over my head!"

I was thankful that my own fate had been kinder. Few of the girls from Vienna were as lucky as I. Some were speedily dismissed when their employers found out how little they knew about housework; they grew despondent, homesick, depressed, and suicide was not uncommon. Some young women from good homes became prostitutes, others wore out their youth trying to hold on to jobs like Gerda's, because that was the only security they knew.

Two weeks before Mrs. H. spoke to me, I had finally succeeded to pry Gerda loose from that degrading and exhausting job. She moved into the Coles' house and was beginning to recover from the strain. She had learned to do housework the hard way, and knew a great deal more about it than I.

"It'll be great to work together!" I told Gerda. "The H's are a wonderful family. They'll treat us like their own children, not like servants, and we'll have plenty of free time!"

But that's not the way it worked out. From the first, it was clear that things would be different this time around. We were not invited to eat with the family but had to wait on them and grab our meals when we could. At night, after washing the dinner dishes, we had to clean out all the fire places and prepare them for the next day. We rose at dawn in the freezing house to light them and to take early morning tea to the family who was still in bed. The work was gruelling. At first, I did all I could to justify the change in Mrs. H's behavior, but after three months, Gerda and I were at the end of our strength. We spent our days off at the Coles, and Mom urged us to quit "the 'orrible aitches," as she called them.

And so we moved back to the Coles. I was determined not to do housework again, and despite the danger of being caught by the Foreign Office who sent refugees back to Germany if they did not remain in domestic jobs, I applied for a position as secretary to an Austrian film producer. To my surprise, I was hired despite the fact that my short-hand and typing skills were negligible. As it turned out, these skills were secondary, for my new boss liked to dictate his letters standing behind my chair and rubbing himself against my shoulder. I stayed barely a week.

After that, I did sewing at the home of a well-to-do woman. In my early teens, I experimented with Mama's treddle machine, using pieces of fabric from her rag bag. I was making simple skirts and blouses and found that sewing came so easily to me that I laughingly told Lilo I must have been a seamstress in a former life.

I quite enjoyed altering dresses, shortening hems and doing odd bits of sewing for Mrs. Mellis and her daughter. If the threat of deportation had not hung over me, I would have happily continued to sew; but I had a feeling I was being watched, and so I took another domestic job. It depleted my energies so much that I slept around the clock on my days off, not even waking to eat a meal.

Years later, when I cheerfully did much harder work, I realized that it had been my attitude, not the chores, that drained my energy. But the only thing that kept me going in my refugee days was the conviction that the life I was forced to lead was only temporary. What gave me that assurance, I don't know, but not for a moment did I believe that the condition I found myself in was permanent. My prince would come and rescue me, and we would live happily ever after. I was sure of that.

Seven

The romantic ideas that had been instilled in me did not loosen their grip until much later in life. My expectations for the "prince" were programmed by fairy tales, novels, and films. A woman's success in life was measured not by her qualities of heart, mind, and spirit, but by her power to attract the other sex. The heroines in the books, plays and movies that shaped my self-image were all beautiful, wore lovely clothes, had their hair done once a week and were both virtuous and seductive. Their character was noble, and if they fell, it was because they met up with a cad.

The hero was the exuberant Zorba the Greek and the bookish Englishman; the worldly, cynical Rhett Butler and sensitive Ashley. Tormented or heartless, masterful or kidding around, he was larger than life—a mythic figure, an archetype.

In the reality I knew, I met neither princes nor heroes. In that reality, you settled for what you could get. I thought that once I had the freedom I had longed for in my strict home, I would meet the man of my dreams pronto. But alas, my chances were no better in London than they had been back home. When a man ten years my senior began paying attention to me, I was pleased and flattered. Hans was a refugee like myself. He was safe, familiar, and his practical business sense promised a good income once the restrictions placed on him as an alien would be lifted. For the present, my interest in ultimate questions had given way to the simple need to survive, but books were still my main source of satisfaction. To Hans, they meant nothing. After some months of "going out" with him, I knew that we were incompatible, and I regretfully declined his proposal of marriage.

In Paris, Oscar and Gretl met a wealthy American who sponsored their affidavit for immigration to the USA. Their papers were due to arrive any day, and their letters assured me they would do all they could to bring me to America once they were there. My sisters were both in Antwerp. They urged me to visit them.

The Belgian Consulate was willing to grant me a visitor's visa for a fortnight, but I needed a re-entry permit from the British Home Office, which was not easy to obtain. In the end, I held a duly stamped paper in my hand. I was delirious with joy and counted the hours to my reunion with my sisters.

The crossing from Dover to Calais was rough, and I was relieved when I could leave the boat. As I sat in the train watching the unfamiliar landscape rushing by, the rustling sound of a newspaper caught my attention. It came from the seat opposite mine. Turning my head, I saw that a hole had been poked in the newspaper. A very blue eye was watching me through the hole. I was amused. That's a new approach, I thought.

In Brussels, I had to change trains. Trying to get the attention of a porter, I discovered that my schoolgirl French had not equipped me to deal with the realities of a railway station.

"Where are you going?" the tall, gaunt young man who had observed me through his paper, said in flawless French.

"To Antwerp."

"Excellent! I am also going there! May I offer you my help?" And without waiting for my reply, he lifted my heavy suitcase off the rack. "Just follow me, Mademoiselle," he said. "I will take you to your train."

I briefly thought of the letter in my purse in which my mother warned me not to talk to strangers—particularly male strangers!—on the trip. But as he placed my suitcase on the luggage rack and sat down beside me, I was convinced that I had nothing to fear from this attractive stranger. His dark-blond hair was longer than customary and gave him the look of an artist. His blazing blue eyes looked at me in a way that concealed nothing, neither his admiration nor his sincere wish to help.

When I had answered his questions about where I came from and what I was doing in Antwerp, he asked: "Will somebody pick you up from the station?"

"Certainly! My sisters are probably waiting there already!"

"Where do they live?" he inquired. "In case they don't meet the train."

"Not a chance!" I laughed.

"But it could happen! Tell me where they live so I can help you get there—just in case."

But of course they were waiting! I rushed into their arms and forgot all about the stranger. He put my suitcase down beside me and left.

The excitement of the trip and of seeing my sisters again affected my health. I ran a temperature and had to stay in bed for a week. It was lovely to be spoiled and indulged by my sisters; apart from the physical discomfort, I did not mind this period of bedrest at all. On the third day, Fanny and I were chatting away when the doorbell rang. She went to answer it.

"Who is your admirer?" she asked when she came back.

"My admirer? What do you mean?"

"A tall, skinny blond man asked about you. He seemed quite concerned when I told him you're ill. Where did you meet him, you minx? You only just arrived!"

"It must be the man who helped me on the train," I said. When I told Fanny how he knew my address, she laughed.

"Very clever! Seems like a resourceful young man! Are you going to see him if he asks you out?"

"I might," I replied, trying to sound indifferent. But I was interested and intrigued.

The next day, Fanny brought a beautifully arranged basket of fruit to my bed. "My admirer?" I asked. She nodded. "He said he'll call you next week. I told him you'll be fine by then."

When he came, I had completely recovered. A strong attraction developed between us. We saw each other every day, and he helped me to get my visitor's visa renewed. He and his brother had left their home in Russia in their late teens to study at the University of Liege. His views leaned towards communism, but being Jewish had made living in Russia dangerous and uncomfortable. His name was Misha; here in French-speaking Belgium he was called Michel.

Michel was twenty-eight when we met. To me, he seemed everything the men I had known before were not. He had been on his own for many years, and he was manly in a way that made the Viennese men I knew look effete. In order to support himself and his frail, studious brother, he soon abandoned his studies and did all kinds of work, including a year as a stevedore in Antwerp's busy port. At present, he was a traveling salesman for a fabric factory, making a hand-to-mouth living that allowed him to indulge his taste for fine restaurants, but not much more.

My family wanted me to find a man who could offer me financial ease. My sisters tried to dissuade me from getting engaged to Michel, and my parents, whom they kept informed by letter, begged me to wait. "Being in love is not everything," they wrote. "Your young man has not created a situation that allows him to support a family. With him, you'll live in poverty. Don't be in a hurry. The right man will come along, and love will follow when there is plenty of money and security."

The "right man" had already appeared on the scene. I was introduced to him by a Belgian family who knew my sisters. He was an American, in town on business.

"He's a multi-millionaire, one of the richest diamond merchants in the business," the Belgian lady told me. "Women are wild about him, but he's not easy to please. I know he'll fall for you. Good luck!"

I went out with Martin a few times, and he did fall for me. I found him nice but unexciting, especially by contrast with Michel, whose charm and mercurial temperament captivated me.

Unable to renew my visa one more time, I left Antwerp after three months. Nothing was settled between Michel and me. My family's resistance to our marriage had made Michel wonder if he was ready to take on the responsibility of providing for a wife who had been raised to expect a life of ease.

When I came back to London, my room at the Coles' was occupied by a young couple fresh from Vienna. I could have shared Margie's room, but did not want to impose on her already cramped space. I was forced to look for a domestic job. The idea depressed me, but it was the only thing I could do.

I took a sleep-in job with the Goldbergs, a business couple who lived in a comfortable flat with two sons in their early twenties. The sons fell all over themselves trying to help me. Mrs. Goldberg, a short squat woman with a painfully stiff neck, watched the attentions the boys paid me with a baleful eye.

"Look at your sons!" she would say to her meek husband. "You ever see them carry a dish for me?" She turned her upper body from the hip so she could look at me. "Do me a favor, darling—when you dust the furniture, don't just give it a tickle. Wipe it! Like this!" And she would show me how to dust not only the visible parts of the sideboard, but less obvious places like the frames of paintings, the legs of chairs, the bases of lamps. I really learned to clean in that flat!

One day, the mailman handed me a receipt for a package from Belgium. The receipt advised me that I would have to pay duty at the customs office, but I was not prepared for the sum the official named. The sender was Martin. It was a big, expensive box of chocolates. In the following weeks, more chocolates arrived. Fuming at the expense these unwanted gifts caused, I was forced to accept them. Then a letter came from America:

"I'm planning to be in London next week and am eager to see you. May I pick you up from your place of work on Tuesday at 7 pm?"

And so it happened that Cinderella was picked up by an American millionaire in a chauffeur-driven Rolls Royce. I can still hear Mrs. Goldberg's stiff neck snap as I emerged from my room wearing my black velvet evening coat with the ermine-lined hood.

In the car, Martin asked me to stretch out my hand. "How would you like this as an engagement ring?" he asked, placing a large diamond on my ring finger. "It could be set in a circle of small diamonds, or do you prefer rubies?"

"Slow down, Martin," I told him. "You know I'm not ready to commit myself."

And after a week of dances, theater and nightclubs, I knew that I would never be ready, no matter how tempting the lifestyle he could offer me.

Eight

When I had been at the Goldbergs a month, I was fired. Holding her neck stiffer than usual, Mrs. Goldberg told me that she did not like the way I cleaned.

"I hired a new girl, she's coming on Monday, I need your room, you understand, darling." She gave me an icy look. "You're a smart girl, you don't need to be a maid. Go catch a rich husband. A good maid you're not."

It was true. I had dragged my resisting body around the Goldberg apartment like a heavy burden. Every step seemed too much. But what to do next?

When my anxiety reached the boiling point, I remembered the letter my friend Renate, a stunning redhead, had sent from Paris. "I'm seeing an interesting man," she wrote. Renate was always seeing interesting men. "He is either an international confidence man, or a millionaire playboy, I don't know which. He likes being seen with me and takes me to lots of parties. He knows some important people, and when I told him about you, he said I should write you about an acquaintance of his, a Mr. Specter, who is very rich and takes great interest in Jewish refugees. Go to him. André will write Specter to expect you."

Specter's office was located on the Strand, in one of London's finest cinemas, which he owned. The man behind the huge desk was short, bald, slight, and elderly, and not at all like the tycoon I expected to see.

"Come sit," he invited, pointing to the armchair facing him. He peered at me through thick glasses. "Such a young girl! A mere child!" he exclaimed. "So how did you manage to escape to London? Where are your parents? Are they safe?"

His speech held something of the sing-song accent of the Jewish ghetto. It was obvious that he himself had come to England as a refugee years earlier. I didn't know how he made his fortune, but I was sure that this mild-mannered man with the anxious look was no international swindler.

The emotion his face mirrored when I told my story was sincere. "All right," he said when I explained my predicament. "How would you like to live in a nice Jewish home where they would treat you like a daughter? You shouldn't be a maid—a nice, educated girl like you! You speak English almost as good as me!"

Better, I hoped. But his kindness fell like balm on my wounds, and visions of a warm, secure, friendly home filled my mind.

"So go watch the film while I make a few calls." He told his secretary to send in a page, and the uniformed boy escorted me to a seat in the darkened theater. The movie was already half over, but I hardly watched the screen, wondering what was in store for me.

After a while, the page tapped me on the shoulder.. He put a tea cart laden with dainty sandwiches and mouth-watering pastries next to me. "From Mr. Specter," he whispered as he poured my tea. I felt very grand and wished the lights were on so that people would notice the special treatment I received.

When I returned to Specter's office, he shook his head. "I didn't reach the people. They're away on a trip and won't be back for a few weeks."

This was bad news. The reality of my problem came back to me full force. I had to leave the Goldbergs in three days and didn't know where to go. There was no room at the Coles and I didn't have enough money to go anywhere else. Mr. Specter saw the expression on my face.

"Don't worry," he said. "I have a solution. You can stay at my flat temporarily."

Oh no! I thought. He's just a dirty old man! And I trusted him! How could I have been so wrong?

Mr. Specter was observing me. "What's the matter?" he asked. "Afraid I'll rape you? So maybe I have nothing better to do? There is an empty room in the servants' wing. If you want, you can stay there till something better can be arranged. If not, I give you a couple of pounds, you can stay in a hotel, but a pretty young girl shouldn't stay in a hotel alone."

I looked at him again. The idea that he might have sexual designs on me was ludicrous. "I'd love to stay at your flat," I said gratefully.

The flat faced Hyde Park. I was let in by a neat, fresh-faced maid who introduced herself as Cathleen. As she led me through the large foyer, I caught a glimpse of a sumptuous living room. In the kitchen, modern appliances gleamed spotlessly, competing for luster with the copper pots that hung along one wall.

Cathleen introduced me to Sheila, the cook, a comfortably plump woman. "We were just havin' a cupper," she told me. "Would you like some?" I had grown fond of the English "cupper," that universal cure for everything that humans have to face, and so I sat down with Cathleen and Sheila to get acquainted.

The women had been prepared for me by Mr. Specter. They plied me with questions about my family, Vienna, the Nazis. While not too well informed, they knew enough about Hitler to be aware of the atrocities against Jews. Both of them had been born and raised in Ireland, and they knew something about oppression and violence and poverty. "We're ever so happy to be workin' for Mr. Specter," they told me. "Such a nice old gentleman! Generous! Gives us a big bonus for Christmas and presents for our birthdays. A real gentleman, that one is!"

Since his wife's death a year earlier, the flat rarely saw visitors. "There's hardly enough work for the two of us," Sheila told me. "That's why Julie was let go. She had the room you're goin' to stay in, you know. The place was much livelier when the Mrs. was alive."

"Coo, I'm not complainin'! I like havin' a bit o' free time," Cathleen said. She had the rosy cheeks and healthy glow of a country girl. Sheila chuckled. "She likes to go dancin', that one!" she said, looking fondly at Sheila.

After tea, Sheila showed me the flat. As she led me through room after room filled with costly antiques and authentic paintings, the impression of wealth was overpowering. The surroundings intimidated me, and I was glad to return to the servants' quarters.

My simple room seemed opulent compared to the ones I had recently known. The bed was cloud-soft and inviting, and the bathroom I shared with the two women was immaculate—the most modern bathroom I had seen in England so far. The plumbing in most English homes was badly in need of repair, and unlike America, where a daily bath is a religiously observed ritual, in England, as in the Vienna I knew, a once-weekly bath was more the rule.

Two weeks passed before I saw the old man again. Then one evening Cathleen told me he wanted to see me in the dining room. He looked very small as he sat at the long table eating his solitary meal.

"So? How're you doing?" he asked.

"Fine," I said hesitantly. "Only..."

"I know. A girl like you needs a family. I'm trying, believe me, but people are nervous, nobody knows what will happen, the Germans could start bombing any time. Be patient. You can stay here as long as you want, the girls like you, you're in nobody's way. Go, have a good time, see your friends, watch the pictures...You need stockings? Girls always need stockings. Here." He drew out some bills and thrust them at me. "Come. Take. Don't be proud."

Another week passed and then another. I was living in a kind of limbo. I took long walks in Hyde Park and often stopped to listen to the soap box orators. Their inflammatory anti-government speeches amazed me. Even in pre-Nazi Austria, freedom of speech had never been that free.

Sometimes I strolled along Regent Street and looked at the rich displays in the shop windows, or watched the buskers perform on the sidewalks outside movie theaters. But my life seemed to be in suspension. I longed for Michel and for my sisters. I did all in my power to obtain a Belgian visa again, but it was impossible. Desolate, I abandoned the idea.

The clouds of war grew more menacing. There was no longer any doubt that England and France would declare war on Germany. In mid-July, Specter called me to the dining room. "Things look bad," he said. "I'm going to close up the flat, put everything in storage. I'll go to France, wait out the war behind the Magenot Line. So what are you going to do? I can't take you along, you know. I'm too old to look after a young girl."

"When are you leaving?" I asked, swallowing hard.

"Next month. So why don't you go to Belgium? Stay with your sisters, you'll be safe. What do you say?"

Tears came to my eyes. "There's no place on earth I'd rather be," I sobbed. "But I can't get the visa. Believe me, I tried!"

"Don't cry," he said soothingly. "So tell me what you need, maybe I can help. I know a few people here and there, I can pull a couple of strings..."

He could, and he did. On August 2nd, 1939, I held the Belgian visa in my hand, and two days later, I was on my way. I said a tearful good-bye to the Coles and my other friends, and this time, I took all my belongings with me. War or no war, I was determined not to return to England.

Nine

When Michel and I saw each other again, the spark struck with the old intensity. He had started a small business that turned warm, woolen fabrics into colorful scarves. The Belgian winters are cold and damp; the scarves appealed to the practical sense of fashion-conscious women and les echarpes Graboi were an instant hit.

"Your parents can rest easy," he told me. "I can support you now. I don't want to live without you. I found that out while you were gone. If you feel the same, we should get married as soon as possible."

I agreed. This time, I was sure my family would not oppose me. My sisters and their husbands held visas to America and were getting ready to leave. My parents would see that it was better for me to be with the man I loved than alone in a world on the edge of World War II.

I was more in love with Michel than ever. His prominent cheekbones were topped by large, luminous blue eyes that seemed to look directly into my soul. I was carried on clouds of illusion, projecting into the passionate, romantic young man all the characteristics of the heroes in my books. There were moments when signs of problems surfaced, but I tried to ignore them, and thanks to the language barrier between us that persisted until my French matched his, I was unaware of the cultural gap that later yawned between us. Ours was not a marriage made in heaven, but for the next few years, our mutual infatuation glossed over our differences. Today I am well aware that what we call love is often only the craving to be loved. But in the springtime of my in-lovedness, it seemed impossible that I would wake up one day and realize that the abrasions of marriage are intended to polish our rough edges and bring our latent strength to the surface.

Before I could tell my family that we meant to get married, one important question had to be settled.

"Would you consider leaving Belgium?" I asked Michel. We were sitting on the terrace of a restaurant that overlooked the Schelde, Antwerp's picturesque river, and were eating mussels and pommes frites, the way only the Belgians know how to make them, as Michel informed me.

"Why do you ask?" He looked surprised.

"My parents want me to leave Europe. Everybody else will be in America— Oscar, Dolly, Fanny… We all want to get away from the threat of war!"

"So do I. But I like it here. It's been my home for many years. Besides, Belgium won't get in the war."

"In Vienna, nobody thought that Hitler would annex Austria," I replied dryly. "Anyway, I want to go to America. As soon as I can get the affidavit."

"The affidavit? What's that?"

"You need a paper from an American citizen who'll vouch for you. He must guarantee to support you should you fail to do so yourself. That's why he must have sufficient means—he has to be rich, in other words."

"And there are people in America who're willing to take such a chance on a stranger?"

I nodded. "It's amazing how kind these Americans are! I can't wait to get there!"

Michel wanted to know more about America and listened with interest as I talked on. What I knew came from reading Dreiser, Steinbeck, Sinclair Lewis, Edna Ferber and other contemporary authors, and from the movies. I knew enough not to believe the glitzy Hollywood films, but the honesty, the naivete that came through exercised a great attraction on me. Europe was jaded, cynical, tired. The land across the sea drew me like a magnet.

"How soon will you get this affidavit?" Michel asked.

"As soon as my brother can find a sponsor for me. It'll be harder than for the rest of the family, though. Both of my sisters have husbands with business experience, and my brother has a degree in law. I have nothing—no working experience except as a maid, and there is no shortage of domestic help in America. A sponsor would be taking a big chance on me. But I know I'll get it. My quota is good."

"Your quota? What's that?"

"The quota depends on the number of people who immigrate from the country of your birth per year. The Austrian quota is still wide open. Once I get the affidavit, I'll be on my way."

"If I decided to go to America, my quota would be as good as yours. Not many people have left the U.S.S.R. in recent years!"

"And would you go?"

"Why not? If it would make you happy..."

Being of age, I did not need my parents' consent, but I was anxious to get their blessings. To reassure them, I slightly exaggerated the extent of Michel's business success. My parents were pleased. "We are happy to know that your Michel will be a good provider," they wrote. "Love is good but security is very important. God bless you, and may good fortune smile on you always."

A letter Mama wrote to Oscar at that time shows her love and concern for me:

Vienna, September 4, 1939

Dearest Oscar,

You have not written in a while, but I want to take this opportunity to write you. We are both well, thank God. And now it seems to be serious with Gusterl and Michel. I had a feeling that it would be, and yesterday we had a letter from her in which she tells us that it was Michel who drew her back to Antwerp. She sounds very happy. We share her happiness and wish her and her Michel all the luck in the world forever and ever—they deserve it, they really had to fight for it! Gusterl says he is the dearest and best man on earth, and she begs us for our blessing, which we give with all our heart. Michel also wanted to write us, but Gusterl thought it would be best if she prepared us first. Altogether we are very pleased that she made her choice according to her own wishes. Papa and I are feeling very anxious because we are wondering if they are already married and we could not be there, it is the same feeling as when you and Greterl were married in a foreign land. But the main thing is that the two of them hold together, and we are sure that he is a fine man because it is inconceivable that our Gusterl would fall in love with someone unworthy!

We are wondering when Fanny and Willy will join you in America. Do they have their visas? Papa just visited your parents, dearest Greterl; they are both well. And now I wish you both the best and send you my loving thoughts.

Your Mother

We were married in a simple ceremony conducted by a rabbi. The wedding had no legal value, since Belgium did not recognize religious marriages, but it was the best we could do before my sisters left, because I could not get the many documents I needed from Vienna in time. In 1939, it was unthinkable for a couple to move in together before they were legally married. I was living in "sin" and felt deliciously wicked. When we were married in a civil ceremony a year later, I was almost sorry.

We moved into a tiny house that stood in the courtyard of one of Antwerp's newest and tallest apartment buildings. People called it the skyscraper because its twelve floors made it tower above the low buildings in the rest of town. Most of its tenants were rich diamond merchants who could easily afford the high rent.

Our little house had been constructed for the architect of the tall building. It served as his office while the skyscraper was being built. The real estate agent was reluctant to show it to us. "It wasn't built to be lived in," he said as he opened the door.

I loved it. Its peculiarities only added to its charm. There was no kitchen, but the addition of a stove turned a small downstairs room that held a sink into an adequate cooking facility. The large room upstairs became our living-bedroom. What made it special was that it was our own little house. Best of all, the rent was low. The money that came in for the scarves was immediately reinvested in the business, and there was not much cash available for our personal use. Michel christened our home "le pigeonnier" because it was not much larger than a pigeon coop—a fine nest for a pair of lovers.

I was playing house. Domestic virtues did not come easily to me. My English experiences had left me less than enthusiastic about dusting, sweeping, and washing dishes, but my real nemesis was cooking. Our meals consisted of Wiener Schnitzl and potato salad. To keep them from being too monotonous, I managed to burn the meat sometimes, leaving it underdone at others. Michel soon gave up pretending to like my cooking.

"Why don't you ask Tanya to teach you?" he said. My sister-in-law was a good cook, especially when it came to preparing Russian dishes. I enjoyed her food, but did not like her. She was a mean-spirited young woman who missed no opportunity to belittle my lack of domestic skills. But my culinary deficiencies threatened to erode my marital bliss, and so I swallowed my pride and asked Tanya's help. She gave it, though not without gloating, and soon my cooking improved.

Two weeks after Hitler invaded Poland, England and France declared war on Germany. So began what was called "the phony war" or "the war of nerves." For months, the war was fought only with words. The French basked in the security of the Magenot Line, and meanwhile, continued to arm.

In Belgium, as on the rest of the continent, it was business as usual; but the air was tense. People said they wished the war would already begin in earnest. The calm before the storm was hard to bear.

I spent most of my days typing invoices for Michel's business. The work was dull, repetitive and cheerless, but I shared it with Michel and that was all that mattered. "We're building our future," he said. Marriage had changed him. He was no longer the devil-may-care traveling salesman I first knew, but a hard-working, purposeful man. Abandoning his communist leanings, he went wholeheartedly after financial success. I respected his ingenuity and perseverance, but I did not want us to build our future in Belgium.

"What about America?" I asked.

"Let me make some real money first. It takes money to start a business in America. Don't worry, we'll get there. I promise."

And so we continued to manufacture scarves, and the money kept rolling in.

Ten

We were making love on the night of May 14th, 1940, four months after our wedding, when an unearthly brightness lit up the room. A thunderous noise filled the air, and simultaneously, the sirens all over Antwerp began to wail. German planes buzzed overhead and spewed bombs at us.

For the next three days, we ducked in and out of air-raid shelters. Our nights were spent in the basement of the "skyscraper." The wealthy tenants all talked of leaving Belgium. "How?" we asked. One man told us he had bought an ambulance and would drive it north with his family. Others said they would aim for Switzerland.

"France is as safe as Switzerland," somebody said. "The Boches will never cross the Magenot Line."

"Do you think Belgium will fall?" Michel asked.

"A few more bombs and we will surrender," the other replied.

He was right. The Belgian Army was ill-trained, small, and it quickly became disorganized. At the beginning of the phony war Michel had enlisted, but the army never got around to calling, much less training, the volunteers.

The bombs kept coming with increasing frequency. We were feverishly preparing to leave. Michel stored the merchandise in the pigeonnier, and when we locked it behind us, almost everything we owned was inside.

Like most of Antwerp's inhabitants, we headed towards the French frontier. On the second day, our little Fiat broke down. No-one could be found to repair it. Ours was not the only car that stood abandoned, and we joined the endless throng of refugees walking on foot toward France.

Before the Fiat broke down, we had been stopped by police who demanded to see our papers. When they discovered that I was a German citizen (my Austrian citizenship was automatically changed to German after the Anschluss), they arrested me as a German spy. In vain I protested that I was Jewish and had fled from the Nazis. "That's what all the damned parachutists say," the officer growled. Me, a parachutist? Rumors of German parachutists who infiltrated the countryside were rife among the fleeing crowd, and paranoia was at fever pitch.

After many hours and a great deal of anxiety, Michel's army registration and his guarantee for his "fiancée" got me out.

Soon, we were on the road again. Heavily laden with suitcases, bedding, even pieces of furniture, masses of refugees trudged along the road. It was not long before the muddy ditches on both sides of the road began to fill up with their possessions. Bird cages, paintings, silverware and precious heirlooms were left behind as people hastened to save their bare lives. Overhead, the German Messerschmidts played a game of cat and mouse. Every so often they swooped down to spray us with their machine guns, then they disappeared behind a cloud. When the drone of their motors announced their descent, we took cover in the treasure-lined ditches. Some of us died there, the rest plodded on. We slept anywhere—in haylofts, in barns, on the ice-cold kitchen floor of a farm house, in deserted train stations. We had discarded everything but one suitcase, filled with my clothes.

"Ditch it!" I told Michel. "Do you think I'll ever care about clothes again?"

"Yes," he replied.

On the fourth day of walking I was unable to rise after taking cover in the ditch. "I can't go on," I told my husband. "Please leave me. Save your life. I can't walk another step."

"Nonsense," he said. But I meant it. When he saw that his efforts to rouse me had no effect, he said, "Wait here. I'll be back," and he was gone.

I don't know how long I lay there when Michel shook me. He had stolen an old, rusty wheelbarrow from a nearby farm and helped me into it. Loading the suitcase next to me, he trundled me off.

The next day we reached the French frontier. A multitude of refugees pressed against it to enter the protection of the Magenot Line. My German passport was met with a stony "Pas admis!" by the frontier guard, and we were forced to turn back. Frightened and disheartened, we walked back the way we had come. By dusk, we reached La Panne, a Belgian seaside resort where Michel had often come for a weekend of sun and fun. When we found a room in one of the majestic hotels, we did not know that we were only a few miles and a few days away from the deadly battle of Dunkerque. That first day we took a long, blissful bath and then lay down in the comfortable bed with its clean linen.

"I never want to get up again," I said as I stretched out, luxuriously naked for once after many nights fully clothed.

We both fell asleep almost instantly. It was dark when the air-raid siren sounded. Hastily, we slipped on our clothes and went down to the cellar of the old, solid building, where the other hotel guests were already settling down for the night.

The next days were spent in search of food. Our forays were punctuated by the shrieks of sirens, sending us scurrying for the nearest shelter.

Then came a night when I told Michel once again that I could not go on. "I need one night of sleep in a bed," I cried, "one whole night, undressed, lying in bed! I don't care if I die! At least I'll die in a bed!" I was curled up on the bed in the fetal position, sobbing.

"We can't stay here. You know that. Come on. If we go down now, we can get a place near the wall. It's easier when you can lean against a wall."

"No! You go! Leave me alone! Leave me alone!" I pulled the blanket over my head. Michel pulled it away and roughly grasped my shoulders.

"Get up! You're coming down with me! Get up this minute! You must!"

"I'm not going!" I sobbed. "I'm not leaving this bed!"

Michel grabbed me in his strong arms and half carried and half dragged me down the four flights of stairs.

That night, there was hardly a pause between bombs. When they were not coming from directly overhead, we could hear the noise of more distant cannons and bombs. Some of the people in the cellar were praying, others huddled together in terror. A woman in the corner shrieked shrilly without stopping. Michel and I were holding hands. Each time a bomb hit nearby, I squeezed his hand until he told me to stop, I was making him crazy. We knew that we were safe so long as we could hear a sharp whistle while the bomb fell. "It's when you don't hear it that it's coming straight at you," people said knowingly.

At 2 a.m., it came. An earth-shaking boom, not preceded by a whistle. "We were hit!" somebody yelled. Children were crying. Pandemonium reigned, but miraculously, the cellar remained intact. The hotel had been built to outlast the centuries.

At dawn, we peered through the narrow windows high on the wall of the cellar and watched as German snipers cautiously crept along the ruined buildings, rifles at the ready.

At last, the "ALL CLEAR" sounded. Dazed, we emerged from the cellar. The elegant lobby on the street floor was a pile of rubble. It had been a direct hit. The strong, solid cellar had saved our lives. All that remained of the stately building was a flight of stairs that led nowhere.

Michel walked up these stairs and looked down into the hole left by the bomb. "Guess what!" he called down to me after a while. "I see your suitcase! It looks unharmed." He came down. "I'm going to look for a rope," he said.

"A rope? What for?" I asked, puzzled.

"I want to try something. Be back soon."

Desolate, I looked around at the devastation. The street was littered with debris. Dead horses, legs stretched stiffly in the air, were lying in the rubble. With a shudder, I saw two bodies in the dust not far from me. I sat down on the ruined wall of the hotel and covered my eyes. "God," I prayed, "if there is a God, let me die right now. I don't want to live in a world where such things can happen!"

When Michel came back, he not only held a coil of rope in his hands, but also two apples, which he had found. And as we sat on the crumbling wall and ate our apples, the absurdity of the situation suddenly hit me with such force that I broke into mad laughter.

"You know what?" I brought out between hiccups. "He's following me!"

"Who?" Michel asked.

"Hitler!" I yelled. Michel quickly covered my mouth with his hand. A group of German soldiers were crossing the square. Sobered, I controlled myself. The hysteria that had gripped some of the people in the cellar had caught up with me, but I knew that I had to master it or endanger my husband and myself.

Michel fashioned a loop at one end of the rope and walked up the stairs.

I watched as he threw down the loop time after time. "I have it!" he called down excitedly at last. He slowly pulled up the rope and above the abyss appeared—my suitcase!

Only two weeks had elapsed since the first German assault on Antwerp. Belgium had fallen to the Nazis. We were trapped. Wearily, we started the trek back to Antwerp, not knowing where else to go. This time, there were fewer people on the road. The refugees had dispersed in various directions or chosen to stay where they were. From time to time, we saw German soldiers marching, and many German army trucks passed by, spraying us with dust. Sometimes we got a ride in a vehicle driven by a Belgian. Once we were picked up by a German officer in civilian clothes. At first, I panicked when I realized who he was, but his face was so open and free of guile that I soon chatted away with him in German. He showed us photos of his wife and child, and I responded by telling him about my parents and begging him to get word to them that we were safe, which he promised to do.

What I remember best of that long walk is the kindness we encountered everywhere. Farmers whose homes were undamaged took us in, fed us, and let us sleep in their spare rooms. The comfort of those warm, soft beds! Sleep, uninterrupted by shrieking sirens was a life-giving gift. My young body responded, and this time I kept step with Michel.

Eleven

The "skyscraper" was occupied by German officers. All the tenants had fled, leaving their luxurious apartments ready prey for the conquerors. Miraculously, our pigeonnier had been left intact. I was frightened by our close proximity to the Nazi officers. We had to pass through the lobby of the big building to get to the street, and there were always one or more of them around. Michel assured me I had nothing to fear.

"They're under strict orders to leave the Jews alone. There have been no arrests and no Jew baitings. The Germans obey orders. They won't touch us till they get the go-ahead."

I believed him. As soon as he had settled me in the pigeonnier, he disappeared. He went to "sniff around," as he called it; I knew from experience that he always brought back accurate information from his "sniffs," and so I relaxed and tried to enjoy the temporary security. I slept long nights, my brain and body drinking in the surcease of immediate danger, the silence, the soft bed.

On the first morning, we were awakened by a curious noise. Compared to the wailing of the sirens and the screaming of the bombs, it was a harmless sound, yet it sent fear signals to my brain. It sounded like a rhythmic clapping or slapping, and in my mind's eye I saw Germans slapping Jews. Michel ran to the window. He made a curious sound.

"Come here! Quick!" He was doubled over with laughter.

Slipping on my robe, I came to the window. Hung over the railing of each of the balconies on each of the twelve floors was a colorful assortment of

Persian rugs. The slapping sounds came from twelve immaculately groomed orderlies who stood precisely aligned, one above the other, wielding their rug beaters in unison.

The next morning we watched as, precisely at 7 a.m., all twelve balcony doors flew open and the twelve orderlies stepped out. With one motion, they flung their rugs over the railing, and the beating commenced. Their precision was awesome. When I saw the Roquettes many years later, they brought back memories of the rug-beating Germans.

It felt good to be back in the pigeonnier among our few possessions. The imitation oriental rug, the copies of a Modigliani and of Picasso's "Three Musicians" had been left alone by the invaders. No doubt they found better booty in the skyscraper. We, too, were left alone. The officers were courteous and polite. They held doors open for me and greeted me with the respectful "Küss die Hand, gnädige Frau" (I kiss your hand, gracious lady).

Only once did we experience the terror that lurked behind the civilized facade. In the fall, the officers bought a pig. The orderlies built a pen for it at the far end of the courtyard, and twice a day they passed the pigeonnier with pails of food. The pen was kept spotlessly clean. I don't know how the pig felt about all this cleanliness, but its girth soon showed the effects of all the food. I felt a great warmth for the animal. Its grunts sounded earthy and real. I hoped it didn't realize it was being fattened for the Christmas feast.

One day, an orderly found the pig dead. A great hue and cry was raised. Suspicion fell on Maurice, the janitor, a shifty-eyed Belgian. To clear himself, he directed the Germans' attention to my husband. The Jews hate pigs, don't they? And who had a better opportunity than Michel to steal out at night and kill it?

The officer who knocked on our door was the tall, sharp-featured man with the greying hair who never failed to bow to me.

"Küss die Hand, gnädige Frau," he said, without bowing this time. "I would like to speak to your husband. Is he at home?" His voice was frosty. Michel was upstairs and came down when he heard our voices. The German lost no time getting to the point.

"We are investigating the death of the pig. Did you, Herr Graboi, have anything to do with it?" When Michel denied it, the German's tone grew menacing. "We are conducting an investigation, and if it appears that you caused the pig's death, you will be executed," he announced. "If you admit your guilt now, it will go easier for you."

When Michel continued to deny that he killed the pig, the officer assured him that the truth would come out. "We will see who murdered the pig!" he stated. He clicked his heels, bowed, and left.

We spent several anxious days. To our immense relief, the autopsy proved that the pig had died of natural causes, and Michel was safe.

For the rest, my memories of that year contain few life-threatening situations. Occasionally, an English plane strayed and dropped a bomb on Antwerp. We applauded wildly even though we ourselves were endangered. But it happened rarely. The English were after military targets, not civilian populations. At night, gigantic searchlights swept the skies. If they revealed an English plane, the noise of anti-aircraft guns filled the air. When they struck, there was a blinding flash as the burning plane streaked downwards like a falling star.

With his usual courage, resourcefulness and enterprise, Michel set about refurbishing our meager finances. Carrying a sample case full of scarves, he criss-crossed the ravaged country by whatever means he could find. Most of the railroads had been destroyed. He hitchhiked, rode a bicycle, and walked. Somehow he managed to get around. He visited the shops that were left intact, and once again, the scarves sold well.

Most of my time was spent hunting for food. It was a pursuit that took as much of my energy as it took Michel's to sell scarves, especially since I often came home empty-handed. Food was scarce in Antwerp, cut off as it was from supplies by the usual routes. Michel was slender to the point of gauntness, but his appetite was huge. I was often at my wits end how to put a nutritious meal on the table. Flour could be bought only on the black market, if you had connections and had the money, and I quickly learned how to bake bread. But it often took days before I could get more flour, and without bread, potatoes, rice or other filling staples, I could not cook a meal to satisfy my husband's needs.

One day, as I wearily trudged from store to store, I noticed a barrel full of chestnuts in a corner. I was surprised. A luxury item like imported chestnuts seemed of little use in times like these. My mouth watered as I remembered the taste of riced chestnuts topped with chocolate sauce and whipped cream, a specialty at Gerstner's, the posh Konditorei on the Kaerntnerstrasse, where I had often gone in my teens. How delicious it had been, and how filling!

On an impulse, I bought a pound. After some experimentation I discovered that I could mash the boiled chestnuts and mix them with sauted onions. This made an excellent replacement for the potatoes Michel missed so much. I could also shape the mashed chestnuts into patties and fry them like hamburgers, and I could rice them and serve them with sugar and cinnamon—et voilà! an elegant meal. I went back to the store and bought the whole barrelful. The storekeeper let me have them for a song. "You're welcome to them, Madame," he shrugged. "I'm happy to see them go. Are you planning a big party, maybe?" He was trying to hide his amusement at what seemed like a crazy purchase.

I believe it was thanks to the chestnuts, the onions, which were plentiful, and another readily available and nutritious food, namely the humble peanut, that we remained in good health.

Antwerp is a curious town. The population is mostly Flemish, the sturdy peasant stock that inhabits the lowlands. Not fifty kilometers away is Brussels, where French is the dominant language. Brussels tries hard to be a "petit Paris," but Antwerp struck me as a dull, provincial town. The men spent most of their days away working, while the women kept immaculate homes and cooked large, robust meals. The Antwerp of the first year of my marriage appears in my mind as a lackluster town full of complacent, mediocre people.

The first year of marriage can be difficult, even under the best circumstances. Add wartime, the presence of the Nazis, and the difference in our cultural backgrounds, and it is easy to see that my memory of that year is clouded by unhappiness. Some fundamental differences between us had begun to appear. I felt alone and vulnerable with a man whom I did not basically know.

Twelve

"We should get our visa applications started right away," I said a few days after our return. Michel was curiously evasive whenever I brought up the subject of the U.S.A. I thought it was due to his attachment to the country where he had spent so many years, but he had agreed to go to America before we were married, and I was sure he would be as anxious as I to leave Nazi-occupied Belgium. "Let's go to the American consulate tomorrow!" I pressed on.

Michel evaded my eyes. "There is something I must tell you, Gusti." He was ill at ease and groped for words. "I was born in Kisheneff, not in Odessa," he brought out, defiantly.

"I don't understand," I said, puzzled. "What's the difference?"

"Kisheneff is a small town in Besarabia, not far from Odessa. Do you know about the pogroms?" I shook my head. "Many Jews live in Kisheneff. The Kossaks would ride into town and kill Jews. They killed my father." There was a look in his eyes I had never seen before.

"Oh!" I said. "You never told me."

"There's something else I never told you. After World War I Kisheneff fell to Rumania. Odessa still belongs to Russia. That's why I lied."

I still did not understand. "What does it matter? You're a Russian. You speak Russian with Lyowa and Tanya, not Roumanian!"

"There is a difference. You yourself told me that the American quota depends on your country of birth. And Rumania..."

My heart sank. "How long do we have to wait? Five years?"

Michel shook his head.

"Ten?" Again, he shook his head.

"Fifteen?"

"Twenty-five," he said. "But don't worry! I'll get us to America somehow, believe me!"

And I did believe him. So far, he had pulled us out of every scrape. My confidence in his resourcefulness was complete.

We were shocked when the Magenot Line crumbled like termite-infested wood before the German assault. Little Belgium, squeezed between Germany and France, had only been a minor obstacle to the advancing Nazi juggernaut. Their real objective was France, and especially Paris, where their triumphal march along the Champ d'Elysee sealed their victory. The country was divided into occupied France and Free France, though the "free" part, under Field Marshal Petain, collaborated openly with the Germans.

We had lived roughly a year under the German occupation when Michel came home one day, looking grave.

"It's time to leave," he said. I nodded. We had been preparing for departure for some time. The Nazis had begun to arrest non-Belgian Jews, and Michel learned that Austrian Jews were next.

I packed a small bag for each of us. Michel had sold all his scarves at a loss, but it enabled us to leave with enough money to see us through a year, with luck.

The guides who would smuggle us into France were a red-headed brother and sister team. Once more we locked the pigeonnier behind us, leaving everything we owned inside. We departed at night in a truck that took us and two other couples to a farmhouse close to the border in northern France. While we waited for the sheltering darkness of the night, the guides instructed us to make no noise when we followed them and warned us that if we were discovered, we would all be shot.

We set out just before midnight. It was a starless, moonless night, and the only way we could stay close to our guides was by holding on to each others' coats. We were walking through a swampy field, our feet sinking deep into the mud. When one of the women slipped and fell, she brought all of us down with her. The guides quickly helped us to get up and made us cover our mouths with our hands lest any sound escape us. Far away, we could see the lights of the guard house, serving as a constant reminder of the danger we faced.

After what seemed many hours we came to a solitary, deserted house. There was no sign of life to be seen and we were astonished when our guides opened the door and ushered us in.

"Welcome to France!" said a friendly voice. An elderly man carrying a candle came from one of the inner rooms. "Come and get warm. You're safe here."

We followed him into a cozy kitchen where wine and a warm meal were waiting for us. It tasted wonderful, and after washing up we lay down on bunk beds and slept soundly until the next day. Early in the morning, we boarded the train for Paris and arrived there around noon.

Paris! How often I had dreamed of visiting that Mecca of literature, art, culture! "Liberté, Fraternité, Egalité!" What noble ideas! I was anxious to get a glimpse of the city that figures so prominently in the literature of the world. But first we checked into a small hotel on the Rive Gauche, where another team of guides waited to take us to unoccupied France.

The guides were two young Frenchmen who obviously enjoyed their mission of helping people to freedom. "You can walk around freely in Paris as long as you are unobtrusive," they told us. "The Boches do not ask for papers on the street—yet! But they will soon, so it would be foolish to stay here any longer than absolutely necessary. Have a good time and don't get back to the hotel too late—we make an early start in the morning," they told us.

"I'll show you Paris," said Michel who had often been here and felt at home.

But the Eiffel Tower and the Champ d'Elysee were full of uniformed Germans, and in mid-afternoon we returned to the hotel, where we promptly fell asleep. When we woke up, it was dusk.

"It's still early," Michel said. "We don't want to stay here all evening. Let's have a bite at a bistro and go to the Follies Bergères. You'll see a piece of the real Paris!"

I put on the one extra dress I brought with me. We arrived after curtain rise and sat in our gallery seats watching the glittering show. It was an extravaganza a la Hollywood. The main attraction was the bare breasts of the women. Their head-dresses and the costumes that covered part of their bodies were gorgeous, and as they paraded around the stage with slow, stately steps they looked like lovely mechanical dolls.

I have neither the temperament nor the desire to be a rebel. Externally, I conform to the prevailing mores, but in my heart of hearts my attitude to the naked human body is, so what? We all have one, equipped with one or two of each—breasts, belly buttons, sex organs that are either male or female. So why all the fuss? I had seen films of primitive African tribes who were unselfconsciously naked and did not appear to be titillated by each others' bodies. How much saner their attitude seemed to me than that of their white brothers!

I think I've always been aware of my body as something separate from me. The body is not me, my essence self, but something I wear, like a dress. I love clothes, enjoy wearing attractive fabrics, colors, styles—not from vanity but from an instinct that makes me want to create beauty wherever I can. A journal entry, made when I was in my sixties, expresses it well: "I decorate my body the same way that I decorate my home, care for my garden, my car, arrange food on a plate in an eye-pleasing manner. If everybody would care for their own little bit of geography in this way, what a beautiful world it would be!"

That night at the Follies I was more interested in watching the Germans watching the show than in the bare breast parade on stage. The arrogant behavior of the invaders proclaimed them the masters of all they surveyed. They talked loudly and called out to the gorgeous dolls. "Today Paris, tomorrow the world," their demeanor shouted. Hatred for the master race rose up in me like a sickness.

"The show did not impress you?" Michel asked when we left the theater. He liked to tease me about my sexual innocence and had expected me to be shocked. "Guess you're more sophisticated than I thought. Shall we have a drink before we turn in for the night?"

I was not tired after our long afternoon nap, and Michel hailed a cab. "Take us to rue Blondell," he instructed the driver. From the outside, the place we entered looked like an ordinary coffee house, but the waitresses were completely naked. The woman who brought our drinks was neither young nor pretty. Her sagging breasts touched the table when she bent down to serve us. "What would you like to see?" she asked Michel.

"What do you have?" he enquired, looking sideways at me with a mischievous grin.

The waitress wheeled off a menu of sexual acrobatics that ranged from activities performed by couples to single acts such as the woman who picked up coins with her vagina. This time Michel had me. I turned beet-red. "It's up to Madame," my husband told the waitress. "What would you like to see, cherie?"

"The last one," I said, trying to look bored.

And in fact, after my first shocked amazement I was bored. How silly! I thought. I truly could not understand why people would want to waste their time and money on watching the bare breasts at the Follies and the agile vaginas of the whores on rue Blondell.

As we walked out of the door, a man entered. Giving me a long, appreciative look he asked, "Voulez-vous tirer un coup?" I understood the words, but not their meaning, and looked questioningly at Michel. Tirer means to pull, and coup means hit. Why should I want to pull a hit? "C'est ma femme," Michel told the man and drew me away. Greatly amused, he translated the man's words. I was not flattered.

The next morning, our small group of refugees and the two guides took a train to a town just this side of Free France. Another border to cross! This time, we would cross in plain daylight. Our guides told us that the guards had been bribed and would give us no trouble, but they took the precaution of giving each of us a basket filled with eggs, butter and other farm products, and on the women's heads they tied kerchiefs in the manner worn by the women of that region. "Pretend you are French peasants in case anything goes wrong," they told us. This was not very reassuring to me as I was only too well aware of my imperfect French. However, I had no choice.

We crossed into Free France without mishap.

Thirteen

We decided to stay in Lyon where Michel knew an elderly couple who had befriended him on earlier visits to that town. Soon after our arrival, we made contact with other refugees who showed us how to avoid the traps that awaited those without a carte d'identité. We located blackmarket sources and restaurants where we could get food without stamps. We were told what places to stay away from, and what places were safe. Many Spanish rebels came over the Pyrenees to escape General Franco's army and were hiding in Lyon, and there were many Jewish refugees from occupied France. The Spaniards and their sympathizers were the prime target of the police raids, but enough Jews suddenly disappeared to make all of us very cautious.

I have almost no memory of the city of Lyon because we stayed mostly in a dark, shabby room in a fleabag hotel that required no identity papers. We bought a small kerosene burner on which I prepared most of our meals, washing the dishes afterwards in the ubiquitous bidet that graces even the poorest hotel rooms in France. It was the only humorous note in an otherwise grim and joyless time.

One day, Michel did not return from one of his "sniffing around" expeditions. As night began to fall and there was still no sign of him, I grew more and more alarmed. After a sleepless night I went to see Monsieur Alban, Michel's elderly friend. When I told him what had happened, he looked grave.

"What do you think?" I asked anxiously.

"A police net, most likely, I'm afraid."

His words only confirmed what I already suspected, but I was hoping against hope that it was not true.

"How can I find out?" I asked, in despair.

"Let me make some phone calls. I know a police captain. He is an honorable man. Maybe he can tell us."

By noon, the answer came: Michel had been located in one of the foulest prisons in Lyon.

"Can I see him?" I asked.

"I'm afraid not," the old gentleman replied. "They don't allow visitors."

I was desolate. "I must get him out of there! Where can I get help? What can I do? Help me, Monsieur Alban!"

"You can do nothing for the time being," he replied. "There is no point in getting caught yourself. I will do all I can. Don't worry, child. We will find a way. Stay with us here tonight. Maybe by tomorrow there will be some news."

But there was no news the next day, and the next. Mons. Alban spent much of his time trying to pull strings for Michel's release, but after four days, there was still no ray of hope. Mme. Alban, a kindly, ample-bosomed lady, hovered over me like a mother hen, but her ministrations did nothing to ease my fears.

On the fifth day, Mons. Alban sat down with me. "I don't want you to get your hopes up too much, but there may be something you can do."

"Anything!" I said. "Please tell me!"

"There is a priest, his name is Father Bernard, who has been helpful to some Jewish refugees trapped in police raids. I don't know if he can do anything for Michel, but it's worth a try. Go see him tomorrow. He is a kind man. He will surely do his best."

Tears streaming down my face, I thanked Mons. Alban. Early the next morning, I went to Father Bernard. He listened compassionately as I sobbed out my story. When I told him the name of the prison, he blanched.

"That is a very bad place," he said gravely. For a long while, he was silent. "All right," he said at last. "I will see what I can do. Try to be calm, Madame. We are all in God's hands. You will hear from me tonight."

But it wasn't until the next day that I heard from him. In mid-afternoon, Mme. Alban called me to the phone. "You can pick up your husband tonight," Father Bernard said. "It's all arranged. No, don't thank me, child. Your husband is innocent. It is God's will that he should be free."

I was incoherent with relief when I told the Albans the good news. Mons. Alban came with me to pick Michel up. The man who came out of the prison gate did not look like the man I knew. He looked wasted. His cheekbones, always prominent, stood out like bullets in a face gone ashen. Slowly, painfully, his story came out. Most of the prisoners in the overcrowded cell had been Spaniards. Every few hours, the guard would come for one of them, and not much later they would hear a shot in the yard below, a scream, and then silence.

"I expected them to come for me any moment," Michel said, shuddering. "I was sure that my life was over!"

The prison stay undermined Michel's optimism and the self-confidence that had carried him before. His usually buoyant spirits gave way to a deep depression which did not leave him for days. We had survived by his courage and resourcefulness. Now he grew grim in his determination to get us to America.

"But how?" I asked. "What chance do we have with your quota?"

"I'll find a way!" he vowed. "Believe me. I'll get us out of here!"

But for two long months, not a ray of hope appeared on the horizon. The only good news was that affidavits arrived for us, signed by my brother's sponsor. We handled them reverently. "They are an omen," we said.

At last came a day when Michel returned triumphantly from his "sniffing around."

"The American Consulate in Marseilles changed the quota of a Roumanian woman to that of her Polish husband!" he exulted. "We're going to Marseilles."

And so we quickly gathered our few belongings and set off for the colorful Mediterranean seaport. Early the next morning, we went to the American Consulate. A line that extended for several blocks was already waiting there. "Will they let us all in when they open?" Michel asked the man who stood next to us.

"Let us in?" the man laughed. "If we're lucky, we'll get close enough to the door to get a glimpse inside by tonight!"

"Then what's the point of staying here all day?" Michel wanted to know.

"The point? To see America, of course!" the man replied.

"That's right," the woman in front of us chimed in. "The Consulate is American territory. I want to see how free people live!"

We did not get close enough that day to see America. That night, Michel shook me awake long before dawn. Shivering with cold, we took up our vigil at the end of the short line that had already begun to form. By noon, we reached the door. "Your papers," the guard said. We handed him our affidavits. "Not those," he said, handing them back. "Your identity cards!"

We were stunned. Without proof of residence in France the Consulate would not consider our case, it appeared. And our chances of getting it were nil. "Go to Nice," the people who witnessed our plight advised. "It's easy to get identity cards there."

And so we went to Nice. Thanks to the off-season rates we found a nice, clean, inexpensive room close to the beach. Few refugees had found their way to Nice. There were no police raids. The ocean was immense, and there were flowers everywhere. I knew the French Riviera by name and had often heard of Nice, that fabulous place where the beautiful people went to play. I expected a village, like the resorts in Italy and Yugoslavia where I had vacationed with Mama. Instead, I discovered that Nice, while still small by most standards, is really a town. Bathed in sunshine most of the year, its white buildings and lovely gardens please the eye and convey a mood of optimism.

Our spirits began to lift and we took hope again for the future. We bought bathing suits and some clothes. Michel had been right when he told me I would be interested in clothes again if we survived. I looked longingly at the lovely dresses in the shop windows on the Promenade des Anglais, entranced by the subtle yet colorful prints, the rich textures, the variety of styles. One shop in particular caught my eye. A simple off-white silk shantung suit hung from the well-padded shoulders of the mannequin. It would go well with my tan, I thought.

"That suit would look great on you," Michel observed. "Do you want it?"

"It's much too expensive. We can't spend money on such luxuries!"

But we bought the suit. It helped to lift the oppressive feeling of exile from my soul. However, we were still without identity cards and food stamps. The granting of these papers had been revoked two days prior to our arrival, and so we were really no better off than before. The fear of arrest was ever present, and since everything except fruits and vegetables was rationed, we were forced to pay the exorbitant black market prices.

"Let's try to get legal," said Michel. He had regained his jauntiness. "They say the police here can be bribed. I bet we can find an official who will make us legal for a price."

"What if we pick one who can't be bribed? He'll report us, and God knows what will happen then!"

"I think we should take that chance. If we don't, we'll never get the papers we need for the Americans. Come, put on your white suit and be sure to smile at the official while I talk to him."

The man who rose from his chair when we entered the small office was short, pudgy and balding. The size of the office and the simplicity of its furnishings made it apparent that the official who occupied it did not make much money. Michel took the risk.

"We are refugees. We are hoping to go to America, but meanwhile we must survive. We need identity cards and food stamps. Can you help us?"

Deliberately, he opened his wallet and took out some large bills.

"Refugees?" the man said, waving the bills aside.

The smile on my face froze. We picked the wrong one, I thought, panicking. Michel's hand shook as he returned the bills to his wallet, but he bravely went on to tell the official our story. While he listened, the man glanced at me from time to time, his pale, watery eyes mirroring compassion. When Michel spoke of my escape from Vienna, he exploded angrily. "Those swine!" he exclaimed. Relief flooded me. He meant us no harm.

"I doubt that I can get you identity cards, but I will try to get food stamps for you. You must be hungry. How can you manage to get a decent meal without food stamps? Allow me to take you to dinner tonight. In the meantime, I will see what I can do."

The smile I gave him was radiant, and Michel's handshake expressed the gratitude he felt.

At dinner, Mons. Pelissier continued to question us about our experiences. He had read about the war, the Nazis, and the occupation of half of France, but here on the Cote d'Azur none of it seemed quite real. We were the first refugees he knew, and the kind-hearted man was very moved by our story. How he managed to supply us with food stamps I will never know. He was our guardian angel throughout our stay in Nice. We saw him often, sharing an evening with him or a Sunday afternoon walk. He was a bachelor, lonely, and touchingly grateful for our company.

One morning, Michel waved a newspaper at me. "It says here that Admiral Leahy and his wife are coming to Nice. There will be a celebration in his honor. The ceremony will take place in front of the Town Hall at three o'clock. Why don't you write him a letter in your best English describing our predicament and asking for his help? We can try to give him the letter this afternoon. What do you say?"

I liked the idea and set to work right away. While I was writing, Michel had copies made of our affidavits. We added these and our best photo to the letter and got ready to leave. At 2 p.m. we joined the crowd that was gathering to await the arrival of the honored guests. Admiral Leahy had done a great deal to encourage the supply of food from America to France, and he was very popular. The plaza was a sea of flowers; hundreds of school children stood ready to sing patriotic songs. It was a beautiful spectacle, but it was marred for us by the presence of the police who formed a chain in front of the onlookers, making any approach to the high guests impossible. That's that, I thought; we might as well go home. But we stayed anyway and were deeply moved by the way the crowd received the Admiral. "Vive l'Amerique! Vive Roosevelt!" they shouted, and hundreds of children's voices called "Merci! Merci!" The Admiral and his wife smiled kindly. Mrs. Leahy especially seemed to me to exude goodness. I sensed that she would understand and respond to our plight.

"I wish I could give her the letter," I told Michel.

"We can send it to her," said Michel who was never one to give up easily.

I agreed. Following my hunch about Mrs. Leahy I made some changes in the letter and we sent it registered, addressed to her Excellency Mrs. Leahy at the embassy in Vichy. When no reply came, we stopped thinking about the letter; it had been a slim hope at best. We directed our thoughts elsewhere to seek a way of gaining entry to the U.S.A. Our funds were running dangerously low. To save money, we made our meals on a small kerosene burner.

Michel was an early riser and would generally have coffee ready for me when I woke up. One morning I was still asleep when I heard him yell "Fire!" When I opened my eyes I saw that his hair and eyebrows were on fire. Immediately, I sprang into action. Tearing the blanket off the bed, I covered his head with it. The flames were instantly extinguished, and Michel got away with singed hair and eyebrows which gave off a burning smell for weeks.

My brother and sisters had settled in New York and started businesses of their own. Their letters expressed their deep concern for me and their fervent hope that we would soon be united. My brother was in constant touch with organizations that helped to bring Jewish refugees to the States, but without the visa they could do nothing for us.

We had not heard from my parents since we left Antwerp. No mail from Austria got through to Free France. Anxiety about their well-being was my constant companion, and I asked my siblings for news of them in every letter. Oscar wrote that they appeared to be well, and that their letters were full of love for me and the hope that their "Nestheckchen," the baby in the family, would soon join the others in America.

Fake visas were doing a brisk business on the black market, and when the opportunity to buy a visa for a South American country came our way, we eagerly seized it. We also bought steamship tickets on a freighter leaving in mid-May for Martinique where, we were told, we would find transportation to South America. Our hearts were heavy, all our hopes were centered on the U.S.A., but at least we would leave Europe and the shadow of Hitler behind us, and that had to be enough.

One day, the clerk at our hotel gave Michel an envelope that bore the words "Embassy of the United States." Michel's hand trembled as he handed it to me. "Read it aloud," he said impatiently. "What does it say?"

Translating into French as I scanned the letter, I read:
Vichy, April 21 1941

Mrs. Gusti Graboi,
Hotel de la Plata,
rue d'Italie,
Nice

Dear Mrs. Graboi:

Mrs. Leahy has asked me to reply to your letter of April 10, which she read with the greatest sympathetic attention.

Inasmuch as the Embassy is not competent under American law to intervene in immigration matters, especially in those connected with the priority of quota numbers, your letter and its enclosure are being forwarded to the American Consul General at Marseille with the request that he give your case and that of your husband all consideration compatible with immigration laws and regulations.

Very truly yours,
Woodruff Wallner
Secretary of Embassy

We were both silent when I finished reading. Our hopes seemed dashed. I don't think we expected our visas to come tumbling out of the auspicious envelope, but we did expect something more positive when we opened it.

"You know," I said after a while, "this may be better than we think. I'm sure Mrs. Leahy's voice carries some weight with the Consul General. '…with the request that he give your case and that of your husband all consideration…'" I read again.

"You're right!" Michel exclaimed excitedly. "By God, I think you're right!"

It took us no time to pack our bags. Monsieur Pelissier took us to the train. His eyes were more watery than usual.

"Here," he said, handing me a small, awkwardly wrapped package. "Don't open it until you are on the train, Madame. God bless you both and may you be happy, healthy and wealthy wherever your fate takes you. Will you write?"

"Of course we will!" I put my arm around the little man and kissed him on the cheek. My unexpected gesture caused him embarrassment. He quickly shook hands with Michel and left.

When I opened the package, I found two items that were rarer and more precious than jewels at that time: a bar of chocolate, and a cake of perfumed soap. Tears sprang to my eyes. That was the man we had set out to bribe!

Mons. Pelissier, Mrs. Coles, Mrs. H., Mr. Specter, and all the other kind people I had met since leaving Vienna did much to heal the wounds inflicted by the Nazis. All these people came from different countries and were of different faiths, and thanks to them I have never again been able to hate an entire race—not even the Germans. I met people, not representatives of a particular country. And I learned that there are good people and bad people and a lot of people in between all over the world.

Armed with our precious letter, we went directly to the head of the long line at the Consulate. The guard's manner changed when he saw the letter. Deferentially, he admitted us at once. After a short wait, we were ushered into an airy, carpeted office where a clean-cut young man introduced himself as the vice-consul, and invited us to sit.

From a file he extracted a familiar-looking letter. I recognized my hand-writing.

"So you want to go to America?" he smiled, showing perfect teeth. "Your affidavits are in order, I can see no reason to deny you the visa. But how will you get to the States? There are no ships, you know. The visa is only good for a year; it will expire before you have a chance to use it. I think you should wait till the war is over. You're safe in Free France. Stay here, have a good time… Do you play tennis?" he asked Michel.

Dumbfounded, Michel shook his head. "Too bad. I'm always looking for a good partner. But anyway, come back for your visa when transportation becomes available."

"But we have transportation," Michel said. "We have booked passage to Martinique, and from there we can get on a ship to the United States."

"You have? Well, that's a different story. Okay, we'll get the visa ready." He looked at his watch. "Almost time for lunch. I know a nice little bistro. Why don't we lunch together? I'd like to hear more about your escape from Belgium. Okay?"

No meal ever tasted better to us. We toasted our good fortune with an excellent wine, and though conversation was difficult because I had to translate for Michel, we were all three in high spirits.

We were jubilant when we left the Consulate, visas in hand. It seemed years since we had left Antwerp without a hope of getting to America. In reality, barely three months had passed. It was a miracle. Our joy knew no bounds.

"Soon, we will be with you!" I wrote to America. "I know you don't expect our thanks for all you have done—the papers, the food, the money (they had sent food packages and a small sum when we wrote that we were almost broke)...Our heartfelt love to you all, my darling old chaps, who are really the dearest and most caring family in the world. Soon, we will embrace you. America, here we come!"

And so we made ready to leave the Old World.

Fourteen

In mid-May, we boarded the S/S Wyoming, an old, disreputable freighter that lay at anchor in Marseille alongside two other ships of the same ilk. All three were to leave for Martinique simultaneously, each carrying its load of refugees. The ships had been hastily converted to carry passengers. They were ill equipped to handle the people who crowded aboard.

The passengers were not like those who had traveled to America by steerage in earlier days. These people were not leaving their countries behind to better themselves in the New World. They came because madness had taken hold of their compatriots. Most of them were well educated and had been used to relative ease. Nurtured by old European cultures, they were merchants, artists, scientists, shopkeepers, architects, doctors, teachers. It was this wave of immigrants that brought European culture to the New World. Good-bye, Europe, I thought, as I stood at the Wyoming's railing. In my heart, I gave thanks to the continent that had given me much—as much as it had taken. The tears that welled up in my eyes surprised me. All I had felt since we received the visas was joy, excitement, curiosity about the future, and relief. I wanted to put the last years behind me—the bombs, the hunger, the fear, the uncertainty. I had already lost two homes; change was becoming almost commonplace in my life. I tried not to linger in the past—not to forget it, but to keep it tucked away. I had not expected to feel any regret at leaving Europe.

My nostalgia did not last. Soon, I turned my attention to the ship. Conditions on the old freighter were deplorable. There were two dormitories below deck; one for the women, one for the men. The air was stifling. There were always lines before the eight toilets that served four hundred passengers, and the washing facilities were equally inadequate. The food consisted mostly of lentils. They gave us gas and left us bloated but still hungry.

Michel strode the deck like a Viking. I was seasick most of the time. It was a relief when we docked for half a day in Oran to take on cargo. My seasickness subsided, and I enjoyed watching the colorful Arab porters carrying crates up the gangplank on their backs. Ah, fresh food, I thought. But when the evening meal came, it was lentils again—pureed, this time with nutmeg and ginger. Apparently the cook had a good supply of spices and used them to vary the taste. It reminded me of my innovations with the chestnuts; surely, they had tasted better than these nauseating lentils!

Our next stop was Casablanca, where we took on more cargo. But the hours we were supposed to stay in port grew into days. We were forbidden to leave the ship, and so were the passengers on our two sister ships. We were told there were cases of typhus on the three ships and that we had to remain in port until we were cleared by the health authorities.

A rumor was spreading through the ship. They will take us to a concentration camp, people whispered. Some anti-Vichy papers had been found, they said. Those of us with forged visas to South American countries feared to be discovered. The paranoia level on board ran high.

"They're not looking for forged visas. They look for spies, money, weapons. The Vichy government may wish to present Hitler with some choice Jewish flesh, but they won't dare to put people with American visas in a concentration camp," said Herr Morgenstern, a dapper, intelligent German Jew whose far-ranging culture I greatly admired.

"I certainly hope they're not after anybody!" I said, thinking of the few well-known names among the passengers. "They just want to clean the ships. We'll soon be on our way, wait and see."

But day followed day, and the boredom and the bad food were as hard to bear as the fear. We must have been at anchor three or four days when Michel spotted an Arab in a rowboat who was watching us.

"I have an idea," Michel called to Johann, son of an Austrian aristocrat and a Jewish mother, who had the charm, wit, and superb manners of the upper-class Viennese. "Let's try to get him to bring us some food."

"Right!" Johann agreed, joining Michel at the railing. The two men pantomimed 'eating' to the Arab below. They brought their hands up to their mouths, chewed and rubbed their bellies. The Arab was watching them wide-eyed. "I don't think we're getting through," Michel said after a while.

"You're right," Johann admitted. He sucked in his cheeks and hunched up his shoulders, the picture of a starving man. The Arab still did not seem to understand. Exasperated, Michel began to shout some incomprehensible words at him. The Arab turned his boat around and hastily rowed away.

"What did you tell him?" I asked.

"Food! Hungry!"

"In Arabic?" Johann asked, impressed.

"No. In Hebrew. He understood."

"I don't think so. I think you scared him away," Johann said reproachfully.

"Want to bet?" Michel sounded confident.

And indeed, after a while the Arab was back. Triumphantly, he held up a loaf of bread. "We need a rope!" Michel exclaimed.

"I know where I can get one," said Johann and ran off. He quickly returned and threw one end of the rope down to the Arab. We held our breaths while the man tried to tie the thick rope around the bread. At last, he succeeded. Johann eagerly pulled it up, but just as the precious cargo cleared the small boat, a big wave splashed over it. The bread Johann hauled in was soaking wet. Disconsolate, we eyed our spoiled treasure.

"It's not his fault," Johann said, trying to master his disappointment. He tossed some coins into the Arab's boat. The man rowed back to the dock.

A short time later, a throaty call drew us back to the railing. Half a dozen small boats rocked on the waves below. In each of them sat an Arab who held up a loaf of bread. The one who had originally brought the bread pointed to a large covered basket. "That's the idea!" Johann said. Again, he let down the rope. This time, the Arab had no trouble tying it to the handle of the basket. Our mouths were watering when we withdrew the freshly baked loaves.

"Come quickly," we called to nearby passengers. "Let's spread the word!" Soon, a brisk trade was under way, and for a while, the mood on the ship rose.

In the end, the Captain got wind of it and sent the Arabs away. "Please, Messieurs and Mesdames, remember the quarantine," he told us. "Nothing is allowed to leave the ship, including money. It could be contaminated!"

The next day, I watched as some Arab porters were carrying baskets of fresh food up the gangplank.

"Don't get your hopes up," said Ilse who was standing next to me. Ilse was Johann's wife. She was a strikingly attractive young woman who had been to Gurs, the dreaded Vichy French detention camp in the Pyrenees. "It was worse than Dachau," she had told me. "At least the Germans keep their death camps clean!"

I peered longingly at the fresh fish, the succulent fruit and crisp vegetables the porters brought up. "It's for the Captain's table," Ilse said knowingly. "For us, it's lentils and more lentils. God, I'm sick of them!"

"So am I," I said, weak with desire for the fresh food. Suddenly, one of the porters approached us. Setting down a small basket beside us, he pointed to a man who stood on the pier. He was wearing European clothes, but his features were Arabic. He smiled at us and bowed, putting his hand to his heart. I made a questioning gesture. He pointed to the basket, then to us, and then he turned away to continue giving orders to the porters, whom he apparently oversaw.

We opened the basket. It contained cheese, tomatoes, cucumbers, fruit, cans of sardines, and yes, even a small bar of chocolate. We could hardly believe our good fortune. In vain we tried to attract the attention of our benefactor—how could we thank him? But when he did not look up, we hungrily bit into the luscious peaches whose fragrance spoke of their perfect ripeness.

We briefly debated if we should share our treasure with others on board or keep it for ourselves and our husbands; we easily agreed on the latter course of action. However, privacy was impossible on the Wyoming, and our little hoard was quickly gone.

When I look back at the docility with which we all stayed on board I can easily understand why the German and Austrian Jews went to their deaths so unresistingly, so politely, keeping things civilized. They believed in justice, in the law, in the rational behavior of man. Even the criminals among the Jews did not use physical violence. Brute force was alien to European Jews; they simply were not prepared to handle it.

On the 14th day, a notice appeared on deck:

Because some disease-carrying rats have been found on the three ships, all passengers are to be ready to debark at 8 a.m. tomorrow. All luggage is to be packed and put on deck. Passengers will be housed in hotels in Casablanca at the expense of the steamship company until suitable vessels can be provided to take you to Martinique. We hope your stay in beautiful Casablanca will be enjoyable and we will do all we can to assure your comfort.

"They'll put us in a detention camp," Ilse said darkly.

"Nonsense!" I shot back. "They can't simply abduct us! There are laws!"

"Why don't you ask the Captain? Maybe he'll tell you the truth!" Ilse challenged.

"All right, I will!" I replied, sure that the captain would not hide the truth from me. I mounted the stairs to the bridge.

"What brings you here, Madame?" the Captain asked. He was a friendly middle-aged man who never failed to wink at me when he passed.

"A rumor is going around that we will be put in a concentration camp. Is that true, Monsieur le Capitain?"

"A concentration camp! Mon Dieu! What an idea! I assure you, Madame, that rumor is false. There is no substance to it, believe me!"

"Are you sure?" I persisted.

"Absolutely. I give you my word as a Frenchman and as the captain of this ship. Please do not be concerned, Madame! You will love Casablanca!" He gallantly kissed my hand and led me to the door.

Completely reassured, I reported his words to the others. Soon they spread through the ship, and that evening an almost gay mood prevailed. People wanted to believe the Captain. "We are going to see Casablanca at the expense of the steamship company," they said. "That's not bad!"

The next morning, we all left the ship. The port seemed deserted. But as soon as everybody was off the three ships, we were surrounded by armed soldiers. They herded us into trucks that bore us to the North African desert. After three hours, we stopped before a group of barracks that stood in the sand, dismal and grey in the glaring sun. A man in the uniform of the French colonial officer addressed us:

"I bid you welcome, Mesdames and Messieurs. I must say, I was not prepared for so magnificent an assemblage. Women and children too, I see.

We have had all sorts of criminals here, but none so attractive. I do hope the ladies will find our accommodations to their liking." He doffed his kepi to us and continued in an icy tone. "We do not want you people here. In fact, nobody wants you. You are un-de-sirables, Mesdames and Messieurs. I do not yet know what unspeakable crimes you have committed; you are Jews, that is enough. You are lazy. I shall strive to overcome my dislike for you enough to teach you to work. This, Mesdames and Messieurs, is not the Ritz. Here, you will not be able to buy decent people to work for you with your blackmarket money. You will work, Mesdames and Messieurs. You will work till you drop. My guards will be right beside you in case somebody feels like taking a siesta. They will only tickle your delicate Jewish flesh with their bayonets, for we have orders not to kill you—not yet. Of course, should anyone be foolish enough to try to escape, it would be a different matter. And since I am the sole judge of what constitutes an attempt at escape..." He underlined his words by cracking his horsewhip against his shiny boots. "I am sure your imagination can supply the picture. So. Now we know where we stand. Any questions?"

No hands were raised. We stood silent, as if turned to stone. "Very well then. Women and children over here." He pointed to the barracks on his left. "The men over there."

Slowly, we separated into two groups. An elderly couple stood tightly enlaced, unable to let go of each other. The Commandant raised his whip threateningly. With a sob, the woman tore herself away. Children were crying. A tangible sense of doom hung over us all.

Inside our barracks, the narrow cots with their lumpy mattresses did not offer us much comfort. With a feeling of utter helplessness, we selected our beds and lay down on them, craving the oblivion of sleep.

To our surprise, the Commandant, after that fire-spitting speech, left us entirely alone. Had it not been for the barbed wire and the few armed guards that patrolled us, we could have believed ourselves free, though stranded in a God-forsaken desert. No attempts were made to force us to work. On the other hand, we were given no help in maintaining the camp. If the sanitary conditions on the Wyoming had been bad, here they were abominable. Our numbers had increased by some two hundred passengers from one of the other ships. There were four outhouses for the 600 people in the camp. Long lines waited before them at all hours. Dysentery was rampant, as could be expected. There were three doctors among us, and they did their best. But conditions were so bad that those who had been in Nazi camps muttered that they had been more humane because sanitation was better.

Our worst enemy was the heat. The dry desert heat seared our lungs. I discovered that I could be relatively comfortable by draping a wet towel around my head turban-like and making frequent trips to a long wooden trough that had been used to water horses before our arrival. It was our only source of water for drinking, washing, and cooking.

When it was clear that it was up to us to maintain a semblance of sanitation in the camp, we quickly organized outhouse details and held each other responsible for keeping our sleeping areas neat and clean. Michel was part of the provision detail. Accompanied by an armed soldier, he and three other men went to the open-air market in Oued-Zem, the small Arab settlement near the camp. The produce they brought was fresh and tasteful, but there was never enough to go around and we were hungry most of the time.

"You should see the way that bastard strides down the street! If an Arab doesn't get out of the way fast enough, he strikes him with his whip!" Michel told us when he came back from the market. The behavior of the French soldier enraged him to such a degree that I was afraid he would lose his temper and do something that would get him in trouble.

The camp had no kitchen. Food was prepared on long tables outdoors, where we also ate. It was better that way. The corrugated tin roofs of the barracks retained the heat in ways that made staying indoors during the day impossible. I worked in the 'kitchen'. It was quite pleasant sitting at the long table chatting with the others while we prepared the food.

One of the things that made the camp bearable was that it gave me the opportunity to act out a fantasy I had carried with me since the age of fourteen, when I first read about the French women whose salons played such an important role in the cultural life of their time. There were some artists, scientists and intellectuals among us, and a group of them met evenings to discuss topics ranging from astronomy to politics, literature, philosophy and art. I listened raptly and pretended, as we sat on rough wooden crates, that we were in my elegant salon. When I told them about this fantasy, they devised an elaborate ritual around my 'soirees' and made believe that the cups into which I poured lukewarm tea from my thermos were of the finest, most translucent china.

My free time was spent reading. The books the passengers had brought along circulated among us, and I read everything I could lay my hands on. There was a dog-eared copy of Gone with the Wind that absorbed me so completely that I forgot my surroundings. My 'salon' and the books I read taught me that while my body may be imprisoned, my spirit can roam free.

It became apparent that the authorities realized that detaining a large number of refugees with American visas could mean a heap of trouble. They let our mail go through and allowed us to establish communication with the American Consulate in Casablanca and with the agencies in the United States who were instrumental in helping Jews escape from the Nazis.

We had been interned about six weeks when it became known that a delegation consisting of the four most respected men in camp had received permission to go to Casablanca to intercede for us. At the same time, a telegram arrived from my brother in New York. "Have booked passage for you on the Marco Polo leaving July 2 for New York. Your tickets are at travel agency Vigie in Casablanca. See you soon."

We were ecstatic, but how were we to get to Casablanca to collect our tickets?

"Go show the telegram to the Commandant," Michel said to me.

"Why me?" I asked. I did not relish the idea of facing that cruel man.

"It'll be harder for him to say no to you than to me," Michel replied. "You know how men react to your smile."

"Not with this face," I protested, pointing to my swollen cheek. The day before, the one dentist in the camp had tried to lance my abcessed tooth with a sterilized safety pin, with the result that my cheek blew up to twice its ordinary size. I looked terrible and felt worse.

"Don't worry about your cheek," Michel said. "It may even help if he sees that you need medical attention."

And so I reluctantly went to the Commandant's office. My attempt to smile brought tears to my eyes. Wordlessly, I held out the telegram to him.

"I see," he said after scanning it. To my amazement, the ogre's manner was mild. "Here, wipe your tears, little lady." He handed me his clean white handkerchief. "Let's see what we can do. I cannot just let you go to Casablanca.

But maybe...Can you type?"

Surprised, I nodded. I did know how to pick out letters with two fingers.

"Good. You will go with the delegation. As their secretary. Satisfied?" This time, the smile on my face was spontaneous though hardly dazzling, thanks to my swollen cheek. "Your husband will remain here as my hostage. You must return with the delegation in three days."

Overjoyed, I returned to the barracks. Ilse noticed my elation.

"You look like you have some wonderful news," she remarked.

"I have! I'm going to Casablanca with the delegation!"

Ilse whistled. "Well! How did you manage that? As if I didn't know!" Her expression left no doubt about what she 'knew.'

I was not surprised. I had met with that attitude before. As I look back now, even I find it hard to believe that none of the men who helped me expected anything in return. Not one of them made sexual advances. Specter, Pelissier, the Arab in the harbor, the German officer who gave us a lift...And the women. Mrs. H., Mom Coles... They all acted from the goodness of their hearts, selflessly helpful, extending themselves without asking, "What's in it for me?" Perhaps I was protected by my guardian angel, or perhaps it was my youthful innocence that called forth the best in people. But I have since learned that hard times bring out either the best or the worst in people, depending on what's in their hearts.

I did not waste time defending myself to Ilse. Let her believe what she wants, I thought. I was painfully aware that my good fortune made the others feel their captivity even more keenly and tried to be as invisible as possible as I prepared for my departure.

Michel and I held each other very tight when I took my leave. "Forget about the camp while you're away," he told me. "Enjoy your freedom while you can. Only be sure to bring back the tickets!"

"You can count on it!" I assured him.

"Get a good meal!" he called after me as the armed guard motioned me to enter the waiting truck along with the four delegates. It took us to the whistle stop of Oued-Zem where we were left to wait for the train.

We were free!

"What were you doing in Oued-Zem, Mademoiselle?" asked the colonial officer who made room for me on the crowded bench. "Seems like a strange place for a European lady!"

Herr Schiller, one of the delegates, a venerable old man with a bushy mane of white hair, explained our situation to the officer, who turned to me. "And you, Mademoiselle? Are you also a delegate?"

I smiled. "I'm not wise enough for that. I'm going to pick up my steamship tickets at the travel agency Vigie."

"The Vigie Agency?" His face held a strange expression. "I advise you to be careful in your dealings with them, Mademoiselle. The agency has a rather dubious reputation."

My heart sank, but I quickly recovered. "They won't try to cheat me. My brother paid for the tickets. They'll have to give them to me," I said with conviction.

The officer smiled. "I hope you are right. Do you have a reservation in Casablanca?"

It had never occurred to me that I might need one. "Oh, I'll find a room. I'm not fussy. Anything will do for the three nights I'm staying—as long as it's inexpensive."

"But my dear young lady, there is not a free bed in Casablanca! The city is full of refugees who wait for ships to take them to America!"

I was not prepared for this emergency, but after all I had been through, it seemed only a minor obstacle. "Something will show up," I said confidently.

"Well, you cannot stay on the street," the Frenchman said. "Tell you what. I will take you to my hotel, maybe they can arrange something for you. The manager knows everybody in Casablanca."

But the manager did not even know of a free closet. I grew afraid. "Well," the manager said when he saw my anxious face, "we do have a free bathroom. The tub can be made up into quite a comfortable bed…"

"I'll take it," the officer said. "Give the lady my room. She will only stay three nights. No, don't thank me, Madame," he insisted when I tried to express my sincere appreciation. "I'm not very proud of my government when it interns innocent people."

I hardly saw the kind officer again during my stay in Casablanca. Two weeks later, when I left the hotel, he was still sleeping in the bathroom. "It's really quite comfortable," he assured me whenever we passed in the lobby. "A lot more comfortable than your bed in Oued-Zem, I'm sure!"

A familiar line stretched from the door of the Tourist Bureau Vigie for several blocks. I decided to go straight to the door. "I'm picking up my tickets. The money was sent from America," I told the burly Arab who barred the door.

"Money? America? Good. Go," he said, letting me pass.

I approached one of the clerks and handed him my brother's telegram. His face was blank. "I regret, Madame, but there is no such ship."

"You lie!" I shouted. The French officer's warning rang in my ears. "I demand my tickets! I will not leave without them! If you don't give them to me I'll call the police!"

"But my dear lady, I assure you there has been some mistake!" the clerk insisted.

"The mistake is yours!" I yelled. Everybody in the office was looking at me. I didn't care. Let them all know that the agency was crooked. "You won't get away with this! Let me talk to your boss!"

"Certainly, Madame!" He was relieved to pass me on and led me to a door in the rear.

"Come in," a man's voice called in answer to his knock.

The man who rose from the desk was tall, grey-haired and slender. His acquiline features were underscored by blazing black eyes. "What seems to be the trouble, Madame?" he asked politely.

I showed him the telegram. "I want my tickets," I said. He laughed out loud. "Somebody is pulling your leg, I'm afraid. There is no such ship. Here, see for yourself." He handed me an official-looking document that listed all the ocean vessels then in use. It began to dawn on me that my brother had invented the Marco Polo in the hope that it would help us to leave the camp. He is very clever, that brother of mine, I thought. In fact, his ruse worked. Only...what do I do now? Do I go back to the camp right away? What will the Commandant do when he finds out that he was tricked?

Feeling utterly helpless, I told the grey-haired man about the conditions for my temporary release from Oued-Zem and asked him for a letter describing the situation to the Commandant. "What else can I do?" I asked, disconsolate.

"I am a supporter of the Vichy government, and I am certain they are right to hold you people in the detention camp. But I admire your courage. I will see what I can do for you. Meanwhile, let me show you our lovely city while you are here."

His name was Monsieur Castella. He was the brother-in-law of General Franco of Spain. Because of the severe shortage of gasoline, the red convertible he drove was the only private car in Casablanca. The sights he showed me were enchanting, and the black-market restaurants to which he took me served gourmet meals. Had it not been for my thoughts of Michel and my fears for our future, the next three days would have been a sheer delight.

"I'm a crook," Monsieur Castella told me. "No doubt you heard that I bleed the refugees dry with promises of ships that never come. It's true. That is how I make my money. My money gives me power over the town. I am the most powerful man in Casablanca, did you know that, little lady? I have them all in my pocket, the politicians, the officials, the police force…"

"I don't believe you," I laughed. We were driving through the faubourgs of Casablanca in his red convertible; the air was intoxicating, the sights eye-filling. A balmy wind blew from the ocean.

"You don't? How can I prove it to you?"

"By getting my husband out of the detention camp," I said without hesitation.

"Easy!" he bragged.

When we came back to his office he bade me wait while he made a call.

"Come," he called after a short while.

"Well?" I asked, not daring to hope.

"I will pick you up at your hotel at 9 o'clock tomorrow morning. Your husband's train arrives at 9:15. You are both free."

The film Casablanca had it all wrong. It wasn't Claude Raines who was the most powerful man in Casablanca. Slim, debonair Monsieur Castella was.

With Michel's arrival a rapid exchange of telegrams began between us and America. Our money had run out; my brother and sisters, themselves not yet established in America, sent what they could.

"You will sail on the next ship that goes to America," Monsieur Castella promised us.

Two weeks after I left the camp, the ship appeared. The S/S Guine was a modest Portuguese liner, but to us, she appeared as a luxury cruiser. The crossing was uneventful. I enjoyed the food, the deck chairs, the clean toilets. After seven days, we arrived at New York Island, New York, America.

Fanny, Dolly, Oscar, Mama, Papa and Gusti *Mama and friend*

Gusti feeding pigeons in Venice *Michel Graboi, Antwerp* *Gusti at Oued-Zem, 1941*

Gusti and Michel, Antwerp, 1940

Michel in Casablanca

Gusti in Casablanca

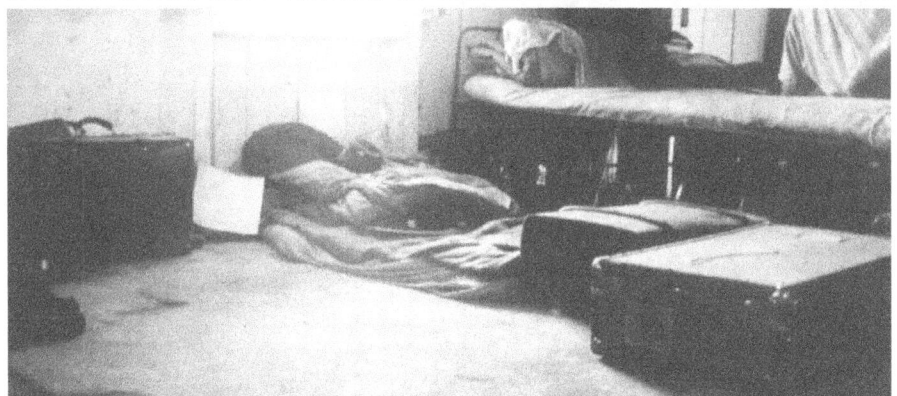

The kitchen, the washing facility and sickbay at Oued-Zem

Mama and Gusti, Italy, 1934

Gusti and Fanny, Hungary, 1936

Gusti and Gerda, Vienna, 1937

Oscar, Fanny, Willy, Gusti and friend skiing in the Austrian Alps

Far right: Fanny and Willy on their honeymoon, Capri, 1934

Gusti and Fanny, Yugoslavia

*Gusti and Michel asking NRS for help,
New York, 1941*

Exiled by Nazis

Pretty arrival on the S. S. Guine was Gusti Grabo who lived in Antwerp till last February when the Nazi occupation forced her to flee to French Morocco. She sailed from there.

*This appeared in the
New York Daily News*

Mama and Papa in Vienna, shortly after the Anschluss

Part Two

Fifteen

I could see them as our ship glided into port. They stood on the pier, waving wildly. There they all were, my sisters and brother and their spouses. Patiently, they stood in the broiling sun while the American authorities, who came on board, conducted endless formalities. A few reporters also came aboard. I stared at them. Two of them actually looked like the reporters I had seen in American movies—straw hats pushed back from sweating foreheads, loud ties, brash behavior. They seemed bored. Nobody famous was arriving, it was just a routine visit in the hope that something would turn up.

"You a starlet?" one of the brash reporters asked.

"I beg your pardon?" A starlet? What did that mean?

"You in the movies?" he queried.

That I understood. "Afraid not," I said, flattered.

"Never mind," he said. "Want to get your picture in the paper?" Indeed I did.

When I finished posing, I returned to the railing to continue to pantomime to my siblings down below. On Fanny's hand gleamed a ring that shimmered in a rainbow of colors. Pointing to it, I made an admiring gesture. Looks like the streets in America are really paved with gold! I thought. My family looked prosperous. Their clothes were smart and well-made and looked expensive to me.

In the late afternoon, I finally stepped off the gangplank into Fanny's open arms. When she took my hand, I felt something pass from her to me. "It's yours," she whispered. It was the ring. Her generosity stunned me.

"How can I take it?" I said, overcome.

"It's nothing," she said. And indeed, as it turned out, it was a bauble from the 5 & 10 Cent Store, so well made that it could have fooled more expert eyes than mine.

"Come on," Fanny said when I had finished hugging everyone. "I want to show you our car."

"A car!" I gasped, hardly believing my ears. But it was true. The vehicle she proudly pointed out may not have been a Rolls Royce, but to my European eyes it looked quite luxurious. It was a modest grey sedan with hardly a dent marring its exterior.

Fanny motioned me to enter as she slipped in behind the wheel. "It has a radio," she informed me. A radio! I had never been inside a car with a radio. "Wait, I'll show you!" my sister smiled, enjoying my awed look. She inserted a key in the dashboard and turned it on. With a lurch, the car shot back. We both screamed. I looked through the rear window. We were nearing the water! Had I escaped war-ravaged Europe only to drown on my first day in America?

Out of nowhere, Willy came running. He had been busy helping Michel with our luggage. With the agility of a trained athlete he leaped on the running board—the cars of that era all had running boards—and grabbed the steering wheel through the open window. "Turn the key off!" he yelled at Fanny, who seemed paralyzed.

We were inches away from the water when the car stopped.

"Thanks for the welcome!" I gasped. "I was safer in Europe!"

We laughed and cried, and the others came running to make sure we were still in one piece. And so, between getting my picture in the paper and nearly being drowned, my arrival in the United States did not lack drama.

It turned out that Dolly and Oscar also had cars, but only the men knew how to drive. Even American women still ceded the wheel to the men when they went out together, and in Europe, a woman who knew how to drive was a rarity.

Although I was impressed with the modest apartments of my siblings with their refrigerators and running hot water, I soon found out that none of them had struck it rich, but that they all worked very hard and lived frugally in order to build up their businesses.

"Have you heard from Mama and Papa?" I asked as soon as we sat around a table laden with delicacies in Oscar's apartment. All were silent.

"No, not for several months," Oscar said quietly after a while. My heart sank.

"Is that because no mail from Austria reaches America?" I asked, hoping that this would explain their silence.

"No mail from our parents has reached America," Oscar replied in a flat voice.

"What did their last letter say? Where they all right?" I wanted to know.

"Their thoughts were all for us. You know how they are. They never complain," Dolly sighed. We were all quiet, afraid to raise the question that preoccupied us most—were our parents still free or had they been taken to a concentration camp?

Several years later Oscar told me that they were taken to Treblinka, one of the most infamous camps in Poland.

"I never told you about it—what would have been the use? You knew in your heart what happened to them, didn't you?"

"Yes. It was good of you to spare me, Oscar. But then you have always protected me, haven't you, big brother?" I said tenderly.

Soon after my arrival Fanny informed me that she had changed her name to Nita.

"Nita! How did you get that?"

"Simple. Fanny—Fanita—Anita—Nita. You see? I'll thank you to remember to call me that from now on. Know what 'fanny' means in English?" We both laughed.

"Well, Gusti isn't quite that bad, but I also need a new name. Gusty! Brrr! A gusty wind! But what about all your papers? You're still Fanny legally, aren't you?"

"No, that's the nice part, you can change your name when you apply for citizenship," she declared.

"What shall I name myself?" I asked Michel.

"Nina," he shot back without a moment's hesitation.

"Nina? Why?" I asked, surprised.

"Nina, Ninotchka…You've always looked like a Nina to me," my Russian husband replied.

And so Gusti became Nina, and it didn't occur to any of us how alike Nita and Nina sound. Perhaps there is a genetic bias for the sound "Ni" in my family, for when my daughter was born, I named her Nicole.

Through an interminable summer, we slept in Nita's living room. The dry heat of the desert seemed almost pleasant by contrast with the humid inferno that is Manhattan in the summer. The screaming police sirens were a constant reminder of the air raid sirens we had left behind; they often made us jump out of bed at night to seek shelter. The packed subways, the haste, the masses of people surging ceaselessly hither and yon left us bewildered, helpless, almost paralyzed. I remember nothing of those three months except the heat and our pathetic efforts to get away from it on weekends when we all piled into Nita's car and joined the long row of vehicles that aimed for an oasis of trees, fresh air and surcease from the rushing, pushing crowds. Instead, we were caught in the inevitable traffic jams caused by overheated, stalled cars.

It was a foregone conclusion that Michel and I would go into business for ourselves, like the three other couples. Looking back, it seems strange that we never considered other alternatives. But in reality, we didn't have many options. We wanted security desperately after our recent deprivations. Michel's business experience with the scarves was the only thing we could draw on. But before we could think of starting our own business, Michel had to learn English. It was understood that I, like my sisters and my brother's wife, would help my husband in the business, but there was no question about who would be the boss. My command of the language was helpful because it allowed me to translate for him, but it would be he who would conduct all transactions.

Sixteen

We had to get away from New York, at least for a while. We needed to catch our breath before tackling the business world. Where should we go?

"Let's go to California," I suggested.

"California?" That's on the other side of America," Michel said, surprised.

"The sun shines there all winter. The pace is slow, we can get used to America, and you'll have a chance to learn English."

"Why not?" Michel mused. "At least we won't need any winter clothes."

And so it was decided. We took the Greyhound bus to Los Angeles where we rented a small furnished apartment and went hunting for jobs. Michel took one as an unskilled laborer in a furniture factory, and I as a sewing machine operator in a dress factory.

I didn't know how different the heavy power machines were from my familiar electric home sewing machine. When I put my foot on the pedal, the fabric flew through the needle with the velocity of a rocket ship. But with the help of the Polish woman who sat to my right, I soon learned to apply the right pressure and to read the notches, snips and other signs by which the pattern pieces were marked.

One day before my 23rd birthday, on December 7th 1941, the bomb fell on Pearl Harbor. America was outraged, and many Californians panicked. The war was coming awfully close to our shores! Michel and I, much as we hated war, were relieved that the U.S. forces joined the Allies to fight against Hitler. American intervention was our only hope, and to this day I give thanks that the Nazis were defeated and did not manage to conquer the whole world.

Michel attended night school, and his English made rapid strides. By spring, we felt ready to tackle the New York business scene. This time, the Greyhound bus was full of war brides. At every stop, one of them would tell me her whole life story in the ladies room.

"My husband's in the Navy. You should see him in his bell bottoms! I'm gonna stay with him till they ship him out. We've only been married three months. Want to see my ring? I met him at a dance, he was with another girl, but I got him! We're gonna settle near my folks when he comes back. Get our own farm with the money he gets from the government. Kids? You bet! We're gonna have six. I'm from a big family myself. I'm so excited! I'll be with Johnny in three days, can you beat that?"

And they would talk on and on about the future they saw in such rosy hues, cherishing the dream of " they lived happily ever after." War was not a reality to them. They adored their husbands' uniforms, glowed with patriotism, and were full of romantic hopes.

For months Michel and I had been tossing ideas back and forth concerning items we could produce. With the small sum we had managed to save we could not afford to make a mistake. To avoid competition, we had to find something no one else was making. We had to aim for a market that consumed large quantities of goods, and the supplies for the item had to be readily available.

As soon as his English allowed, Michel began to read Business Week and related publications. "I have it!" he called out one day, looking up triumphantly from the magazine he was reading.

"What?" I asked eagerly.

"Here, read this." He passed me the magazine.

The article described a new process, called "peroxilyn coating," which transformed regular cotton cloth into waterproof fabric that could be wiped off with a sponge.

"Very interesting, but what does it have to do with us?" I wanted to know.

"We decided to focus on the infants' and children's market because American parents spend a lot on their kids, right? Well, if we can come up with something that is attractive and practical, the shops that cater to the toddler trade will want it."

I saw what he meant. "Something for the nursery that can be wiped off with a sponge…"

Before long, the idea of a peroxilyn-coated pinafore began to take shape in my mind. The one I designed had a doll's face pinned to the bib. Michel liked it enough to invest in several yards of the new material. I made a few samples on my second-hand sewing machine, and Michel, secure in his rudimentary knowledge of English, presented them to some Fifth Avenue stores.

Soon we had enough orders to rent a small loft downtown. We added stuffed toys made of the same fabric to our line of goods, and our firm became known in the trade.

Our staff grew rapidly. It was my job to oversee the 60 odd sewing machine operators. Michel supervised sales and advertising and spent a good deal of time away from the shop. Most of the operators were black. I was shocked by the race discrimination in this supposedly tolerant country and wanted to show our employees that not all whites are bigots. I addressed them by their family names, prefaced by "Miss" or "Mrs." in the formal European way. I had heard that no white American would sit down to a meal with blacks and was determined to make up for this dismal practice.

At lunchtime, I sat with the women at the long work table and tried to make conversation. To my surprise, they seemed reluctant to reply. After a few days it began to dawn on me that my presence, far from giving them comfort and satisfaction, put a damper on the enjoyment of their lunch. After that, I ate my lunch in the office where I could see them without being seen. The laughter and rough horseplay I observed quickly assured me that I had best not try to play nice white lady and to leave them alone.

In 1944, our son Daniel was born, and fifteen months later his sister Nicole. My son's entrance into the world occurred on a night when a hurricane raged in the city. Windows broke with a crash and all kinds of objects whirled through the air as Michel drove me to the hospital.

I had prepared myself for motherhood by reading everything I could find on child rearing. But when I actually held the living, breathing babies in my arms I realized that I must trust my own instincts rather than the authorities whose books I read. I was awed by the differences in the children's personalities that manifested from the moment they were born. The books looked at the newborn as a tabula rasa, to be shaped by the environment. Heredity was given some play, mostly in terms of disease, but the all-encompassing responsibility for the child's development was placed squarely on the shoulders of the mother. A generation of guilt-ridden mothers who mistrusted their own judgment was thus foisted on the young. We were warned not to frustrate the child, to give it freedom it was ill equipped to handle at a tender age, to be "permissive." As mine grew to school age, I discovered that they wanted and needed limitations, and that while it was easier not to say NO to them, they really felt more cared for and protected by a judicious use of that word than the children who were left to their own devices.

Michel and I had very different ideas about raising our children, and we had many painful clashes about it. Overnight, I had turned into the proverbial Jewish mother, fiercely protective of my brood, convinced that I knew what was best for them. I felt I was tuned into their needs in ways no one else could be.

True to my European upbringing where even people in modest circumstances had household servants, I hired a placid, big-bosomed Dutch nanny to look after their physical well-being, while I nurtured their growth in all other respects. I still went to the business regularly to help Michel, but the children were the center of my universe. "Everything else is trimming on the Christmas tree of life," I used to say. The rock on which I stood was my children and my home.

Because of my closeness to (Fa)Nita, our social life revolved around her and her husband's friends. These were a group of Viennese refugees who for the most part were either on their way to financial success or had already reached it. The men played bridge and golf on weekends; the women played canasta and poker. Neither Michel nor I took any interest in these pursuits, but my desire to be with my sister was so great that I continued to tag after her as I had done as a child.

Life seemed pretty tame in those years. The security we found in our new homeland soon began to lose its charm. We needed a new challenge, something that would enliven the humdrum everyday existence that now seemed our lot.

Our business was prospering. It was time to move away from the city, to build our own house. We bought a corner lot in the estate section of an exclusive Long Island community and commissioned a pair of young architects to draw up plans.

Bill Brieger and Stanley Saltzman had recently graduated from Harvard where they studied under Marcel Breuer and Walter Gropius, both famous for their innovative ideas. Auntie Rosa's villa in a suburb of Vienna had been designed and furnished by Marcel Breuer, and I had greatly loved and admired the beautiful house. My taste in architecture was shaped by the authentic old buildings of my youth as well as by radically modern Bauhaus-inspired structures. I had expected the architecture in the New World to be bold and original, but except for the skyscrapers—the real ones, not our Antwerp midget—I saw little that was not an imitation of Old World styles. I was particularly struck by private homes that mimicked French Provincial, Tudor, or Baroque.

"Why build a house with all modern conveniences and then try to make it look old? That's like building a carriage with a motor inside," I remarked to Michel. We were amused by the veneration in which America holds "antiques"—stuff that to us was no more than yesterday's junk. It seemed strange that this vital, youthful, brazen and naive people should be so attached to the past.

The blueprint Bill and Stanley submitted surpassed my wildest expectations. My heart beat with pleasure as I watched the handsome redwood and fieldstone structure go up. The flat-roofed house with its garden and swimming pool satisfied deeply my craving for beauty and comfort. For the next few years I was absorbed in living out my dream.

What was that dream? Where did it come from? Did it originate with me, or was it programmed into me by the culture? By fate? Or by the Cosmic Travel Agency I would visit one day in the future on the kind of trip I then knew nothing about?

Looking back, my dream seems to have been pieced together from movies and books. It had all the trimmings of a glamorous and romantic Hollywood production: an attractive husband, two lovely children, a beautiful home; a butler with white gloves who served me breakfast in bed (he pulled back the heavy drapes to let the sun stream in, and then he set the breakfast tray with one fragrant rose in a slender vase on my lap, saying "Good morning, Madam!" in a cheerful voice), and a housekeeper with whom I conferred about the menu for the day. There was travel, interesting new friends, music, art, sports, gay parties...In short, it was the American dream.

Michel made the outdoors his domain. He created a garden of exquisite complexity and charm which turned our corner lot into a property that seemed much larger than it was. He built dry walls, designed and constructed a bamboo fountain, and planted trees with Jones, our elderly gardener who tended the beautiful flower beds that graced the terraced grounds. My husband, who had never lived in the country, became a passionate gardener. His favorite reading material now was how-to gardening books and seed catalogues.

One morning, I woke to find the pear tree that had stood on the lawn outside my bedroom window gone. In its place was a small, graceful, exotic purple-leafed tree. To surprise me, Michel had switched them before I woke up! I remembered the story about the French king who had a beautiful garden planted for his queen overnight, and I felt like that queen when I surveyed my home and my garden.

Our new set of suburbanites was a loose-knit group of young couples. We were the yuppies of that day—bright, well-educated conspicuous consumers. I became known for the parties I gave, and Michel and I were much in demand for those given by our friends.

Our move to Long Island put physical and mental distance between me and my siblings. Until then we had all lived within a few blocks of each other on the upper westside of Manhattan. I had always been especially close to Nita, but now I found myself growing away from her more and more. We were different, far more different than I had known in the past when I tried to pattern myself after this adored and yet feared sister. Nita was an imperious beauty with flashing dark eyes and the kind of bone structure that even old age cannot erase. She was domineering, strong-willed and demanding; her whims had to be instantly indulged. At the same time her warmth, generosity and charm endeared her to all who knew her. Her powerful personality exerted a strong pull on me, and the process of discovering who I was apart from her was painful and long.

When Michel formed a business partnership with Oscar, it had a negative effect on my closeness to my brother. The two men were too different to allow for a smooth collaboration, and although the business profited from their divergent talents, it drove a wedge between us on the personal level. Loyalty to my husband forced me to curtail our social interactions, but my feelings for this dear, cultured, highly intelligent man never changed.

With our move to Long Island my life changed dramatically. The pattern it took was similar to that of the other young couples in our set. The men commuted daily to their businesses, law offices or medical practices. The women were housewives; that is, we did not work outside the home. But we worked! We ran the household, chauffeured the kids, went to meetings, did volunteer work, had our hair and nails done once a week, shopped for clothes, gave dinner parties, hired and fired the help, met our husbands in New York for dinner and a show; we swam, played tennis and golf, took adult education classes, gardened, and supervised the activities of our children. We were the wives of successful men, envied by our less privileged sisters who believed that happiness would automatically be conferred on them if only they too had such financial ease. In reality, I soon began to see that misery often hides behind smoothly coiffed and flawlessly made-up exteriors, and it dawned on me that psychological wounds are no less painful than physical deprivation. Suffering, whether caused by emotion or by lack of food and shelter, is always equally severe.

I became a patroness of the Five Towns Music and Art Foundation, a non-profit organization that brought cultural events to our community. Along with public performances there were chamber music concerts in private homes. Ours was one of these. I kept very busy maintaining the house on a relatively small budget by doing many things myself such as sewing miles of curtains and drapes, embroidering cushions, making some of my own and my daughter's clothes. The butler-chauffeur and the cook-housekeeper fantasy lasted only a few years. After that I made do with a sleep-in maid and a man for the heavy cleaning once a week.

Life was good. I enjoyed the luxury, the security, and the leisure that allowed me to indulge my taste for the arts, and I was very proud of my two children and my home. My relationship with Michel, now that we had settled into a comfortable lifestyle, had begun to reveal deep and insurmountable differences between us, but I consoled myself with the thought that my marriage was no worse and no better than those of the other couples I knew. The war years and the hardships of our refugee existence receded into the past, to be remembered only rarely. I lived in the present. Past experiences had no power to detract from it.

Seventeen

In the fifties, my self-image depended heavily on my looks, and on the attention I received from men. I had long since stopped trying to make intelligent conversation with men—they simply did not take me seriously except in the role of an attractive woman. I myself had come to believe that my looks were my sole asset and I carefully nurtured the image I found most successful in social interactions. I dressed in the style then in vogue: narrow-waisted, full-skirted dresses with bodices that revealed half of the breasts. Looking back, I can see that I split myself in two—the self I presented to the world, and the private self inside. Outside, I was flippant, sarcastic, blasé. I didn't talk about the things that really mattered to me but stayed on the surface, making brittle remarks. There were women even then who knew how to be more than just attractive females, but I was not one of them. I derived great satisfaction from my ability to convert my body into the enticing picture of an elegant, sexy, flirtatious woman who made clever remarks.

In my youth, a woman's main survival skill lay in her ability to attract and hold a man. From early childhood on she received cues from her environment that taught her the wiles that could capture and entrap a man. The man would promise to support and protect her and the children they begot; to hold him, once they were married, she had to maintain her looks. She kept her figure, wore alluring clothes, and made sure her hair was coiffed in the latest style. Looking chic was a major occupation for middle and upper-middle class women, engendering an industry that was an important factor in the nation's economy.

That's how it was for me in the early '50s. In retrospect, I can only marvel how blindly I went along with the prevailing fashion. I teetered on high heels, wore my hair in the casual-seeming Italian style that was the result of nights spent with fat rollers pinned to my head, and squeezed myself into the Merry Widow that displayed my breasts like two oven-ready buns on a tray. I was enfolded in the social matrix like a fish in water. I fit in, was liked, even admired by the people in my social set, and I, in turn, liked and enjoyed their company.

At parties, I flirted with the men, but left no doubt in their minds that anything more was out of the question. There were reports in the papers about wife-swapping parties in the suburbs, but in my set, such activities were unknown. Our large circle of acquaintances may have included more than one man or woman engaged in an extra-marital affair, but surprisingly enough, this worldly and sophisticated group did not, at least to my knowledge, indulge in sex parlor games.

I was acquiring the reputation of a fine hostess; it was a mark of distinction to be invited to the parties I gave. I enjoyed planning them, but secretly longed for the kind of talk I had known in my "salon" in Oued-Zem. Our Roman party was a big success. The guests arrived wrapped in togas, their heads crowned by laurel wreaths. At the door they were greeted by our friend Mel who handed them a drink he had concocted. After that, Nubian slaves (two stalwart young men whose torsos we smeared with coconut butter) carried them on a litter around the torch-lit pool, and then threw them in the water.

We never found out what Mel put in that drink—he would not tell us, but the effect was as sudden as it was startling. A lovely blonde with the look of a fragile china doll who was known to be a non-swimmer kept leaping into the water, and time after time a fiftyish lawyer who had once been a lifeguard dove in after her and saved her. A tall brunette who was usually rather cold and distant embraced everybody, and a loud argument broke out between two men. I kept dancing around the pool and letting myself fall in sideways.

"Nina and Michel Graboi's parties at their Lawrence estate rival Elsa's soirees," enthused Irving Cahn in Host. But no matter what my life looked like on the outside, there was an emptiness inside that I tried to fill with activities.

My love for the theater began when I was fourteen. The Deutsche Volkstheater staged a new production of Goethe's Faust, and my sister invited me to see it with her. Mephisto was played by Max Pallenberg, one of the finest actors on the German stage. The dry, pedantic way in which our great classics were presented to us in school had spoiled them for me, but the opportunity to see Pallenberg was not to be missed.

The play stirred me profoundly. At midnight, when Fanny and her husband dropped me off at home, I crept to the bookshelf and took down the volume that contained Faust. Trembling with anticipation, I opened the book. The voices of the actors still rang in my ears, the action unfolded again before my eyes. I was so deeply engrossed that I did not notice when dawn came. By the time I got ready to go to school, I knew the Prologue in Heaven by heart. The play opened new vistas for me, and from then on I never lost respect for the awesome potential of the performance media.

In the '50s, the Broadway stage was neither inspiring nor ennobling. It was the time of the anti-hero and the kitchen-sink drama. The actors paraded the currently fashionable neuroses on stage, thereby helping to create more of the same. Whether it presents heroes or anti-heroes, the theater cannot help creating role models. The role models of the '50s held up a mirror of failure, impotence, alienation and nihilism in a claustrophobic world inhabited by families at war with each other and themselves. When it didn't show the great musicals of that day, the stage was awash with slice-of-life dramas that portray our weaknesses, our neuroses, our self-absorption.

As an avid theater-goer, I felt betrayed by the contemporary stage. Instead of lifting me up, it played on a narrow band of emotions in a trivial and pedestrian setting. There were exceptions to this dismal fare, but they were rare, and almost always foreign or old.

I hungered for the kind of theater that would send me out stimulated, expanded, inspired. I wanted to see plays that dealt with great, universal themes and gave me heroes and heroines that were models of what we can become. I wanted plays to make me think as well as entertain me. Books did that; I felt that the theater should do no less.

In the fall, I enrolled in a class offered by The Five Towns Music and

Art Foundation. The teacher was Helen Waren, a talented actress who had appeared on Broadway and on T.V. Her reddish hair and strong-nosed profile did not add up to beauty, but there was something compelling about her. Her voice was modulated on a bell-like tone, and her eyes and animated features commanded attention.

The class began as a speech class, but Helen's real purpose soon became clear. She wanted to test herself as a director, and she wanted the opportunity to do unconventional theater, away from the financial pressures of the Broadway and off-Broadway stage.

There were nine students in the class, all women. In four short months Helen transformed us into the feisty, lusty women of the cheeky Greek comedy Lysistrata, who refuse to sleep with their husbands until they end the war. Helen knew how to evoke qualities in us of which we ourselves were unaware. She was a fine teacher and an excellent director.

I was enthusiastic about the project and threw myself into helping to make it a success. Rehearsals were held at my home. I spent much time and effort assembling the people, props, and services required to stage the play. Besides acting the part of Kalonika, I made the costumes for the play from sheets donated by the cast.

The performance was so well received that several men joined us, allowing us much broader scope in the plays we staged. We now became The South Shore Drama Group, a community theater with Helen as artistic director. I was nominated president, a very flattering title whose real meaning was that I had to do most of the organizational work.

In '54 and '55, the terrace of my home became the stage for "A Summer Evening," where we performed for an audience of 200. One time, a storm knocked out the electricity. By late afternoon, it had not yet returned. The problem of lighting the stage was solved by two fire engines who threw their powerful beams at the terrace, bathing it in a strange, hallucinatory light.

The longer I knew Helen, the more my respect for her grew. I felt that she deserved a better showcase for her talents than our amateurish community theater.

"Why don't we start a small repertory theater here on the island?" I asked her at the end of the second year.

"Are you serious? Do you know how many people tried to do that?"

"A lot of people also try to start a business, but Michel and I did okay. We can do it, Helen, I'm sure. All we need is a space. We could do experimental plays and…"

"Stop!" Helen interrupted me. "Let me think about it. It's a crazy idea, but maybe…"

She called the next day. "I've been giving your idea some thought," she said. "A repertory theater is out. There are far too many problems, and besides, we'd need a lot of money to even start. But here's another idea: how about summerstock?"

After mulling it over and discussing it with Michel, I thought it was a fine idea. Instead of leaping headlong into something as ambitious as a year-round repertory company, we could try out some of our novel ideas in summerstock.

"I like it," I told Helen. "I'll start looking around for a space."

"A small space. Less than 199 seats. That makes us off-Broadway. No union."

We began to meet regularly to discuss our plans. "There's only one problem," Helen told me after several weeks. "I'm pregnant."

For a moment, I couldn't find words. Pregnant! That meant she would be very pregnant by the summer. What would happen to our plans? "That's wonderful! Congratulations!" I brought out, ashamed of my selfish thoughts.

"Yes, we're very happy about it. The doctor says I must take it easy. It could be a little risky at my age, you know." I did know. Helen was past forty, and this would be her first child.

"We'll have to forget the summerstock theater for this year," I said regretfully.

"No, we don't. You met Stanley; you know what a fine director he is. How would you feel about him coming in with us?"

I tried to hide my disappointment. Stanley Waren, Helen's brother, had impressed me as a very cold though capable man when he directed a play for the South Shore Drama Group. I did not care for his personality and had a feeling that we would clash. But the idea of the summerstock theater had taken hold of me, and so I reluctantly agreed.

I searched Long Island's south shore for a suitable location, but had to tell my partners week after week that I'd come up empty-handed again. By March, when I still had not found a place, we began to consider alternatives.

"What about a beach club? Maybe we can rent space in one," Stanley said.

"That's a good idea," Helen agreed. "We'd have a ready-made audience. The beach club patrons are always looking for entertainment."

"Well, I'll check it out," I said hesitantly. I didn't have much faith in the idea, but was willing to give it a try.

"The only available space is the Capri Beach Club," I told my partners two weeks later.

"Great! What's it like?" Helen asked.

"It's big. It can seat 700. It's not raked—we'd have to put in pitched flooring. Believe me, it's not what we want. And forget about the patrons as an audience for our plays. They wouldn't care for the kind of theater we want to do."

I parted from Helen and Stanley with the uneasy feeling that they would want to go ahead with it. Stanley had shown strong signs of interest, and Helen, as always, was ready to support him. The powerful love-hate relationship between the brother-sister pair was causing me a good deal of anxiety. The two generally ended up agreeing, but this was often preceded by a passionate argument. Most of the time, Stanley won, and I, who frequently disagreed with him, was outvoted by the two of them. I hoped that the Warens would see how ill a 700 seat theater lent itself to the purpose of staging avant-garde plays, but I knew that if Stanley wanted it, Helen would go along.

And that, in fact, is what happened. I was far too committed by then to back out, but when Stanley explained that we would have to follow the custom of other straw-hat theaters who booked "package deals," I nearly withdrew.

"Think of it this way," Helen said. "It's true that we'll have to take warmed-over Broadway fare and stars who have seen better days, but we can still choose plays that appeal to us. Our resident company will be directed by Stanley, and you know how good he is. It'll be a great experience; and maybe we'll earn enough to start a repertory theater next year. I think we should do it. You'll love it, Nina. You'll see."

It was too late for me to get out of it. And so, with a heavy heart, I made the arrangements.

Eighteen

My relationship with my partners began to deteriorate as soon as the contract was signed. Now that we were getting down to business, there were endless verbal fights between the brother-sister pair. The atmosphere was thick with hostility and I could see that I had unwittingly walked into a battle that had gone on for years. I was called upon to take one side or the other, and this generally brought down the wrath of both on me.

My workload kept getting heavier and heavier; I often wondered why I had allowed myself to enter into this venture. I was interviewed by the Long Island Press, the Nassau Herald and the South Shore Record and gave parties for visiting stars. I was well known in the community but I knew that what people saw was not me but the "chic, continental Mrs. Michel Graboi" described in the papers. My life, in reality, was filled with feverish activity with scarcely a moment to catch my breath. I felt guilty about neglecting my duties as wife and mother, and guilty about not having stuck with my original plan for a small theater and experimental plays.

As the season neared, I became more and more apprehensive. My partners convinced me that to be realistic we had to book box office draws, that is, stars in tried and proven plays. And so, like most straw-hat theaters, we booked "packages." A package consists of a play, a star, her or his leading man or woman, and an advance man. The advance man comes a day or two earlier and makes sure the sets are okay, there are rooms booked for the stars, the props are at hand, etc. The stars arrive Saturday and rehearse with the resident company Sunday and Monday. The performance opens Tuesday and runs for a week.

During the pre-production period, I worked to exhaustion. We interviewed prospective apprentices and members of the resident company, a task I found disheartening. The three of us seemed to sit in judgment over these people, to have power over their lives. We bickered with agents, hired a stage manager, a box office manager, a publicity person. I spoke to charitable organizations and sold them benefit performances. I found a printer for the weekly programs and induced local stores to advertise in them. Sets were built on our driveway and I fed the apprentices and the backstage crew lunch. In addition, there were tea parties, luncheons and cocktail parties to lure people into buying season tickets.

As we got ready for the opening, I was appalled by the way the apprentices were exploited. They were housed in a run-down boarding house and had to perform all the menial tasks connected with production. When we hired them, they were told that they would appear in the plays, but what it boiled down to was some meager walk-ons that gave them no opportunity to act. Stanley and Helen assured me that that's the way it is in the theater, and I didn't doubt it, but I continued to feel bad about it throughout the summer.

Our first star was Sylvia Sidney. In her youth she enjoyed great popularity in parts that suited her waiflike appearance and large mournful eyes. Now she was past her prime, but her name still carried enough weight to give us a full house for our opening week.

I was too busy with a hundred chores to pay much attention to our leading lady, but I gathered from the gossip that Miss Sidney was testy, demanding and prima donnaish. My illusions about the theater were quickly dispelled. On the other side of the curtain, life in the theater is frantic, chaotic, competitive, and often desperate. I thought of the actress in the Dorothy Parker story whose life, as she states, is a mess. The fear of aging, of "losing it," is built into a career based on good looks and personality. Some of our stars fell into that category, and their behavior was rooted in that fear.

The stars had done their parts innumerable times. Their slightest gestures had become automatic; they were secure and polished in their roles. The resident cast, on the other hand, rehearsed for five days under Stanley's direction, and as his interpretation of the play was often at odds with that of the director who had rehearsed the stars, the resulting performance looked like two different plays.

The most dramatic of our stars was Magda Gabor, the eldest of the famous Gabor sisters. Magda was as beautiful as Eva and Zsa-Zsa, but her personality was less flamboyant, though not for lack of trying. She started her engagement at the Capri Theater by throwing a tantrum over the color of the stage set, which was supposed to match her dress. Our overworked apprentices had to stay up all night until it did. We prepared ourselves for a hard week with our temperamental diva, but as it turned out, Magda was the most frightened and nervous of all our stars. On opening night, she was a wreck.

"How does my hair look?" she asked me anxiously. I had gone backstage to attempt to calm her down.

"Perfectly lovely," I assured her.

"And the dress? Is the back wrinkled? Does my bra show?" She was turning around before the mirror and wringing her hands.

"You couldn't look more beautiful," I assured her. "Believe me, you look great."

"Are you sure? Do I have too much rouge? What about these beads? Do they go with the dress? And the shoes! I look terrible, I know I do! Mama will notice everything! She has the eyes of a hawk!"

Mama Gabor, still showing signs of the exquisite beauty she had passed on to her daughters, had arrived early. Richly bejewelled, she sat front row center.

"Is that why you're so nervous?" I asked Magda. "Because your mother is out front? But she must have seen you in this role before! Didn't you wear the same shoes then?"

"No, she didn't see me before. And if anything is wrong with the way I look, she'll give me hell."

Before my eyes, the glamorous diva had become a little girl, frightened of what Mama would say. I could see how Jolie had browbeaten her beautiful girls into the most rigorous attention to every detail of their appearance, and how her withering criticism had kept them in line.

Magda's performance was uninspiring, but the taste of the Capri Theater audience was not sophisticated, and they applauded her heartily. Apparently Mama was also not too displeased, and the rest of Magda's week with us went well. One evening Eva brought Zsa-Zsa's daughter Francesca and Ephram Zimbalist to the theater and to the party at my house afterwards. The little girl fell in love with my daughter's doll collection and would not leave until Nicole gave her one of her favorite dolls.

Stanley Waren and I did not get along. His arrogant manner and nonchalant way of going over my head with decisions of which I did not approve led to many heated arguments. Helen was absent most of the time, putting in an appearance only for opening nights. The audience complained about poor visibility, the air conditioning regularly gave out on the hottest nights, and the plays themselves failed to excite me.

I could not wait for the season to end. I had seen through the cloud of glamour that surrounds the theater and its famous stars, I had seen the fear of aging in Sylvia Sidney's eyes and sensed the need for approval behind Wendy Barrie's lovely smile. Zero Mostel was a clown who drowned himself in drink, and Brian Donlevy's Hollywood star status had done nothing to make him feel more secure.

I saw the lies the newspapers print, the ease with which public opinion can be shaped, and the exploitation of the young that goes on in the name of art. I saw the audience's lack of discernment and the way the opinion of one or two men—the critics—can make or break a play. I saw the fakery of the theater and of the image famous people project.

I had already seen that a comfortable lifestyle is no guarantee of a happy life. It seemed that the wealthy are no better off than the poor. Where the latter suffer from lack of material goods, the former suffer emotionally. I felt that the people starving in India were no worse off than the rich Americans. All have an equal load of suffering, and now I knew that the famous suffer too. It seemed that there was nothing one could do to ensure a happy life; I saw the futility of the scramble for money, power and fame in which people are so passionately engaged, and none of it seemed to have any meaning.

I myself had achieved a measure of fame in my community. I was admired, envied, talked about, sought after, and within myself I knew it all to be ashes. I was in despair. Nothing seemed to make sense. The picture people painted in their minds of Nina Graboi and her glamorous life had nothing to do with my reality. That reality held many soft curves and gentle cushionings, but it was empty of meaning, purpose, reason to live. With time, my marriage had become threadbare. It became increasingly clear that in most respects, we were painfully incompatible, yet divorce was still rare in those days, and Michel would not hear of it.

In my heart, I knew that I would leave my husband once the children were in college. We had been good partners when we escaped from the Nazis, when we built up our business, when we built the house. Now we were sparring partners. My marriage had assumed the shape of a battlefield from which I sought escape by plunging into activity. As for the children, they were at an age when the home was no longer the center of their world. More and more their minds were being shaped by the outside world, and I knew that whatever good or ill I had done them was already done. Try as I might, I could not discover the meaning of my life in my family.

The theater had seemed the most promising of the activities in which I engaged. Here I was, after a successful summer which could, had I wished it, have led to a career; yet I was feeling a deep depression. It was fall. The leaves were at their most enchanting, cascading green, red, and golden from the trees. I was driving through the quiet Five Towns back streets with their magnificently landscaped estates.

"So what!" I heard myself yell. "So what!" So what. Endlessly. It seemed that I could not stop. I got in my car when the kids came home from school and drove around, shouting, "So what!" behind the closed car windows.

So what if I have a beautiful home, two lovely children, so what if I give great parties, know famous movie stars, wear elegant clothes…Unless there is more to life than climbing up the ladder of worldly success—unless there is more than being born and dying, suffering and joy—unless there is more to me than this body that will age and someday die—more than successes and failures, ephemeral pleasures and heavy pains, life is not worth living. The ladder of worldly success is not worth scrambling up.

But then what? What can give life the meaning that the world cannot supply?

It was the beginning of a search that would last for the rest of my life.

Nineteen

In 1955, it was not fashionable to believe in God. To the philosophical avant garde, God was dead. Science laughed at the superstitious beliefs of the ignorant; many of the college-educated turned away from religion. Those who still went to church or synagogue did so more to maintain a tradition than from a sincerely felt need for intercourse with the divine.

I was thirty-six years old. I knew that if I was to go on living, I had to find a meaning and a purpose that went beyond my personal and family concerns. We grow from the restrictions of childhood into an adulthood in which happiness and fulfillment seem always around the corner. We always wait for this to happen or for that, to find the right sex partner, to make a million, to do something that will bring us power and fame. "If only I had…" "If only I could…" It seemed to me that life was a tale told by an idiot, signifying nothing; and I wanted to die.

I had become familiar with death in World War II. I survived the Nazis in Vienna, the German bombs in Belgium, the detention camp in North Africa. In those years, death was not an abstraction but an ever-present possibility. Thousands around me died, and the next one could always have been me. I was not troubled by metaphysical speculation. I was too busy surviving. Seeing the young, the old, the crippled and the strong, the good people and the bad die in such numbers made it seem absurd to believe in God. In those years, the longing for material comforts and political security was uppermost in my mind. And now that I had it, I soured on life.

The immediate trigger for my depressed state was the Capri Theater experience. But other disillusions had preceded it. Our life style brought me in contact with people much higher up the ladder of success. Through them, I saw one of the bitch goddess's faces. Another peered at me from the mirror held up by the people who knew me. "The woman who has everything."

Everything! At the end of that summer all my "if onlys" had become "so whats". I wanted to die, but I was not suicidal. There was something in me, a kind of optimism, that made me feel that there is more, that something is rescued, something lives on…I thought of the birth of my children: who was that I who sang while my body screamed with pain? Did it have an existence independent of the body? And wouldn't that mean that there is no death?

My questions were awkwardly formulated, naive. It was a first groping for answers. I, who had never gone to college, now plunged into philosophy. I read Bergson, Spinoza, Spengler, Kirkegaard, Nietsche, Heidegger, Schopenhauer, Kant and Plato without finding what I was searching for. Here and there were some tantalizing hints, but nothing I found satisfied my craving. I was still hovering on the edge of depression, and the discourse of the venerable gentlemen did not strike home.

It would have seemed natural to reach for the Bible at that point, but I was not yet aware that there was anything religious in my search. What I wanted was proof that we don't just muddle through and then are gone without a trace. I wanted to know if the human race has a goal, if all our random activities have a meaning—if we are not just rabbits born to eat, procreate, and die.

One day I happened to pick up a magazine in the dentist's waiting room. The word "reincarnation" caught my eye in a short review of a book that had just come out, called The Search for Bridey Murphy by Morey Bernstein. The author was described as a business man who practiced hypnosis as a hobby. The book is the case history of a housewife who, under hypnosis, became Bridey Murphy, an Irish woman who lived in the 18th century.

Reincarnation! Like an echo from long ago, I remembered Lilo's mother. Was reincarnation possible? And if it was, what did it mean? If we are more than our bodies—if something, our essence perhaps, lives on, then our dreams about life eternal and about God may be true.…

I was not ready to believe, but I decided to suspend judgment while investigating further. In order to track down some of the titles in Bridey's bibliography, I took out membership in the American Society for Psychical Research.

ONE FOOT IN THE FUTURE

The Society was housed in a small ground floor apartment on upper Fifth Avenue. I was not without apprehension as I approached the secretary who sat in a room crowded with filing cabinets. She looked reassuringly ordinary, but I could not keep the goose pimples from rising. ESP spooked me; it was with an effort that I kept from turning around and running away.

The collection of books filled the walls of what must have been the apartment's dining room before it became the headquarters of the Society; scant as it was, it held priceless treasures for me.

For the next year I drove to the city twice a week and returned with armfuls of books. I read about the research conducted by Professor Rhine at Duke University, the studies of Gardner Murphy, Karlis Osis and other reputable scientists. I read about telepathy, telekinesis, astral travel, poltergeists, levitation and prophetic dreams; I read about communications with the dead in the cross-correspondences of Myers, Gurney, Sidgwick and Verall (Evidence for Personal Survival from Cross-Correspondences). It was obvious that something more than fantasy was going on. Little by little, my skepticism began to abate. What really convinced me was the sheer volume of the writings that attested to these phenomena.

If only one percent is true and the rest is either elaborate fantasy or deliberate hoax, it proves the existence of forces outside the known reality, I mused. I found a good many of the books questionable, but the level of intelligence and honesty in the rest left a deep impression.

This process took place long before mysticism and the occult became part of pop culture. Not one among my large circle of friends and acquaintances shared my interest. Well-educated and aware as they were, parapsychology lay outside their sphere. In the first flush of my new discoveries I became evangelical and made a nuisance of myself by talking about it endlessly. I was convinced that the world would change overnight once everybody saw that we're not here today and gone tomorrow, that we have been and will be here again, that there is no death, and that we are more than skin-encapsulated bags of bone and flesh.

I myself had no extra-sensory talents. Not a single incident of telepathy or clairvoyance had appeared in my life. The authorities claim that we all have the potential for it. I wanted to test it. With cardboard and crayons, I designed a deck of Zehner cards. There are 25 cards in the deck: 5 circles, 5 squares, 5 crosses, 5 stars, and 5 wavy lines. Finding my friends reluctant to participate in my "research," I recruited my children, aged 10 and 11. Danny and Nicky took to it enthusiastically. The boy showed considerable talent for right guesses, and he was equally good at guessing the nature of drawings we placed in sealed envelopes. The number of "hits" he registered was better than the law of averages predicts, but the experiment was inconclusive.

The children were especially delighted with my attempts to hypnotize them. With the proper solemnity, I would light a candle and bid them to stare at it while I intoned the words Bernstein spoke to Bridey. It was probably fortunate that I never succeeded to hypnotize them, much less regress them to a former life. They missed no opportunity for horseplay, and our sessions were brought to a halt by our laughter.

I avidly continued to read the arguments for and against Psi and reincarnation. I also read Walt Whitman, Ouspensky, Gurdjieff, Edgar Cayce, and Richard Maurice Bucke's Cosmic Consciousness, A Study in the Evolution of the Human Mind. In the mid-fifties, books of that nature were as hard to find as people who were interested in them. In the sixties the heavens opened up and scores of books, both old and new, showered down upon the waiting world. How much easier my search would have been if I had waited! But at that time, very little information was available about non-ordinary states. There was William James who got high on nitrous oxide in the dentist's chair and had an unforgettable glimpse of another reality; and there was C.G.Jung. Elsewhere, psychology dismissed transcendent states as oceanic feelings and regression to the womb.

Before long, I read my first book on Hindu philosophy. It was like a blow to my solar plexus; it jarred me awake. Here, at last, was what I sought. Instead of an object of dispute and often ridicule, here, reincarnation was taken for granted. The teachings were logical, unsentimental, yet filled with the spirit of non-harmfulness, compassion, understanding, love. To my western ears, Hindu philosophy sounded naive. The world I knew, the "real" world, was ruled by money and desires. But the words in Patanjali's Yoga Aphorisms struck a deep chord. Unlike Christianity and Judaism, which insist on unquestioning faith, Patanjali tells us to believe nothing without first testing it. This was just right for me. It was the way I had chosen long ago, when I was still a child.

"God will punish you," Mama used to say when I did something naughty. Poor dear Mama, so busy raising her brood and running the house! She did not like to punish us, nor did she want to bother Papa with the task of disciplining us when he came home from work. So "God will punish you!" was her stock response to our transgressions.

I must have been about five when I decided to put God to the test. Conquering my fear, I tossed my ball against the dining room wall, which was strictly forbidden, and waited, trembling, for God to strike. Nothing happened. "Maybe He'll punish me tonight," I thought. But when night came and still I had not been struck by lightning, I saw that I could safely ignore Mama's warning.

I approached Patanjali's Yoga Aphorisms in the spirit of testing an hypothesis. Up to that time, only my intellect was involved in my search. Outside of my abortive experiments with telepathy, I had made no attempt to achieve the state of mind which Bucke calls Cosmic Consciousness and the Hindus Samadhi. I began to check out some of the startling statements Patanjali makes. "The mind is a chattering monkey," he says. What? Is he kidding? I have a fine, well-disciplined mind. I was proud of it, much prouder than of my looks. My identification with the body was tenuous, but my mind...My mind is me, I, my true self...or isn't it?

Making my mind blank is child's play, I thought. Am I not master in my house? It was quite a blow to find out that I couldn't keep my mind empty for more than a few seconds. Snatches of songs, conversations, irrelevant thoughts intruded and ran off with my concentration like a team of wild horses—as Patanjali warned.

With a will I went to work to subdue the chattering monkey. With closed eyes I concentrated on the seated figure of Buddha. Listing the features of the image I visualized, my mind wandered. I discarded the Buddha and concentrated on a lotus flower. The Hindus see it as the perfect symbol of the human condition, rooted as it is in the mud, yet growing towards the sky. Again, my mind wandered. I'll have to try something more familiar than the Buddha or the lotus, I thought.

When I substituted a rose, I tripped out on a reverie of rose gardens, the roses my first admirer gave me, romance, violets, strawberries, must remember to buy lamb chops for tomorrow night, parsley, where was I that summer when I picked blueberries…And like a drunken monkey, my mind took off on the meaningless ramblings that are our ordinary mode of thought.

I had somewhat better luck with the image of a cow, on which I settled next. The goal of concentration is to exhaust the mind by focusing on the attributes of the chosen object. The friendly bovine gave my mind much to inspect. Being a good deal larger and more complex than a flower, it offered a long list of attributes. I thought of the milk it gives, the leather made from its skin, its double stomach, the dung that heats the huts of poor people in India, breaded veal cutlets…No. I quickly chased that last thought away. But despite such lapses, the image of the cow was more successful in helping me to empty my mind than the lotus, the rose, and the Buddha.

Patanjali is right, I realized. My mind is a chattering monkey. It was another statement he makes that I found harder to accept. He claims that the self we know is not the real self. The true Self is the Atman, the God-within-the-creature. Yoga, according to Patanjali, is the effort to separate the Atman (the true Self) from the non-Atman (the apparent self).

"Nonsense," I thought. "The one thing that I know is that I'm me, I, myself. How can he tell me that that sense of I-ness is not the true me—that it is an illusion?"

It was around that time that I went to the Bar Mitzvah of Gerda's son. Gerda had gone directly from England to America and was living with her husband, her mother and her two sons in a modest apartment in the Bronx. Most of her numerous aunts, uncles and cousins had been able to escape from Vienna and were gathered at the Bar Mitzvah. The tight-knit clan had known me as a teen-ager, and they told little stories and anecdotes about me. Did I actually do or say that, I wondered? But the I that wondered about that I of the past was not really the same I any more. In between, there had been Hitler, England, Belgium, marriage, the bombs, Oued-Zem, motherhood, the Capri Theater…The me I had believed immutable had gone through numerous transformations.

I began to see that there might be some truth in Patanjali's startling words. Another insight was provided by the way others saw me. The glamorized version of Nina Graboi was strictly in the eyes of the beholder. To myself, I was much less enviable. A vast gap between who I was and who I could be had opened up. I saw that we humans carry within us the potential for a greatly expanded awareness of reality that embraces levels which are not accessible to ordinary consciousness. The cosmic nature of the reality that the books described dwarfed the microscopic portion of it that I knew. More than anything, I longed to look into the invisible realm.

An unexpected result of my meditation was that the insomnia that had plagued me since adolescence disappeared. I stayed awake until my cow stood before me, nameless and attributeless, in her pure form. It was then that I allowed myself to sink into sleep, a deep sleep that was more refreshing than any I had known before. Eventually, after a year of practice, I caught a glimpse, a faint hint of the possibilities. I experienced a sense of peace and a feeling that my body grew lighter. It did not last long, but it was enough to give me a taste.

My fascination with Hinduism had yet another effect. It made me turn away from the social life that had played such a large role before. I was consumed by desire to be of service. I fired the excellent housekeeper who came close to being the "pearl" I had long sought. I cooked, cleaned, and scrubbed for my family; I stopped wearing make-up, flirted with the idea of shaving my head, and yearned to simplify my life. I wanted to conquer the ego, the false self that feeds on desires. But after a few months I realized that it was precisely that ego that made me impose a lifestyle on my family for which they were not ready. So I hired another housekeeper (not nearly as good as the one I had let go), and began giving parties again.

In the late '50s, I took classes in Hindu philosophy and comparative religions at Hofstra University and the New School for Social Research. I was also reading books on anthropology, and a new image of humankind began to emerge for me.

Throughout this, I kept paring away at the accretions of my conditioning. I subjected all my beliefs to radical doubt and questioned the values by which I lived. Were they truly mine? Or had they been foisted on me, as on everybody else, by the culture? I had questioned before, but not nearly enough. I discovered new possibilities, alternative approaches to almost everything I had hitherto taken for granted, and I saw the hypocrisy and the phoniness of much that made up the image I presented to the world. I called it "peeling the onion" and worked diligently to free myself of robot prejudices and responses.

These inner events took place over a period of years, and they are still going on. The ego, or the false self, is a thousand-headed hydra, as I was to find out in the course of time. But once started, the work on myself continued independently of the activities that now replaced the intense studies of that first year.

Twenty

We spent the summer after the Capri theater in Europe. There, my life took a new direction. In Paris we saw a play named L'Oeuf (The Egg) by the existentialist playwright Felicien Marceau. Here was a play with more profound meaning than the domestic dramas Broadway dished up. It is the story of a young man who, alone among all the others who are inside the egg of the world, is outside. Excluded. Not part of the good times, adventures and amorous conquests everyone else seems to have. At the office, his colleagues regale each other with tales of their passionate nights. The people around him, the magazines he reads and the movies he sees—all make him believe that he alone does not feel fresh as a daisy when he wakes up in the morning; he alone cannot get the girls or the raise.

One day it dawns on him that the others are lying. And he begins to lie. Each of the trivial and accidental happenings in his life are transformed into tall tales, and suddenly he is inside the egg with the rest. Now tall tales are no longer enough. The big lie taught him that nothing is true, and his acts become more and more outrageous until they finally end in murder. He kills his wife for no other reason than that it is the most absurd and gratuitous act he can think of.

I brought a copy of the play back to the States and translated it. About a year later I happened to read that Alexander Ince, a Broadway producer, had taken an option on L'Oeuf. I sent him my translation and received an invitation to come and see him.

The walls of his office in Manhattan's theater district were covered with posters of shows and photos that showed him with celebrities. The rotund man behind the desk beamed welcome. His bald head was surrounded by a white fringe that showed his age more than his unwrinkled face.

"Come in, come in, darling," he called as I stood in the door. "Take a seat, be comfortable. Very pretty, very pretty!" I didn't know if he meant me or the manuscript that he extracted from his littered desk. It was my translation of L'Oeuf. "Not bad," he nodded as he leafed through it. His accent was heavy and unmistakably Hungarian. "Quite good. Too bad. I have a contract with Maurice Valency. He is working on it right now. So you see…"

Yes, I saw. Maurice Valency was the best-known translator of French plays. His renditions of works by Anhouil, Giraudoux and other eminent playwrights were both critically acclaimed and successful at the box office—a rare occurrence on Broadway. "Well, thanks for reading mine anyway," I said, rising to take my leave.

"Wait," he said. "What's your hurry? Sit. Smoke a cigarette. Talk. What do you see in the play?"

I told him. I explained the play was important because it gave such a vivid contemporary demonstration of the logical conclusion to which total nihilism leads. I said I knew I could bring it to life in English. "But you have Valency under contract. He's sure to do a splendid job. What do you need me for?" I asked.

"So I have him under contract. What if I don't like his translation? Nobody is infallible, you know. Here, give me." He pointed to the manuscript under my arm. "Yes, here it is," he said, opening it to a page in Act Two. "This is how I want you to change it."

For the next months he kept me revising and adapting my translation to what he thought was the American taste. We had many arguments about it, but he was the expert, so I often went along. In the end, he used neither Valency's translation nor mine—though not without incorporating bits and pieces of both—but that by someone of whom I had never heard. In its final form, the play was almost unrecognizable. Despite the famous comedian who was hopelessly miscast as the lead, it failed miserably on the Broadway stage.

Ince introduced me to Ninon Tallon, a literary agent who had a small monopoly on French plays. She encouraged me to do more translations, and in the course of reading and rejecting numerous plays I came across one that set my imagination on fire.

In Les Naturellesdu Bordelais (The Natives of Bordeaux), Jacques Audiberti created a world in which the pursuit of love-making without love ends in the metamorphosis of the human race into huge, ice-cold metallic crickets. The broadly burlesqued sexiness of the play has at its core an indictment of our society's soulless sensuality, in which the partner is unimportant, interchangeable and thus dehumanized.

The Natives is multi-layered. Translating it revealed aspects that were at first buried beneath the author's delirious flow of language. Audiberti's use of sounds, rhythms, and his coining of new words makes it difficult to grasp the play fully on the printed page. The atmosphere is a hypnotic mixture of hallucination, ferocity, eroticism, realism and fantasy—all in such a constant state of flux that a plot-synopsis becomes completely inadequate to convey the play's action and mood. Above all, it is superbly theatrical.

I felt a great affinity with Audiberti's unique combination of earthiness and mysticism and wanted very much to make him available to the American audience. Writing before the age of psychedelics, his work has all the characteristics of the psychedelic experience and foreshadows the impatience of psychedelic art with formalized structures.

Bitten by the Audiberti bug, I translated several more of his plays. When I proved to my satisfaction that I could remain faithful to the author while interpreting him so that his words sang in English as they did in French, I felt it was time to meet Mons. Audiberti.

The mental image I had built up of him was larger than life. He would be a giant, given to great, booming belly laughs, bursting with energy and élan vitale. I wrote to the Societé des Auteurs et Compositeurs in Paris to ask for his address. They wrote back that this was not possible as he frequently changed his domicile, but they would forward my letter. In due time I received a note from Audiberti assuring me that he would be happy to meet me. His signature was exactly what I had expected—big, sprawling, eccentric, bursting with energy.

The newspapers were full of his name when I arrived in Paris. His new play had just opened and was met with boos and hisses from the volatile French audience—a distinction he shared with other great playwrights whose works later became classics. The papers called him "a man of mystery" because he managed to elude the most cunning reporters.

It took a fortnight before the Societé could track him down; they gave me an address but no phone number. There was no answer to the telegram I sent, but I had come to Paris to meet him, and so I decided to present myself unbidden at his home.

Armed with a loaf of long French bread, an apple, and a bottle of fine wine, I hailed a cab. The apple was in memory of his lovely play called Pomme, Pomme, Pomme, and the bread I intended to insert in the door should he refuse to let me in.

The house in St. Germain des Pres did not look inviting. I had to cross a large, untidy courtyard full of yowling and fighting cats to get to the apartment. French bread at the ready, I rang the bell. The door was opened by a slovenly middle-aged woman who let me enter without ado and bade me wait in the dark hallway while she went to announce me.

Feeling extremely foolish, I stood clutching my French bread. After a few moments, she returned and ushered me into a room at the end of the hallway. In the semi-darkness I made out a figure on a bed piled high with articles of clothing, books, newspapers and ashtrays.

"Entrez, Madame," a feeble, rather high-pitched voice came from the bed. "You must forgive me, I am not feeling well. Please sit down."

I looked around for a chair but could see none that was not covered with an assortment of trash. Audiberti motioned me to sweep the stuff off. "So you are an American," he said. "You do not look like one." The hand he extended was flabby, clammy and limp. The eyes that peered at me from a large, balding head were small and watery in a pasty face. For the next two hours, he talked about his troubles. "She is a demon, that woman. She took everything! My money, my collection of rare books, my house…I had a house in the country, a villa! She squeezed me dry, like a lemon! What you see here is the shell of my former self. She ruined me. There is nothing left. I wish I had never met her!"

It took a while before I understood that he was talking about his wife. As he raved on and on I felt like the little housewife who came to worship the famous actress in Glory in the Daytime. So this was the man into whose brain I had crept, whose poetic mind had left me breathless, whose creativity had seemed almost superhuman! Sitting there with my illusions in tatters, I had only one desire—to leave! When I finally rose to go, he held me back. "You say you are an American? I don't believe it. You don't act like one. All Americans are loud and ill-mannered. You're not. How come?"

Whenever anyone attacks America, I become more American than apple pie. "No American would be as rude as you, Monsieur," I said with all the dignity I could muster. "I came all the way from the U.S. to discuss your plays with you, and all you do is talk about your troubles. You never gave me a chance to say a word! Believe me, we are more civilized in America! I bid you good afternoon, Monsieur!" Outraged, I walked to the door." Just a minute, Madame," he exclaimed. "I realize that I have been rather boorish. Will you accept my apologies?" Not very enthusiastic, I nodded. "Will you tell me what that bread is doing under your arm? Did you expect to find me so destitute that I could not afford to buy my own bread? And the apple. Was that to tempt me, like Eve?"

His expression had changed. There was a mischievous twinkle in his eyes that made him look like a cunning peasant. The effect was very comical.

"The bread was to help me force my way in," I said. When I told him the strategy I had worked out to be admitted, he laughed loudly, though not with the booming sound I had imagined back in the States.

"I can see that I have to make up for my rude behavior," he said. "Will you allow me to take you to dinner tomorrow? We will talk about the plays then, I promise."

The restaurant was a meeting place for Paris's artists and intellectuals. It was like a club where only members can get a table. The walls were filled with signed photos of illustrious people, Audiberti's among them, and he himself was received like an old, honored guest. Things went much better than the day before. We spoke at length about his plays and I was happy to see that he entirely approved of my conception of his work. When I left Paris, it was with the assurance that I had carte blanche to translate his plays; I was elated, and in the next two years I translated three more of his plays.

I genuinely enjoyed this work, but it also acted as a smokescreen for the increasing alienation I felt from my lifestyle and from Michel. It had long been obvious that my husband and I saw the world through different lenses. No doubt he suffered as much from this state of affairs as I did, but he stubbornly continued to oppose the idea of a separation or divorce.

The thought of meeting another man did not enter my mind. The men I met at parties failed to excite me. Not one of them matched my interests, and short of a meeting of minds and hearts, the idea of a love affair left me cold.

What preoccupied me was the thought of what I would do to support myself, once I left my marriage. I hoped that the plays I had translated would bring me an income and open the way to the profession of translator of plays, but I was beginning to see that it would not be easy to sell Audiberti to an American public, let alone a producer. I had plunged into the work because I was fascinated by it; I knew that the plays were excellent, but my judgment deserted me when it came to their commercial worth. I pursued their sale for the next year, then I gave up. Regrettably. Today, the plays still moulder in my drawer. They were ahead of their time then; now, they may well be behind.

It was a time in my life when I felt myself aging and helplessly trapped in a marriage that had become abrasive. My feelings of that period are captured in a curious, unfinished manuscript that I recently discovered among some of my old writings. The gloomy words show the autumnal feelings in my heart, but they also speak of the longing to escape from the prison of my marriage and the prison of selfhood:

ELISE stands in the doorway of her house watching her children, a boy of fifteen and a girl of fourteen, get on their bikes. The sun shines on their happy faces. They laugh, wave to their mother and ride off. ELISE's face is in shadow. She enters the house. The camera follows her as she walks from room to room. Except for the children's rooms, the house is in semi-darkness. In the boy's room she picks up some clothes, folds them, hangs them up, then does the same in the girl's room. She looks around. Nothing else to do. She goes to the living room, selects a book and sits down. For a few moments, she scans the pages, then rises, arranges some flowers, turns on the radio, etc. Her movements are aimless, slow. The NARRATOR begins to speak when she enters the living room.

NARRATOR: She hangs suspended between her yesterday and her tomorrow, between a world of lights and shadows, of unfulfilled destiny, of hopes not yet spent. Her spirit roams the frontiers of her world, looks for a corner where it can alight and feel at home. But it retreats, it cannot come to rest. Once, when she was a child, a servant took her to a church. Cool and harsh was the bench on which she knelt, cool and harsh the scent of incense in her nostrils. Her spirit found no bridge to build from church to God.

[ELISE's dining room. A dinner party. She sits at the head of the table and talks animatedly to the two men at her side.]

NARRATOR: Familiar faces, a familiar role. Each task in her day determines how her face must look, what dress to wear, what feelings to pretend. Every hour slides smoothly out of its compartment and brings with it the responses she must make. Once the air had been filled with the scent of lilacs and apple blossoms; but it is fall, and the leaves must borrow the breath of the wind to make them dance. There are treasures in her soul. To whom can she show them? Who can she share them with? The children took what they needed. Now they are fleet, their beds will soon be empty. The husband has vanished long ago, been banished into half-oblivion. Gray is the color of her love, as gray as ashes. The treasures in her clamor to be shared.

ELISE [Her face is clearly visible for a moment] [Yearning]: I love, love, love…[Her face is in shadow again.]

NARRATOR: Love. Undifferentiated love, love without an object, love for nature, art, thy neighbor…The treasures in her soul grow dusty. Her body, which was made for love, shrinks from the whip of time and screams reproach at her for each lost hour. She has been frugal of herself, much too fastidious, too hard to please. Passion was a climate of her soul, her body lacked existence of its own, she has subdued it, made it flaunt its beauty only as a game. She has remained a virgin, waiting still deep in her womb for her soulmate, her other half. And when he did not come, she turned to death. Ravisher, conquerer, come carry me off, I'll be your bride, your mate, your wife…Her daytime self knows nothing of her nighttime thoughts. Death, in the daytime, is a vandal, a thief, the enemy her reason hates and fears. Her soul prepares a shroud while yet she seems to dance through life. Her mind is drawn towards the unknown. God—is there a God? Is there an order in the universe? Is mundane living just a shell that hides another dimension?

ELISE: Perhaps once I was stone, and the water washed over me, enfolded me wordlessly and was my mate. Perhaps I was a flower once, and the bee came and drank my nectar wordlessly and was my mate…

NARRATOR: She tries to feel the wordless oneness of the water and the stone, the flower and the bee. She longs to break the prison walls of her solitude to flow, to merge, to feel herself at one with…what? She does not know.

ELISE: How empty life is! What purpose does it have? Yesterday I was born, today I live, tomorrow I shall die. A wave in the ocean, a heartbeat in time, a link in the chain. Wealth, beauty, husband, children—all merely foam cresting the waves…Do I really live? I know what it is to be a child, a woman, a mother. But what is it like to be a fish? Or a seagull? To feel with a seagull's heart, to suffer seagull hunger, to beget seagulls and feed the seagull young… Or a shell. A shell has no heart, it is only a house. What is it like to be a house chained to the body of a creature? Does the shell know God?

NARRATOR: So much of life she cannot be! So many forms, colors, shapes, feelings, even those she once knew—where are they now? Some she remembers, can reproduce at will. The first time she held her babies in her arms…Picking violets in the meadow…Her first dance…Her wedding night…The shutter clicks, the image is supplied. But not the feeling. That she can never feel again. [Shot of a child bouncing a red ball.] Her red ball once held her entranced for hours. Her heart jumped with joy as she bounced it, and bounced it again. Where is that joy now? Where the hate, the love, the pleasures and the pains of her yesterdays? Life holds her yet, but her spirit is in flight. Life has been kind to her, responded with a smile of welcome to her presence. But is that all there is? she asks.

[ELISE floats on the water, her long hair trailing behind her.]

ELISE: To dissolve, to return to eternity's womb, cease to be one and be one with all…What does it feel like to be water, a shell, a gull, an old man?

[The CHILDREN leap into the water, swim up to their mother and splash her. She splashes back.]

NARRATOR: How they pull her back! And how gladly she follows!

[ELISE and the CHILDREN race. Mother and daughter swim side by side, the boy soon forges ahead.]

NARRATOR: Her son, tall and strong, can out-race her, out-swim her by far. Her daughter still lingers by her side, not ready yet to cut the cord. She loves them, yet she bids them farewell. Softly she has severed the ties, strand by strand, heartbeat by heartbeat. Her children are not her children, she knows. They are the son and daughter of life.

[ELISE sits in her garden. She has a book on her lap but stares off into the distance.]

NARRATOR: To live life, not to read about it. To break through concepts, to experience, to feel, to be engulfed. Evil, for instance. She knows that it exists; there are murders committed, weapons forged, there is vice, lust, greed, arson. But the feel of it, the touch of it, the slime and the stench and the passion of it—she's a stranger to them, they never entered her world. The people she knows, the sights she sees are aseptic, safe, sound, protected. A cotton-candy life, a furred-bunny life, a cosy, rosy garden-party life. A middle-road life with the sharp edges blunted.

* * *

Rereading these pages, I am struck with a sense of unfamiliarity with the feelings I then harbored. Here was a woman not yet forty who believed her life to be over because her children had grown! Did I really experience these sentiments? It seems so alien to me now; again, I am reminded of how little of what I call myself is permanent.

Twenty-one

"This is Gregg Price," Ninon Tallon said, putting her arm around my shoulder. "You two should meet. He levitates."

"He what?" I asked, startled.

"He rises up. Absolument. Let him tell you."

She turned back to her other guests, leaving me to face the young man who possessed this remarkable gift. Short of the movies, he was the most handsome man I had ever seen. He looked like the young Tyrone Power, except that there was something brooding in his face, which only enhanced his amazingly good looks.

We were standing in Ninon's foyer. The living room was packed with celebrities, leaders in the world of the theater—producers, directors, playwrights, a sprinkling of actors. I came because Ninon had told me I would meet people who could be helpful with the Audiberti plays, but as soon as I entered I knew that I had made a mistake. I no longer felt at home at cocktail parties, and even less so with famous strangers. I was ill at ease and soon gave up trying to mingle with the guests. I was on the verge of leaving when Ninon brought Gregg to me. When I saw him, I quickly changed my mind.

"Can I get you a drink?" he asked.

"Thanks. Make it a scotch on the rocks."

"Coming up. Don't go away." He dove into the crowd and returned almost at once with two glasses.

"Did you levitate?" I asked.

"What? Here?" He laughed. "I was a waiter once. I know how to pilot drinks through a crowd."

"You levitate. And you were a waiter. What else do you do?" I asked.

"I'm an actor. Presently unemployed. I've done some TV crap, but I'm determined not to do that again. I won't act unless the play has some depth, some meaning. I'd rather be a waiter!"

"Bravo!" I said. "I admire your integrity. What kind of plays interest you?"

"The classics, and the avant-garde. The kind of plays they do in Europe. There's an Italian playwright who was never performed in the U.S. He's fantastic! Extraordinary! You'd love his plays!"

"Are they available in English? I don't read Italian," I observed.

"There's one that's been translated. It's not a very good translation, but you can read it if you like."

"Great! As it happens, I own the rights to some French plays that I translated. Would you like to see them?"

When we parted, it was with the promise to exchange plays.

I was excited by this meeting. It was good to talk with someone whose interests were so similar to mine. I didn't know what intrigued me more—his levitating or his ideas about the theater. With keen anticipation I looked forward to seeing him again.

A week later, he called. "I keep remembering our talk. Can we get together tomorrow?"

We talked about extra-sensory perception, Bucke's Cosmic Consciousness, Hermann Hesse's Steppenwolf, Teilhard de Chardin. He knew a great deal about the lives of the Saints, and I marvelled at the passion this young Adonis brought to a subject so far removed from the world of the theater. The play he brought me confirmed my perception of him as a sensitive and intelligent young man, and he, in turn, thought Audiberti's plays and my translations were superb. We met in romantic places—the swan pond in Central Park, the Cloisters, the garden of the Museum of Modern Art. He bought coffee in containers, and we strolled around or sat on the grass. He was always talking, gesticulating, acting out monologues from plays. I was charmed.

"I can't afford to take you to lunch," he once said when I suggested we meet earlier.

"You're broke?" I asked. He nodded, a bit shame-facedly. From then on, it was I who bought the coffee. He was a God-send—someone with whom I could talk about the theater, ESP, religion, philosophy. We talked endlessly as we wandered about.

"So when will you let me see you levitate?" I asked. We had met four or five times by then and my curiosity had reached a peak. "I know you can't do it in a public place, so why don't you come to my house? I promise you a good dinner. My husband will enjoy meeting you."

"Yes, but I won't enjoy meeting him! I want you, can't you see?" And with that, he flung away his half-filled coffee container and clasped me in his arms.

It took me by surprise. The subject of love and sex had not come up between us, and if the thought of a romantic entanglement had occurred to me, I had speedily dismissed it. He attracted me, that was undeniable; but he was eight years younger than I, an age difference that made anything other than friendship seem out of the question. Older woman—younger man was not an acceptable combination in the '50s; I was programmed by my generation to recoil from the thought. But as he murmured passionate words into my ear I realized that our meeting had been bound to lead to sex from the beginning, and my blood quickened under his touch.

Sex had long become a reluctantly performed duty in my marriage, one I avoided as much as I could. The constant friction between us robbed it of all attraction for me, whereas it seemed to arouse Michel, who often roughly demanded his marital rights. When our house was built, I had insisted on separate bedrooms. In my heart, I was not married to Michel, and the fact of my infidelity with Gregg caused me no qualms of conscience. I entered into the affair with gusto.

Gregg was a delightful lover. With exquisite precision he knew how to make my body sing. He did not levitate—there seemed no time for it when we were together. For months I swam in a fog of desire whose flame was fed by his phone calls between our meetings. His beautiful, sonorous voice poured endearments into the receiver which I feverishly pressed to my ear. Tingling with desire, I could hardly wait for the next tryst.

I played with the idea of running away with him. "Run where?" he asked when I mentioned it. "I have no money. Do you?"

I did not. I did not think of the money I had access to as mine, and while I felt no guilt about sleeping with another man, using Michel's money to support my passion would have seemed the height of treachery.

We had been seeing each other for several months when Gregg seemed preoccupied one afternoon.

"What's happening?" I asked.

"There's something I want to talk to you about. I hope you won't be shocked. You're one of the most sophisticated women I ever knew, but, forgive me, there are certain areas where you are quite naive. No, not naive. Innocent is a better word."

"What are you driving at?" I asked apprehensively.

"I'm talking about sex. No, don't turn away. You're as delicious a woman as I have ever known and I can't tell you how much it means to me to be your lover. But sex can be even more exciting with more than one partner. There's…"

I felt the blood leave my face. "You mean…is there another woman?"

"No; not another woman. I'm talking about group sex. I sometimes go to group sex parties. It's a lot of fun. We all get to know each other in the Biblical sense. Know what I mean?"

"Are you talking about orgies?" I asked, dazed.

"If that's what you want to call it. Some of the people in the group are high society, some are famous theater people. It's all very high-class, very discreet. There's one coming up on Friday. I'd like you to come."

I was revolted. I had come to terms with the taboos my affair with Gregg violated, but this was too much. When I looked at him again, he seemed to have changed, and I wondered why I had never before seen the coarseness that disfigured his beautiful face. When he tried to take me in his arms, I pulled away.

"No, thank you," I said coldly. "That's not my cup of tea."

"Are you sure? You're a hot, sexy woman. Why deprive yourself and others of pleasures that can be shared?"

I never saw Gregg after that. It was immeasurably painful to be cut off from the source of a passion that was both physical and mental. He satisfied something in me that had gone hungry for what seemed all my life. Dozens of times I picked up the phone to call him, but each time my recoil won out.

It was no good trying to change my mind. The taboos I'd grown up with were too strong.

Twenty-two

In my youth, I was told that I must love my parents, my brother and my sisters. I was about fourteen when I announced to my assembled family at the dinner table:

"I don't have to love you."

There was a shocked silence. My family was used to the unorthodox views of their youngest, but this went even beyond my usual heresies. Seeing their stricken faces, I realized that they didn't understand.

"I love you," I quickly added. "It's just that I don't have to love you. I mean, I'd love you even if you were strangers!"

What I was trying to say was that I had discovered that love cannot be given on command. I really did feel love for my family, but I had already seen that the circle of love that is supposed to enfold a family is often a circle of habit and sometimes an arena for fights. Even in mine, so close and loving, there were currents and undercurrents and times when I wished more than anything to be free of the bonds forged by love.

As a young girl, I thought that being in love with the man I married would guarantee a life of eternal joy. I soon learned that there weren't too many couples who lived out the fairy tale. Wedded bliss, I found out, isn't all it's cracked up to be; the happiness it's supposed to bring is, except in rare cases, simply a myth.

My marriage had already begun to unravel by the time the children were born. We thought they would bring a renewed sense of purpose and partnership to our union, but our disagreements over their upbringing put perhaps more of a strain on our relationship than all the other factors combined.

The one bond of love that seems inalienable is that of a mother to her child. Motherhood is one of the greatest blessings in life, I had always been told. And in many ways, it is. That it is also one of the heaviest burdens is kept secret from one generation to the next. The charming smiles, the adorable gurglings of your infant son or daughter are paid for with sleepless nights, and later with the inevitable clashes between you and your growing child. "Little children, little worries. Big children, big worries," isn't that how the saying goes? Yet so strong is the imperative of nature that women uncomplainingly carry out this task and hand down the myth of the joys of motherhood to their unsuspecting daughters. Today I know that the unconditional love a mother is supposed to bear her child is as much of a fable as that child's unconditional love for her. There is as much ambivalence in the mother-child relationship as with the rest of the family members. The nuclear family, so vital to the well-being of the growing child, is also the breeding ground for the psychological damage that characterizes so much of today's civilized society.

By the time I was in my thirties I had already seen through these myths. "Peeling the onion" of my conditioning revealed much that I had unthinkingly accepted as "the way things are." How far I had yet to go before I could look at reality with eyes unclouded by convention was brought home to me one afternoon as I strolled with my now teen-aged children through Washington Square Park.

We had come to the city to meet Michel for dinner. We left home early to walk around Greenwich Village for a while. The Flower Children were not yet visible in the suburbs. I had encountered the scruffy-looking youngsters with the big smiles and the flowers in their hands at bus terminals and on the streets of the city, and I wanted my kids to get a good look at them. It was not only their unkempt appearance that repelled me. The most unsavory aspect of the Flower Children was that they smoked pot and took LSD, that dreaded new drug that turned sane people into raving maniacs. By the early '60s, the subject of drugs brought fear to the parents of teen-age children. Like everybody I knew, I unquestioningly believed what the media said and missed no opportunity to warn my children against acid and pot. And now I wanted them to see for themselves what these drugs did to youngsters who fell under their evil spell. I parked on Washington Square.

Wide-eyed, Danny and Nicky scanned the unkempt, oddly dressed kids who walked around the park or sat in small groups on the grass.

"They look weird," Nicky said.

"She's pretty," Danny remarked. He was staring at a girl who leaned against a tree. She was part of a group that was laughing and talking loudly, but she seemed separate, in a world of her own. Her curly black hair had not been touched by a comb in months. Her long skirt was clumsily patched, leaving some holes open to display a dirty slip under frayed edges. Her blouse was purple and missed several buttons. I wondered what my fastidious son saw in that sloppy girl. He was a conservative dresser who favored beige chinos and button-down shirts. It seemed strange that he could find a girl so careless about her appearance appealing.

"She's a mess!" Nicky said disdainfully.

"What makes you say she's pretty?" I inquired of my son.

"Her face shines," he replied.

I looked again. This time, I did not see the dirty, patched clothes, but a radiant face with eyes that held a far-away look as if seeing something that was invisible to me. Yes, she was lovely. I knew what Danny meant.

And I also knew that my prejudice had kept me from seeing it. But this brief look behind the apparent did not change my view of the Flower Children. Anxious to demonstrate the ill effects of the drugs, I drew my kids' attention to a group that sat on the grass. The pungent odor of smoke that emanated from them was definitely not tobacco. "They're smoking pot!" I said indignantly. The youngsters were passing something from hand to hand. They wore a wild assortment of outlandish clothes that were a deliberate attempt to get away from the sanitized, wrinkle-free garments worn by their spotless elders, away from the ties and the fashions society blindly obeys. There was a challenge in their get-up: hey look, they seemed to say, we're free! But in their non-conformity they conformed to a new dress code, one that included love beads, wrinkled and often torn clothes, blue jeans, and long, and if possible, matted hair.

"Poor kids, they probably had unhappy childhoods. They must have, to go so far overboard!" The current dogma held that it is always the parents, and in particular the mother's fault if the child is maladjusted. I assumed that these wretched, unbathed kids who sat on the grass smoking a forbidden drug were the result of poor parenting.

"They're just rebelling," Danny said.

"Maybe. But taking drugs is one sure way to mess up their lives," I said with conviction.

That I myself would one day sit on the same grass with a similar group, passing a joint from hand to hand while staring at a spider web was quite inconceivable to me at that time.

In 1962, TIME Magazine reported an experiment made by Walter Pahnke, a graduate student at Harvard's Divinity School. On Good Friday, he assembled 20 divinity students in the basement of the Boston University Chapel. In a double-blind study, 10 of the students were given psilocybin (the synthetic form of the hallucinogenic mushroom psylocibe), and the rest placebos. Later, teams of scientists were asked to rate the written reports of the students. The results were clear. Nine of the ten who received psilocybin had mystical or religious experiences, while those who got the placebos, did not. When the reports of the students were placed side by side with the writings of mystics and visionaries of the past, there could be no doubt that they described genuine self-transcendent experiences.

Inevitably, this study evoked my interest. Once more I saw to what extent my mind would go to block me from looking at what was unfamiliar. I realized that there was more to these drugs than the sensation-thirsty media let us know. It was the first time that I heard of an experiment with exceptional states of consciousness. My studies of extra-sensory perception and Eastern philosophies, plus my own meager experiences during meditation, had convinced me that these states exist. But I had always believed that only rare individuals such as saints, prophets and geniuses are granted mystical visions. Still, there was Bucke's theory that cosmic consciousness is on the increase, and the theories of Teilhard de Chardin who claimed, based on his research in paleontology, that humanity is evolving towards the OMEGA POINT, a point where a quantum transformation will take place in human consciousness and we will emerge as a new breed.

We are growing, becoming more spiritual, these men said. Could the drugs help us, who are now located between the animals and the angels, to one day leave our larval state and become butterflies? With all my heart I wanted to believe in our potential to evolve, to emerge from our brutish past.

And with all my being, I longed to experience what the divinity students had experienced. Looking for more information on the drugs, I learned that they had been called "psychotomimetic" because they were supposed to mimic psychosis, but the word "psychedelic," that is, mind-manifesting, was the term now widely used. Aldous Huxley's Doors of Perception and Heaven and Hell as well as Alan Watts' The Joyous Cosmology spoke eloquently of the dimensions the psychedelics open up. Some day, I vowed, I would experience them. But the time was not yet. I was not yet ready.

Twenty-three

I have no idea when it was that my passion for the theater subsided. One thing is certain: it subsided. It did more: it disappeared. One day I was avidly reading and translating plays, and the next they were gone, never to be looked at again.

Little by little, I became entirely absorbed in my search. I learned that the human psyche is capable of extraordinary states that are accessible under certain conditions. I searched the psychology books for a model of these. In vain. The literature gave much information about mental illness. About mental health, almost none. Freud based his findings on his work with patients, and the whole profession followed his lead. I often wondered how mental health professionals think they can cure their patients when they don't know what mental health is.

Somewhere, I felt, there must be models of mental health. There must be models of that "moreness," that extra factor that allows some to see more, to be more conscious, more creative, more compassionate, more aware. And if there are such models, we should study them. We spend the majority of our time in the service of the body. Feeding it, dressing it, transporting it is a never-ending task. It is for its sake that we toil, and when we have satisfied its basic needs we toil some more to clothe it in rich clothes, house it in opulent homes, and transport it in luxurious vehicles. We are concerned with our image, that is, with unreality itself. Lives are consumed in the hopes and fears of what "they" will think. And while we enslave ourselves to often unloved work to provide our senses with fleeting pleasures, we remain ignorant of our true nature—our eternal Self.

It was that Self that I longed to discover. In order to get in touch with the ground of my being, I had to strip away the accretion of prejudices and preconceptions that cluttered up my psyche, making it impossible to see what was really there. I peeled my onion with passionate intensity. At Erich Fromm's bidding I looked at everything as if for the first time. Gurdjieff taught me to recognize that I'm a sleep-walking robot, that I must call HALT to my drowsy psyche and begin to examine myself with waking eyes. William James assured me that the self I think I am does not exist, and Patanjali demonstrated that my mind is a chattering monkey over which I have no control.

It was now ten years since I had read The Search for Bridey Murphy. The "more" that I had hoped for, existed. I had come to believe in it, and I was convinced that homo sapiens, as described by psychology, is an incomplete and lopsided view of the human race. It must not be thought that this period of self-searching went by without intense inner conflict. The whole edifice of my value system, my past beliefs, was being shaken and pulled apart. I vacillated between yes and no, between spiritual ideas and practical views. Often, I doubted the reality of the things I read. If psychology did not recognize cosmic consciousness and higher states of awareness, maybe these states did not exist?

And then a new voice was heard in the West. Dr. Abraham Maslow opened the way to a new look at mental health. He studied several persons whom he saw as self-actualizing and fully human. What he reported about their "peak experiences" rang uncannily like the reports of the mystics. Here at last was someone trying to establish a model of the healthy psyche, and included in it, almost like a stamp of authenticity, was the mystical experience!

Maslow presented his work as a hypothesis, not as scientifically proven fact. His criteria for self-actualization stressed emotional maturity, non-rigidity, inner-directedness, a high ethical and aesthetic sense, balance. Though strongly individual, his subjects lacked the ego defenses that surround most of us like barbed wire. They saw life in much broader terms than the narrowly personal ones that imprison so many of us, and they were generally more creative.

I was doing volunteer work at the Post-Graduate Center for Mental Health in Manhattan when I read Maslow's Towards a Psychology of Being. I spoke to Dr. Arlene Wohl, one of the Center's directors, about the need for research with fully functioning, mentally healthy individuals.

"Sounds interesting," she remarked. "Why don't you write a proposal?"

"Who? Me?" I asked, surprised.

She nodded. Doesn't she know that I have no academic background? I wondered. But if she thinks I can do it—maybe I can!

With the zeal of the innocent, I set to work on a task for which I was wholly unprepared. But Maslow's concepts were inspiring. I hoped they would clear the air of Freud's pessimistic views and make way for a fresh look that would teach us to tap the enormous reservoir of potentialities buried beneath the threshold of awareness.

After months of studying and weekly meetings with Dr. Mary Collins, the Center's director of research, I wrote two papers entitled Evolution in Search of a New Breed of Man and Alienation: A Shortcut to Dynamic Growth? I called the proposal A Study of Full Humanness and sent it plus the two papers to Dr. Maslow, who sent back praise and encouragement. Dr. Collins was also pleased, and at her suggestion Dr. Wohl invited me to present it to the Center's staff.

I prepared carefully for the staff meeting and approached it confidently. But it didn't take long to see that the assembled Ph.D.s meant to have their sport with this lay woman who championed that crazy Dr. Maslow.

I began to read the introduction to the study, but after my first words Dr. Wohl interrupted me.

"Put that away," she ordered me. "Kindly address us in your own words. We're not interested in what you wrote."

I felt myself blushing. Haltingly, I began to speak. "I've studied the literature and found almost nothing about positive mental health. I believe that..."

"How many years did you study?" a man asked. His expression showed his contempt for my lack of academic credentials.

"Please hear me out," I pleaded. "The ideas of Dr. Maslow address a serious shortcoming in our approach to mental health. If a surgeon didn't know what a healthy leg looked like, how could he set a broken one?"

Had I been less passionately involved in my thesis I would have been aware how sacrilegious my words must have sounded to these people. I was attacking the roots of their professional training! Naive as I was, I thought they would be delighted to discover that Maslow's work pointed in a direction that would make psychology more effective. Instead, they greeted my words with derision.

"Maslow has a superman complex," said one of the Ph.D.s.

"Who does he think he is? Nietsche?" said another.

The tittering that went around the room silenced me. Without another word I rose and left the room.

I was deeply hurt by the outcome of that staff meeting. I was too early, but not by much. Humanistic psychology, which Maslow founded, was soon to become an influential branch of that discipline. According to Freud, our best and highest aspirations are merely symptoms of neurosis. He defines genius as nothing more than sublimated sexual drives, and our subconscious as a sewer inhabited by monsters and vile incestuous desires. Our only hope to become—what? hopefully not creative geniuses!—to become productive, lies in making the unconscious conscious. To do this, we must reach back into our childhood and focus our attention on the wounds of the past. When this focus becomes a habit, the barbed-wire fences of the self-concentration camp are built.

I believe that these fences must be knocked down before we can see ourselves as we really are—as beings whose feet are planted on the ground, but whose heads and hearts can reach the stars.

My hope that Maslovian psychology would put an end to the interminable preoccupation with childhood wounds has not materialized. For many people, their personal drama remains a subject of endless fascination. I believe that our lives can be much richer and more rewarding if we turn our attention away from the past and look at what we can become instead of what we are prevented from being. There are vast untapped potentialities in the human psyche; what stops us from exploring them is the obsessive way we dwell on past injuries.

Rationalism, pragmatism and Freudianism foisted limiting ideas of human nature on us. Most of these still remain, but there has been enormous progress in the decades since my ill-fated presentation at the Post-Graduate Center for Mental Health. Today, there are many who strive to transcend the preoccupation with the small self to reach out for the greater Self—the Self that embraces all of humankind and connects us with the spirit.

The failures of the past can turn into triumphs of the future. To lead us away from the shallow view of human nature that is still prevalent today, we must direct our gaze to the greatness that slumbers within. And despite the chaos that abounds in the world, it is my unshakable belief that the new breed of humans which is now incubating will be more like Maslow's self-actualizers than Freud's domesticated primates, ruled by neurotic drives.

ONE FOOT IN THE FUTURE

Twenty-four

In the spring of 1965 I attended a weekend seminar on Tibetan Buddhism in Bucks County. The speaker was a Lama, the head of a Tibetan monastery in New Jersey. The venerable old man was flanked by two young Americans who, yellow-robed and shaven-headed, translated for him. One of them, a tall, thin fellow with a pale face, sat with his eyes closed most of the time. To my western eye, his motionless body conveyed an impression of dull-wittedness despite the fluency with which he translated the Tibetan words of his Lama.

From my readings, I was familiar with the concepts of which the Lama spoke. In particular, the idea of Shunyata, or The Void, had impressed itself deeply on my mind. Everything arises out of the void, everything is contained within the void. "Is it because it is full of all there is?" I asked. I conceived of it as similar to a cacophony of voices, all speaking simultaneously, so that it is impossible to make out what anybody says. If all is contained in the void, then it seems void because it is so full. "Fullness is emptiness, emptiness fullness," says a Buddhist text.

The eyes of the tall young man opened. The glance he shot me obliterated my earlier impression of doltishness. Keen intelligence shone from his eyes. When he finished translating my question, the Lama looked at me approvingly. He nodded and gave a lengthy discourse on Shunyata. Encouraged by his response, I ventured another question.

"What does Tibetanism say about evolution?" I asked. I wanted to know if the vision of Teilhard echoed the ancient teachings. Again I received that look from the young man. But the Lama avoided my question and launched on an unrelated subject. Later, during a break, I passed him in the garden of the seminar house. "Very clever lady," he said in English, smiling. Clever? I wondered what he meant. Cleverness was regarded with suspicion by the teachers of mysticism—a sign that the small mind or the ego is at work. His remark made me keep quiet for the rest of the seminar, but my elation did not diminish.

Here, for the first time, I was among people who shared my all-consuming interest in transcendent states and spiritual teachings. It was clear that the other seminar attendants had given much thought to these "impractical" matters. I was not alone! As I introduced myself to them I learned that most of them held positions in the academic field or were psychologists who had become interested in the "more" that was not dealt with in orthodox psychology. I was overjoyed to have found like-minded people at last and resisted the impulse to embrace them all only by an effort of will.

One person stood out from the rest. This was Virginia Glenn, whose impact on my life was to change it forever.

Hobbling over on swollen legs she flashed me a bright smile.

"Do you know Alan Watts?" she asked.

"I don't know him, but I read his books," I replied. "Do you?"

"Yes. He's tremendous," she announced. Nearly blind eyes peered merrily at me from behind thick glasses. A smear of bright red lipstick was incongruously planted in a flat, pallid face that somehow suggested Iowa as her place of birth. (It was.) Her short stubby nails were adorned with flaking red nail polish, and an outlandish straw hat sat rakishly on limp, sparse hair. A voluminous satchel crammed full of pamphlets, newspaper clippings and letters completed her outfit. Add to this a high-pitched voice loud enough to be heard in a large auditorium even when she whispered, and you have Virginia Glenn. The external Virginia, that is. The inner Virginia was an enigma.

She was in her middle thirties when I met her. By the standards of a society that believes health and wealth are the supreme goods, hers should have been a miserable life. Her formidable array of physical disabilities brought her a pittance from the government, enough to pay for the small crowded room she sublet from an old lady, though sometimes not enough for food. She had a severe case of diabetes that could be held in check only by a rigorous regime of diet and insulin. But Virginia often forgot, and then a call would go out to her friends that she was on the critical list again at St.Vincent's Hospital, but not to worry, she'd pull through. And around her bed would come crowding the men and women who were to make substantial contributions to the human potential movement.

When she came out of her coma, she immediately began to chatter about this lecturer or that, or about a book that had caught her fancy. The amazing thing was that she never read these books, nor, I believe, did she understand more than the gist of the lectures she attended. To her, they were uniformly "tremendous." The astonishing sophistication and discrimination in her choice of pioneering scientists, psychologists and philosophers was due to an intuitive gravitation to excellence rather than an intellectual grasp of the material. She didn't need that. For her, it was enough to know that they talked about "the things we're interested in," as she put it. Her vocabulary was quite limited and abounded with platitudes. She was the only person I knew who used "lo and behold" as an intrinsic part of her everyday speech.

I know very little about her life before we met, except that Somerset Maugham's The Razor's Edge served the same function for her as Bridey Murphy did for me. From that reading on, which occurred somewhere in her twenties, her interest was so single-mindedly focused on the numinous that she ignored the physical pain that should have made her a bed-ridden invalid instead of a powerful, dynamic catalyst in the emergent consciousness revolution.

Virginia's most outstanding gift was her ability to bring people together. Her connection with the shapers of the '60s movement began with Alan Watts. Her hero worship for the Zen philosopher earned her the nickname "The 200 Watt Lightbulb"; and Watts, in turn, held her in warm regard. After her death on July 4, 1970, he wrote:

> Somewhere between general mysticism and transpersonal psychology is a branch leading off to parapsychology, psychic research, astrology, spiritual healing, and magic. The only term anyone has been able to invent for this dimension of life is "These Things," as in asking, "Are you interested in these things?"

Virginia Glenn was very definitely interested in "These Things," and in her relatively short lifetime managed to bring together many of the great workers in these fields who had hitherto only read or heard of each other...

...What always interested me was her discrimination and good taste in a dimension thronged with charlatans...Above all, Virginia's genius was to bring together people who...would fertilize each others' insight and imagination. She must have been a catalyst of hundreds of friendships.

After...her death..., I made her an ihai or memorial tablet inscribed in Chinese characters with the posthumous name, Raku-ge Bosatsu... Bosatsu is Bodhisattva, a title she surely deserved. (Virginia Glenn— 1931-1970, in Bulletin of the Society for Comparative Philosophy, Nov.1970.)

At the end of the Bucks County weekend, Virginia invited me to attend a study group that met once a week at the apartment of Bill Erwin, a young psychologist. There were rarely more than a dozen people present. Virginia, who organized these meetings, invited speakers who addressed us on topics ranging from psychology to physics, medicine, religion, and philosophy. The group of regulars included Ida Rolf, the originator of Rolfing, a robust, energetic, formidable old lady fighting for the acceptance of her unorthodox approach; Stanley Krippner, Director of the Dream Laboratory at Maimonides Medical Center and one of the foremost authorities on ESP (extra-sensory phenomena), and Jean Houston, the Valkyrie-like young professor of philosophy, who with her husband Robert Masters wrote The Varieties of Psychedelic Experience, and later became High Priestess of higher consciousness. Most of the regulars were professionals—therapists, counsellors, doctors—who alternated with the speakers Virginia invited in presenting talks to the group.

Guest speakers included Joseph and Teresina Havens of the Society of Friends; T.X. Barber, who spoke on hypnosis; Eugene Nemeche, a psychiatrist who was an expert on C.J.Jung; movement therapist Melvene Dyer-Bennett; Barbara Marx Hubbard and Earl Hubbard (then her husband) on art and the sacred; James Klee on Eastern philosophy; Colin Wilson, author of The Outsider; George Peters, who ran an LSD Rescue Service in Chicago; the renowned endocrinologist William Wolf; and whenever he was on the East Coast, the philosopher Alan Watts.

Considering the industry that developed in the '70s around New Age seminars, perhaps the most outstanding feature of our Saturday afternoons was that no money was exchanged. We were all, speakers and participants alike, invited by Virginia, and the idea of remuneration never entered into it.

I lived for these meetings, and for the lectures I attended with Virginia. In the morning, she would call: "Did you know so-and-so is giving a talk tonight?"

"Who is he?" I would ask. The name she gave me would generally be unknown to me. "What does he talk about?"

"Wait. I'll tell you." Papers rustled as she dug into her satchel. As usual, she did not find what she was looking for.

"Well?" I would ask.

"Oh, you know. The things we're interested in." And with this scant information I would meet Virginia for dinner and then on to the lecture. I was rarely disappointed. Though I don't remember most of the speakers' names, what I learned from them became an intrinsic part of my mental vocabulary.

After the lecture, Virginia would hobble on her swollen legs to the stage and squeal in her penetrating voice: "That was tremendous!" Beaming, she patted the lecturer on the shoulder. "We just loved it, didn't we, Nina?" she said, turning to me. And then she would ask in her "Do you know Alan Watts" voice: "Do you know Nina?"

In these lectures, as well as in the Saturday afternoon talks at Bill Erwin's, there were frequent allusions to the psychedelics. I learned of their importance in the research of altered states, of their benefits, and of their dangers. Orthodox science decried their use, but some of the more adventurous scientists, artists and intellectuals eagerly explored the new mental frontiers.

My own desire to experience these states kept growing, and I toyed with the idea of one day taking LSD under the supervision of a competent psychologist. But I was not yet ready for it. There was still more onion to peel. I was determined to approach LSD as a key to the Divine; bringing any personal baggage to it seemed sacrilegious. I would wait until my slate was clean, or at least cleaner. The mystical experience was not a band-aid for my unfulfilled dreams. What I longed to catch a glimpse of was a dimension that includes, yet far exceeds, the human world. I hungered for the experience of the more without which life, to me, was not worth living. I believed the words of mystics and poets, but I wanted to experience them myself. The intellect can be the best man at the wedding, but he cannot consummate the marriage, I told myself. However, while still in the process of preparing for the experience, I was anxious to read and listen to the voices that spoke of Eastern philosophies and of breakthroughs in various disciplines. What they said brought science and mysticism closely together and gave me ever deeper insights into my all-absorbing interest.

The most pressing aspect of my life, however, was the question of my marriage, and it had to be resolved before I could continue my quest.

ONE FOOT IN THE FUTURE

Twenty-five

The decision to leave my partner of 27 years was not taken overnight. It had been two decades in the making. The strength to act on it came only after a long struggle. Even today, when divorce has become commonplace, it is still not a step lightly taken. I was 47 years old, had no job experience, no professional training, and no financial resources of my own. Separation spelled fear, divorce spelled panic, and the question "What will I do?" rose to haunt me each time I considered this step.

The emotional side of the question was even harder to deal with. As a wife, I felt delinquent. But it was no longer just the discord in my marriage that compelled me to seek a separation; my thirst for the freedom to pursue my path increased steadily, and the intensity of my desire for self-transcendence was matched by my husband's desire to divert me from my goal.

It's easy to think of a marriage that failed as invariably unhappy. In mine, the storm signals appeared early and continued to ravage us through the years. But the picture of unvarying unhappiness does not apply. There was ambivalence. There were good times and bad, and the hope that things would improve deserted me only in the darkest moments. In between, there were times when we came close, and others when it seemed that what separated us was a bottomless abyss.

Things had been tense between us for years, but it was only after both of the children were away in college that the emptiness between us began to yawn. I experienced the empty nest syndrome forcefully, and in ways I had not expected. I had crying spells. My life was over. I was useless. I was getting old. In short, I recapitulated all the cliché responses of motherhood bereft.

From Smith College, Nicky wrote:

"Mom, I hope you don't miss me as much as I suspected when I spoke to you on the phone. Please try and get something to keep you occupied. There should be many things in your life besides your children to sustain you. It's not hard to make one's life fruitful and productive. With your talents, there's no reason for your life to become stale, weary and unprofitable as soon as your children leave home…"

To help me over this rough time, Michel tried to reawaken my interest in the things I once enjoyed. "Let's meet for a drink at the Plaza and see a show. The new musical that just opened has great notices—I'll get tickets, you'll love it, you'll see!" I shook my head. "Come on, Nina, it's time you started to enjoy life again. I know you don't care for such things any more, but a drink, a good dinner and a new hat will do more for you than your philosophy. Let's have a good time! We only live once!"

Normally, this would have prompted me to launch on a discourse about reincarnation, but in my dejected frame of mind I was willing to try his way. For a short period, something like a second courtship ensued. We rented a studio apartment on the corner of 12th Street and 5th Avenue in the city so we could stay overnight; we met in bars, strolled through Central Park, the Village, along 5th Avenue; we went to shows, nightclubs, the ballet. I shopped for new clothes and had my hair done in a new way. Temporarily, Michel's practical mind triumphed over my spiritual longings, and for once, I meekly followed his lead.

But after a few weeks of "enjoying myself" I stopped trying to enjoy what I didn't enjoy and settled down to face facts.

Fact number one: the children are fine, they are where they should be. Ergo, what I'm going through is self-pity, an emotion I detest.

Fact number two: I can stay with Michel, keep the status quo. But "you'll be dead in two years if you do," said a voice within me. "Okay, okay," I replied. "That means I should leave and face the fear of poverty and a lonely old age. A fine choice!"

In the last year I had considered and rejected many ideas of how to make a living, but none seemed right. I knew that whatever I did would have to be more than just a way to pay the bills. It would have to be in some way of service to the new breed. I'd rather die than work just to keep myself going, I thought. There is only one purpose in my life, and that's to help with the birth of the new breed. But how? What can I do?

While I was going through this conflict, Eugene Lion, a director I knew, decided to include my translation of Audiberti's one act anti-war play Les Patients in an off-Broadway production. In view of the fact that my interest in the theater had waned, it was an anti-climax. But Gene was an old friend, and he knew about my problem. We often talked about what kind of work I could do that would be meaningful as well as give me enough income to get by. Eugene was a gifted and creative artist whose passion for artistically admirable but financially disastrous plays was equal to mine. It was this that had cemented a friendship that outlasted the death of my theatrical ambitions.

"Why don't you open a lecture bureau?" Gene said one day.

"A lecture bureau?" I was perplexed.

"Sure. It would be a natural for you. You'd be doing something useful and interesting, and you'd be earning enough to support yourself."

That Eugene was hardly a financial wizard didn't stop me from giving serious thought to his suggestion; the more I thought about it, the better I liked it. Using the New York apartment as my office, I named it The Third Force Lecture Bureau. It was to provide a podium for the voices that spoke of the new step in human evolution which I believed was taking place. With Virginia's help I made a list of people to contact that looked like a Who's Who of the intellectual New Age elite. My clients included Alan Watts; Ira Progoff; a group of psychedelic artists, poets, and film makers named USCO; Joseph Havens, a psychotherapist, and his wife Teresina, an authority on Eastern religions; Walter Weiskopf, professor of economics who lectured on human values; Paul Krasner, editor of the counter-culture magazine The Realist; Charles Tart, ESP and hypnosis researcher; Peter Stafford, who later wrote The Psychedelic Encyclopedia, and other researchers in "the things that interest us." Perhaps the most surprising name on my list of clients was Yoko Ono, who billed herself as an artist who staged "happenings." She was still married to the film maker Anthony Cox and had just given birth to their first child.

One morning, Virginia called. "Timothy Leary is giving a talk at the Hotel

Albert. Would you like to go?"

Despite my interest in psychedelics and the years of peeling the onion of my conditioning, I was still middle-class enough to recoil from the tinge of disreputability that adhered to the notorious Dr. Leary. But if Virginia was going…

"Sure," I said. "Meet you at 6:30?"

The dreariness of the hall in the down-at-the-heels hotel did not help to put me at ease, nor did the unkempt, noisy youthful audience. Leary himself, feet clad in bright red socks and white tennis shoes, sat on the edge of the stage , long legs dangling. His body was lean and youthful, and his animated face held a benign and dreamy look. I cannot now remember a thing he said, but I vividly recall the interruptions from backstage, whence rude noises, squeaks and laughter frequently burst forth. I expected Leary to rise momentarily and charge backstage, brandishing his microphone. But no—not a muscle tensed in his relaxed body, not a harsh word left his smiling lips. He simply waited until the ruckus subsided, and then continued to talk. This impressed me far more than anything he said. In the world I knew, nothing like that had ever happened.

By the end of the lecture, the impression I had drawn from the sensationalism of his public image changed. Virginia, of course, knew Leary. She insisted that we wait for him after the lecture so she could introduce me. For the few minutes that I faced him, he gave me his undivided attention while his eyes held my gaze. I came away from our first meeting with the distinct feeling that there was more to the infamous doctor than I had expected.

In the spring, I met Leary for the second time. Virginia had somehow wangled two invitations to the press conference he was giving at the Harvard Club. I don't know how it came about that I sat next to him, but as I watched him turn a hostile group of reporters first into curious, then friendly, and at last attentive students, my respect for this man who crackled with energy and good spirits grew.

At the end of the conference he turned to me and flashed me his brightest smile. "Thanks for the good vibes," he said. I was surprised. How did he know that my feelings about him changed while he spoke to the reporters? He never looked at me!

I don't remember if I had a mental picture of Leary before I met him, but if I did, it would probably have been of a sunken-eyed fanatic, a Svengali out to enslave the kids with dope, a mad scientist with glittering reptilian eyes and a hypnotic voice, a sexual aberrant who staged orgies. That's how the press presented him.

But that was not the Timothy Leary I got to know in the next year—a year that would shake most of what was still intact of my belief system and precipitate me into a new birth.

The year was 1966.

Did I have a premonition of the importance of that year in my life? The number six came to my lips whenever I wanted to emphasize something. "I asked you six times!" I would tell the children. "It took me six hours to get through at the market!"

"Six, six, everything is six!" Nicky teased.

"Yeah, Mom, it's always six," Danny piped in.

Always six. Why?

Twenty-six

At that press conference I also met Larry Bogart, Leary's public relations man. He wanted to hear more about The Third Force Lecture Bureau and called me a few days later to set up a meeting. His office was at 866 United Nations Plaza, and in the course of our conversation he mentioned that there was a small office for rent across the hall.

"Why don't you take it?" he said. "A lot of people go in and out of my office. I'm sure some of them would be of interest to you. You'd be able to recruit them as clients if you were here."

It seemed like a good idea, and so I rented the office. I was buoyed up by the people who agreed to be represented by me, as well as by those who didn't but sent letters of encouragement:

"Congratulations on your venture. I certainly hope it succeeds. May I suggest that you consult with Tony Sutich and John Levy of AAHP (American Association for Humanistic Psychology, later called Association for Humanistic Psychology) for more suggestions. Also Mike Murphy of Esalen Foundation, Big Sur. He runs an educational institution and knows every lecturer in the country who would be of interest to you. As for me, unfortunately, I give less and less lectures rather than more… I really do wish you well and would be glad to help in other ways." Signed Abraham H. Maslow.

"Thank you for sending me the information about The Third Force

Lecture Bureau—I agree with the purpose described in your statement. I do not intend to lecture next year, but you are welcome to use my name in your list of lecturers if you wish. With all best wishes for your venture, I am sincerely, Laura Archera Huxley."

The people Larry Bogart sent to me were interesting eccentrics. There was a Rosicrucian, one or two mediums, a man who was writing a book about the Tarot, a numerologist. Larry, who is an authority on soil conservation and air pollution, had never taken a psychedelic and had no intention of doing so, nor was he personally involved in the occult, but he deeply believed in the Bill of Rights and often took on unpopular causes. One of the people he sent me was the astrologer Dane Rudhyar, whose books have become classics today. The tall, white-haired man had the air of an Old Testament prophet. His eyes expressed great wisdom; I felt that I was in the presence of a superior mind. Unfortunately, I was unable to secure any speaking engagements for him or any of the other proteges of Larry, as their fields of expertise were regarded as nonsense by the establishment. I did not have much more success with the rest of my lecturers, as most of them were too controversial to be much in demand. It soon became apparent that I could not hope to support myself with the lecture bureau, but I persevered because I deeply believed in the need for the voices of these people to be heard.

One of the ways Bogart devised to raise money for Leary's defense was a raffle. Some of the donations were highly original. There were light machines, sculptures, paintings—creations of what was becoming known as "psychedelic art." I stood staring at a very large oil painting with strong colors, bold shapes, and a haunting quality of almost recognizable forms, when Timothy Leary walked in.

"If you were on LSD now, you'd see colors like you've never seen before," he said, putting his arm around my shoulders. "You'd see worlds—oceans, forests, skies...You'd see the dance of the cells and of the atoms..."

"I'd see all that in the painting?"

"Well, not necessarily in the painting," he admitted. "But you'd see!"

I was getting to know Leary better. Often, he would come to my office for a cup of the coffee I brewed in my electric pot. "I hate the city," he would tell me. "Someday, they'll tear up all that concrete and put the metal back underground. There'll be grass and flowers growing on Times Square in five years, take it from me!"

Although invariably friendly and genial, the famous smile was often absent from his face. It was clear that his visits to the city to see lawyers and confer with publishers plus his uncertainty about his future weighed heavily on him. I was anxious to talk to him about the visionary aspects of the LSD experience.

"Do you believe that humanity is taking a new step in evolution?" I asked.

"I do. And I believe that the psychedelics are playing a crucial part in it. It's no accident that LSD was discovered the same time as the atom bomb. If the leaders of all the nations took LSD, there would be no more wars, no more oppression, no more hunger!"

Though I could not help feeling that his faith in the power of LSD to change humanity for the better was misplaced, I thought that I understood what he was talking about. Like myself, he believed that the human race is presently evolving to a higher level of consciousness and a greater spiritual awareness. His research with LSD seemed to bear out the fact that our nervous systems are equipped to receive a vastly greater spectrum of reality than we realize; and once the veils of perception are cleansed, wars, racism, competitiveness and violence will be seen as old, outgrown, pre-human traits.

I gave him my paper, Evolution in Search of a New Breed of Man. "We've seen the same thing," he commented when he returned it. If what LSD research stated was true, the drug was capable of increasing human awareness to the point of cosmic consciousness.

I also met Richard Alpert (a.k.a. Ram Dass) and Ralph Metzner in Larry's office. I felt an immediate rapport with the outgoing, ebullient Alpert. Metzner, more somber and somewhat dour, revealed a profound knowledge of scholarly subjects related to religious and esoteric lore. All three of them impressed me as exceptionally intelligent and well-meaning individuals, and I was proud to add them to my list of speakers.

In the '60s, the names Leary, Alpert and Metzner were as well known as those of the Beatles. Although they are best remembered for their connection with LSD, they were actually in the vanguard of the consciousness revolution that originated in the '60s. Their primary interest was the expansion of human consciousness, opening it up to the dimensions that co-exist with ours but are normally hidden from us. Though all three are still now, at the beginning of the '90s, teaching different aspects of higher consciousness, their names are insolubly linked with the '60s, and the role they played in the lives of the baby-boom generation can never be forgotten.

In 1963, Drs. Timothy Leary and Richard Alpert were fired from the psychology faculty of Harvard. It was obvious that their LSD research was the cause, though it was not the official reason. The scandal-hungry media eagerly grabbed at the news and immediately, the names Leary and Alpert became famous—or infamous, depending on one's point of view. Leary's smiling face became a familiar sight. The two ex-professors were joined by Ralph Metzner, a Harvard graduate who had studied at Oxford after leaving his native Germany. Together, the three formed IFIF (The International Foundation for Internal Freedom), went to Zihuatanejo in Mexico with a band of fellow explorers, and then moved to the vast Hitchcock estate in Millbrook, New York, where they continued their research, held workshops for professionals interested in transcendent states, and wrote The Psychedelic Experience, a modern version of the Tibetan Book of the Dead.

What the trio stood for sent shockwaves through the American consciousness.

It is surprising that three such disparate personalities should have come together: Leary the archetypal Irish rebel, Alpert the Jewish intellectual, and the scholarly, reserved German Metzner. They were a strange but effective combination. Leary's showmanship, charisma, sparkling wit and daring imagination put him center stage. He was the one who spoke most fearlessly against the status quo and gave the most lyrical expression to the mystical experience.

No less charismatic than Leary, the boyish Alpert was in awe of his older colleague. "I thought I could do nothing better with my life than to serve him," he later said about his initial feeling for Leary. Prior to his association with Leary he felt he was fat, arrogant and bourgeois. The young psychologist saw his role in the trio as steward of the group's financial resources, but his sense of responsibility often clashed with Leary's devil-may-care attitude. He really didn't come into his own power until after his trip to India where he met Neem Karoli Baba, the guru to whom he owes all, as he says.

Ralph Metzner was the editor of The Psychedelic Review, a serious, scholarly magazine that reported on ongoing research with mind-altering drugs. He was the least known and the least knowable of the three. Leary described the young graduate student at the time of their meeting with the following words: "He had a reputation for being one of the smartest students in the department. He was an experimentalist, a precise, objective, and apparently very academic young man."

Leary the scientist, Alpert the intellectual and later the mystic, Metzner the scholar: what held these three together was their shared faith in the power of the transcendent experience to remove the blinders that keep us at odds with each other. A world where all humans have access to the mystical experience would be a world transformed, they believed. Everyone would then directly see what Jesus, Buddha, Moses and Mohammed preached. Instead of obeying The Law, they would become the law. The New Age, the Aquarian Age, would then begin. For this, they were willing to give up their promising careers, risk their safety, lose the approval of their academic peers, and earn the enmity of the dominant culture.

When the Harvard Psychedelic Research Project was organized in 1960, its members, some 35 highly respected professors, poets and philosophers, spent long hours debating who should take psychedelics. Aldous Huxley and Gerald Heard, two of the group's core members, argued that only select individuals should be given these drugs. Heard pointed to the ancient custom of pledging initiates to secrecy, and Huxley felt that while the drugs were powerful sacramental tools for the philosopher, they would be of no benefit to the ordinary person.

Leary, Alpert and Metzner, however, were more egalitarian, and they believed in the power of the drug. After their break with Harvard they decided to expand their experimental design "from selected laboratory samples to hundreds of field studies involving millions," as Leary put it in Politics of Ecstasy. By 1963 they were popularizing LSD in articles, lectures, books, and interviews.

The transformation of the three Harvard academicians took place at a time when the spiritual dimension was sneered at in academic circles. Religion was viewed as superstition by generations schooled in the rational tradition of the age of enlightenment. Life was seen as a series of meaningless coincidence; we were alone in an uncaring universe that obeyed mechanical laws. The doors of orthodox science were closed against the intrusion of the non-rational, and experimental psychology strove to emulate the physical sciences. A veil of ignorance covered the hidden, intuitive aspects of the psyche. What was valued was will, logic, objectivity.

By the late '50s, a few philosophically inclined scientists began to plead the case of the right hemisphere of the brain, that non-verbal, image-making powerhouse of creativity. But the dominant theoreticians ignored their words as well as Maslow's theories of self-actualization. The accepted paradigm was materialistic and mechanistic. What couldn't be demonstrated in the lab didn't exist. The success of this approach was evident in the technology that came out of it.

The baby-boomers, the generation born after Hiroshima, watched Mighty Mouse and Superman on television, but in school they were taught that the miraculous does not exist. Modern technology almost kept pace with the Sci-Fi comics they read. Their world was not the same as that of their parents, and a chasm opened up between the generations.

The time was ripe for the Harvard trio. Organized religion had little to offer western society. Faith in an invisible divinity was not enough. What LSD promised was the direct, unmediated experience of self-transcendence—the mystical enlightenment where we know what the philosophers and the prophets talk about.

The knowledge of psychedelic substances has been traced back to the Eleusian Mysteries and beyond. Whether in the form of plants, mushrooms, herbs, or chemicals, psychedelics were known to produce states of consciousness that made healing, religious ecstasy and prophecy possible. From evidence gathered in the last decades, they apparently cause temporary alterations in the brain chemistry (as does fasting, breathing methods, whirling, etc.—all time-honored means for consciousness alteration). What happens is the removal of what Aldous Huxley called "the reducing valve." In the past, only small numbers of initiates were familiar with techniques that open the inner eye.

The essence of the experience the Harvard trio was so eager to make available to all was the encounter with the divinity within. "Find the wisdom within yourself," Leary would say. "Unhook the ambitions and the symbolic drives that keep you addicted to the dominant tribal games."

While I continued to see Leary's enthusiastic advocacy of LSD as reckless, I could not help sharing his dream of a world free of violence, hate, wars, competitiveness. I did not believe that LSD had the power to transform a combative, violent, competitive race into gentle mystics and philosophers, and I felt that those who were not ready to perceive another reality might be harmed by premature exposure. But I had to agree that in its present form, our society is quite insane, and that we are headed for self-inflicted destruction unless something happens to change the world. LSD? Maybe. "Anyway, it's worth taking a chance," Timothy believed.

But Leary's charismatic sales pitch never failed to point out the dangers of LSD. "If you don't get along with your boss and your mother-in-law in your normal consciousness, don't think you can handle the cosmic energies you'll encounter on a trip," he warned. But not many listened.

In view of the ego-shattering effects of the drug, it is surprising that so many of the young, unprepared trippers came away unscathed. The Harvard trio turned the world on. Thousands, and then millions, entered dimensions of consciousness that permanently altered their concept of reality.

When I announced that Leary, Alpert and Metzner had joined my list of clients, I received several unfriendly letters. I was not surprised to get one from Maslow in which he said :

> "…the workers with psychedelic drugs have now fallen into a kind of left wing and right wing, the more far out and the more sober and scientifically responsible being with the latter. I very definitely identify with the latter group and think of the former ones as a positive danger not only to science and research, which they are, but also dangerous to many individual human beings. I would urge you not to load yourself up too much with proselytes and drug pushers. The group of researchers that I respect most and that I am associated with is on the West Coast…"

I was to encounter the same objection to the trio's activities frequently. They were shared by most of the members of Virginia's group as well as by Michel, who strongly opposed my association with them. As for me, I felt myself lifted up and carried off on a current that held the very essence of the future. I was suddenly at the source of the events that were shaking up the world in the '60s. And I loved it.

Twenty-seven

"Please pack an overnight bag and come to the office as soon as you can!" Larry's voice sounded urgent.

"But Larry, you know I wasn't planning to come in today," I answered, somewhat annoyed. It was 7 a.m.; the phone roused me from a deep sleep. "What's happening?"

"I can't explain. Believe me, it's important! Will you do it?"

I hesitated. I had planned to take care of some shopping in the morning, and later I had a dentist's appointment that I hated to cancel. But Larry must have a good reason. He had never asked me to do anything before.

"Sure, Larry," I said.

"And bring an overnight bag. You may have to go to Washington."

"To Washington! Why can't you tell me what's going on?"

"I'll tell you everything when you get here. Just try to come soon!"

I hastily packed an overnight bag and drove to the city, wondering what Larry had in mind.

"It's Timothy," he explained when I arrived at his office. "He's supposed to appear at a senate hearing in Washington tomorrow. The investigation is headed by Robert Kennedy, and I have word from an inside source that it's a trap for Tim. You know how reckless he is, he's sure to play into their hands. I've tried to talk him out of it, but that stubborn Irishman won't listen to reason."

"I see. But what can I do about it? Do you expect me to muzzle him?"

"Of course not. Listen, he'll be here soon. You can help convince him not to go. But if he insists, I want you to go with him and act as a buffer between him and the reporters. They'll be out for his blood. Your presence will help to gentle them down. You can make them see the real Timothy Leary, the man who wants to raise the level of consciousness, not turn kids into dope fiends."

"Sounds like a tough assignment, but I'll try," I promised.

"I prepared a press release to explain his absence, just in case. I want you to go over it with me. I have not given up, you know. I'd hate to think of Tim in prison!"

We spent the next hour polishing and amending the press release. What we came up with was much milder in tone than any statement Timothy himself would have made. "He'll never let us put this out in his name," I observed.

"I won't show it to him until the last minute," Larry replied. "I just hope we can stop him from going."

When we were through, I went to my office and brewed a pot of coffee. There was a knock on the door and Timothy stuck his head in.

"Can I leave him here?" he asked. Without waiting for my reply he pushed a peculiar figure into the room. A fair-skinned shaven head surmounted a tall, gangly body draped in an ocher sheet. Blue eyes peered at me from behind half-closed lids. Not knowing what to make of this apparition, I offered him a seat and busied myself with papers while I gathered my wits. A strange noise made me look up. My visitor's knees were shaking so hard that his bones rattled. He was obviously in a very agitated state. I looked at him more carefully. There was something familiar about him that I could not place, and then I had it: he was the American who had translated for the Tibetan Lama at the Bucks County seminar. But what was he doing with Leary?

Little by little, the following tale emerged: while studying at Harvard, the young man had known Leary and felt a strong connection to him. He himself had turned on long before he met Leary, and he knew the power of the psychedelic drugs. Seeking to understand the mysteries they opened up, he chose to enter an ancient Eastern religious tradition and eventually was ordained as a Tibetan monk. He no longer used psychedelics, but his interest in their effect continued, and he felt great concern for all the young people who were sent to prison because of the prevailing drug laws. He was living at a Tibetan monastery, but the day before, he had received a strong psychic message that Leary must be stopped from further public appearances, because they endangered Leary himself as well as the young people who listened to him.

"All that publicity, all that excitement about the drugs—it must die down," he said, his knees beating a precise tattoo to his impassioned words. "He must be stopped from going to Washington! I didn't know about Washington when I hitchhiked to Millbrook. Now I know why I had to come."

Hitchhiked? I thought. In that get-up? Apparently. And when he learned about the investigation, he got in the car with Timothy and was now asking me to help him stop Tim from going.

"Larry doesn't want him to go either. He's in there right now trying to argue him out of it. And if you and Larry can't convince him, I doubt that I can do anything."

"He trusts you. He thinks of you as a friend. Anyway, it's very important that you try."

"I'll try. If he goes, it will show that he wants publicity so much he'll do anything to get it. I don't have much respect for that, and I don't think I can really be friends with him if that's his game. But I don't believe it. He's after bigger game."

"I know. He's so sure that what he's doing is right—he just won't acknowledge the fact that he's putting himself and the hippies who listen to him in jeopardy."

"I agree. I'm not comfortable with his proselytizing. I don't think LSD is for everybody. Guess that makes me an elitist."

"And Timothy is an egalitarian. What's good for one is good for all, he believes. But he's wrong. And he must be stopped."

"Guess you're right. Would you like some coffee?"

"I don't drink coffee, thank you. But could I have some tea?"

I heated some water and put a tea bag in a cup. "We've met before, you know," I told him.

"Yes, I remember. You were the one who asked about evolution."

"What a memory! And do you also remember that I never got an answer?"

"I do. The teachings about evolution are part of Tibetan esoteric lore. It's not a subject to be brought up in a public seminar."

"Oh? Then maybe you can tell me about it now—we're alone. Do the Tibetans believe that the human race is presently evolving spiritually?"

"Yes and no. I can't answer that. You'd have to know a good deal more about the teaching."

I told the monk of my interest in Hinduism and Buddhism, and soon we were deep in talk. The time flew. I was overpowered by a deep longing for the unseen and the unknown, the dimension beyond opposites. The odd-looking young man in my office suddenly appeared beautiful. A warm affection for him welled up in my heart. I felt more at home with this exotic stranger, than with the people I saw every day. He told me about the practice the monks followed, and he spoke about the head Lama of the monastery with deep love, respect, devotion and awe.

"Do you live there all the time?" I asked. He nodded. "Isn't it hard to leave such a quiet retreat and come out into the noisy, dusty, hurly-burly world?"

"It is. But I had to do it. Tim will do great harm to himself and to others if he persists."

Just then Timothy entered the room. "Oh, you're still here?" he asked the monk.

"As you see. What have you decided?"

"I'm going. The plane leaves at 5:47. Are you coming with me?" he asked me. "Larry said…"

"No, she won't. If you go, Nina said she couldn't be your friend any more," the monk interrupted. Timothy shot me an angry look, then turned to the monk. A heated argument broke out between the two men. Finally, the monk rose.

"You're not getting rid of me! I'm coming back to Millbrook!" he told Tim. Then he turned to me. "Thanks for the tea. We will meet again," he said. The door closed behind him.

Timothy sat down. "Thank God he's gone! That scarecrow has harassed me since three o'clock this morning! Can you imagine! He appeared in the middle of the night in my bedroom and ranted at me from the foot of my bed till it was time to get up! And then, when I got in the car to leave—somebody from Millbrook was driving—he pushed me into the back seat and sat in front with the driver! I'm a peaceful man, but really, that freaky monk is going too far!"

I handed him a cup of coffee. He looked like he needed it. The warm drink seemed to calm him. "He said he saw knives and black shadows around me in a vision. I'm in great danger, he said. I must stop talking about LSD or I'll wind up in prison…"

"And so you will, if you keep going."

He shrugged. "I don't believe it. But it's a chance I have to take."

"Do you want to be a martyr?" I asked. I really did not understand him, but I marvelled at the depth of his commitment.

"What you learn from LSD can make you a better person—more alive, more awake, more intelligent, loving, creative, productive…" He leaned back, the famous smile spreading over his face. "Don't worry. It won't happen. I won't get more than a fine out of the Laredo bust. Half an ounce of grass—what can they really do?"

"They already did! A $30,000 fine and a maximum sentence of 30 years isn't exactly chicken feed!"

"It'll never stick. I have a good lawyer. He assures me we'll beat it. He'll make it a test case for the individual's right to control his own consciousness. For his religious right!"

"I hope you win, but I urge you not to go to Washington. More negative attention is the last thing you need now."

"First that monk, then Larry, now you. All right, tell you what I'll do. I'll talk to my lawyer. Whatever he says, I'll do. Fair?"

"Yes, fair, Tim." I agreed. He smiled, winked at me, and was gone. All afternoon, he and Larry remained closeted in the office across the hall. I stayed in my office, waiting for word.

At four, Timothy emerged. "You won," he said. "I'm not going. My lawyer agrees that it would be dangerous. But someday, maybe ten years from now, you'll be sorry about the part you played in this."

"I will? Why?"

"Because then you'll have taken LSD," was his cryptic reply. I looked puzzled. "Never mind. Listen, how would you like to drive to Millbrook with me tonight? You brought an overnight bag, didn't you? Did you drive in?"

I nodded, a bit dazed. I didn't know if I was ready for a visit to the weird mansion, but yes, I wanted to go. And so, not without trepidation, I drove to Millbrook with Timothy Leary—or rather, he drove. True to my status as a female I mutely handed him the key to my car.

The sun had almost gone down when we reached the throughway. I saw little of the landscape through which we sped. I was more interested in my companion. I talked to him of my strong objection to the indiscriminate spread of LSD. "You can't deny that it has a negative effect on some people," I argued. "It's not all just scare tactics by the government and the press!"

"Sure, acid has done some damage, but the percentage of psychotic breaks is so negligible that it hardly counts. Most of the ones that freak out were already on the verge when they took LSD. It would have happened sooner or later anyway. Some people should no doubt stay away from it, especially those who have rigid character structures and belief systems. LSD breaks down structures, and some people break under the blow. But in general, the level of intelligence goes up for LSD takers; they become more than they were."

While we were talking, I was painfully aware that Timothy was tailgating. He kept dangerously close to the cars ahead of us and put his foot down on the brake only at the last moment. Knowledge of the limitations of my brake kept me pushing my right foot to the floor and emitting squeals of terror. Timothy pretended not to notice, and I was relieved when we arrived unharmed at the entrance gate to the Hitchcock estate.

As we drove along a dirt road through a darkly wooded landscape, I fell silent. There was mystery in the air. It seemed a long way from the gate to the famous mansion.

The big house loomed strangely in the moonlit night when it finally came into view. We drove through an arched porte-cochere. After parking the car, Timothy ushered me into a large kitchen. Seven or eight people were seated on cushions around a low table. They greeted him warmly. Most of them were in their early or mid-twenties and very beautiful. They wore loose, colorful garments and strands of beads. There was a kind of radiance and lightness about them that made me feel dense and bulky by contrast. I felt ill at ease. Fortunately, they ignored me.

At first, the almost worshipful respect with which they surrounded Timothy seemed ridiculous to me. But as I watched his face relax, I was glad that this burdened man had a place to come where he was received with such unquestioning love. The Leary I knew in the city was involved in legal battles, smeared by the press, and despite his great charm, intelligence and breeding, still slightly disreputable in my eyes.

"How did it go in Washington?" asked a tall, bearded man.

"I didn't go. Nina and Larry Bogart talked me out of it. My lawyer thinks the hearing may have been a trap, as Larry's Washington contact claims. But I still think I should have gone."

"I'm glad you didn't. Remember Teddy Kennedy? He couldn't even hear what you had to say!"

"Yes, but Bobby is different. I could have made him see the light."

"Don't be so sure. It's all politics. They want your ass, and they'll try to get you one way or the other," said a blue-eyed boy with long blond hair.

"They've got me already. What more can they want? Anyway, I'm glad to be home. The city is awful. But that'll change when the baby-boomers assume power in a decade or two. Nobody'll get busted for smoking flowers any more."

"What's that about getting busted?" asked a man who had just entered. He was older than the rest, probably in his mid-thirties. There was an edge to his voice and appearance that set him apart from the others. Though he was not thin, his face had bony angles and his eyes held a searching expression that made him look as if he suspected everyone.

"Hail the conquering hero!" Timothy said. "Meet Art Kleps, Nina. He's just back from testifying at Senator Dodd's Sub-committee on Juvenile Delinquency. How'd it go?"

"I made mincemeat out of them. Gave them hell!" Kleps said, obviously satisfied with himself. He launched into a long replay of the hearing. There was something about him that made me uncomfortable; and besides, I was getting tired. Soon I excused myself and was shown to a room upstairs in the mansion's former servant quarters.

On the floor was a mattress covered with an Indian spread. Before the window stood a small shrine with a Buddha flanked by a vase that held tall branches of apple blossoms. On the wall were some garishly colored posters of Indian divinities. It was a lovely room, but utterly different from anything I had ever seen. My head was full of the stories I had read. Drugs. Orgies. Freak-outs.

I locked my door.

In the middle of the night, a spine-tingling howl pierced my sleep. Terrified, I remembered where I was. Oh God, what poor tormented soul was crying out like that? It must be somebody on LSD! Let me out of here! I want to go home!

At dawn, I went downstairs. In the kitchen, a young man I had not met the night before was filling a baby bottle. He gave me a friendly smile.

"Good morning! I was just making some coffee. Would you like some?" he asked.

I nodded, and he added some water to the kettle on the stove. "Coffee should be ready by the time I come back," he said. "I'll just take this upstairs to the baby. Make yourself at home."

Curiously, I looked around. The kitchen presented an interesting mixture of art and utility. The equipment was vintage; you had to know a special trick to coax the stove into action. There were two of everything: stoves, sinks, refrigerators, cold storage rooms. Through the center of the room ran a counter that was decorated with a fantastic variety of mosaic designs. I learned later that this had been a communal venture, each person doing their own thing.

Between the windows, a large clock showed a handless face. On the walls were some more of the brightly colored Indian posters, and all available surfaces were adorned with art work that alternated between childish splotches, surprisingly masterful designs, and bold, striking forms. Like the mosaics on the counter, they seemed to run into each other, metamorphose, and become one.

The water on the stove was boiling. I longed for the normalcy of a cup of coffee, and when the young man failed to return, I searched the shelves of the large pantry for the coffee but could not find it. It was my first time in a communal kitchen, but even after many exposures I still grope my way around helplessly when confronted with the strange logic that seems to prevail in such arrangements. Fortunately, the young man reappeared.

"Here, let me do it," he smiled, producing a coffee can from the refrigerator. He motioned me to the low table. My bones creaked protestingly as I lowered my body to the floor. Holding the steaming coffee mug in my hand, I felt myself relax. Despite its strangeness, the kitchen was reassuringly homey, and the young man with the baby bottle did not seem very threatening either.

He sat down with enviable ease and grace. "I'm Joel," he said. "Here's some honey, or do you prefer brown sugar?"

"Thanks. How long have you been at Millbrook?"

"A few months. The baby was eight months old when we came."

"Where did you live before?"

"In Berkeley. I was studying physics when I started to turn on. Naturally, I dropped out. I was dealing grass and acid; the police chased me all over San Francisco. It was fun for a while, but when the baby came, things got crazy. That's when we came here."

It was hard not to show my shock. A dealer! Dope fiends were bad enough, but a dealer! Hesitantly, I looked at Joel again. He was smiling at me, unaware of the effect his words produced. No, there was nothing of the hollow-eyed, sneaky, cruel look of the perverter of youth on the face of this handsome, friendly, intelligent Jewish boy. He could have been the son of one of my Long Island friends. It was impossible to be intimidated by him, and so I broached the subject that was uppermost in my mind.

"Did you happen to hear something last night? It sounded like the cry of someone in distress," I said.

Joel laughed. "Did it wake you up?" I nodded. "That was Fang," he smiled.

"Fang?" I repeated, unable to suppress a shudder at the name.

"Yeah. Want to meet him?" Joel asked. He was laughing.

Not particularly anxious, I indicated assent. Joel motioned me to follow him and led me into the next room, a spacious dining room with French windows that opened on to a terrace.

"Fang!" Joel called from the door..

A beautiful large dog with a brown, white-flecked coat appeared. Joel patted him. "That's Fang," he said. "Fang likes to howl at the moon, don't you, Fang?" The dog hung his head and licked Joel's hand. "Why don't you take a look around?" he suggested. "Fang will go with you."

It sounded like a good idea. Nobody seemed to be up yet. While Joel went upstairs I descended the steps from the terrace. Turning around, I looked at Das Alte Haus, as the original owner had named it. He was a German industrialist whose means must have been as inexhaustible as his imagination.

It is impossible for me to do justice to a description of the baronial estate. Amazing, bizarre, splendid—it was all of that. Its vast wooded acreage held a lake, a waterfall, two hills that were christened "lunacy hill" and "ecstasy hill" by the Millbrook community, and numerous baroque buildings. Besides the 64 room mansion where I had slept, there was a tennis house that had been turned into a meditation room by the Leary group, a bowling alley, a splendid house called "the bungalow" where the Hitchcocks stayed when they came for a visit, another roomy house that was later inhabited by the ashram headed by Bill Haines, a gate house that Art Kleps would make his home, and sundry other structures that either stood abandoned or served a variety of purposes for the community.

In the center of the lawn below Das Alte Haus was a huge fountain. All I had seen the night before when we drove up were the revolving lights that illuminated its spray. Now I noticed that large goldfish were swimming in it, their reddish scales glittering in the morning sun.

Fang and another dog of the same size followed me. They wanted to play, and I threw sticks for them. Gradually, people started coming out on the lawn. Spreading out straw mats, they sat on them and did Yoga exercises. One of them beckoned me to join them, but I did not feel ready for this. At 8 a.m., a bell boomed and the people rose and entered the house. I followed them. There were perhaps twice as many as the night before. We lined up for breakfast, which was dished out in the kitchen. I stood between a woman with a jolly face whose brown hair was braided into two long pigtails, and a youth with the sunburned look of an athlete. Everybody seemed to take my presence for granted and I began to feel at ease among these strangers. They did not talk much, but there was a lot of eye contact and a lot of smiles.

I carried my dish of oatmeal to the dining room. Its furnishings were as catholic as the kitchen's. Mattresses and low tables were lined up along the walls, but there was also a large table surrounded by chairs. Gratefully, my 47-year-old body sank into one of these.

As I looked around, I noticed that none of the women wore any make-up. Despite the simple dresses they wore, they managed to look regal, perhaps because of the way they carried themselves and the frank, unembarrassed looks they gave me. Nobody questioned me about myself, and I saw that I didn't have to question anybody either. Social games were suspended here. Nobody tried to impress, and nobody expected me to impress them. What a relief!

I left shortly after breakfast. The lesson I took away with me was that I still had a long way to go in unlearning the cliché thinking of which I already thought myself relatively free. That Leary himself, after countless acid trips, appeared saner, healthier and happier than most people I knew had not been enough to offset the brainwashing effects of the media propaganda. Though my middle-class certainties had long given way to the desire to view the world as if for the first time, I now saw that even after years of self-examination, my societal conditioning was still firmly in place. I had come here expecting to find a band of lunatics, crazed by the ingestion of forbidden drugs. Instead, the impression I came away with was that of a kind of Shangri-La, and of people who came closer to living the spiritual life than any I had known before.

"Got to keep peeling the onion," I thought as I drove back to Long Island.

Gusti (now Nina) and Michel, Los Angeles, 1941

Nina, Los Angeles, 1941

Dolly, her children Susie and Kurt, Nina, Gretl, Michel, Long Beach, N.Y., 1944

Nina and Michel, Palm Beach, 1950

Nina and (Fa) Nita, Palm Beach, 1952

Nina, Lawrence, 1951

Nina, Highmount, N.Y., 1953

Palm Beach, 1952

The house in Lawrence under construction, 1948

Nina and Michel, Atlantic Beach, 1954

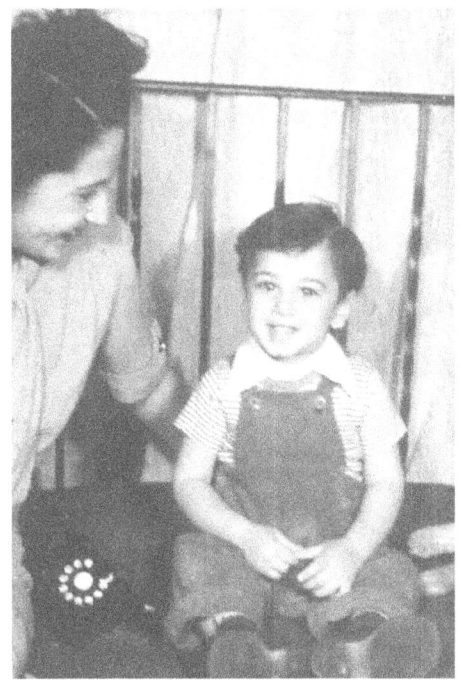
Danny, 1946

Nicole, 1947

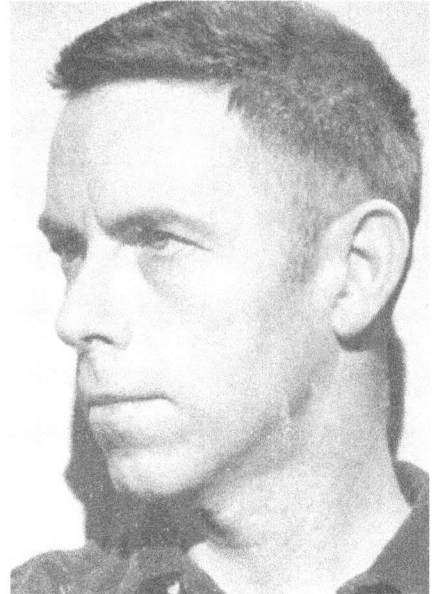
Alan Watts, 1954

Richard Alpert (Ram Dass), 1965

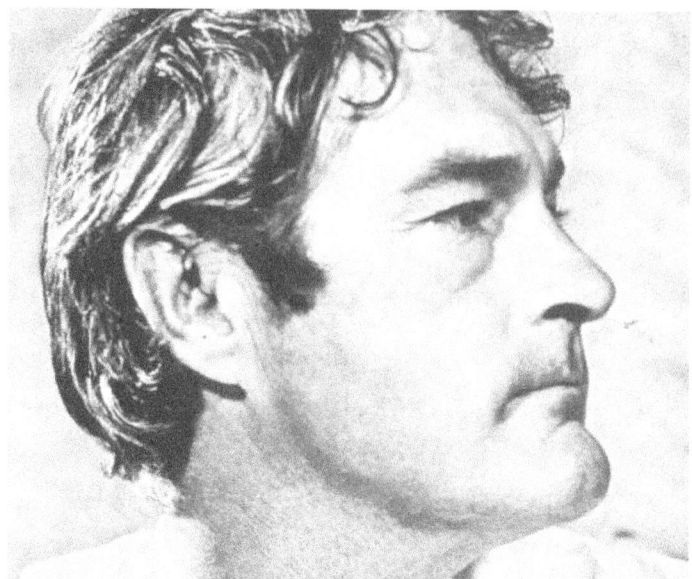

Timothy Leary, 1965

Left to right: Leary, Frosh, Rolf Von Eckartsberg, M.J. Herher, Gerd Stern, Paul Lee, Houston Smith, Sidney Cohen, Abram Cohen, Abram Hoffer, Sterling Bunnell, R. Alpert.

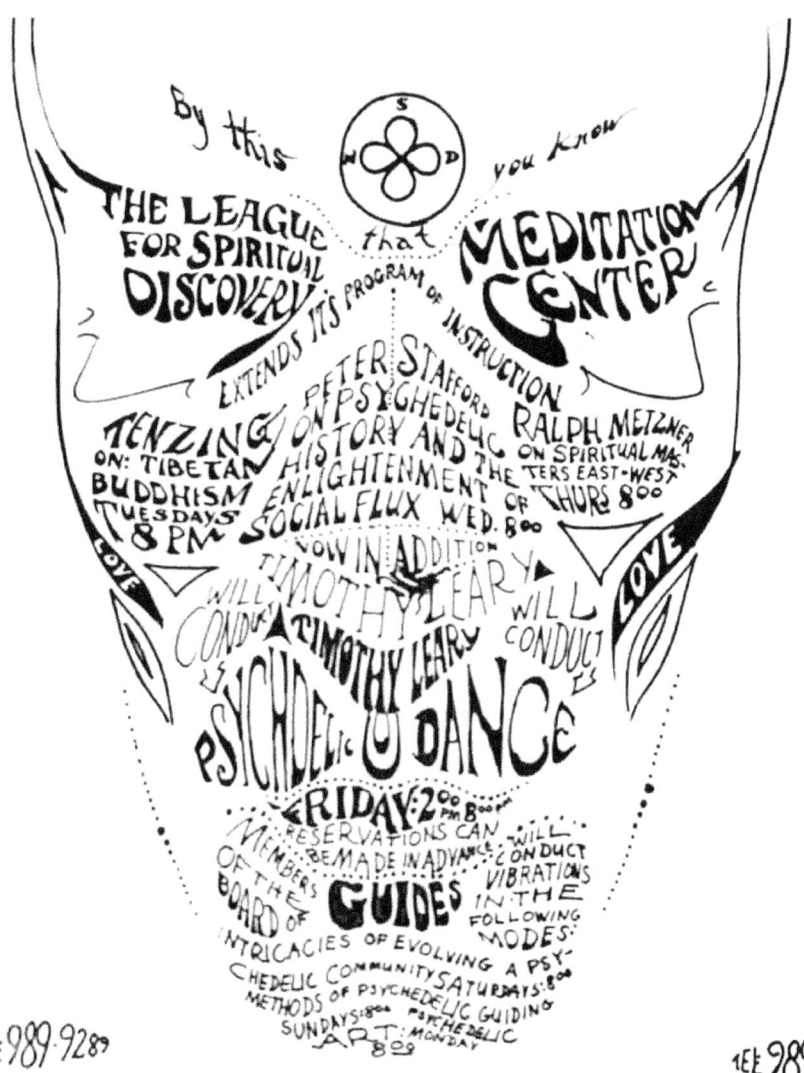

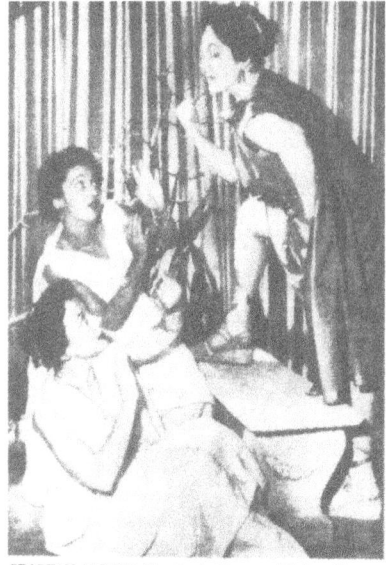

SPARTAN ADVICE: Mrs. Louis Strauss of Valley Stream, right, gives with Spartan advice as Mrs. David Lutkoff of Hewlett, left, and Mrs. Michael Graboy of Lawrence cower in fear. It's all part of the show rehearsal by the Five Towns Music and Art Foundation Theatre Workshop.

Nina

Lillian Saxe, Mildred Strauss, Bunny Ehrenberg, Sue Lutkoff and Nina in Lysistrata, 1954

Rehearsing "Glory In the Daytime" for the Five Towns Music and Art Foundation's dramatic workshop performance on March 15 L. to R. Lillian Saxe, Nina Graboi and Bunny Ehrenberg.

ONE FOOT IN THE FUTURE

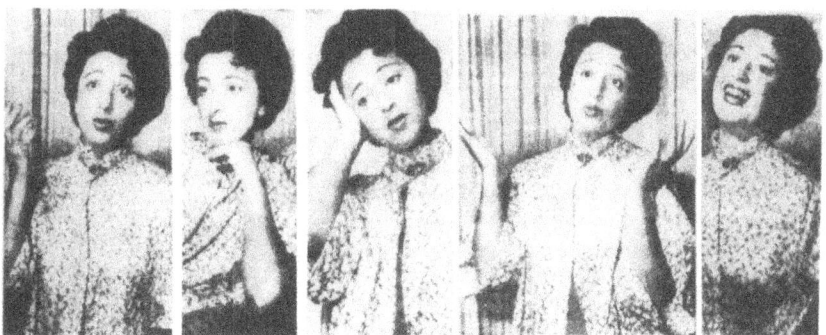

LONG ISLAND DAILY ***, WEDNESDAY, JUNE 29, 1955

"I had never been in a kitchen ... once the French thought I was a German spy ... but somehow I just know we would get out ... my crazy optimism!"

Actress Tells Own Real Life Drama

By NINA LAKRETZ

Glamorous Nina Graboi, actress and co-producer of Atlantic Beach's new Capri Theatre, has lived a life as fantastic and adventurous as any of the plays she will bring to the stage this summer.

While still in her teens, she dodged the Nazis through four countries, was jailed — by error — as a German spy, and suffered through an internment in a concentration camp.

Once, because she had no ration card, she lived on a diet of peanuts.

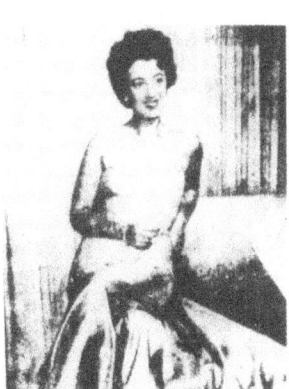

Mrs. Graboi, theatrical business manager, at work.

Today, 31 years later, she and her husband, a successful toy inventor and manufacturer — live in comfort and quiet in an ultra-modern home in exclusive Lawrence.

Quiet, that was before Mrs. Graboi and two theatrical professionals embarked on the summer theatre project.

Nina Graboi, together with Helen Waren and her brother, Stanley, an NYU drama teacher, head the production staff. Mrs. Graboi handles the business and social end of the infant venture.

Since February the Graboi house at 285 Ocean Ave. has been turned into a small-sized madhouse. The only quiet spot is the garden where Nina Graboi lounged the other day and talked about her adventure enroute to the U. S.

. . .

"WHEN I WAS 16, my parents decided to leave Vienna and go to England," said she. "The Nazis were coming and they were Jewish. . . .

"For the next three years, we lived in six or seven countries on a tourist's visa.

"I had never been in a kitchen before, except to get a glass of water," she laughed. "My parents were well-to-do."

Her family and Nina were able to stomach Nazism by the odd bits of food. A striking brunette with flashing eyes and high spirits, she also had many admirers.

Nina Graboi, Lawrence matron, as a hostess at home.

ONE OF THEM was a young salesman, debonair Michel Graboi whom she met in 1940 and married soon after.

They lived in comparatively peaceful Belgium until Hitler's army caught up with them.

"Then," said Mrs. Graboi, "we had to run. The Germans were exterminating Jews. . . .

"Once, in our flight, the police jailed me as a German spy. I was still an Austrian citizen. Lucky for me they decided they were wrong ... and let me go. . . .

DISGUISED as French peasants, the Graboi sneaked into France. Luck was with the young couple. They schemed to obtain U. S. visas and boarded "what looked like heaven to us ... a rat-infested cargo ship headed for America."

"But before we were halfway there, the ship was halted and its passengers taken to a concentration camp in Casablanca.

"But somehow," said Mrs. Graboi, brightening, "I just knew we'd get out of it. It's my crazy optimism — but I felt we were living through a horrible dream and that someday I'd wake up and be safe and comfortable again."

A few weeks later, the Grabois were released and permitted to continue to the U. S.

THEY WERE penniless when they docked in 1942. But a few years later, Michel Graboi began a toy business that clicked immediately. In 1951 they built the glass, wood and stone home that Ina-ug-trions have been admiring ever since.

They now have two children, Nicky, 10, and Daniel, 6.

With business success came leisure for Nina. Prodded by a combination of boredom and the reawakening of a childhood ambition, she took courses in speech and drama and did a few TV jobs.

Last year she launched the Shore Shore Theatre Arts, which she describes as a non-commercial Theatre.

"We hold readings among ourselves and learn through each other's criticism. Also we gave five public performances a year."

193

The mansion at Millbrook, N.Y.

ONE FOOT IN THE FUTURE

York Times. THURSDAY, JANUARY 19, 1967.

Followers of Dr. Leary Build 'Village' Shrine

Not a trip on a flying carpet, but a meditation. Inside a former store at the corner of Perry and Hudson Streets, volunteers take time from renovation work for a bit of spiritual harmony. Store is to be a psychedelic shrine.

Work Put Aside for Meditation When Sundown Nears

By JOHN P. CALLAHAN

They were six volunteers scraping, brushing, hammering and sawing yesterday to transform a dilapidated corner store in Greenwich Village into a psychedelic shrine—the first meditation center to be established by Dr. Timothy Leary and his followers in this city.

"We are a mixed sort of group," one of them observed.

One was a pregnant woman from New Jersey accompanied by her husband. Another was a senior from Brandeis University. Near her sat a philosophy major from the University of Washington, a former monk who kept very much to himself and a 29-year-old man with his degree in psychology.

Time for Meditation

Curved portion of fascia board over store's door says "League for Spiritual Discovery"

195

Don't be (a litterbug!) — Bottom of drawing by Eddie Schwartz is missing.

Part Three

ONE FOOT IN THE FUTURE

Twenty-eight

In the months following the Millbrook visit I had the opportunity to get a closer look at the outrageously dressed hippies who came to lick stamps, make phone calls, type letters and perform other office tasks for the Timothy Leary Defense Fund. I could detect no anti-social behavior in them, but they seemed exceptionally free. Along with the rest of the law-abiding citizenry, I had previously seen them as a menace to society. Now I went to Washington Square Park to sit with them around the fountain or on the grass. I listened to their music and to their talk and discovered that they came much closer to my own way of thinking than my circle of suburban friends. The states of consciousness I had read about were familiar to them. They talked about the brotherhood of humanity, about peace, an end to competitiveness and to "hype." The personal concerns that are blown up out of proportion and occupy most people's energies were absent from their conversations, which centered around universal themes. I thrilled to the new spirit that spoke through them. The New Breed? I wondered. But mixed in with the wisdom and the brotherly love there was also much that was childish nonsense, and so I could not be sure.

    I began to go to Millbrook regularly on the weekends. From the moment my car entered through the massive iron gates at the gate house, I experienced a change of normal reality. Everything was suddenly magnified, extraordinary, marvelous. The chirping of the crickets was not just their ordinary night song, but a choir of voices raised to praise God. The ancient trees that lined the winding road that led through fields and past a lake to the mansion were murmuring spirits who whispered dreams into the soft night air.

The sprawling mansion was lit up by spotlights that made the huge cosmic face painted on its facade look like a living creature. Golden Buddhas sat on window sills, and a giant bell hung on one side of the massive stone terrace which surrounded the house. Alexandra Zarro, who lived there for a period of eight months in 1967, described the scene inside with the following words:

> I just couldn't believe that what I saw before my eyes was actually happening, here, on planet earth. Dayglow witches, diaphanous goddesses, minstrels and princes, excited kids, zonked-out cats and dogs all flowed through the hallways. The whole house vibrated, shook and laughed to the music of the Grateful Dead which poured out of speakers from every single room. I was on a magic carpet being borne to a land of colour and dreams that I had only experienced in early childhood when my mother read me the Arabian Nights, or when I looked at the pictures in the Olive Fairy book. The variety of costumes set my imagination on a tailspin. The girls in the bathrooms weren't just putting on a little mascara but were painting their faces with day-glow and water color and stage paint, placing flowers in their hair and adorning their ankles and wrists and waists with bells and beads…The children were in on it completely, dressing up and asking the women to help them rouge their lips…and the men in their velvet jackets and satin and paisley pants, boots, and necklaces. Never had I seen such beautiful, glowing, alive people; and I had just come from the big city with my little weekend dress and gold pin…from the land of gray and black and spike heels and little purses and uptight executives… the land of the dying. Here there was life, pulsing, breathtaking, vibrating life. Stoned out of my head on nothing but what my eyes beheld, I lay back in the tub while children poured drops of scent into the water and the candles flickered and gleamed and the music went on…

The more I saw of the group's activities the more I became aware that new life styles, new physical, mental and spiritual ways of being were explored and practiced by the community. Some of the most innovative and fascinating experiments in individual and group consciousness were taking place. They experimented with modes of interaction that would later become known as New Age therapies, with Eastern methods of meditation, and with diets that were at odds with the meat and potato diet of America. To quote Alexandra again:

> What happened is almost impossible to describe because it happened in America. If the setting had been Indonesia it would not appear so bizarre, but outside Poughkeepsie, N.Y. a bunch of Americans were flipped out of their conditioned mind sets into the world of magic, myth and Mysticism. Millbrook was not just an experiment in social living such as Skinner's Walden Two or The Farm. It was ultimately a journey into Source…A grandiose setting is not enough to create a magical atmosphere. It was the mental set of the inhabitants that had stretched the borders of reality to include those realms that were previously restricted to night dreams and beyond. An ancient cast of characters had been liberated from bondage and a new movie was being written. The Americans who passed through the gate and entered the spell of the magic circle were now goddesses and priests, ascetics and erotic nymphs, holy men and clowns, witches and saints. There was nothing normal at all about the situation except that you could get coffee and peanut butter sandwiches in the kitchen. But sitting next to you might be an elf or a giant.

The Millbrook group cared deeply about ecology. They grew vegetables, milked two goats, separated the non-organic from the organic garbage which they saved for compost. Most of them were vegetarians and ate brown rice, but everybody "grossed out" on ice cream once in a while. Depending on who did the cooking, the food varied from abominable to delicious, and it was either feast or famine at the mansion. One weekend sumptuous meals were served, and the next there would be nothing but granola. At these times, the pantry shelves and the great refrigerators stood empty except for the sacks of cat and dog food, which were always in ample supply.

I found many of the books that had meant so much to me in the mansion's library. In addition, there were science fiction books like Stranger in a Strange Land and novels by Hermann Hesse. There were also books about the Tarot, astrology, and the I Ching. These subjects were new to me, and I was delighted to discover these ancient systems.

Some thirty people were living in the mansion at that time; their ages ranged from one to fifty. From the affectionate ease with which they treated each other it was apparent that they had shared some deep experiences. Thrown together because of their common aim to explore alternate realities, they seemed more like a family than a group of strangers. They wanted to bring the spiritual dimension into their daily lives, and in their LSD sessions they sought to attain a permanent spiritual transformation.

The individuals in the group could hardly have been more diverse. They varied in their backgrounds, their education, their socio-economic status, and their ages. Most of them were well educated and highly intelligent; some had degrees in science, psychology, or in the arts, and all had a great deal of knowledge about eastern and western religions. There were also some without much education but with a keen awareness of visionary states. But all, without exception, were preoccupied with the mind-manifesting substances they took once or twice a week. Except when they recounted some trip experience, their talk was rarely personal. Instead of detailed accounts of private dramas they talked about transpersonal topics such as the various world religions and drugless methods for entering the LSD state.

I was spellbound by these talks. Once more, like in Oued-Zem, I was listening to people who talked about the things that mattered most to me. To myself, I appeared abysmally naive and ignorant. I was still a psychedelic virgin, and these experienced trippers awed me. Here at last I was in a milieu that spoke to my heart and my mind.

It was rumored that orgies took place in the mansion. The place was no monastery, but neither was it as licentious as some claimed. I never saw a sign of group sex, but there was no lack of lusty love-making and temporary pairings.

Many have tried to describe the Millbrook estate, and there is some truth in all the reports, no matter how conflicting. It was a cross between a madhouse, a country club, a research institute, a monastery, and a Fellini movie set. You were guaranteed a magical mystery tour as soon as you entered the door under the porte cochere. In the hall, you were greeted by a sign that asked you to "kindly check your esteemed ego at the door." "A strange mutation of Thoreau's Walden," one reporter called it. It was paradise to some, hell to others, and it always changed, never presented the same face twice.

Unlike Ken Kesey's West Coast acid scene, the Millbrook group's focus was on self-transcendence, not on blowing society's mind. Instead of the public freak-outs of the day-glow Pranksters, they walked around wearing robes and discoursing like Ivy-League intellectuals. Outside their "trips," most of them seemed reasonable, cooperative, and intelligent.

The Millbrook estate belonged to the three young heirs of the Hitchcock-Mellon fortune, the twins Tommy and Billy and their sister Peggy. On their occasional visits, they stayed at the bungalow. Billy and Peggy often spent time with the community, and it was not unusual to find the attractive young heiress washing dishes or paring vegetables in the untidy, cluttered kitchen.

The heartbeat of the community was the Meditation House, an octagonal structure that had once served the German millionaire who built the estate as the tennis house. It held a fireplace and was ideal for the group meditations that brought the community together mornings and nights. There was a low bedstead covered with the ubiquitous Indian spread, and an altar with the statue of a serene, half-smiling Buddha.

Dawn had hardly risen one weekend when I was awakened by an eerie noise. Is it Fang? I wondered. No, this noise was of a different order. I ran to the window. In the early morning haze Malcolm, another weekend guest, strolled on the lawn. He was dressed in a Scottish kilt, and strung over his shoulder was the bagpipe that produced the offending sounds. I looked at my watch. Five a.m.! What an outrage! Somebody will stop him soon, I thought as I lay down again.

But nobody did. It did not occur to me to ask him myself. I was a guest; it was not up to me to interfere in the affairs of the community. When the bell called us to the Meditation House two hours later I rose without having gone back to sleep.

I walk across a broad stretch of lawn still dripping with dew. The fire in the Meditation House has already been lit, and the room is fragrant with incense. The beginning of a circle has formed on the floor. I take my place on one of the cushions. Nobody speaks. We sit silently, holding hands. The only sounds in the room are the sparks sent out by the burning logs, and the scratching paws of the lively tiger kitten that lives in the Meditation House. Today, she plays in the center of our circle, and this pleases us, for we know that the kitten enters the circle only when the energy is high.

We sit thus for perhaps fifteen minutes, feeling our combined energy travel through our joined hands. At last, somebody speaks. "I welcome Jenny into the circle," the voice says. "Jenny," we all repeat. "Please send healing to my mother Diane," says another, and again we repeat, "Send healing to Diane, John's mother." Other names are brought into the circle. The atmosphere is charged with energy. I'm beginning to feel that I must be on an acid trip—did somebody slip something into my juice at breakfast? No, it can't be, I quickly remember; I haven't had any breakfast yet! Is that what it's like to be high? I wonder. An image arises before me. I'm in an echo chamber that takes in the chaotic vibrations of the outside world and sends them back balanced, attuned, cleansed.

The breakfast bell summons us to a hot dish of oatmeal and a cup of Pero. There is also coffee for those who want it, and I'm one of them. I carry my dish to the terrace and join Michael Green, a prodigiously talented painter who is a strong, spiritual voice in the community.

"Why didn't anybody stop Malcolm? He woke me up at five! Didn't you hear him?"

"I heard him."

"Everybody must have. That bagpipe was loud enough to raise the dead. So why was he allowed to go on?"

"Well, playing the bagpipe is his thing."

"At five a.m.?"

"At five a.m." Michael smiles.

"I don't understand. What gives him the right?"

"Nobody tells anybody to stop doing anything. Everybody is free to do their thing. So he wakes us up once in a while. It's okay."

This does not surprise me too much. I have seen the community ignore outrageous behavior before. I detect a strong influence of Summerhill where juvenile delinquents were given complete freedom and allowed to act out. The Millbrook community functions along similar lines. Once a week they have meetings where their grievances can be aired, but for the most part, they seem very tolerant of each other's foibles.

"The community sort of selects itself," Michael explains when I ask how they handle the trouble-makers who are bound to appear thanks to the open door policy. "We turn nobody away. The ones who can't act harmoniously don't stay long. They come for a day, to party. When they find out that there is no party going on, they split."

But all was not harmony at the mansion, even among the permanent residents. An incident that has remained engraved in my memory happened one evening when a small group gathered in one of the large upstairs rooms. The talk centered around astrology when Ken Jones began to fling words full of sexual innuendo at some of the women. He was obviously drunk and eager to pick a fight. When the women did not respond to his taunts, he turned to Susie Blue, a young black girl who was hired to take care of some of the small children. Everybody liked Susie. She was always cheerful and ready to help with any chore. "Bet you fuck good," Ken threw at her. The girl's face changed. She looked away. "Bet you know how to suck a guy good." He leered.

"Leave her alone," Marshall said. But Ken was not to be stopped. "Want to know what Nigger pussy feels like? Ask Susie. She'll give it to you. Won't you, Sue?"

By now the girl was in a rage. She rose, approached him and put out her hand to slap him. But he was quicker. His fist shot out and struck one of her eyes. Blood spurted. With a scream, I fled from the room, afraid that that madman would come after me. I was deeply shaken by this act of violence and by the racism that informed it. Millbrook was the last place on earth where I expected to find this scourge.

But the next morning at breakfast, Susie appeared calm and unhurt. "How is your eye?" I asked her. "I thought he blinded you!"

"No way. He didn't hurt me," Susie reassured me.

"But there was blood coming out of your eye," I protested.

"Oh, that was a pimple I'd been scratching. It opened up," she smiled.

How strange, I thought. How differently we perceive the same incident! Is it true, as these people say, that we create our own reality? What is reality? What is illusion? I no longer knew. When I listened to their halting trip accounts, it seemed obvious that what I called reality was only a minute fragment of an immense whole. "I'm like an ant that thinks it knows reality," I mused.

In the last months some of my 'givens,' the taboos and assumptions by which I lived, had been badly shaken. I questioned myself about the validity not only of my beliefs, but of my perceptions. As I learned about the varieties of experience that a minute amount of LSD can produce, I realized that these had more to do with the taker than with the substance itself.

The only thing we can know is what we ourselves experience. Does that mean we create it? I wondered. It was not a thought I was comfortable with. Surely, I did not create Hitler! Or hunger, wars, or illness.

But reality had to reside somewhere. I was determined to find it.

ONE FOOT IN THE FUTURE

Twenty-nine

The Millbrook population was always in flux, but a core of permanent residents remained. There was Bhavani, an American woman in her mid-forties who followed a strict Hindu discipline; tall, broad-shouldered Marshall, a former probation officer with the rugged looks of a woodsman, his wife Patricia and their two small children; pretty blonde Carol and her son Eric, a fun-loving, mischievous boy of 10; Betsy Ross and her brother Bob, whose passion was organic gardening; Diane Di Prima, the poetess with the flaming red hair that shone like a beacon from among the trees with which she liked to commune; Jackie Cassen and Rudi Stern, two multi-media artists who created the light shows that later accompanied the psychedelic celebrations staged by the Leary group; Michael Green, the great painter; Art Kleps, the belligerent alcoholic blessed with a fine sense of humor; Jean McCreedy with her two pre-teen sons who successfully balanced the unorthodox Millbrook life with that of a straight public school; and Rosemary, Timothy's exquisitely beautiful girlfriend who moved with the grace of a dancer.

One weekend I notice that something has changed in the way people approach the Meditation House. As we cross the lawn I see that they all carry small gifts—feathers, flowers, small striated rocks, pieces of fruit.

"What's going on?" I ask Bhavani.

"Rosemary spent the last 24 hours alone in the meditation house and tripped during the night. We're welcoming her back. We'll all take turns doing this, so there'll always be someone who holds up the torch for the rest of us." Her lovely serene face is wreathed in smiles. Clearly, she approves of this new custom.

"Will Rosemary be all right by now?" I ask, trying to keep my voice from betraying my anxiety.

"All right?" Bhavani throws me a curious look. "Why shouldn't she be?"

"I mean, will she be 'down'?" I quickly add. My old conditioning has surfaced again.

"Don't worry," Bhavani reassures me. "She'll be quite rational."

We arrive at the meditation house and stop to remove our shoes. Most of the others are already seated, and as I take my place in the circle I note that we all face the bedstead on which Rosemary sits. The radiance of her face is almost unearthly. Smiling, she lets her eyes wander around the room, nodding to each one of us.

"Welcome back," Timothy says. "We can see that you had a safe journey and that you're bringing some new insights back. Will you share with us what you have learned?"

"I was lying here on the bed, but all of a sudden it felt as if I were walking through the woods. I saw all sorts of animals—an owl, a fox, a small spotted deer, a coyote—and they were trying to say something to me. No, not say—they didn't talk; but they tried to make me understand something that was very important to them. 'This is our home,' they seemed to say. 'Don't rob us of it, don't try to take the earth away from us. We belong here. Don't let your people harm us.' I promised that I would bring their message to my people, and they disappeared. I felt very peaceful, very happy; I knew that they trusted me to do what I could to protect them. And then I heard the OM. It filled the air, it came from all sides; not loud; softly, almost like a vibration made audible. It came from the trees, and the trees seemed as alive as the animals." Rosemary's sensitive face is suffused with emotion. "The plants and the animals have consciousness, just like us. They can't talk, but they have feelings, and they want to live. So what I want to communicate to you and to the world is that we must take care to preserve our precious fauna and flora."

She has finished. We all sit quietly for a while. Then those who brought gifts put them down on the bed, embrace Rosemary, and leave. The rest of us file out after them.

That evening, another ceremony is held for Michael, who will spend the next 24 hours in the Meditation House. Again, we sit in deep silence as we let our thoughts embrace him and wish him an enlightening trip.

The more I saw of the life at Millbrook, the better I understood that the people there were suspended between consensus reality and the multi-faceted realities that the LSD experience opened up. I could see why they tended to neglect dull, repetitive chores. Dust covered the intricate woodwork in the baronial rooms; children's toys, animal hair, bones the dogs brought in, and even dog shit littered the floors. I was used to a home environment that was pleasing to my sense of cleanliness and of esthetics, and the mess made me more than a little uncomfortable. But I came back, again and again. They were engaged in a ground-breaking experiment; concern with household chores seemed lifelesss and trivial by comparison.

When I arrived one weekend I found the community engaged in feverish activity. They were painting psychedelic designs on the walls of the many bedrooms in the servants' wing. Bathrooms were being scrubbed. Plants suddenly graced the downstairs rooms, and the dust disappeared from the woodwork. The community was preparing for the summer seminar that brought some 25 students to Millbrook.

I was strolling through the mansion looking for something I could do to help.

"What are you making?" I asked Jean, who was measuring the mattresses that were lined up along the walls of the dining room.

"I'm trying to make decent covers," she replied. "The Indian spreads are pretty, but when people sit on them they get all mussed."

"Here, let me," I said, grasping one end of the measuring tape. "I'm pretty good at this sort of thing. If you can use me, I'd like to help."

"Great!" she said, relieved. "Frankly, I don't really know how to do this."

Soon we were cutting and pinning the fabric and talking about the subject that preoccupied us both, namely, the mystical experience. "Did you read *Mysticism* by Evelyn Underhill?" Jean asked.

"Sure!" I said, enthusiastic. "A great book!"

"It is. Remember what she said about the dark night of the soul? Boy, was she right! I mean, you can enter Heaven and see how the universe works, and then you can fall straight down into hell, and you don't see any more, you're blind again, blind as a bat...almost as blind as before."

"But never again as blind?" I asked.

"No, never as blind," Jean replied pensively.

"I wouldn't mind being almost blind! If I could see, even once, I'd know forever after that IT exists!" I said wistfully. "Do you think I'll see too, one day?"

"Sure you will. You already see a lot!"

"I see with my mind. But you know, the intellect is like the best man at the wedding. He can take the groom to the altar, but he cannot consummate the marriage!"

"That's a nice metaphor!" Jean squeezed my hand warmly. "Well, maybe you'll have a nervous breakdown like I did!" She laughed. "No, you won't. You're too balanced. But don't worry. You're on the right track. Are you thinking about taking LSD?"

"Yes, but I'm not ready. I want to be sure...I'll take it when the time comes."

"That's good. I respect your decision to wait for the right time. Just make sure to let me know when, so I can send you good vibes."

I thanked her. I felt warm affection for Jean McCreedy. Something about her appearance set her off from the rest. A tall, attractive woman, she, too, wore a loose, long robe, but somehow you seemed to see her in a well-tailored skirt and shirt. Her pert Irish face was crowned by neatly cut short hair, an oddity in a place where almost all the women wore their hair long. Her looks still reflected the prim, successful Washington secretary she had been, but her life was radically changed. On one of my previous visits I had asked what brought her to Millbrook.

"I was lucky. I had a nervous breakdown."

"That's lucky?" I asked, dumbfounded.

Jean laughed. "It sure was for me! If I hadn't cracked up, I'd still be sitting in my suburban house struggling with my marriage and my job. It was the best thing that ever happened to me!"

"But how did you come to Millbrook?"

"Well, as it turned out, my nervous breakdown was a religious experience, only I didn't know it then. It was my good fortune to have a therapist who was a wonderful, understanding man. He helped me to recognize the breakdown as a massive decrystallization of my basic programs and beliefs. During therapy, I had a series of spontaneous spiritual experiences. Then later, I became aware of the experiments that were being done with LSD. The accounts people gave were a lot like the experiences I had had without it. I became determined to somehow connect with Leary and his group of researchers. I came to a seminar in 1965 and Timothy invited me to live here. I went back to my home in Arlington and loaded a truck with all my belongings. When I arrived, I watched my furniture and belongings distributed throughout the 64 room mansion. My first big lesson in non-attachment! Basically, I was so excited to be here, I just didn't care!" She laughed again without a trace of resentment. "The fact is, there's really nothing I need that I don't have. I work as Timothy's secretary in exchange for rent and food. Clothes and other stuff sort of show up here as if by magic. We lack for nothing."

"But don't you miss having your own things around you?" I asked, astonished by her nonchalance.

"I did, at first. But I'm so grateful to be out of the rat race—the mad rush for more money, more promotions, more status! To be allowed to explore my own consciousness…My God, what a blessing!" Her voice rang with conviction.

I felt accepted and at home with most of the Millbrook residents but was especially drawn to Jean. Perhaps it was her well-scrubbed neatness, or her ladylike behavior. Where some of the others seemed suspended in the air, Jean could always be counted on to take care of things. No one seemed saner or more capable. It was like her to replace the untidy spreads with fitted covers.

Jean basted the covers, I sewed them on the machine, and we talked.

"You talk about ego loss when you trip. What does that mean?"

"We also call it death of the ego. It's when you lose all sense of the identity, the personality you wear. When you're pure energy. When you dissolve. I don't know. I can't describe it."

"Well, I sort of understand. Hinduism calls the ego, or the self, an illusion. Is that what you mean?"

Jean nodded. "You know, I figured something out about the ego. It's really our way of expressing ourselves on the earth plane. If we could see it for what it is, we wouldn't have to try to shed it. It keeps our bodies running and keeps track of our vital statistics. The spirit doesn't have a name, or an address, or a year of birth. The ego itself is necessary, and how and what we express through it has great impact. It's when we identify with it, when we think that's all we are, that it becomes destructive.

"You're right," I agreed. "The trick is to remember! Does it get easier once you've taken LSD?"

"Not necessarily," Jean admitted ruefully. "It's a process. LSD, or psilocybin, or peyote can speed it up, but we still have to work at it. What the psychedelics do is to allow us to see what it's like when we leave the prison of the body and of the personality that we've built up over the years."

"Does everybody experience that?"

"Oh no. It all depends on readiness. Acid doesn't give you something that isn't already there. Some who are not prepared experience the loss of ego as a living hell. LSD is a hard master. I really don't think it's for everyone. It has to be treated with great respect. That's why what you're doing is so right. Set and setting, as Tim always says. It's the most important aspect of the trip—especially the first one!"

"Set and setting? Yes, I've heard him talk about it. What exactly does it mean?"

"Set is the attitude you bring to the experience, your preparation, and your expectations. It's also the mood you're in. And setting is the place and the people you take it with. But as Timothy says, if you're having a fight with your husband or your father or your mother-in-law, don't think you can tackle the energies you'll meet on a trip. It's best to be free of hang-ups and personal problems when you take LSD—as free as we can be, that is…" She grinned. "Wouldn't it be nice if we were all as advanced as we know we could be?"

"Wouldn't it! And wouldn't it be nice if the kids listened to Tim's warnings instead of turning on on street corners! A bad trip is almost guaranteed the way they do it! Of course, not everybody can have as ideal a setting as Millbrook. I hope I can do it here when the time comes."

"Of course you can! We wouldn't let you do it anywhere else!"

The slip covers were finished. They fit snugly, and our handiwork was admired and praised by the community.

I was gently told that for the next month all the rooms would be needed for the seminar participants, which meant that my visits were over for the time being. This suited me fine as I was preparing for an exciting visit to San Francisco.

Thirty

It began with a brochure Virginia extracted from her voluminous satchel. "There!" she said triumphantly as she held it out to me. "Doesn't that look tremendous?"

"It certainly does!" Excitement gripped me as I let my eyes run over the announcement of an LSD conference to be held on the Berkeley campus. The list of speakers included some familiar names, foremost among them those of Leary, Alpert and Metzner.

"Wish I could go," Virginia said wistfully.

I was electrified. The conviction had been growing in me that the leading edge, the evolutionary spearheads, were to be found among the kind of people Virginia had exposed me to. Whether they were scientists or psychologists, the lectures to which she took me shared a viewpoint that was at odds with the ruling mechanistic orthodoxy that had blocked research into human consciousness for so long. LSD and the psychedelics played a prominent role in the exploration of the frontiers of the mind. The Conference was sure to attract many of these researchers, and I longed to be there.

"Why don't we go?" I asked Virginia.

"Well…If I can find the money…"

"Maybe I can help you out," I offered.

"Oh, I couldn't do that," Virginia said firmly. "But we'll see. Things sometimes happen in unexpected ways…"

I was determined to go. My relationship with Michel was nearing a crisis. He would not hear of a divorce. I felt trapped. A painting I once saw haunted me. A woman in a long, diaphanous dress is rising up in the air, and a kneeling man hangs on to her skirt. "I'm that woman," I thought. "If he would only let go!" I had to get away from the arguments and discussions that now happened between us almost every day. The trip to Berkeley would give me a badly needed breather.

I hoped that Virginia could come too; I knew how much it would mean to her. Two weeks before the conference, she called. "You won't believe this!" Her voice thrilled. "I just got a check in the mail—enough to cover the round trip! Now all I need is a place to stay."

A few days later she called again. It took a while before I could make out what she was saying. She was almost hysterical. At last, I got it. It appeared that she had just spoken to Alan Watts, who invited both of us to stay on his houseboat in Sausalito. "Isn't he wonderful?" she gushed, excitement making it almost impossible for her to speak.

I had met the philosopher when he came to one of our Saturday meetings. Afterwards, a few of us went out to dinner with him, and I discovered that he was just as spellbinding a speaker in private as on the podium. His encyclopedic knowledge, his lightning-quick wit, and his profound familiarity with Eastern religions as well as with Christianity and Judaism were an inspiration. He was as earthy and sensual as he was spiritual; his interests covered not only esoteric subjects but embraced the flesh and our "inevitable rascality," as he was fond of saying.

One evening he and a few guests came to dinner at my New York apartment. The candle on the table was sputtering, and as I reached over to pick it up, some of the wax spilled on Alan's pants.

"I'm so sorry," I stammered as I looked at the rapidly drying mess.

"Don't worry," the great man said. "Have you got an iron? Good. Plug it in and bring me a bunch of paper towels."

"Sure," I said, admiring his composure. "Shall I get you a robe so you can take your pants off?"

"No, don't bother. Just heat up the iron," he replied. He wadded up the paper towels and stuffed them into his pants; then he applied the hot iron to the soiled spot. "See?" he said when the last trace of wax had disappeared. He extracted the wad of paper and held it out to me. It had absorbed all the wax.

The philosopher's down-to-earth common sense was delightfully different from the image of a mental giant I had formed before I met him. His enormous gusto for life drove him to the excesses that would eventually kill him, but they never interfered with the brilliance or the volume of his work.

Like Virginia, I was excited and honored by the philosopher's invitation and could hardly wait for the day of our departure. He had asked us to come a few days earlier, because he and Jano, his wife, were going to Esalen the day the conference began. "You're welcome to stay on as long as you like," he told me on the phone, "but we won't get to spend any time together unless you get here a few days before."

Virginia's eyes gleamed behind her thick glasses when we boarded the plane. A few days earlier she had once again landed in the hospital with acute insulin shock, but had pulled out of it in record time to be ready for the trip. Her body was thinner than before, but her face had lost none of its corn-fed rotundity. Now it was lit up from within.

"Just imagine, Nina! We'll be staying with Alan!" She always managed to give the hallowed name a special intonation. By the time we arrived at the San Francisco airport she had asked numerous passengers her eternal "Do you know Alan Watts?" Her high, shrill voice was clearly audible above the noise of the engine as she held forth about her idol. Never did her 200 Watt bulb shine more brightly, nor was she ever more inspired.

The cab drove us through the Golden Gate park, across the bridge, and along the bay in Sausalito. At last, it stopped before a dilapidated hulk.

"This can't be the right place," I protested.

"Sure is, lady," the cabby affirmed.

Virginia and I looked at each other. Surely, this could not be where the philosopher lived!

"Wait here," I told Virginia. "I'll go look."

I walked across the rickety board that spanned the muddy path from the dock to the boat and found myself facing a door that looked ready to collapse. Hesitantly, I rang the bell.

"Ah, there you are!" Alan said warmly. He was wearing a richly embroidered silk robe that seemed incongruous framed by that door. "Come in, come in," he invited, stepping aside.

Relieved that we were in the right place, I called Virginia and asked the driver to bring our bags.

The S.S Vallejo, as the old tugboat was named, hid a pearl behind her craggy, grey exterior. Inside, she was of the rarest beauty. "Oh my!" Virginia exclaimed. Alan laughed. "We call it The Oyster. Quite a surprise, eh?"

The Oyster was sparsely furnished, Japanese style. The paintings and art objects were of predominantly Eastern origin. A large statue of Buddha sat serenely on a low dais and was surrounded by Tibetan bells, gongs, and other devotional objects. Behind it, a very old Tibetan tanka graced the wall, and a stick of incense burned in a dish filled with sand.

That evening, Alan showed us another side of his multi-talented nature by cooking a superb Japanese meal. His wife Jano, who was not feeling well, joined us for dinner and Alan entertained us with stories and anecdotes. It was an evening of pure enchantment. As I looked out on the moonlit bay I marvelled at the good fortune that brought me in contact with Alan and the other people I had recently met.

As I had told Jean, I wasn't ready for LSD, but marijuana was said to be a mild psychedelic, and I was anxious to try it. I knew that Alan smoked it and hoped he would turn me on in the temple-like atmosphere of The Oyster. I had mentioned my interest in the herb to him in New York, but two days went by without a sign of its presence on the boat. I was too shy to ask and resigned myself to the thought that I'd have to look elsewhere for my opportunity.

"There's a party at some friends' houseboat tonight. Would you like to come?" Alan asked us on the third day.

It looked like any party when we entered the spacious, elegantly furnished room on the lower deck. The people were well dressed and attractive, and closer to my age than most of the Millbrook group. The stereo played rock-and-roll, and hors d'oeuvres were set out on a table that held the usual assortment of liquor. There was a curious odor in the room, and I saw some clumsily hand-rolled cigarettes pass from hand to hand. Marijuana! My opportunity had come.

An attractive late thirtyish man greeted Alan. The cigarette in his hand exuded an unmistakable aroma.

"This is Roger, Nina," Alan introduced us. "Nina has never smoked grass. Would you like to initiate her?"

"With pleasure! So you're a novice?" Roger's smile was warm. "Come!" He took my hand and guided me to a quiet room upstairs. There were no chairs in the room. We sat on cushions, our backs leaning against the wall. "What kind of music do you like?" Roger asked.

"Oh, mostly classical; but the Beatles are great," I said.

"Okay, I'll put a record on." He went to the phonograph that stood in a corner of the room, and soon the sounds of Strawberry Fields Forever filled the room.

"Inhale deeply," Roger instructed me. Without hesitation I took the joint he proffered. "Hold the smoke in as long as you can. Feel it filling your lungs," he told me. I obeyed. He handed me the joint again. Again, I inhaled deeply.

As I inhaled for the third time, I felt my belly ballooning out; and then Roger and everything around me disappeared. I was spinning backwards through evolution, my awareness of myself as a woman with a name, a past, a family, an address, gone. I was ape, lion, tiger, horse, dog, rabbit, fish, insect, and then a primitive organism that scrabbled out of the mud onto dry land. Then the process was reversed. I evolved through innumerable forms back to my human one, and then I was giving birth. Later, I was a black girl dancing to the beat of a drum in an African Kraal. I was totally unconscious of my surroundings until I became aware of Virginia staring at me open-mouthed as she watched me stamping my feet and shaking my hips. It made me self-conscious, and I stopped. It was like plummeting down an endless shaft, this coming back suddenly into consciousness of myself in this body.

Later, I looked at the night sky, leaning backward over the boat's railing. "All I have to do is let go and I'll sail through the air like a bird, unhampered by gravity," I thought. And just as I was going to let go a chair appeared in the air and I sat down on it. Later I found out that it was Alan who caught me and carried me into the room where he put me down on a couch.

There was also an episode where I danced again, leaping through the air like Pavlovna only to be reminded by my aching legs of the 47-year-old body I was presently wearing.

The labor pains I experienced that evening were as real as the ones that brought my children into the world. I didn't know to what I was giving birth at that time. Much later, I realized that it had been to myself—my new self, from which much that I had earlier taken for granted now began to fall away.

I will not attempt to describe the rest of that memorable evening. Suffice it to say that it tore down once and for all the prison gates of my 3-D reality. Now I KNEW that there was more. And I knew that others of the psychedelic brother-sisterhood knew.

From that time on, the external bonds that still held me to my former life began to crumble. I entered the phase that Timothy Leary calls Post-Larval, and my novitiate in that delicately balanced schizoid state where we are not yet at home in the new reality but no longer believe in the old, began.

Thirty-one

The conference was originally to be held on the Berkeley campus, but at the last minute it was moved to an off-campus building in down-town San Francisco. Public hysteria, fed by sensational reports of LSD-induced psychoses, caused Sandoz, the Swiss firm of pharmaceuticals who produced the chemical, to terminate all research contracts and to recall all supplies of LSD and psilocybin, even though the law making LSD illegal was not yet in effect. The climate surrounding the mind-altering drugs grew more and more hostile, and the university administration's move was probably prompted more by fear of riots than by opposition to the drug researchers themselves.

The conference had been organized by Richard Baker, who would later become known as Baker-Roshi, head of the San Francisco Zen Center, and chaired by Frank Barron, professor of psychology specializing in the field of creativity. In his opening address, Barron called for more research; Dr. Sidney Cohen warned that irresponsible enthusiasts like Leary and Ken Kesey would ruin the chances for serious work with the psychedelics in the same way that hypnosis was lost to us for fifty years. Abram Hoffer reported that his work with alcoholics showed an almost two-thirds rate of cure, and Erich Kast described LSD therapy with the terminally ill as a very positive experience for a large majority of the patients to whom it had been given.

Allen Ginsberg, whose name had been crossed off the list of presenters with the explanation that he was not a scientist, appeared in the lecture hall on the first day of the conference and was given a standing ovation to protest the decision to eliminate him.

The diversity of opinions expressed by the speakers was summed up by one of them who stated that "everything you hear about LSD is nonsense, including what I'm telling you." Given the conviction with which detractors as well as enthusiasts spoke of the drug, it was hard to imagine how the objectivity necessary to conduct unbiased research could be reached. LSD had struck a nerve in users and non-users alike, and the climate surrounding it was one of stark emotion.

A perfect demonstration of this was an exchange between Ginsberg and a pale, tight-lipped man in suit and tie. It was during an intermission. The two stood confronting each other in the yard. The contrast between the poet in a rumpled, non-descript shirt, his bushy hair and shaggy beard innocent of the barber's shears, and the other's conventionally correct attire spoke eloquently of the two separate worlds these men inhabited.

"I'd like to see all of you in jail," the man shouted. "You're all crazy, you're a menace to decent people! The sooner we lock you all up the better for society!"

"But why?" Ginsberg asked. There was wonderment in his glowing eyes. It was not a rhetorical question. He really wanted to know.

"Because that's where you belong! Decent people shouldn't be exposed to you! You're scum! You're making dope addicts out of our kids! Thank God we still have law and order! That's why they'll put all of you dopers in prison!"

"But what about the kids they'll put in prison if the drug laws make criminals of them? Doesn't that bother you?" The poet's voice was low and pleading, and the absence of hostility in his eyes and his demeanor formed a striking contrast to the other's menacing tone. To my surprise, the man now seemed to respond to the gentle words of the poet. His face softened, his voice dropped, and he came a step closer to Ginsberg.

"Look, I don't want to see kids go to prison. But it's for their own good. Better they spend time in jail than go on using drugs. You can understand that, can't you?"

"No, I can't." Ginsberg's sad, dejected face expressed such puzzlement that the other shrugged and held out his hand.

"I'm sorry," he said. It sounded sincere. All his hostility gone, he shook hands with the poet and walked away.

The talk Leary gave was brilliant and well prepared, but his indiscriminate enthusiasm for the drug and the claims he made for its power to elevate the consciousness of the user made me uneasy. I was much more in agreement with Richard Alpert (yet to become Ram Dass) who suggested that the government establish an Internal Flights Agency, which would prepare and licence prospective LSD takers and weed out those to whom the drug might prove harmful. It was already known that people with rigid character structures, heavy investment in dogmatic belief systems, and pre-psychotic tendencies were poor risks for the powerful mind-altering chemical, and I felt that much misery could be avoided by screening them out.

In the evenings, there were light shows at the university and parties at the homes of some of the local conference participants. My marijuana experience freed me to dance in ways I never had before. Instead of the stiff, formal ballroom dancing where, enlaced by a partner who led me in the fox trot, the rhumba, or the waltz, I allowed my body to move spontaneously and to merge with the music. People followed their own different drummers, sometimes swaying in rhythm with a partner, sometimes not. Richard Alpert engaged me in a teasing, swirling dance where we never touched, but moved in unison. Never before had I known such self-abandoned rapture, and I wanted to dance, dance, and keep dancing for the rest of my life.

At one of these parties I saw Roger again.

"How do you feel?" he asked. "Back to earth again?" He smiled knowingly. "You had quite a night!"

"I wonder what you must have thought of me. Was I acting very strange?"

"Well, let's just say you didn't act the way you do ordinarily, I imagine. But I'm curious. What went on inside you? I never saw anybody react the way you did to three tokes of some fairly mediocre grass! Seems to me you were ready for it!"

"Oh yes, I was ready. But not for what I experienced! It was awesome!"

"I could see that. Look, we can't talk here. Would you like to come for dinner at my house tomorrow? Good! I'll pick you up at 7?"

The car wound its way up a narrow serpentine road until it stopped in a clearing with a house that seemed to belong to the landscape. It perched on a steep mountain with a dazzling view. The house was a study in contrasts. In the center of the living room was a sunken area that held a low table surrounded by cushioned benches. Like on the S.S.Vallejo, the Japanese style dominated. Off the living room was an exquisite little temple. In the dim candle light the shrine looked like a precious jewel. A timeless quality pervaded the house. I could have imagined myself in the home of a Samurai or merchant prince in Japan had it not been for the bathroom, which displayed an almost vulgar modernism—a chrome and tile extravaganza, defiant in its exaggerated up-to-date appointments, as if to say, "Hey, don't forget me! This is the West, in the 20th century!"

The house charmed me. "Did you buy it or was it built for you?" I asked Roger.

"I built it myself. I'm a carpenter. It's just right for my daughter and me. Did you know that Alan wrote The Joyous Cosmology here?"

"No, but I can well imagine! A writer's paradise! How beautiful it is here! Everything is so beautiful! The whole world! I never knew...Tell me, Roger, does it just seem so to me because of—you know—the other night?"

"Oh, so it opened your eyes? Congratulations. I'm honored to have been present at your initiation. Grass never did that for me!"

"I still can't believe that's all it was. If that's what's called 'a mild psychedelic' I wonder what a strong one would do! Are you sure there was nothing in that joint besides grass?"

"Absolutely nothing, believe me. Care to tell me what went on?"

"I'd like to," I said, relieved to be able to talk about it. And so, lying in a hammock under the redwood trees, I told Roger about the experience.

"Sounds like an acid trip," Roger remarked when I finished. "I knew something unusual was happening when I saw you dance. You were so graceful, you seemed to become the music. And the part where you were giving birth...I could see that you were in pain, and it frightened me, but there was nothing I could do—you didn't even hear me. You were gone!"

"Yes, that's how it felt. I lost contact with the present...I was elsewhere, though to say 'I' is a lie. I don't know where 'I' was..."

Roger nodded. "I know what you mean. I've experienced it on acid, but never on grass. Speaking of grass, would you like to smoke?"

"Would I!" I wasn't sure that I was ready to repeat the experience so soon, but on the other hand I was irresistibly drawn.

I inhaled cautiously. By the third toke I began to feel something. It was as if a veil fell from my eyes. The shapes and colors in the room stood out more brightly and clearly, and everything seemed imbued with life. But apart from that, nothing came. Delightful as it was, it was a purely visual experience and remained so until Roger took me in his arms, when it became a tactile experience of a kind that overshadowed any love-making I had known before .

We slept together in the hammock under the stars. When I said good-bye to him the next morning, I had no illusions that a lasting romance would follow this brief fling. It was true what they said about the herb. Under the right circumstances, it can become an aphrodisiac. I'd have to be careful in the future about who I smoked with, unless I wanted my life to become a series of one-night stands. And this I emphatically did not want. As pleasurable as the love-making had been, the experiences of my first smoke were incomparably more memorable. It was that area that I wanted to explore, and the episode with Roger was soon forgotten.

♥ ♥ ♥

"There's a new rock and roll group who call themselves The Grateful Dead. They're supposed to be very good. They're giving an all-day party tomorrow. Would you like to go?" Ralph Metzner asked. It was Saturday. There would be no conference the next day. It sounded good.

"Sure," I replied eagerly. Another opportunity to dance!

The next day at noon Ralph and his friend Paul Lee picked me up on the S.S. Vallejo. Paul, an assistant professor of philosophy at UCSC was a warm, witty, friendly man in his late thirties. He and Ralph knew each other from Harvard, where Paul had studied theology with Paul Tillich.

"Everybody will be on acid," he told me on the way to Mill Valley, where the party took place.

"They will?" I tried to keep apprehension out of my voice.

"Don't worry," Ralph said. "Nobody will commit mayhem."

"I'm not worried about that. It's just that I've never taken it and don't want to be the only one who's not high."

"I won't turn on either," Paul said. "I'm scheduled to give a talk at the conference on Monday. I can't afford to space out."

"Good," I said, relieved. "Do you mind if I stay close to you?"

"Right! We'll stick together, you and I. I'll protect you from the dope fiends." His good-natured face crinkled up in a smile.

The party was held at a spacious estate with a swimming pool. The lawn was covered with people of mixed ages who strolled around, lay on the grass, or dove into the pool.

"Half of them are naked!" I exclaimed in shocked surprise. I was still a suburban housewife, and public nakedness was not in my repertoire of acceptable behavior.

"Aren't they!" Paul said. Though neither he nor Ralph seemed disturbed by it, they kept their clothes on. But nakedness was not to be the most shocking thing I saw. As I walked around, I observed that several couples were making love in full sight of everybody. It was a strange, and to me repulsive sight to see these bodies, most of them a sickly white, rolling around together on the ground. It seemed to me that they were not particularly enjoying themselves but were performing the act more like a duty—to demonstrate their freedom, I thought. None of the others seemed interested in their activities; people walked by without paying attention to the copulating pairs.

"I have an announcement," a voice came from the loudspeaker. "I'm afraid all of you will have to move your cars. We're blocking the road and the neighbors are complaining." A loud groan of protest went up from the group.

"This is the test," Paul said. "If they can get up and move their cars, we may get through this thing all right." He and Ralph went to move the car, leaving me alone and apprehensive among a crowd I felt none too comfortable with. Nobody took any notice of me; the cars were moved without a hitch except for one who drove into something and smashed a headlight. I selected a spot on the lawn near the band and sat down. Considering the lasting phenomenon The Grateful Dead have since become, it is surprising that I have no memory of the music. I was so busy scanning the whole scene that I paid no attention to the band except once, when Paul whispered in my ear: "Look at the guy with his head inside the speaker! Know who that is?"

"No," I admitted. "I can't see his face."

"That's Neal Cassidy. He likes his music loud!"

Near us, two dogs were fighting. A large, naked man approached them and restrained one while talking to the other in a low, reassuring voice. A little girl, maybe two years old, ran close to the swimming pool and was scooped up by a woman in a shapeless, clumsily patched shift of indeterminate color.

Neither she nor any of the other women wore make-up. There were no colorful costumes in this crowd. They looked almost intentionally unattractive and unkempt. Had it not been for the elaborate sound system of the Grateful Dead and the motorcycle that attempted doggedly to drive up an almost vertical hill, I would have thought I was back in the stone age.

"See that man over there? That's Owsley. He must have been giving out acid before we came."

"I'm trying very hard to be non-judgmental, Paul. But my God! They're going backwards! Is that what LSD does?"

"For some, I guess. But don't be too hard on them. They're protesting our repressed, artificial way of life. Back to nature doesn't have to mean back to the stone age."

"It does if they want to do away with technology. Go back to no cars? No refrigerators? No printing press and no TV? What would happen to our culture? And what about the global village that Buckminster Fuller talks about? Only through technology will we realize how totally interdependent we are!"

"There are levels of consciousness that have nothing to do with technology," Ralph remarked. "What these people want is to go back to a simple, natural lifestyle that doesn't threaten the earth, or impose sexual repression on them. Perhaps the technology they want is spiritual, not material. Machines keep us from exercising our natural gifts. We're out of balance. Something has to happen to heal the split between us and nature."

I left the party with the uneasy feeling that there was a regressive aspect to the Aquarian Age movement—a nostalgia for the past that is counter-evolutionary. I thought of Evolution in Search of a New Breed of Man, the paper I wrote for my Study of Full Humanness. It began with a quote from Genesis, "Look not behind Thee…," and went on to say: "Today, civilization is faced with the dilemma of Lot's wife. If we turn back to the past and try to linger in it, we are lost. Our only hope for survival lies in a resolute forward look, and in the courage to leap ahead into the unknown. Behind us is a sentimental past; nostalgia will get us nowhere."

I was beginning to see that there were several different kinds of hippies. There were the Millbrook types who believed that they could change the world by elevating their own consciousness; their main interest was spiritual. There were the acid test Ken Kesey types who saw life as a continuous party and thought that by blowing the collective minds of society they could create a new and better world. There were the political types to whom revolution was the only answer to existing injustices; and the back-to-nature types who wanted to set back the clock to a simpler life more in harmony with the earth. And even within these different factions there were numerous subdivisions; the only thing they all had in common was long hair and idealism. It was the latter more than anything else that endeared them to me.

Despite the uneasiness I felt at the Grateful Dead party, my overall impression of the San Francisco Hippies was very positive. My love affair with the Flower Children continued, and I was grateful for their easy acceptance of me despite the difference in our ages and the fact that I was still a semi-straight suburban matron. My stay in San Francisco in the summer of '66 has remained a landmark as the date of my rebirth. Henceforth, all that went before became merely background, a life that could just as well have been somebody else's. The woman who returned to the East Coast was not the same as the one who left, and the change was irreversible.

Thirty-two

The reality I knew had cracked, and through the cracks shone another order of reality. This new reality was not simply an extension of the old. In some ways, it was upside down. My worldly sense of values was turned around. I had had a glimpse of eternity, and beside it, the daily concerns that had once preoccupied me dwindled. What I had vaguely sensed as a teen-ager when I speculated that I had been put into the wrong body, and in Oued-Zem, when my "salon" and the books I read transported me out of the concentration camp, and at the birth of my children when my body writhed in agony while I, inside, was singing—this sense that I'm not my body had now become an experienced reality for me. The I that became insect, fish, bird, and mammal was not Nina Graboi. It was not Nina Graboi who danced to the drumbeats in the Kraal, or leaped lightfooted through the air. A letter written by Goethe to his friend Eckermann states what I now knew:

> The thought of death does not in the least disturb me, because I am firmly convinced that our spirit is altogether indestructible and thus continues from eternity to eternity. It is like the sun, which to our eyes seems to disappear beyond the horizon, while in actual fact it goes on shining continuously.

Two weeks after my return from San Francisco, Ralph Metzner invited me to smoke D.E.T. (diethyltryptamine) with he and his girl friend, Gray Henry.

"What's D.E.T.?" I asked.

"It's a mild version of D.M.T. (Dimethyltryptamine)

"Is it anything like LSD?"

"It's as strong, but lasts only one hour instead of 8. Want to try it?"

"I'd love to," I replied without hesitation. If Ralph thought I was ready for it, then I was. My respect for the Harvard trio had sky-rocketed since the conference. If my one marijuana experience had taken me to such undreamt-of dimensions, what must they have seen on their many trips!

Ralph lived only a block and a half away from the 12th Street apartment where I now spent much of my time. I was both frightened and elated as I walked to his house. I had not smoked grass since San Francisco—I was still digesting and processing that experience. Would tonight be equally overwhelming? I was glad that I wouldn't have far to go to get home.

The large, high-ceilinged room was fragrant with incense, and candles threw mysterious shadows on the walls. A Judy Collins record was playing, and Ralph and Gray were leafing through a book of Escher prints.

"Ready for the great adventure?" Ralph asked me.

"I guess so," I said, unable to keep my voice from quivering.

"You'll be fine," Gray said reassuringly. "I've done it several times, and believe me, it's not like anything you've ever known. But you come down from it, alas. There's only one problem. It tastes awful." She shook herself. She was in her mid-twenties, blond and buxom, a student at one of the leading colleges. Ralph was deeply in love with her and tried to win her away from another young man who was his perfect antithesis. Where Ralph was studious and reserved, the other was the typical tempestuous macho South American who asserted his mastery over the gently reared Gray at every turn. I was stunned to learn that she eventually married him, but at the time of which I speak she had still not made her choice and spent a great deal of time with gentle Ralph.

I had not met her before that evening but felt an immediate rapport with her. Set and setting were auspicious. I conquered my fears.

"Let's do it," I said to Ralph.

"All right. Now remember, it hits fast. Inhale deeply, and be prepared to fall back. Don't worry. We're here. Nothing can happen to you. You'll see and hear strange things; they could be fearsome, or they could be beautiful. Either way, it'll be over in an hour, I guarantee it. Here, sit on this couch. Okay?"

He put some dry parsley into the bowl of a glass pipe and sprinkled a white, crystalline powder on top. Holding it out to me he lit a match under the bowl. One last bolt of fear shot through me, and then I inhaled.

I gasped. The smoke tasted as if all the noisome chemicals in a lab had been combined. But I was aware of this for only an instant. Then...

What follows is the account I wrote of the experience the next day:

July 28, 1966

The doorway to my home is a honky-tonk. I pass through a gate where my brain gets compressed before it explodes from its shell and enter a familiar scene of throbbing sounds, perfumes, brightly lit colored glass baubles and cheap glossy silks. Pan waits for me there, leaps to welcome me and engulfs me in a wild, sensuous dance. His breath and his hands travel over me in flashes of hot light. Niagaras of dazzling gems pour from his hair and mouth. How enticing he is! The warm bath of the senses tempts me, but I'm eager to go on. TIME is still real for me at this stage. I must hurry.

I see layers, not neatly arranged one on top of the other but interlaced, now one now the other rapidly exposed to view and then merging again with the rest. How many are there, each different in kind and yet the same? Enraptured, I know them all to be real, realities that co-exist in an eternally playful dance. Everything is always simultaneously true and untrue, I suddenly know. And this knowledge comes to me while I watch through my hand how the faded blue of a wall turns to shimmering azure as my fingers spread and close. Closed fingers—dull faded blue. Open fingers—shimmering azure. Same wall. Same fingers. Same eyes. Each time the transformation is complete.

I have done this before. Or have I? Is this not the same trick of the mind by which I seem to anticipate everything my companions say? This is important. Must try to articulate. I speak for the first time—voice raucous, strange, a stranger's voice—whose?

"The mind flashes signals ahead that shape the next moment. That's why I think I've already been there."

"Would that explain déjà vu?" somebody asks.

Yes, maybe, but more, much much more. The relation between mind and brain is blindingly clear, an equation on a blackboard spelled out in an infinity of sparks. I know, at the same time, that I was here before. That I never left, in fact. That everything that happens "down there" is the robot manifestation of the life "up here." There are no phonies and no lies. The puppet thinks it cheats, puts on an act, when everything it does is willed by the master above. Not by God, but by the individual soul that controls the clay puppet. Fully conscious at all times, the soul lives outside time; undying and unborn, its home is a warm yellow glow where it sits bodiless watching amused how the puppet, its empirical self, goes through the motions it is bid to make.

Someone in the room mentions a name. Oh no! It can't be. My name! Or rather, the puppet's name. How funny! I laugh and laugh and look at the Nina-person down there who thinks she is me. I feel indulgent affection for her. How limited she is! And how pompous! She actually believes herself to have a degree of autonomy. Let's see. There was something she wanted to do. Or rather, something I wanted her to think she wants to do. Face her monsters, that's it. She reads a lot, you know. Knows all about the importance of coming to grips with buried trauma. Okay, puppet, bring on the monsters!

Hesitantly, the brain probes its recesses and conjures up the husband the woman down there thinks she hates. He walks into the room. No, he toddles! How cute he is! Lovable, in fact! He reaches me and buries his head in my lap. "There, there," I say indulgently, patting his rosy behind. "Run along now and play. Mommy has important work to do." He clings to my skirt. Gently, I make him release me. I motion him to go. He disappears.

The brain is scanning for trauma. Bring on the worst, the darkest, the arch-enemy: Hitler!

Adolf Hitler materializes. Impossible! Instead of brimstone he smells of glue and I see that he is a puppet. Glue oozes from his joints.

I hear myself laugh. The laughter frees me. Hate? Inappropriate, at best...

Here is the young man who started on this trip with me. But how he changed! His hair is grey, covered with ashes, his blind eyes have a milky stare; in his hand is a beggar's bowl. Cross-legged and emaciated, he sits on caked mud. "Oh Ralph, you're a Hindu beggar!" I exclaim. With infinite compassion I fall to my knees before him. "Is that what you see?" he asks. (Later, he told me that he had a vision of himself as a Hindu beggar when he was in India.)

Behind closed lids arise sparkling towers, mosaic-laden mosques, gothic spires. A row of dancing girls. No, dancing atoms. No, energy. Wavelets of energy, dancing to an inaudible rhythm. I open my eyes. Yes, it's everywhere. And I thought objects are solid! How silly of me! I laugh, and the laughter takes me back to the soul who sits watching, amused.

I feel all-powerful, huge, but weightless. I seem to hover above the earth, embracing it with my body. In a minute area of my right pinky nail, I see the Nina-puppet. I lift her arm and bring her fist down on the table. Her hand easily passes through the wood.

The descent has begun. I look at my companions. Oh yes, I remember. There is the young woman Ralph introduced to me as "Gray." How sweet she is! And how familiar! Of course! We were together before, the three of us! In an attic...A nordic country...Hans Christian Andersen...and we played...

Excited, I tell the others. "Really?" they say. They are not impressed. Eagerly, the brain chimes in. Hallucinations, it scoffs. Drug-induced hallucinations. Phantasmagoria, that's all. I silence it. Later, I will have to deal with it. But not now.

Back in ordinary reality.

No, never again ordinary.

Thirty-three

The D.E.T. was sort of a test. I did not flip out, did not try to leap from a window. I was ready for LSD.

"When can I take it?" I asked Timothy.

"Whenever you want. I heard about your D.E.T. trip. You're ready."

"Great! How about next Friday?"

"Sure. I'll assign a guide to you."

I left Manhattan in the late afternoon. Ralph rode out with me. "Got any last minute advice?" I asked him.

"You don't need it. You know what it's all about. Just remember to surrender. Don't try to fight it. Let it happen, whatever it is. Resistance is one sure way to have a bummer."

"Yes, I know. But what happens if I get into a bad place?"

"Your guide will know what to do. I'll look in on you from time to time. Don't worry. You'll have a great trip."

"I'm sure I will, but Ralph—I can't help feeling a little...scared, I guess. Will my fear make something go wrong?"

"Not unless you get paranoid. It's natural to feel some apprehension beforehand. We're playing with awesome powers. I always feel some fear, and so does Tim who has probably tripped more often than anybody else. Trust your Higher Self. You'll be safe."

The mansion was full of visitors and journalists, all clamoring for Tim's attention. Dinner was long over before I could approach him. He knew immediately what I wanted. "Ah yes, Nina! It's all arranged. Your guide will meet you in the Meditation House at ten. He has the sacrament. Love and blessings! Have an enlightening journey." He held my eyes for a moment, hugged me, and was gone.

A cheerful fire crackled in the Meditation House. Two candles were lit before the Buddha. There were flowers in a tall vase, a bowl of fruit stood on a low table, and two crystal goblets gleamed on a tray with a pitcher of water. I sat down on a cushion and tried to empty my mind of the busy thoughts that scurried around in my brain. Soon, the door opened. I turned around to see who my guide was. It was Tenzing, the Tibetan monk!

I had not seen him since the encounter in my office. I knew that he was at Millbrook, but heard that he stayed mostly alone in the woods.

"Are you my guide?" I asked. How wondrous it would be if Tim had assigned this remarkable guide to me!

"No. I merely heard that you are here and came to say hello," the monk replied.

"Why are you at Millbrook?" I asked him.

"To help keep destructive forces away. There is a strong gathering of energies against this place. Unless Tim changes his tone and steps out of the limelight, there isn't much anybody can do to avert disaster."

"Tell me, how do you, as a monk, feel about LSD?"

"I think it can be a key to enlightenment when rightly used. But without the discipline of a religious training, the enlightenment soon dissipates. For those who are unprepared, it can be a trip to hell. But miracles do happen… Some who are totally unprepared enter Heaven, and others…You never know."

"Am I prepared?" I asked.

"Only you can know that," he said. "But judging by what I know of you, I think you are," he added when he saw my questioning expression.

"Thank you. It's important for me to hear it, coming from you."

The monk nodded. "Well, have a safe journey. I'll look in on you from time to time if you wish." I nodded eagerly. "Bless you. Here comes your guide."

It was Nathan. "Tim said I should stay with you," he said. "Is that okay?"

I was happy with Tim's choice of a guide. Nathan and I had never exchanged many words, but something radiated from this quiet, calm man that made me glad to sit next to him in a meditation circle. What was left of my apprehension disappeared and I waited serenely for what was to come. Nathan drew an eyedropper from a small vial. He put three drops of a colorless liquid in one glass and one drop in the other. He handed me the first goblet. "I gave you 150 mm. I'm taking 50. It will help me to stay in rapport with you." He poured water into the two glasses and lifted his to me. "May the spirit protect you and guide you," he said.

And we drank.

What follows is the account of the trip, written a week later:

The setting for my session was the Meditation House. I sat cross-legged before the altar with Nathan, my guide, and we meditated in silence while we waited for the chemical to take effect. Thirty minutes or so later things began to happen. I lay down. "Will you take care of my body if I leave it?" I asked Nathan.

"Have faith," he answered.

I was looking up at the wooden ceiling and noted for the first time the intricate carvings that cover it. "Christ died in this room," I heard myself say.

"And He was also resurrected here," came Nathan's calm voice. My death, and my resurrection, I thought. After that, I lost consciousness, or the place where my consciousness went became inaccessible to what I normally call my consciousness. I was bombarded with images, concepts, information and illumination to a degree that far exceeded my capacity to deal with.

I felt my face changing, as if it were being poured into a new mold, and there were colors, and sounds, and the light! And gradually, a new self-awareness dawned. Not of my ordinary self as Nina Graboi nee Gusti Schreyer, but of the over-soul, the eternal Self of which the Nina-person is but a glimpse, a fleeting moment in the eternity of Being.

Someone entered the room. He looked dear and familiar, and a huge wave of love for him washed over me. I didn't know that it was Tenzin, only that he was dear and familiar.

And then the struggle to get back into the body began. I say the body, because I was not conscious of my physical self. It was a fierce struggle. I was not yet done with the world, I had to get back in the body. Things got confused at this point. I panicked. A parade of bodies appeared before me, but none of them seemed right.

"Who am I?" I asked Nathan.

"I don't know. Where do you live? Are you married? Have children? What's your name?" Nathan inquired, trying to activate my memory.

There is an identity waiting for me. I have to resume it. Somewhere I have a home, a family, a name…Am I married? I look for a sign, a wedding ring (I had taken mine off after my last quarrel with Michel), something that will give me a clue. But there is nothing—nothing I can hold on to. I keep slipping away…

Nathan brings in some logs. Gnarled and rustic, they smell of the earth. "You bring me roots," I say gratefully. "Thank you. Thank you." Nathan looks supernaturally noble and handsome. The wood is something to hang on to. It comes from the earth to which I must return, lest I go mad…

I lose consciousness again, and when it returns I find myself lying on the wet grass. I rise, or seem to float upright. Far, far away I see the Earth, a hazy green-blue ball that is coming closer, there are wavy lines on the surface, the ball is adrift in haziness…I have to land on this far-away ball. The effort is enormous. I'm frightened. Eons pass before my foot finally makes contact with the ground. My first few steps are like those of a baby, I'm relearning to walk. I fall…

Somebody is rubbing my cheek with sandpaper. The sensation is not unpleasant and I open my eyes. On my chest is a small kitten, the tiger kitten that lives in the Meditation House, and it is ardently licking my face. As I look at the cat's face, it changes. Hundreds of jewels gleam on it, and the cat-body becomes that of a snake. The kitten is the snake in the Garden of Eden, seducing me back into life, into the world of the senses!

The sun rises. I'm back on earth. I know my name, my identity, my age. "Good morning," I say to Nathan who has dozed off on the floor.
"You're down," he says. We smile at each other. "Come, let's have some tea."

We walk across to the Big House in the first light of dawn. The kitchen is empty, but in the library we find Jim and Marshall. We sit with them for a while. My consciousness keeps fading and coming back as I try to listen to the talk.

I want a cigarette and go to fetch one from my first floor room. As I cross the hall, the tiger kitten, who must have followed me to the Big House, jumps on my shoulder and stays there while I walk up the stairs. The small animal manages to hold on without putting her claws in my sweater. Silken pads embrace my neck and remain there until I return to the library with the cigarette.

In the kitchen, I busy myself making breakfast. The kitten has followed me and I give it some dry food and milk. I'm suddenly ravenous. With the food comes the full realization of who I am. Relief floods me. "I'm me! I'm Nina! I made it! I'm not crazy!" But almost immediately, a stab of remorse hits me so powerfully that tears spring to my eyes. "My children! My home! How could I forget? How could I go so far away from my family to a place where I have no children…"

I sob uncontrollably. Something has been lost forever—my faith in the safe, secure human laws, my sense of undivided selfhood, my involvement with life. And yet, paradoxically, I feel that my involvement will now be greater than ever—but in a new way, a way that embraces eternity.

A flood of memories rushes in. I see Vienna, the faces of my parents, sisters, brother, Oued-Zem, London, La Panne…

"I nearly didn't come back!" I exclaim.

"But you did," Tenzin says. He has entered the kitchen and is looking for a cup. "Tell me, what did you learn, Nina?"

I think about this for a while. "I learned that I'm more—so much more than this body that walks the earth. I learned that I'm still me, even without a name, a family, an identity, or a body. I almost think that the body is a prison that holds my consciousness inside narrow limits, to make it possible to function on the earth. Once I was out of it, the limitless was my home…" I'm surprised by what I'm saying, and by what that implies. "Does that mean there is no death, Tenzin?"

"You died last night, but you're still here. You can draw whatever conclusions you want from that. To the Buddhist, the aim of the game is to get off the wheel of birth and rebirth. You had a small taste of that last night."

"Yes, but I was very frightened when I couldn't get back in my body. I didn't like that part of the trip!"

"That's because you're not finished with your rounds on the earth. You still have much to learn here, so don't worry—you'll always find yourself back in your body, even if you wish to stay free."

"How many more rebirths will I have before I shed the body for good, Tenzin?"

He laughs. "There is a story about a holy man who walked through a forest in which lived many hermits who practiced austerities in order to advance spiritually. The saint passed a saddhu who, recognizing him as a man of great spiritual power, asked him how many more times he would have to be reborn. '300 times,' the holy man replied. The saddhu jumped for joy. 'Only 300 more times!' he shouted. 'The end is in sight! What a happy man I am!' The saint walked on, and another saddhu approached him with the same question. 'There are 47 more births ahead of you,' said the saint. 'So many!' the saddhu exclaimed. 'I have practiced austerities for many years, I deserve to be liberated after this lifetime!' The holy man sighed. 'Thanks to your impatience, the number has just changed. You will have to come back again 300 times.'"

I am silent, reflecting on my many shortcomings that would keep me coming back for innumerable lifetimes before I would be ready to shed the body for good.

"Why did you want me to bring Tim to you during the night?" Nathan asks.

"What do you mean?"

"You said, 'Bring Tim to me!' When I told you that it's 3:30 at night and he would be fast asleep, you said, 'Wake him up! I have to take his toys away!' You sounded imperious, like the Austrian Empress Maria Therese! What did you have in mind?"

"I have no idea!! What other crazy things did I do and say? Was I awful?"

"No, you were not," Tenzin says. "You were quite beautiful, in fact. You're an old soul. Even my Geshe commented on it. He remembers you from the Bucks County seminar—even remembers the red dress you wore!"

"He does? Thank you for telling me. And thank you for looking in on me last night. I'll never forget your kindness. And yours, Nathan! I feel blessed to have had you as my guide."

The kitten perches on the refrigerator and leaps on my back as I pass. In the hall, a slightly larger tiger cat, the six-toed Isis, is waiting. She is the mother of my little friend, whose name is Jackie, named after Timothy's son, Jack. It seems to me that Jackie is reporting the events of the night to her mother. The two form a circle, the head of one touching the tail of the other. Her report finished, Jackie stretches out, ready to go to sleep, but Isis nudges her. "Your job is not yet over," she seems to say. Jackie immediately races after me and squeezes past me through the door. I am not sleepy, but I undress and lie down, Jackie curled around my neck. "Thank you, Jackie," I say. "You, too, were my guide." Before the session, I had read The Psychedelic Prayers, Timothy's version of the Tao Te Ching. I think of the poem named

THE GUIDE

In the greatest sessions
One does not know that
there is a guide

In the next best sessions
One praises the guide

It is worse when
One fears the guide

The worst is that
One pays him

If the guide lacks trust
in the people

Then
The trust of the people will be lacking

The wise guide guards his word
The wise guide sits serenely

When the greatest session is over,
The people will say—

"It all happened naturally"

or

"It was so simple, we did it
all ourselves."

When I came downstairs I noticed the loving care with which the Millbrook group kept all jarring noise away from me. I felt they were protecting me in unobtrusive ways to allow me to gently re-enter the normal world. Throughout the day, people would come and sit next to me, hold my hand, or just smile at me, and they said "Thank you!" to me—for what? I did not ask. How fortunate I was to be received back into the human community by these beautiful souls, in these beautiful surroundings! My heart went out to trippers who had to come down into a world of ugliness and strife after an experience like mine. I wonder if I'll ever feel such harmony again with any group of people as I felt with them throughout that day.

At noon, Timothy came down. I watched him drift this way and that, in the direction of whatever voice called to him, always cheerful, always totally open to the demands of the moment. The man is like a leaf, I thought, so free, so easy; he is here to serve evolution in her hour of need, and not, as I thought before I knew him, his ego.

When he saw me, he threw me a questioning look. A broad smile spread over his face as he noted the expression on mine.

"Come, there's something I want to give you," he said. I followed him into the house where he went to a closet and withdrew a book from a box. It was a beautiful edition of The Psychedelic Prayers.

"Write something in it," I begged.

"What shall I write?" he asked. I laughed. Words seemed paltry that morning after the night's events. Tim seemed to know what I was thinking and he too laughed. We stood there laughing loudly for a while, and then Tim took pen in hand and wrote across one corner of the inside cover,

"To dearest Nina—What shall I write?........
Laughter,
Laughter,
Love, Tim.
Millbrook, 1966."

Thirty-four

It took courage to take LSD in 1966. I'm not just talking about the legal aspects. It set you apart. It forced you out of your cultural mold and took you on a trip—I keep marvelling at that word's deep meaning—from which there was no return to a pre-acid state. Almost everybody I know who took LSD at that time dropped out of their previous lifestyle and social group. But this did not isolate us. Acid use was restricted to such a small circle of "heads" that we became instant members of a tribe. We recognized each other wherever we went. It wasn't the clothes we wore, or the length of our hair. It was in the eyes, a far-away look, a look of having seen much.

Returning from Millbrook after that weekend was like stepping into a familiar scene with new eyes. What I had once taken for reality now looked like flim-flam. The hypocrisies and delusions in which I, like most people, had spent my life stood naked before me. My gratitude for the moment when the veil parted and I knew that "I" am so much more than I thought was so immense, that I often discovered myself sobbing with joy.

My familiar reality had cracked; a vast new reality that promised liberation from death and meaninglessness lay before me. I believed that if everybody saw what I now saw there would be peace on earth. The demons of hate, violence, illness and war would be banished back into Pandora's box. The scales would fall from humanity's eyes and we would recognize that we are one, and that we are eternal.

I now fitted into my life in Lawrence even less than before. I knew that I had to find the courage to leave. More than ever, I saw how damaging my relationship with Michel had become—to both of us, although he kept protesting his love for me and even threatened suicide if I left.

It was early fall, the leaves were just beginning to turn. My garden embraced me. The trees, the flowers, the shadowed mosses were alive with tenderness. As my eyes wandered through the graceful arc formed by two trees, they were drawn further; a landscape of virginal splendor opened before me. It was still my garden. I knew every tree, every bush; but it was transformed, transfigured into the perfection of a world newly created—a vernal world, inhabited by ethereal beings under whose feet the grass does not bend. I sank into rapture as I watched; I remembered the Zen proverb that says, "Before enlightenment we carry water and chop wood. After enlightenment we carry water and chop wood." Yes, but with what a difference! The world does not change, only our perception of it.

Like a cow chewing its cud, I sit by the pool, integrating. The process is passive. A shaft of energy enters the top of my head and runs through my body in glittering sparks. It's as if a new opening has been created in my brain—I'm seeing into, around, and through objects and people. I'm aware of dimensions that include, but do not end, with the reality that has framed my world.

The phone rings, jarring me back to the everyday world.

"Hi, Nina." A lovely, melodious voice. It is Jennie. The youngest of my social set, she is not as threatened as the others by my new associations. She is calling to invite us to a party. I'm trying to think of an excuse. Quick, what shall I say?

"A small party. Just eight of us," Jennie coaxes. She names names. Two of the couples I know; the men are successful professionals, the wives are being psychoanalyzed. The third couple is coming from Manhattan; he is a well-known theatrical producer. "You'll enjoy meeting him; he could be helpful to you with your French plays."

My French plays! How long ago that seems! Where did it go, that once so passionate interest? But I'm fond of Jennie, and Michel likes parties. I accept.

I sit before the mirror in my bedroom. As I apply make-up I think of the lovely faces of the Millbrook women, so innocent of make-up except when they paint them for the fun of it. Make-up is not part of the persona with which they face the world, as it has been for me and for all the women I knew before. How many years has "putting on my face" been an unquestioned habit? Another layer of the onion lies exposed. When will I give it up?

Not yet, I decide. And certainly not tonight. I will not proselytize, I promise myself. If the subject of LSD comes up, I will either shut up or point out the dangers and the pitfalls of the road I have chosen. I will make it clear that I have chosen it because the world has nothing more to give me—nothing I want, nothing I desire. A sensibility that is anchored in the physical is bound to receive a shock of terror when the "other world" opens up. When such a person discovers that we are spirit and exist separate from the body in another, an eternal dimension, fear and disorientation sets in. It was then and is now my firm conviction that those who present themselves at the portals of that other world should do so only when earthly life has already loosened its grip.

I put on a dress of russet silk and tie a burnt orange scarf around my waist. The colors reflect the glories of the autumnal landscape in Jennie's garden where we take our cocktails before dinner. Nobody talks about LSD. Amused, I observe myself go through the old familiar motions that constitute my party self. How easily the bantering phrases rise to my mouth! I'm aware of the coquettish looks, the flirtatious teasing that draws the men in the room to my side. I know that they desire me, and that they would tire of me as quickly as they had of their wives. To them, I'm mysterious, exotic, glamorous, unknown; to myself I'm an onion with innumerable skins. I'm the amused observer of my own game. Aren't they as tired of it as I am?

Again and again, my thoughts wander to the mythical, magical community at Millbrook where I feel more and more at home. I don't belong here, I think as I join in the party chatter. I long to go home and to remove my party persona like a mask. This is the last one of this kind I'll attend, I vow.

And it was.

♥ ♥ ♥

Leary's appeal against the Laredo bust sentence centered on the issue of religious freedom. He argued that as LSD and marijuana are used as sacraments by him and the rest of the Millbrook community, they should be legally obtainable, in the same way as the peyote which is used by the Native American Church. When he announced that the Millbrook community had incorporated as a religious group named The League of Spiritual Discovery, an avalanche of mail and phone calls poured into the mansion. Everybody wanted to join the new religion. We were stunned by the sheer volume of requests. The LSD revolution had spread beyond the colleges and seemed on its way to becoming a vast grass-roots movement. Timothy Leary, as leader of the new religion, could have become one of the most powerful men on earth. But to the surprise of all who believed him to be power-hungry and self-serving, he wanted no part of it. "Start your own religion," he wrote in a pamphlet that gave guidelines on how to do it. The League of Spiritual Discovery had only two commandments: Thou shalt not alter the consciousness of thy fellow man, and Thou shalt not prevent thy fellow man from altering his own consciousness. "Expanded consciousness is the Fifth Freedom," Timothy Leary proclaimed. Along with his famous slogan, "Turn on, tune in, drop out," these words had a powerful hold on the young.

But while the Millbrook group viewed psychedelics as a primary key to the mystical experience, they continued to search for non-drug ways to reach it. For this purpose they decided to stage a series of performances called Psychedelic Religious Celebrations. These would attempt to recreate the psychedelic experience for the spectators. The first of them was based on the novel Steppenwolf by Hermann Hesse.

"Better not call it that," I warned Timothy, remembering from my adaptation of Siddhartha that the author objected to dramatizations of his work.

"Right," said Tim. "The show will be only loosely based on the book anyway. We'll call it something else."

The something else was The Death of the Mind. On weekends, I found the group assembled in the cellar of one of the buildings on the estate. The structure of the cellar reminded me of the Roman catacombs where the first Christians met secretly to practice their new religion; it lent an eerie sense of underground conspiracy to the rehearsals.

Hesse's Steppenwolf is an outsider, a man split between his instinctual drives and the smooth veneer of culture which he owes to a good mind and an excellent education. He is tormented and near suicide when a series of mysterious events enter his life in the person of a bewitching young woman named Hermine. She tutors him in the delights of life and brings him to Pablo, a musician in the nightclub where she dances with Harry.

It is obvious that the Nobel prize-winning author identified with the protagonist whose initials are the same as his, and the girl's name makes her his alter ego, his female part. Hesse was deeply influenced by C.J. Jung, but that he also tasted of more immediate experiences than his revered friend's words will become obvious in what follows.

Pablo invites Harry and Hermine to join him in his room and greets his guests:

"My dear friends, I have invited you to an entertainment that Harry has long wished for and of which he has long dreamed. The hour is late and no doubt we are all slightly fatigued. So, first, we will rest and refresh ourselves a little.'

Hesse's description of the scene leaves little doubt as to the nature of the refreshments:

From a recess in the wall he took three glasses and a quaint little bottle, also a small oriental box inlaid with differently colored woods. He filled the three glasses from the bottle and taking three long thin yellow cigarettes from the box and a box of matches from the pocket of his silk jacket he gave us a light. And now we all slowly smoked the cigarettes whose smoke was as thick as incense, leaning back in our chairs and slowly sipping the aromatic liquid whose strange taste was so utterly unfamiliar. Its effect was immeasurably enlivening and delightful—as though one were filled with gas and had no longer any gravity. Thus we sat peacefully exhaling small puffs and taking little sips at our glasses, while every moment we felt ourselves growing lighter and more serene.

Now Pablo escorts them to the corridor of a little theater, where Harry wanders from door to door and enters a variety of scenes. The lesson the Steppenwolf must learn in Pablo's magic theater is to laugh at the world, not to take it, or himself, seriously. The world, as Hesse sees it, is the result of the tension between the ideal and the real. "All life is so, my child, and we must let it be so; and if we are not asses, laugh at it." We go through torments to protect our personality; once we see through the illusion, we laugh.

Though the details vary with the taker, Pablo's theater with its innumerable doors recreates the general features of an LSD trip. I was enthusiastic about helping to bring a psychedelic version of the book to the stage. Along with The Magus by James Fowler, Mount Analogue by René Daumal, and Hesse's Journey to the East, Steppenwolf was a cult book among the LSD cognoscenti. Now that I had joined that brother-sisterhood, I could easily see why.

Jackie Cassen and Rudi Stern were in charge of the multi-media show. Many elements were needed for the slide show and the films that would be projected on the scrim. Costumes, lights, music and scenery had to be made and procured by what was basically a group of amateurs. But having observed the level of creativity at Millbrook, I had no doubt that they would carry it off in style.

I helped as much as I could. My 12th Street apartment was a gathering place for the cast and crew. I still lived officially in Lawrence, but spent much of my time in New York. The excitement that surrounded the rehearsals was intense. I watched how Ralph gradually became Harry Haller, and how Timothy with his magnetic voice and nimble body turned into the mysterious Pablo. Beautiful Rosemary was both High Priestess and Hermine, the girl-boy enchantress. And Rudi and Jackie created magic with the light show.

The Death of the Mind opened at The Village Theater, which became the Filmore East. In 1966, it was a shabby theater that featured mostly Yiddish plays. I arrived two hours early with Rosemary and Timothy. A line had already formed at the box office. They cheered when they recognized Timothy, and he flashed them his famous smile.

Backstage, the usual last minute chaos prevailed. Jackie and Rudi carried walkie-talkies and kept testing and retesting them. The film and the slides would be projected on the transparent scrim from the back and the front, and some of the action would also take place behind the scrim. Lights were tested, Peter Walker strummed his guitar, a button needed to be sewn... I had no special function backstage except to help wherever help was needed. Everybody was tense, poised for the leap—the moment when the curtain would go up and everything had to be in place.

Word passed around that Timothy asked us all to gather on the stage. We formed a circle and stood silently, holding hands. From beyond the closed curtain, we could hear the noise in the auditorium.

"Let us remember that we are here to serve the spirit, and not ourselves," Timothy addressed us. He was clad all in white; a glow seemed to emanate from his person. "We've done our best to prepare for this performance; all will go well as long as we stay calm and focused. OM." "OM," we all intoned.

This brief moment of rededication to the spirit had a revitalizing effect on us all. When the curtain went up a few minutes later, the stage and the performers were ready, and the magic spread through the theater and embraced the spectators.

I stayed backstage until intermission and watched the audience from behind the curtain. So many shining young faces! Wearing their most colorful costumes, the hippies had turned out in force. The 800 seat theater was packed, people were standing and sitting on the floor in the aisles. The aroma of incense filled the theater, bells tingled, beads shone, and hardly a short-haired male could be seen. But it wasn't just their get-up that differed from the usual theater audience. In Storming Heaven, Jay Stevens quotes Diane Trilling, who along with her husband Lionel Trilling deeply disapproved of the performance. She was especially upset by the quality of the audience:

> Young, village, but middle-class, good contemporary faces of the kind one wants to trust, the faces of people to whom intellectual leadership might be thought appropriate, except that they had made another choice and the signal of it was in their eyes. The four of us appeal to each other: Is it only the gifted who go in for this sort of thing? Are these the best, the brightest of their generation?

Although the reaction of the critics was mixed, the success of the show was phenomenal. Meanwhile, preparations for The Resurrection of the Christ had begun. To focus the group mind on the subject, a group LSD session was held at Millbrook. From the loudspeaker came readings from the Bible, Gregorian chants, Bach's organ music. We lay with closed eyes on the living room rug, letting the sounds enter us. There was a beatific smile on the faces of some. You knew that they were transported into some inner heaven. Others looked troubled, thoughtful, and somebody, after about two hours, laughed. Two or three people rose and went outside. There was raw emotion in the room. A nerve had been struck, suppressed feelings came to the fore. In the hall, Jackie Cassen was busily draping the walls and the stairway with roll after roll of toilet paper. To express her feelings about the religion that had been drummed into her as a child?

The money from the performances was rolling in, and Tim was flying high. "Can we meet an hour or so early tonight? There's something I want to talk to you about before we go to the party," he said one afternoon. He and Rosemary were staying at my apartment and we were all going to a party at Billy Hitchcock's Manhattan penthouse that evening.

"We're thinking of opening a Center in New York," Timothy said. "What do you think?"

"What kind of a Center?"

"We'll call it The New York Center for the League of Spiritual Discovery. It will be a place where people can get information. The front room will be an art gallery filled with exquisite objects of psychedelic art, and the back will be a shrine where kids can come off the street and learn something about set and setting. There will be classes and lectures and…Do you like it?"

"That sounds wonderful!" I said. My face was glowing. Tim smiled. "Yes, I thought you'd like it. Well, how about it? Want to be the director?"

"What?" I was flabbergasted.

"Here's the way I see it. You've created a sanctuary in this apartment, an atmosphere that is a haven in the middle of the city. It's this atmosphere that we want at the Center. I've also watched you with the hippies. They trust you, they listen to you. You often talk about how important it is to prepare them for the trip… Well, here's your chance."

I mulled this over in silence.

"I'd have to quit The Third Force Lecture Bureau," I observed.

"You'd earn a good salary. I have a feeling the lecture bureau isn't doing so well. Am I wrong?"

He was right. Things had not worked out the way I hoped. My profit margin was too small to allow me to publicize my business, and the speakers were too avant-garde to receive enough bookings. The idea of earning a decent salary was extremely attractive, and so was the thought of working with the hippies. But I had reservations. By now I had seen some of the casualties of the psychedelic experience. Some of the young people had their slight hold on consensus reality broken by the influx of too much that they could not absorb. I did not wish to contribute to the indiscriminate use of the powerful psychedelics. On the other hand, I reasoned, the horse was out of the stable, the kids were turning on, and no amount of legal suppression could stem the growing tide. As head of the New York Center I could do much to prepare those who were determined to try it, discourage those to whom it would be detrimental, and counsel those who were trying to integrate the experience.

"I'm going to accept Timothy's offer," I told Michel a few days later. When I explained the plan to him, I found him, not unexpectedly, very hostile to the idea.

"I won't permit it," he said. "You're sure to get arrested, and I won't have my name dragged in the mud."

"I'm sorry you feel that way. I won't get arrested. We won't do anything illegal at the Center. No psychedelics will be allowed on the premises."

"How will you stop the kids? It's a crazy idea and I won't have it. I won't be responsible for you if you do it. Choose between me and the Center. It's up to you."

"It is?" Here was the cue I had been waiting for. Michel had blocked all my efforts to convince him of the truth of my desire to end our marriage, and I could see no way to do so gracefully. Now he himself was giving me the opening I needed.

"Don't do it, Nina," a friend had warned when I told her of my intention to get a divorce. "You don't know what it's like to be a divorcee. Do you realize how hard it is to find another husband at your age? I'll always be your friend, of course, but people will stop inviting you to their parties—you'll be a fifth wheel! And you'll have no money! No matter how unhappy you are with Michel, it'll be worse for you alone!" As I listened to her cautious words I marvelled at the distance I had come from the kind of life in which the considerations she spoke of were paramount. I did not want to find another husband, and the parties she mentioned had long lost interest for me. The only thing that frightened me was the prospect of poverty, but Timothy's offer was taking care of that.

"My mind is made up," I told Michel. "I'll take the job."

On the last day of 1966 I moved my personal belongings to the 12th Street apartment and spent New Year's Eve with my Millbrook friends.

A new life began.

Thirty-five

My new freedom was intoxicating. To eat when I want, to sleep when I want, to go out or stay home, visit friends or stay alone and read—it was as if heavy chains had fallen from me.

I joyfully took possession of the 12th Street studio apartment as my new home. The Lawrence house had fourteen rooms. The apartment had one; a large, sunny one with a bathroom and a miniscule kitchenette. I decorated it with the new eyes the psychedelics had given me; and with an ingenuity I did not know I possessed. I used fabrics, mirrors, large branches of trees, and objects trouvées instead of money to convert it into a space that was cozy and comfortable as well as pleasing to the eye. I permitted myself one extravagance—a large white sheepskin rug which gave the room an air of luxury and warmth.

Only one thought marred my happiness: my children. How would they take the news of this final separation? I had written a letter to them at a time when I had not yet found the strength to go through with it. The letter was not sent, but I kept it, knowing that one day I would be ready. Here it is:

Lawrence, June 30, 1965

My dearest children:

I'm leaving your father, and in a way you two as well. You're both adults now. You, Danny, have already removed yourself from much of your physical and emotional dependence on your parents and have become the fine human being I always knew you would be. This final breaking up of your home will bring you much pain, but it will not make too much difference in your life at this point. It is you, my Nicky, who will suffer most. I know how ambivalent your feelings towards me are. You want to free yourself of me, but your love for me keeps you from realizing your own self. It is not my nature to efface myself while I'm here, darling. And so it is probably best to break that imprisoning bond between us in this harsh manner.

If it had not been for the joy you, my children, gave me, and the pleasure I learned to derive from books, thoughts, and the little things in life, I should have long ago been destroyed by the disappointment of this unhappy marriage. I know that both of you feel that I'm to blame for this failure. In your eyes I'm unloving and hard, and this despite the unvarying nurture I have given you for twenty years. But this is not the time to cast blame, neither on you who are torn between two impossible loyalties, nor on your father, whose bitter childhood and youth made it impossible for him to come to terms with himself. Though the years have mellowed him, so that the man you see today only rarely shows the characteristics that poisoned my younger years, there is still enough left to make a warm, companionable relationship between two aging people impossible. In the past, the happiness of being your mother more than compensated for the pain of being his wife, especially since there was no way out without turning your lives into a nightmare. I only hope that once you get over the hurt my present step inflicts on you, you will be able to see that, given the circumstances, your youth has been remarkably sunny.

This is why I expect you to take this blow without self-pity. You owe me that much for the strength I have given you through my love. You're on your own now, as free as anyone can ever be to choose yourselves. What you make of your lives from now on is your own business. I feel proud of a job well done. I have no regrets, no guilt, no self-reproach.

As in the past, your father has again threatened to disappear into Europe and to withdraw all financial support from you and me if I leave him. But with me out of the way, I think he will live up to his obligations to you. As for me, I have no fear of the future, and shall not ask your father for anything. My personal needs are very small, and I believe I'll be able to provide for them with my skills in sewing, or by doing clerical work.

You know that I often get emotional, and so you probably see me sobbing away while I write this letter. But you're wrong. I'm as dry-eyed and sober as I hope you'll be when you read it. My zest for life is as great as when I left my home in Vienna nearly thirty years ago. A whole new life is ahead of me. And you, armed with fine young bodies, first-rate minds, and far, far more wisdom than I had when I set out on my own so long ago—your sky will only momentarily be clouded by my defection. You're still too young and too involved with me to be able to stand back and say, "Good for you, Mom!" But I think you won't hold a grudge against me for too long; we've been too close for that.

What you feel about me now and in the future is your problem. There is nothing I can do about it. You owe me nothing, just as I owe you nothing. The give and take between us in the past has settled all accounts. I have had the rare good fortune to be blessed with two children who have made motherhood a joy. You, in turn, have had the benefit of a mother who never saw herself as a victim. Far from embittered by my marriage, I have remained a yeah-sayer to life, and I opened your eyes to the miracles of nature, of books, and of the perpetual wonder of being alive.

I fervently hope that the blow of losing your home at this time will make you all the more eager to found solid, lasting homes of your own, and to bring into them the values of true companionship between two equals, who happen to be a man and a woman, but who, above all, are two human beings who respect each other rather than vie with each other, who are not engaged in a struggle for the supremacy of one sex over the other, one mind over the other, and one body who sees the other as a means of self-gratification. A man and a woman—equal, yet different. One with a keener mind, the other with a stronger nature to withstand the struggle for survival. Does it make any difference who has what? So many problems could be avoided if the so-called attributes of the sexes could be seen for the artificial constructs they are! But when the male, made arrogant by centuries of rule over the female, and the female, expecting to be wooed and protected by the male, enter into a marriage with these role images in their minds, there's hell to pay!

Two incompatible people, drawn together into a marriage of extremes by war, uncertainty of the future, and sexual attraction…and then forever after separated by alien backgrounds, lack of communication and conflicting ways of seeing life. Clearly, your father and I made a mistake. But this mistake, this inharmonious marriage, has produced incredibly harmonious fruit: you, my children, are the beneficiaries of a broad span of genetic goodies. In you, the concrete and the abstract modes of thought are united, and sensuality and spirituality live side by side. Your instincts are keen, and so is your preparedness for the struggle for survival. Your natures are rich— richer than you as yet suspect. And so our misery is your good fortune. Again, I tell you I have no regrets. Out of all the possible combinations of genes, it took your father and me to produce you. There were dark regions in our lives, and then there was this brightness that is you—and it made all the rest worthwhile.

Whether you will hate me or love me in the years to come seems beside the point right now. You will extract whatever is most conducive to your growth from this experience, that much I know. The older generation is at best manure for the growth of the young. I was the rich black soil in which you grew, my children. It doesn't matter if that soil is now a stink in your nostrils—it fed you well!

Love always,
Your Mother

Curious, I thought as I reread it. I wrote it a year and a half before I smoked marijuana, a year before I took LSD. And yet Michel, as well as people who know me, blame "the drugs" for my desertion! True, the psychedelics gave me the courage to do what I had long wanted to do, but they were hardly the deciding factor!

The truth was that I was dropping out of the narrow circle of my family to drop in on the family of WO-MAN. Now all children were my children. I had found my mission in life. It was to be a midwife to the New Breed. I was here to help them get born.

Once again, I did not send the letter. Was it because I began to have an inkling that my idealized view of motherhood did not entirely correspond to the facts? Most of what the letter said was true. But I had already begun to change, and I recoiled from any hint of hypocrisy. I now saw everything as being simultaneously itself and its opposite. And I knew that my love for my children was by no means unmixed with the occasional regret at the burden, the pain, the self-denial that motherhood inevitably entails.

Meanwhile I was scouting around for a space for the Center. I located three possibilities and asked Tim to look at them. To my surprise, he picked the one I found least attractive. It was a large, dilapidated store front in the West Village, badly in need of repairs.

"Why?" I asked him.

"It has atmosphere. Look!" He picked off some of the thick, cracking plaster that covered the walls. Part of an embossed bronze plaque appeared. "Bet the whole wall is covered with them!" He tested the plaster in other spots. "I was right!" he said triumphantly. "You know, I think the plaques cover even the ceiling! We'll scrape off the plaster...It's great! We'll take it!"

I was not too impressed by this discovery, but when I sized up the place I saw that it had merits. The large rectangular space could be divided into two good-sized areas. The plumbing looked in need of work, and the floor was covered with layers of linoleum on which armies seemed to have marched; but there was plenty of light, and I could visualize a shrine in a recessed area in the rear. But I could also visualize the amount of work that would go into renovating the place, and it looked forbidding.

"Hire some strong men. You should be able to get it cleaned up in a week. Really, Nina! It's perfect!"

His enthusiasm was catching. "Okay. Let's take it. I'll turn it into an island of beauty and serenity, and all who enter will experience the spirit of

Millbrook here," I promised.

The storefront stood in the West Village, on the corner of Hudson Avenue and Perry Street. The neighborhood was not specifically ethnic; all kinds of people lived there, which meant the hippies would blend in without being too noticeable. The rent was reasonable for the size of the space, and I particularly liked the fact that it was within walking distance from my apartment. I called the landlord and arranged to meet him.

"We're ready to sign the lease," I told him.

"We?" he asked.

"Well, actually he. Timothy Leary."

"What? Are you crazy? Think I'll rent this place to Timothy Leary? Forget it!" He was ready to walk out.

"Wait!" I put my hand on his arm. "Just listen to what we'll do here!" I drew a mental picture of the Center for him, and little by little I felt him relent.

"The League for Spiritual Discovery is a legally incorporated non-profit religious organization," I told him. "I'll be in charge. I'll be here every day and make sure everything is legal and under control. Believe me, you have nothing to fear!"

"Well…Call me tomorrow. I'll give you my answer then."

When I called the next day the rent had gone up. But it was still a good price for the amount of space, and the lease was signed. Tim paid three month's rent in advance and I hired two men to chip away at the plaster. After the first day it became glaringly apparent that it would take many long days to reveal Tim's cherished bronze plaques. As for the floor, layers and layers of linoleum had bonded together. Impossible to get them off short of chipping away at them with hammer and chisel. Always the optimist, Tim thought we'd find fine old parquet flooring underneath. When I told him how much work it would take to restore the place, he was undismayed. "Hire more men," he told me.

The two men did not come back the next day. "Too hard," they said. I had no better luck with the next ones, and two weeks went by without any appreciable progress having been made. But the budget Timothy and the League members drew up called for a considerable sum to be spent on the Center, and I went blithely ahead setting up appointments with architects and interior decorators when Tim dropped a bomb.

"Did you cash the check I gave you yesterday?" he asked.

"Yes," I replied. "I had to pay the men."

"It'll bounce. All my checks bounced."

I was speechless. It appeared that the check he had been given by Bill Graham, who managed the theater, had bounced because something had gone awry with the agreement between him and the League.

"What'll happen to the Center? Does this mean we have to abandon it?"

"No. Don't worry. I have a plan. I'll tell you about it tonight before the show."

What his plan amounted to was that he'd make an announcement about the Center during the show and ask for volunteers to help set it up. My enthusiasm was not great, but there seemed to be no alternative.

"Okay," I said. "Tell them to call me."

"No, I'll tell them to see you in the lobby during intermission. That way you can pick out the ones you want right away."

Timothy made the announcement in his usual Pied Piper style. The result was that I was nearly crushed to death by dozens of kids who begged me to put them to work. Most of them looked like they couldn't tell a hammer from a saw, but I picked out a few who seemed more promising and asked them to come to the Center. Among them was a young architect who offered to draw up plans for the alterations. What he came up with was a blueprint that called for a hinged wall that separated the inner and the outer room and could be lifted to turn them into one large space for public lectures.

When the kids came to the Center, I handed each of them a chisel. The zest with which they set to work promised much, but before an hour had gone by I knew that it would take months to get the storefront ready. Work was not what the kids came for anyway. What they wanted was to talk about their trips.

The Center was needed. My frustration with the obstacles I encountered grew. When I accepted Timothy's offer I had been confident that my experience with the Capri Theater prepared me for this venture. In reality, nothing I had ever done came close to the role I now had to take on.

The problems I faced were innumerable. There was not only the lack of money, materials, tools, and skilled workers—there were the youngsters themselves, the hippies, the kids who came to help. These baby-boomers were used to getting their own way. They wanted to do "their own thing," and that meant they resisted any hint of authority. Only one thing they all agreed to respect, and this was the taboo against bringing drugs to the Center. They realized how vulnerable we were, and that the discovery of illegal substances on the premises would inevitably lead to us being closed down. But in most other ways they were stubbornly individualistic. My patience was sorely tried when they played their guitars or blew soap bubbles while the rubble piled up on the floor and most of the plaster still clung to the walls. I hated the bronze plaques. Instead of rejoicing each time another one was exposed to view I was tempted to smash them. I cursed the moment Timothy laid eyes on them and wished a thousand times we had never begun to remove the plaster; but once we started, we had to go on. I was sick of the condition of the store and worried about my economic survival, but Tim was away on a lecture tour and there was nobody at Millbrook who was willing to take on my job.

I knew that my real usefulness did not lie in trying to supervise the work, but in talking with the kids. They saw me as a representative of Millbrook rather than as just a woman their mother's age, which, taken alone, could have marked me as the enemy. They were touchingly eager to tell me about their drug experiences, and I saw what a marvelous opportunity this was to help them gain some perspective on the strange territory of the mind into which they had stumbled.

I needed help. I needed a man who could direct the work.

Don Smoot was a member of Virginia's group. He was doing part-time research work at Maimonides Medical Center. I knew of his interest in psychedelics and had always liked the tall, bearded young man; and so I asked him if he would join me at the Center. I offered him a small salary out of the meager sum at my disposal and was glad when he accepted. I thought that his training as a psychologist and his interest in psychedelics combined with his gentle personality would make him the perfect choice for the task of directing the work. It was not long before I saw my mistake. Don didn't know how to direct the kids any more than he understood the complex blueprint for the swinging wall the architect had drawn up. It furthermore appeared that his gentleness was paired with a good deal of indolence. All too often, he did not appear at the Center when he had promised to come, leaving it unattended if I was not there. To my regret, he proved to be an added burden instead of a relief for me, though in one way, he was the perfect choice. The hippies adored him. But I was no better off than before.

A month passed. Then two. Timothy returned from the lecture tour. In November, he came to the city to see the Center. Knowing how he'd feel when he saw it, I invited him to have lunch with me at the apartment first. I had to prepare him.

"So tell me, how does it look?" he asked as soon as we sat down. Carefully, I described the condition of the place to him. He was furious.

"If you had half the powers you claim to have, you'd have been ready to open two months ago with your hands tied behind your back!" he flung at me.

I looked at him in amazement. "I never claimed to have any powers! I can't perform miracles without money or skilled help! What do you expect me to do with a bunch of hippies who do or do not come when they say they will and then do or do not work? Hah!" It was my turn to be furious. What had prompted him in the first place to offer me this job? And what in the world had prompted me to accept? Job, hah! Some job! It doesn't even pay a salary! A damned volunteer, that's what I am! I was suddenly conscious of the absurdity of my situation and began to laugh. In a moment Timothy joined me and we both laughed at the irony that had turned our lovely plans into this penurious venture. Timothy realized how unreasonable his expectations were and his mood changed.

"It sounds pretty grim," he admitted. "Tell you what. We need a rug!"

I was startled. "A rug? What for?"

"You'll see. Can we take this one?" He pointed to my sheepskin rug.

"Oh no you don't!" I said, indignant. I shuddered at the thought of my immaculate white rug among the rubble at the Center. Timothy laughed.

"Well then, let's get one."

We walked to 14th Street and he bought a large imitation Persian rug at one of the cut-rate stores. The volunteers who were present at the Center that afternoon had an unexpected treat. Doctor Leary helped to clear the floor, spread the rug, and put the small statue of the Buddha donated by one of the kids in the center. He added some candles and the flowers he had also bought, and then led us in our first meditation at the Center. The ritual changed the atmosphere. From that moment on the storefront became The Center for the League of Spiritual Discovery. It took on the character of a shrine, a refuge from the ugliness and violence outside. While alterations continued to go on, a space was cleared every afternoon at 4, the rug was spread, and I led the meditation. A few days after this practice began, a loud rumble broke into the silence, bringing us down to earth with a thud. The garbage truck was making its rounds! It gave me the opportunity to talk about how we can use everything as a tool for meditation by merging with it, rather than fighting it. I told them about my experience with the airplanes in Lawrence, how I had attached my consciousness to one of them and had been taken on a trip…

Some of the kids were innocent of any knowledge of meditation. Others were astonishingly sophisticated about mysticism, East and West, the I Ching, Astrology, and other esoteric subjects. Going to the Center now became an adventure instead of a chore. I eagerly looked forward to my contact with these young people. There was much about them that I admired, and also much by which I was, I hoped without showing it, shocked. Every morning, as I walked to Hudson and Perry from my apartment, I wondered what the day would bring.

Renovations proceeded at a snail's pace. I grew more and more impatient. We were needed; the reaction of the few who found us demonstrated that. How to speed up things?

One day, a short, broad-shouldered man came to the Center. The look in his eyes identified him as one of us, and as he wandered around looking at this and that, I saw an aura of crackling energy around him.

"Looks like you could use some help," he said to me after observing the scene for a while.

"Could I!" I exclaimed.

"I'll help," he said. His name was Eddie Schwartz. If there ever was an answer to my prayers, he was it. Under his direction, renovation now went ahead full steam, and the day of the opening was in sight. The architect's blueprint had been discarded for a much simpler version of a hinged wall, and

Eddie taught the kids how to construct it.

Every day I compiled lists of the materials and supplies we needed and posted them near the door. Miraculously, they often appeared within hours, and even my prayer for someone who knew something about plumbing and electrical work was answered in the person of a fast-talking long-haired "freak" who called himself Reb. He fixed the toilets and installed electrical outlets for the light fixtures donated by someone else. The only sore spot that remained was the floor. We had given up on the futile job of removing the old linoleum, and the shabby floor looked even shabbier by contrast with the splendor of the bronze tiles, now fully revealed. I spoke to Richard Alpert about it and about another matter that weighed heavily on my mind.

"I'm not happy with the idea of an expensive art gallery," I told him. "The kids who are served by the Center are not the kind who will be comfortable if they have to pass through it to get to the meditation room. It will send them a signal to buy something before they can enter the inner sanctum, and may keep them away. Anyway, where will I get the money to buy art works? No, I must find another way!"

"You're absolutely right," Richard replied. "The way to support the Center is with love money—money given freely, from the heart. And listen, I have a solution for the floor. I have an uncle who has a mattress factory. I'm sure I can get him to donate enough mattresses to line the floor. What do you think?"

I looked dubious. I envisioned kids' bodies sprawled all over the place. Richard caught my look. "Well, think it over. Forget about the art gallery. Charge for lectures and classes, but for the rest, let people contribute what they can. Do let me know about the mattresses as soon as you can. I'm going to India in a few weeks."

Neither of us knew then that the worldly Richard Alpert who piloted his own plane would come back from that trip as Baba Ram Dass, the ascetic disciple of the Indian guru who transformed his life.

I declined his offer of the mattresses, but agreed with him about the love money. Timothy also agreed.

"The League can carry the rent for the Center a couple of months longer, but it has to become self-supporting after that. If you think you can do it with love money, go ahead!"

Most of the problems that stood in the way of the opening had been solved. Only one remained. One day, as I looked despairingly at the disfiguring expanse of chipped linoleum, a man walked in. His face was flushed red with anger.

"Is this where you teach kids to fry their brains?" he shouted, glaring at me.

I smiled. "Do they look as if their brains were fried?" I asked, pointing to the youngsters who were industriously installing the sliding wall. It was a pleasant sight: four long-haired teen-aged boys wearing beads, colorful shirts and patched pants, cheerfully wielding screwdrivers, hammers and saws. Others were standing on ladders attaching the light fixtures to the ceiling, while others still were setting up the shrine in the rear under my direction. Not even the most rabid opponent to drugs could have found anything here to support his views. For a while, I just let the man watch.

"They're all volunteers," I told him. "They come to help because they want the Center to open. There will be lectures and classes to teach them to have religious experiences without drugs."

"Religious experiences! What are you talking about?" the man exclaimed. It had obviously never occurred to him that the drugs could have anything to do with religion.

I explained the connection in as simple words as I could muster, and the man's face relaxed. "Well, if that's what's going on here…Maybe I should send you my son."

We began to talk, and it appeared that he was very worried about his son whom he had caught smoking grass. "Yes, do send him," I said. In the course of conversation I learned that he was a salesman for a carpeting firm. "You'll need to carpet this floor," he said. "I could give you a reasonable price for… Let's see. How many square feet do you have?"

"A lot. But we can't afford to spend any money on carpeting. We don't have it. I've been praying that somebody will come along who can donate it," I said ruefully.

"You have? Well, maybe I can help," he offered. "How would you like a lot of the three foot squares we use as samples? They're all different colors, but they'd do the job!"

I was ecstatic. The colored squares became an important feature of the Center's decoration. We laid them out in geometric patterns, and the problem of the floor was solved. The opening was set for March 3rd, 1967. My volunteers and I looked forward to it with great excitement.

Thirty-six

The swinging wall is raised. The space looks like a seatless lecture hall. I'm glad the hippies like to sit on the floor—our budget could not have stretched to include chairs. I figure there is room for about 200 people. We're asking for a contribution of $2.00, that means we can make about 400 bucks. We need it! I hope we have a full house. I sweep the carpet one last time and look around to see if anything else has to be done. It is 6 pm. Timothy's lecture is scheduled for 8. I'm alone. My volunteers will come at seven to man the door. The place looks good. Far better than I could have hoped.

The door opens. It is Jean. "May the Center bloom like these flowers!" she says, handing me a bouquet of roses.

I have hardly taken the flowers from her when the door opens again. An avalanche of bodies presses into the room. Within minutes, the space is filled. There goes the money, I think ruefully. It's useless to try to stem this tide. Soon. every inch of floor space is occupied and the door closes behind those who entered last. Outside, people are lined up around the block.

Timothy begins to speak. The room is swept up in his energy field. The hippies love this man who tells them to question authority and to think for themselves. The main thrust of Leary's work is to prod human consciousness into opening up to the untold possibilities that slumber in that billion-celled computer we call the human brain, 95% of which we do not use. A tightrope dancer on the beam of evolution, Timothy trusts our ability to grow, to evolve.

The Center is launched. All is well, except for the money. But there will be other lectures, and next time, we'll be prepared.

♥ ♥ ♥

And there were more lectures. Leary, Alpert, Metzner, Ginsberg and other authorities on psychedelic drugs and meditation techniques gave weekly talks at the Center. Afterwards, a few of us would generally gather at my apartment. I remember one occasion when Rosemary, who did not like to leave Millbrook, came to the city to hear Timothy's talk. Afterwards, the three of us walked to my place. On the way, Tim bought a bottle of champagne. I noticed that he directed some sly digs at Rosemary, who was white-faced and silent. I was not unaware of a side of Tim's personality that could cut like broken glass, but had never seen him use it on the woman he loved. That evening, however, his caustic remarks brought her close to tears. Not knowing what it was all about I was relieved when the other guests arrived: Allen Ginsberg, Richard Alpert, the Hindu teacher Shyam Bhatnagar who used musical vibrations as aids to healing, and his tall young disciple John Shewel.

In high spirits, the men traded cosmic jokes. As usual, Timothy held center stage. Rosemary, even more quiet than usual, attempted a wan smile from time to time, but the hurt, drawn look did not leave her face. Tim drank incessantly. When he had emptied the bottle of champagne (the rest of us having declined), he made such a venomous remark to Rosemary that she left the room, fighting down her tears. I followed her.

"What's going on?" I asked.

"He wanted me to bring his phonograph to the Center, and I didn't. I know how much he'd miss it," she sobbed. "He'd be in a stew if it were gone!"

I had to laugh. "What a dilemma! Part of him wants to give everything away, and another part wants to keep it, so he makes you the scapegoat!" It was funny. Rosemary could see it too and we both laughed when we joined the others.

The talk showed no signs of slowing down. It was near dawn when the party broke up. Allen and Richard had left, Rosemary was waiting by the elevator, Shyam and John were saying good night. At the door, Timothy suddenly turned on me.

"If you weren't so selfish, you'd bring all that to the Center," he said, making a sweeping gesture that covered the objects in my apartment.

I grew rigid, ready for a fight. Sensing the tension between us, Shyam and John came and stood beside me. I took a deep breath and made myself relax.

"Sorry about that, Tim," I said calmly. "I need beauty around me when I come home to recharge my batteries. And you need to hear good music on a good phonograph."

As suddenly as it had appeared, the anger left his eyes. He flashed his famous smile, kissed my cheek, and followed Rosemary.

♥ ♥ ♥

The sign above the front door spells The Center for the League of Spiritual Discovery. The initials L S D stand out in full psychedelic brilliance. Isaac Abrams, the young man whose painting had graced my United Nations Plaza office, has decorated the two pillars that flank the door with designs that flow from his hand almost unbidden. The door is made of fine wood and was once handsome; now it shows wear and tear and forms a strange contrast to the bold colors of the sign. In the front room, book shelves made of rough planks run along one wall. On a low table are reprints of papers about the psychedelics, and on the wall behind the desk hang some posters and psychedelic paintings. It's a Spartan room. Tim was right; it would be greatly improved by some of my possessions; but the colorful carpet squares and cushions do much to offset its severity; the only chair in the room is a rickety one behind the desk. I insisted on it. Sitting on the floor is becoming easier for me, but not more comfortable. "I've lived in a body that's used to chairs for 47 years," I told the hippies to whom chairs are as much a badge of the straight world as short hair.

A few of what I have begun to call "my kids" sit on the cushions. Some of them are reading, others talk. There is much sharing of food and passing around of objects and books. A feeling of camaraderie and good vibes fills the room.

In the meditation room, the Buddha sits serenely in the niche. I lined it with a piece of the midnight blue velvet that covers the swinging wall. When we discovered that the thin plywood of the wall let every sound through from the front room, we sent out a call for help. A few days later, a young man brought a huge velvet curtain that had once covered the stage of a defunct theater. It was the perfect solution for our sound problem and added warmth and dignity to the otherwise bare room.

Along the walls, a few neatly covered mattresses are lined up. The soft rat-tat-tat of an Indian tabla comes from a record player whose sound leaves much to be desired (hence Timothy's wish to give us his). There are fresh flowers; some sticks of incense are stuck in an orange next to the Buddha and send out sparks that dance in the dark, candle-lit room. Timothy's rug lies in the center, surrounded by the carpet samples. The room is no more opulent than the one in the front, but the shadows of the candles play on the bronze walls and ceiling, and the thick blue velvet curtain enfolds the room in a nest-like embrace.

"It looks good, Nina," Timothy conceded. "It's a good setting for the work we can do to educate people about the constructive use of LSD." His faith in the power of the psychedelics to take us a step further on the evolutionary ladder is unshaken. The psychedelics undeniably play a large role in the emerging New Age consciousness. I strongly believe in the need to educate and prepare those who are ready to take LSD, and I hope that people will learn to treat the psychedelics with the reverence, the respect, and the caution they deserve. They can take us to heaven, or they can take us to hell. They can illuminate us, or they can drive us mad.

I'm pleased that Timothy likes the Center. I deserve to bask in the glory of a job well done. But there is still much to do. For one thing, I want the symbols of all religions in the shrine. Religious wars still rage in different corners of the earth. We must learn to treasure the unity in our diversity, or we are lost. But it's best to start with Buddhism—the only religion that never caused blood to be shed. Ultimately, I hope, all religious dogma will be replaced by direct, personal experience.

ONE FOOT IN THE FUTURE

Thirty-seven

"God grant me one more day of openness," I pray every morning as I walk to the Center. Every day challenges my preconceived notions anew. The elements I come in contact with are worlds removed from the predictable world of the suburbs. Each day confronts me with new discoveries.

And they come. They all come to the Center, the spaced-out mystics, the Messiahs, the fanatics, the saintly souls, and the hippies—the true flower children, the bearers of the new consciousness. First there were only the original ones, the crew. Then came the others. They look at the books and the brochures, sit on the floor reading, talking, playing the guitar. Most of them are young, under 25. Their clothes are in varying degrees of disrepair. You have to look funky—neatness is what separates the straights from the hip. That, and the beads, and the length of hair. The '60s are the hirsute decade. Hair, hair, it's everywhere. To these shiny-eyed, alert youngsters, "to belong" means to look as different as possible. Some of them have an undefinable glow—the acid glow, as I have come to call it. They seem almost ethereal, absorbed in the visionary world. The children of an affluent society, their needs have always been taken care of by Mom and Dad. There are two cars in the garage of the split-level home filled with consumer goods, none of which brought happiness to the families who live in them. To the children, the magical world of comic books is more attractive than that of the adults among whom they grew up. There is Superman, and Spiderman, and Popeye the Sailor whose muscles bulge when he eats the magical spinach. No wonder the children are drawn to the drugs that promise the magical mystery tour. Unlike their parents, they believe in magic.

Most of the time I sit behind a desk placed near the entrance door. The people who come in generally stop to talk to me before they look around. With some, an immediate rapport is established; others are suspicious of me and need to check me out.

"What do you think about LSD?" A pair of hazel eyes cooly look me over. He is about 18, wears a faded patchwork shirt, love beads, blue jeans torn at the knees, and shoulder-length unkempt hair. He is waiting.

I'm on trial. I'm middle-aged, wear lipstick and straight clothes. But I know something that all who have taken LSD know, and that is that there are levels of consciousness of which we know nothing in our normal state.

"Acid? It can take you on a trip to heaven, or on a trip to hell. I've been to both. How about you?"

He grins. "Yeah. Me too."

I passed the test. He sits on the floor. His legs fold gracefully into the half-lotus seat.

"You could be my mother!" he says. "You're about her age! Man, she'd die if she knew I take acid!"

"Do you want her to know?"

"Sure, but I know how she'd react. Wish I could turn her on! She's straight, but she's okay—know what I mean? An okay mom. I'd sure like to turn her on!"

"Why?"

"Because, like, she'd see. The games. The ego trips. The hype. The guilt. I mean, she'd really see!"

"Is that what you see on your trips?"

"Sure. That, and a lot more. Colors. Stars. And how everything hangs together. I don't know, man! I can't describe it!"

"I know what you mean! We're all trying to find the right words! When did you first trip? How old were you?" He was 16, two years ago. Has tripped often since then. I ask if he has mostly good trips. He thinks for a moment and then looks up.

"Good? I guess they are, even the scary ones."

"Ah yes, the wrathful deities!" He looks blank. "The Tibetans call our scary visions 'the wrathful deities'. The wrathful deities are the other side of the gods. They need each other, like the cops need the robbers."

The boy is quiet. His head is tilted to one side as he sits deep in thought.

"Does that mean everybody sometimes gets into a bad place?"

"Sure does. Do you trip alone, or with friends?"

"Mostly I turn on with Jim and Rick. We go to the park in Brooklyn. We have a ball."

"What do you mean, a ball?"

"We see things. You know—the trees dance and everything is, like, alive! It's like we don't have to talk to each other because we're all tuned in. Sometimes I see funny things, like lights around people. Some people, I mean. Man, I thought I was flipping out when I started seeing it!"

"That light is called an aura. Some people can see it all the time. Does it still scare you?"

"Nah. Rick sees it too. He even sees it in colors. I just see a light around some people—their heads, mostly. No, it doesn't scare me. Tell you what does scare me: it's when I—when I, like, slip out of my body. Like, I'm over there (he points across the room), or up there (he points at the ceiling), and I see me over here (pointing to himself), but I'm there! I know it sounds crazy, believe me! But it's true!"

He is agitated. "It's okay," I reassure him. "It happens to lots of us! I was lucky," I say, really meaning it. "I'd been reading lots of books about things like that before I began to turn on. That's why I wasn't scared when it happened."

"There are books about that?" he asks, incredulous.

"Sure. Some of them are ancient."

"But acid was only invented in 1938," he objects.

"That's true. But the state of consciousness it produces is as old as humanity itself. There have always been people who ate or smoked psychedelic plants, or practiced yoga, or used other methods to get into altered states. A trip is really a journey into the unknown territories of the mind, whether you get there by fasting, chanting, whirling, meditating, controlling the breath. What they all have in common is that they change the chemistry of the brain. Do you know about ESP?"

"ESP? No, never heard of it."

"It's short for extra-sensory perception. It deals with psychic phenomena—

things like getting out of the body. We probably have some books on the subject. You might want to look at them. Why don't you join them while I find one for you?" I point to the group that sits on the floor. By now we have a small but sufficiently representative selection of volumes on our bookshelves. I pick out Astral Projection by Oliver Fox. As always, I marvel at the ease with which books like this can now be found. The heavens have opened and poured down on us the hidden teachings that were kept secret for so long. Less than a decade ago, books on astral projection, astrology, the Tarot, even the I Ching, were as hard to come by as roses in the snow.

Most of our books are brought by the kids. Again and again, I find books as well as incense, candles and crystals in the barrel that stands near the door. The empty barrel happened to catch my eye when I looked around for something that would symbolize our need for support. I fixed it up to look like a wishing well and posted a flowery sign next to it asking for contributions. At the end of the day I dive in and fish out the day's take. What I come up with is rarely in the shape of greenbacks. The gifts in the wishing well are given with great love, but they don't help pay the bills. Financially, we just limp along. We ask for voluntary contributions to the lectures and classes instead of fixed rates. Occasionally, someone will drop in a $20 note, usually an adult. But my beautiful flower children are dirt poor, so poor that a drunk, who comes in to sing loud Irish songs for us brought me a bag of stewing meat. "Here, Mama, make them a good strong stew!" he told me.

Right now the kids are discussing evolution.

"Survival of the fittest!" I hear Gary say.Ô

"A dog-eat-dog world, you mean? I think you're wrong; maybe it was true once, but it's survival of the smartest now, not of the strongest," George says. He is a slight, bespectacled youngster with the nearsighted eyes of the bookish.

"The fittest can mean the smartest," Karen interjects. "It's still a universal law."

"There are no universal laws. We all have to eat, sleep and shit. And make babies. That's all. Killing is considered honorable in primitive societies, and in our own it's mandatory to kill in war," Stewart says. He wears a tattered army coat and is obsessed with a hatred of war.

"Only the fittest survive," Gary insists. He is a student at N.Y.U. and has a hard time reconciling what he hears in his classes with the insights he gains on his acid trips.

"No, only the most adaptable," Ellen says. Adaptability is something she knows about. She was born into a well-to-do family and ran away from home two years ago, when she was 15. She drifted from crash pad to crash pad until she found a job as a waitress. Now she earns enough to pay for a walk-up she shares with two friends. "I'm never going to be a consumer," she had told me when she first came to the Center. "My mom used to redecorate the living room each time she changed the color of her hair. I think people who amass money so they can buy more things are stupid."

"In the Aquarian Age there will be no need to adapt," Judy states in her high-pitched, flat voice. She has been in and out of mental institutions where she was diagnosed as an incurable schizophrenic. She feels welcome at the Center. Her words are sometimes amazingly profound; the kids regard her with something akin to reverence. Judy's cryptic remarks and her strange sudden laughter make her a kind of guru to the rest.

I slip into the meditation room. The aroma of incense hits my nostrils; soft Indian music fills my ears. In the semi-darkness some twelve people sit in the room. They are deeply absorbed in their own inner world. Some sit with their eyes closed and a beatific expression on their faces. Others look pensive, troubled. One young woman has fallen back on the mattress and lies prone. I approach her.

"Sit up, Helen," I whisper in her ear. As if suddenly waking up, she rises to a sitting position. The kids know they should not lie down in the meditation room. A sign with a figure in the lotus seat and the words "Let us honor the meditation room by sitting up like the Buddha" is pinned to the door, and whenever possible, I remind the meditators of it. Helen smiles at me. She does not resent my reminder. Thank God, the kids have accepted me. I'm still a mother figure to them, but they don't see me as an authority figure, and they know I'm on their side, even if I occasionally scold them.

"I need to talk to you, Nina," a young man whispers as I pass. "Sure, John. Any time." John is one of the most ardent meditators. He started to take acid in his freshman year in college and had some deeply spiritual experiences. Determined to be a saint, he spends most of his time at the Center meditating, or trying to talk about his experiences.

I return to the front room. A stocky, middle-aged man stands at my desk. He wears an overcoat and a tie and is staring at the group on the floor.

"Can I help you?" I ask him.

The man looks baffled. This is not what he expected to find in an LSD Center. He wasn't prepared for a bunch of hippies engaged in calm discussion. He looks ill at ease as he stands trying to glare down at me, but only manages to look perplexed.

"What do you people think you're doing?" he brings out.

"We're teaching young people about LSD," I say, looking calmly into his eyes. "We tell them about its good points and its dangers."

"Aha, so you admit that it's dangerous!" he says triumphantly.

"Certainly. LSD can be as dangerous as an airplane in the hands of a pilot who doesn't know how to fly. The mystery schools of ancient Egypt and Greece prepared their students for years before they were initiated. LSD is strong medicine. It's not for everybody."

"You bet! Then why doesn't your Doctor Leary say so?"

"He does! He always injects a note of warning in his talks! People hear only what they want to hear. Look, here is a transcript of one of his talks." I hand him a paper in which I underline the following sentence:

> There are many predisposing factors—intellectual, emotional, spiritual, social—which cause one person to be ready for a dramatic mind-opening experience and which lead another to shrink back from new levels of awareness.

The visitor's face is thoughtful. There is nothing here to confirm the rumors he has heard about LSD. He tells me about his son. The youngster, a good student and a "regular American boy" has changed, and the father is alarmed. Could it be drugs? We talk for a while, and then he, like most of the others who come through the door loaded with angry thoughts, leaves pacified. Some even become our friends and drop in on us from time to time. The capacity of the kids to welcome anyone into their circle is boundless. How trusting, how gullible, how naive they are! Perhaps it is this quality that accounts for what happened with the policeman.

"Here it comes," I thought when I saw him enter the door. "Michel was right!" But then I rapidly remind myself that we have nothing to fear—we have done nothing illegal here.

"It's just routine," the policeman assures me. "I'm just here to look around, not on official business." His eyes sweep the room, looking for suspicious signs. The kids' get-ups and the wild unruly hair tumbling over their faces gives them the appearance of Gypsies; one of them is playing the guitar, some of the others are singing. Their peacefulness and gentleness cannot be missed.

"What makes them so peaceful?" the officer asks.

"It's their idealism, I think. And their faith. They think we can all change and love each other. They really believe it! They believe we are all one."

"And that's because they take LSD?"

"It could have something to do with it, but it doesn't necessarily work that way. The drug can only bring out what's already there. Would you like to take a look at some of these? They have a lot of information." I hand him some reprints. He thanks me warmly, and leaves.

Two weeks later he comes again. "Can I take some of these along?" he asks, gathering up several pamphlets. "Interesting stuff," he remarks. "You know, all we hear about LSD is the bad stuff. I'll show these to some of my colleagues." The next time, he has a request. Could he bring three boys who are making trouble on the block to the Center?

"Bet they're the ones who cracked our window!" I say, feeling vindictive. One morning when I opened the Center I found a window in the Meditation Room cracked. It looked like it was caused by a small rock or a ball.

"Guess so," he replies. "They're tough street kids. Bullies. Maybe you can straighten them out? Don't worry, I'll keep an eye on them. If they make trouble, out they go. Okay?"

"Oh well," I say. "We'll give it a try."

He says he'd bring the boys by in an hour. The young hoodlums come charging through the door and then stop dead in their tracks. Aged between 8 and 10, they have the round heads and husky build typical of most neighborhood bullies. What stops them is the greeting they receive. Alerted by me about the visitors, the hippies are determined to reform the boys with love. The three toughs are used to scowling faces; here, they look at beaming smiles. It is too much. Struck by a common impulse, all three turn around and flee. At the door, one of them points to his head. "Loco!" he shouts, and runs after the others.

We did not, alas, succeed in reforming the boys, but from then on, they leave the Center alone, though they continue to wreak havoc on the rest of the street.

Like the Millbrook population, the minds of the kids who come to the Center are not focused on "the material plane." They litter. We clean up after them, but we need some way to make them aware of the problem they cause. Gently. A sign saying simply, DON'T LITTER, would bring visions of the police state to the young drop-outs' minds and provoke them to contrary acts. Signs and messages have to be worded in poetic or funny terms and adorned with psychedelic art.

"We need a sign that says DON'T LITTER." I tell Eddie Schwartz.

"I'll make one," he offers. Within an hour, he presents me with the superb drawing of a goddess. On the bottom it says DON'T BE A LITTERBUG. The picture is an example of the flood of creativity that poured out of the young people in the '60s. Eddie did not call himself an artist, though his talent is obvious in that sketch. He tossed it off almost carelessly, playfully, the way much of the art of that period was produced.

Thirty-eight

It was not easy to keep things running smoothly at the Center. One person setting his or her will against the others had a paralyzing effect. When Malcolm woke us up at the crack of dawn at Millbrook, nobody wanted to oppose him. Here it was the same. For a brief span in the '60s, the Saint was the culture hero. Collectively, the flower children projected such gentleness, meekness, openness, and faith that a nation—indeed, the world—fell in love with them. Power-hunger and ruthlessness seemed to have gone out of style. One truculent, nervy kid was enough to change the atmosphere at the Center. Fortunately, the few trouble-makers soon stayed away. Not much fun trying to provoke the gentle flower children. It was as if a force field were activated around us, holding us safe and secure from all negative interference.

Financially, on the other hand, we were barely ahead a few bucks after the monthly rent was paid. For my saintly young friends, the money motive did not exist. As long as our actions are pure and do not come from selfish motives, our needs will be supplied, they believed. So far, they had been right. I felt almost ashamed whenever worries for the future arose in my mind. HERE and NOW, they said, and "The lilies in the field..." I learned from them about faith, and love, and harmlessness, and sharing, and I sailed along with them on clouds of utopian visions.

The kids respected the "no dope on the premises" rule, but they would sometimes take LSD at home or on the street and then come to the Center to trip. The Center was open 24 hours a day; people were manning the hot line and were available to help anyone on a bad trip. Not too many of these happened at that time. Sometimes a wild-eyed hippie would burst in, face distorted, breathing labored. He or she would be escorted to the meditation room, where, once seated, he/she would grow calm. This was true of almost all who came in agitated. If they needed more attention, I or one of the volunteers would take them to a small side room and sit with them until we had talked them down. But this was rarely necessary. It was becoming known in hippie circles that the good vibes that radiated from the Center could be felt for blocks. Our reputation spread. More and more people came flocking through the ramshackle door, and my workload kept increasing. Eddie Schwartz had gone to live at Millbrook with his wife Loraine. I felt lost without him. There was so much to do, what with ongoing classes and lectures that had to be scheduled, networking with other groups, talking to irate parents, interested strangers, freaked-out kids, religious fanatics, the idle curious, mystics, people who wanted to sell something, drunks who came from the near-by Bowery to talk to a captive audience—all needed attention. And in addition, there were the bills.

When I told Timothy that I was getting burned out, he sent some people from Millbrook to help me. The first to arrive were Carol and Bob. Bob was the young man whose passion for organic gardening had transformed a fallow patch into a rich vegetable garden. He and Carol, the mother of 12-year-old Eric, were soon to be married. The hippies called blue-eyed Carol "the Corn Maiden." Her blond beauty made it easy to think she stepped right out of an Indian myth. I was happy to see the couple. They brought the clean Millbrook air to the city.

"You look pooped," Carol commented when we finished hugging. It was true. I had not taken a day off since the Center's opening. "Why don't you take a rest? Go to Millbrook for a few days. Bob and I will look after the Center; won't we, Bob?"

"Sure. That's why we came. We'll stay a week—couldn't take the city longer. While we're here, there's no need for you to come in. We're not going anywhere in this crazy city! This is probably the only sane place. Relax, take it easy. We'll look after things."

I almost wept with relief. I had not known until that moment how depleted I felt. I didn't go to Millbrook; instead, I cloistered myself in my apartment.

More than anything, I wanted to go to the source again, the place of the inspiration for my work with the hippies. I wanted to smoke D.E.T. again—alone this time.

It was late at night when I put a match under the glass pipe. When I came down, I wrote the following:

> A huge book is open before me. An invisible hand turns the pages. It is the book of the history of humanity. On the first page is Adam and Eve. This is followed by page after page of humans in different periods and different clothes. I recognize the same Adam and Eve in them all. As the pages turn, I see conquerors, heads of state, philosophers, and inventors pass before my eyes. And then suddenly, a Joker pops up from behind the book. He looks just like the jokers in the card games I used to play with Nita.
>
> "Hah hah hah," he laughs tauntingly. "Took the wrong turn there, didn't you? Hah hah hah!" The page that lies open shows Gutenberg's invention of the printing press!

What a strange vision for me who dotes on books! Surely this did not come from my subconscious! But from where? And why would literacy and the ability to disseminate printed material have set us on the wrong course? Would it have been better to continue the oral traditions, to keep the art of writing in the monasteries and perhaps teach it to the children of the rich? Is the spread of culture that the printing press made possible an evil, not a good?

I stayed home three days. On the fourth, I had a strong urge to go to the Center. In the front room, a ladder was leaning against a wall, and at its foot stood several cans of white paint. Paint brush in hand, Bob was about to mount the ladder.

"What are you doing?" I yelled.

"Nina! We didn't expect you till next week! We wanted to surprise you!" Bob said, kissing me on the cheek.

"Yes," Carol said. "We were going to have it all done by the time you came back." The Corn Maiden's blue eyes shone.

"Have what done? What are you talking about?" I was filled with foreboding.

"The walls. And the ceiling. We wanted to take these dreadful metal things off, but they're stuck on tight. So the next best thing is to cover them with paint. It'll need a few coats, but we don't mind. You'll love it. We'll have it all done by the end of the week."

I was dazed. "Why do you want to do it?" I asked.

"Well, you know. Metal belongs underground."

"It does? Who says so?"

"Timothy. He says all metal should be returned underground."

I burst out laughing. I laughed so hard that I wound up crying. Carol and Bob looked bewildered. When I explained that it was this very metal that made Tim want to rent this place they looked pained. "Come on," I said, "you're not taking every word Timothy says as gospel, are you?"

"It's not because he says it. I agree with him," Bob stated.

"And so do I," Carol affirmed. "Besides, these plaques are ugly. But if you don't want us to, we won't touch them."

I thanked God I had arrived in time. The faith these young people placed in the words of their prophets! I had watched in astonishment as the gurus gathered devoted followers who listened to their teachings as if these came from them and not from the ancient books that I, too, had read. The cult of the personality would reach a peak of absurdity when the nation elected an actor as president, but the cults that spring up around a charismatic figure show that there must be something in our genes that predisposes so many to turn their hearts and minds over to someone who speaks with authority. It was—is—common for followers to discuss, examine and analyze every move their leader makes. If he places his fork a certain way, it is taken as a code of some kind, expressing something inexpressible and vastly important. This is not to say that I believe no such exceptional individuals have ever existed. But they are rare. For the most part, our leaders still have to peel their own onions; they're still human, and that means that the opposites prevail in them, as in us all.

Timothy himself often warned against believing everything he said. "Tomorrow I may change my mind," he would say. He knew of the idolatry of some of his followers, and he feared it. "Those who see me as God today will see me as the devil tomorrow," he once said. This brought an episode to mind that demonstrates how he wished to avoid adulation. It was at Millbrook. I was tripping in the Denisons' spacious upstairs room. Ruth Denison stayed with me as my guide. The community was planning a group session that night, but I had chosen to trip by myself during the day. I was lying on the bed with my eyes closed. When I opened them, Timothy was bending over me. He was dressed for the group session, all in white. With my vision heightened by the acid I thought I had never seen a more beautiful, luminous human being. The thought must have shown in my eyes because Timothy's face changed into a hideous grimace. He crossed his eyes, stuck out his tongue, bared his teeth, drooled. He looked so weird and yet so comical that I guffawed. Divine beauty, devilish ugliness: twin illusions, they dwell side by side.

Timothy also sent me Herbie Grubb from Millbrook. Herbie wore an Indian headband on his long sandy hair. His pimply face was serious and impish at the same time. Where most of the other youngsters searched in the East for answers to their questions, Herbie's interest was riveted on the American Indian. He was either peering at the pages of books on Indian art or making sand paintings on paper. Sitting on the floor in the front room he would paint and munch on ginger snaps. The boy was very gifted, and his interest in esoteric subjects was deep. I talked with him about the similarities between some of the North American native rituals and those of the Tibetan Buddhists. He listened with deep concentration and began to take books from the shelves that illustrated these similarities.

One day a girl of perhaps 19 came in. She sat on the floor facing my desk, and stared at me. Huge, dark, shining eyes fringed by long lashes sat in a perfectly proportioned oval face. Her small body could have belonged to a Dresden doll; long, silken hair fell in chestnut waves to her shoulders. She was exquisite—a vision of loveliness such as is rarely seen except on the screen. Her eyes remained on my face for a long time.

"You're beautiful," she said at last. I knew that her words referred less to my looks than to something intangible that she had seen. She was full of questions about LSD. The Center was her first contact with the world of psychedelics, but she had read about them and was curious. I was happy to answer her. Her bright, lively mind was uncontaminated by the scandal-hungry press that surrounded LSD. Alexandra came every day, listened to lectures, took classes, and met Fred Blacker, who fell in love with her and carried her off to Millbrook. I quoted her thoughts about the mansion in Part III, Chapter 1.

Various counterculture groups approached me. I became an active participant in some of the meetings where activists, community planners, ecologists, peace groups, counter culture economists and members of the underground press met. The level of intelligence of these young people never failed to impress me; their methods of dealing with the establishment, however, left much room for improvement. They thought they could awaken the straight world from the idiocy of war, competitiveness, acquisitiveness and racism by using the logic of their idealism, but the chasm that yawned between them and the straight world was miles deep. The language they used to express their ideas turned English into the tower of Babel. It was not surprising that no meeting of minds could take place. To me, these eager young messengers of the Aquarian Age looked like Don Quixotes tilting at an immovable force with the weapons of their inexperience. How brave they were! They wanted to raise the world's consciousness, meanwhile living in poverty in squalid "pads" where they discussed ways to accomplish this goal endlessly, far into the night.

We all operated on shoestrings, struggling to keep things going day by day. When Murray Levy announced that he planned to rent Madison Square Garden for a psychedelic showcase, he was greeted with skeptical applause. Madison Square Garden sounded a bit grandiose, but the idea itself was good. We needed a showcase, a place where the straight world could view the psychedelic community instead of reading about it. To them, we were a breed apart. What they knew about us came from the media. Unfortunately, some of what the hippies themselves fed to the media only aggravated the situation. The media were always looking for attention-getting news, and the hippies knew how to provide it. The ploys they used to get their message out were brilliant. They were convinced that if their message were heard, we would all wake up in a better world. Time to put away the dog-eat-dog mentality that dominates our society, they were saying. Time to celebrate our differences, to celebrate life, and to know that we are eternal. But their wisdom, their quicksilver wit, their humor, their jargon, their long hair and the way they dressed were too far out, too threatening to the society. They were getting through to each other, but not to the straight world.

What was needed was to establish personal contact with the public, some of us believed. If we met people directly, we reasoned, if we had a chance to come together face to face, they'd see our deep desire to merge with them, to do away with the we—they barrier. The showcase could give us a chance to do that. It would prove that we are productive, and that we want to spread love, peace, and faith.

It was not Madison Square Garden Levy had rented when he spoke to us again. The closest he came was that the name Madison also appeared in the locality he now proposed. The storefront on Madison Avenue could have fitted in one of the Garden's dressing rooms. A brush with reality had convinced our entrepreneur to lower his ambitions. "It's a dry run," he told us. "Madison Square Garden will come later. Let's see first what we can do." We agreed. An empty storefront was a better proving ground than Madison Square Garden. It was before craft shows and renaissance fairs became popular. There were no models for what we were doing, which left us free to improvise wildly.

We had two hours to set up. At eleven a.m., when the doors opened, the space had been transformed. Rainbow-hued cloths draped over cords separated the space into booths. The booths were set up with flair and ingenuity and displayed new, original products. The effect was dazzling. There were paintings and sculptures, crafts, books, jewelry, games, and music, and there were open, friendly faces and hippies who greeted you with a smile.

We set up the booth for the Center in the rear. We had nothing to sell, but here was a chance to represent The League to the public. After much debate and discussion we had settled on making our booth look like the meditation room at the Center. We brought Timothy's carpet, the Buddha, cushions, Indian bedspreads, and with candles, incense and music we created an atmosphere that was as much like that at the Center as we possibly could.

Around noon, the place began to fill up. We had struck a nerve in this conservative neighborhood. The people could relate to the commercial aspect of the showcase. It's easy to talk with someone who has something to sell. These hippies are harmless, the people decided. They're just trying to make a buck.

Our booth was not trying to make a buck. Lit by candles and a revolving lamp which threw changing colors and patterns on the ceiling, and sending out incense signals to the nostrils of the curious, our booth must have been an exotic sight at that time and in that place. Several of the kids sat with me on the floor. We talked, sang, passed fruit juice and crackers, and talked. We did nothing we wouldn't have normally done, and nothing to attract attention. Some people stopped to stare, waiting to see the freaks do something weird. I was beginning to feel pretty silly sitting there, when a thought flashed through my mind: what if some of my Five Towns friends were to step through that door? What would I do? The answer came at once.

"Come join us," I invited the elegant woman who had been watching us for some time. I pointed to a cushion. The kids made room for her. She sat down, but looked ill at ease. I introduced the kids to her, she gave us her name, and pretty soon she asked about LSD. This became the model for the rest of the three days. Anyone who watched us was invited to join us. Not everybody did, but enough people put their prejudice aside and sat with us. They sat in their stiff uncomfortable clothes and asked questions. Some of them had children who had become hippies, and the intelligent answers our kids gave, as well as their sincere desire to build a bridge for these alienated, worried parents made a real exchange possible. It was rewarding to see faces loosen up as we discussed our differences without anger, without noise, without hostility. Some people wanted to know what we were selling, and in the absence of any merchandise they looked for pamphlets and propaganda material. We had intentionally brought nothing, not even the reprints we kept at the Center. To those who seriously wanted to learn more, we offered to send literature. But we refrained from saying anything that smacked of propaganda, nor did we solicit any funds. One well-dressed woman in her mid-forties handed me a check for $200 as she got up to leave. "My blessings on your undertakings," she said. "You make me feel good about the young generation. Whatever you're doing, I'd like to support it."

By 11 p.m., our booths had to be dismantled and the store emptied. A sky-high insurance fee would have to be paid if we left things overnight. It was fun to be part of the whirlwind energy with which our motley band went to work to set up again in the morning. I loved the creativity and inventiveness of the hippies, and I loved their high, gentle spirit. The beauty they created with minimal means and maximal imagination was the exuberant manifestation of the visions they saw on their trips.

Some of the people we had met at the showcase came to the Center to get more information and to listen to lectures; and for a while, the Center became a bridge between the hippies and the straights.

We were also a bridge in another way. We sometimes received requests for speakers from various groups. "Why don't you go?" Timothy asked me, passing me a letter addressed to him. The letter is of interest not only because it started me on a new activity, but because it represents the kind of liberalism which, though grouping the League with "religious Cults and Sects," was open enough to "neither espouse nor scorn your religion."

When I got on the subway to go to the church, I was as calm as if I were merely going to the Center to speak to "my" kids. I knew my subject. I had nothing to fear. To be on the safe side, I had made a few notes the night before. The points I wanted to stress were as follows:

> LSD is simply a tool like a microscope, not an object of worship. It can be as dangerous as X-rays when misused.
>
> The reason for our interest in Eastern religions is its emphasis on non-duality, and on the reconciliation of opposites.
>
> We need a new approach to education stressing the interconnections instead of the bare facts. We're all one, but not the same. Let us celebrate our differences.
>
> Boy on re-entry after 1st trip: If I wanted to, could I ever go back to being a vegetable?
>
> Integrating what LSD teaches is a life-long process.
>
> Oceanic feelings and ego loss are often called regression to infancy. Why not consider the possibility of adult oceanic feelings?
>
> The League is not a club or a cult; we don't accept members. Start your own religion.
>
> Reaction to LSD is as varied as the takers.

When I went looking for the address I had been given, I realized with a shock that the modest church I expected to find was in reality the cathedral on Riverside Drive. The great Gothic structure with its tall spires evoked my awe. My heart sank. I'm not going to talk in there! I was close to panic. To my relief, the room to which I was shown was small and held no more than 60 or so seats. The faces that scrutinized me as I stood behind the lectern were young, in their twenties and thirties. Some were open, but reserved. Others betrayed the closed hostility I was familiar with from some of the visitors at the Center.

I began by stating frankly that this was the first time I had ever addressed an audience. "You're stuck with me, like it or not," I told them. "You are curious about this new, bizarre psychedelic revolution. Let me begin by telling you how I myself became involved."

After a short history of the events that led to my first LSD trip I added: "Until a year ago I was a law-abiding citizen. Then I smoked marijuana and became a criminal."

There was laughter in the room. I did not look like a criminal. The audience was with me. I went through the points I had outlined and finished to warm and sustained applause. In the question and answer period that followed, they wanted to know what I got out of LSD.

"The main benefit I derived from the psychedelics is that they taught me that 'I' am not my body but an evolving consciousness, clothed temporarily in a body. I died after my third toke on my first joint of grass, and when I came back, I was not I any more but a consciousness that encompassed a vastly broader spectrum than I ever dreamed of. It doesn't last, but once you have known it, you can never forget that it exists. When the experience becomes integrated into your life, the fear of death disappears—and we can only truly begin to live when we no longer fear death."

The questions kept coming for well over an hour. When I was finally ready to leave, a small group followed me into the street to ask in a low voice, "Where can we get it?" Needless to say, I did not give out any information, but I was so heartened by the reception my talk had received that I accepted several more speaking engagements, all of which had the same result.

Meanwhile, at the Center, I was the confidant of the kids who felt they could talk to me about things they couldn't discuss with their mothers. They talked about sex, and I discovered a serious discrepancy between the way the boys and the girls experienced the so-called sexual liberation. Commitment was out. In the communes and the crash pads everybody slept with everybody else. "We're all one," they said. The boys loved it. The girls pretended to, but under a thin veneer of hipness, most of them wanted one man, their man, instead of the one-night stands that were so common among them. Marijuana, which they all smoked, can be an aphrodisiac, as I myself had learned. But on the morning after, when she looked at the man in her bed, the girl sometimes wanted to die. The genie of sex was out of the bottle, and the repressiveness of the preceding decades was replaced by indiscriminate promiscuity.

In my adolescence I was as curious about sex as any healthy teenage girl. Early on, I formed the idea that the woman "gives" herself to the man, like a precious jewel. That she herself could experience the electro-magnetic charge that men value so much was never mentioned in the books I read. A woman was either the victim of her husband's lust, or she loved him enough to submissively "give" herself to him. The message the conventions of the time conveyed was a schizophrenic mixture of post-Victorian morality and the roaring '20s. Virginity was something no girl could afford to lose if she wanted to get married. If she did lose it, she had been robbed of it by some fiendish cad. At the same time, if a girl pretended to have lovers, this added allure to her. A case in point was a movie called THE DREAMING MOUTH, in which the heroine, played by Elisabeth Bergner, tries to deceive her suitor into thinking she had a spicy past; but of course all ends happily when he finds out that she is as innocent as the driven snow. There were disturbing hints of "bad" women who actually enjoyed sex here and there, but female orgasm was kept a dark and unmentionable secret.

All of that had changed by the '60s. As consciousness expanded, so did sensory awareness. The baby boomers were letting it all hang out. The hippies played musical beds. "We're all one," they said, meaning, "Let's all sleep together." Girls frankly admitted their pleasure in the sexual act, played Love Goddess, and joined the boys in the amorous dance. But when the first thrill began to wear off, many of them discovered that "sexual freedom" was more to the taste of the boys than to theirs. In the '70s, they became Earth Mothers. They wore long skirts and cooked, baked, laundered, planted herbs and vegetables, and raised the kids. But by the '80s, they saw that they had once more played into the hands of the men and decided to take on no more sexist roles but to become individuals. Gone was the playmate of the '60s and the Earth Mother of the '70s. The self-confident, independent '80s woman was born.

Today there is a growing awareness that men and women are equals, though not the same, and that only the partnership society of which Riane Eisler speaks in The Chalice and the Blade can produce the peace and harmony between the sexes for which we all so deeply long.

Thirty-nine

At Millbrook, most of the residents were couples. Some were married, others lived together. Several weddings were performed on the estate. The marriage of Carol and Bob in the summer of '66 was an event for which the community prepared for weeks. Carol showed me the pattern for her wedding gown.

"I'm thinking of something soft, like angel skin; in lavender, you know? What do you think?"

"Sounds great!" I said. The Vogue pattern was for a simple but elegant Empire style gown, long slim skirt cut on the bias falling away from below the breasts. It would look regal on her slender young body. I congratulated her on her choice.

"Glad you like it. Do you know how much fabric I should get?"

"It tells you on the pattern. See?" I pointed to the back of the package where the required yardage was specified.

"Ah yes!" she said. "It'll be easy once I get the hang of it. I'll just have to read all the directions."

"You mean…Will this be the first dress you've ever made?"

"Yes," she said, adding confidently, "but I know I can do it!"

I was not so sure. "Well, you can call on me if you need help," I offered.

When I came to Millbrook the following week-end, I found Carol staring at a length of cloud-soft cerulean blue fabric. Spread out on the table were the pattern pieces. Carol was exasperated.

"I can't figure it out!" she wailed.

Before long, I was pinning the pattern pieces to the fabric and sitting at the ancient treddle machine sewing Carol's wedding gown. Word spread. For the next few weekends, I was sewing long robes for the women and loose, wide-sleeved shirts for the men.

The sewing machine was in the Sri Ram Ashram that occupied a building near the mansion. The leader was Bill Haines, a burly man with the manner of a field marshal. He had lived in India for many years and his knowledge of Hinduism was profound. His followers loved him and feared him.

The contrast between the ashram and the Big House was great. The people in the Big House tended to let the material plane slide. A state of anarchy prevailed; all and everything was okay. It was different at the ashram. There were no dirty dishes in the sink; the rooms were neat and clean, and the refrigerator was well stocked with fresh food. It was almost too neat—like a suburban home. Upstairs, Bill Haines' large, sunny room was filled with religious Eastern art, and there was a beautifully arranged and lavishly decorated shrine with one of the Hindu divinities, I forget which. But the place of honor was reserved for a large TV set.

The atmosphere here lacked the laissez-faire of the League, and I couldn't help wondering if some kind of leadership and discipline is not, after all, a necessary ingredient of communal living.

Sitting in the kitchen of the ashram, where the sewing machine stood, I met some of the people who lived there. They were as colorful as the League members.

As a boy, Bali Ram had been a dancer at the court of the King of Nepal. His face was satin-smooth and high cheek-boned, more like that of a Malaysian than a Hindu. His burning eyes seemed older than his face; generations of his ancestors looked out of them. His svelte body revealed the dancer with every step. They must have handed down the art of dancing from father to son, I thought, watching him approach.

"Could you have the goodness to see if this is all right?" the dancer asked, holding up an elaborate costume. I was dazzled. Layers of iridescent silk cascaded from a waist-band; the subtle shading of the colors blended together into a psychedelic dream.

"I'd love to!" I was curious about the Indian. It was rumored that he and Bill Haines were lovers. If so, a more polarized pair can hardly be imagined. I never found out what brought Bali Ram to America. He seemed like a bewildered child. "This country. This America. I do not understand!" he often said.

"Why do you dance?" I asked.

"Why? Because I must! I was born to dance! That is my work in this life. It took lifetimes of practice to bring me to this point. In my next life, maybe, I will dance even better..." The melancholy in his eyes mirrored ages of self-discipline spent in Terpsichore's service. He spoke with that soft Hindu intonation that always gives me a strange feeling of déjà vu.

One of the strangest figures at the ashram was a woman who was called Sarasvati after the Hindu Goddess of Wisdom. Long before today's skinheads, hers was shaved, giving her a weird, ghostly appearance. She played scullery maid and did the humblest work. Her features were not unattractive, but she was slovenly. And she literally grovelled before Bill Haines. "Fuck me, Master," she implored. "Do it to me once...just once...I'll do anything..." She was certain that making love with him was the path to enlightenment. From time to time she disappeared for a few days and returned with a sizable sum of money, which she handed to Bill. "I won it at the races," she would say. Years later I heard that she was getting a Ph.D. in philosophy and was highly regarded by her professors and colleagues.

While I worked on the costumes for the wedding, the others were busy with preparations for the feast. Cases of champagne arrived—a gift from Peggy Hitchcock. Food was prepared and soon the great refrigerators were filled to overflowing. The fountain was cleared of the debris that clogged it up, the sound system was tested, and the whole place took on a festive air.

On the day of the wedding, a strange group assembled on the lawn. The League and their hippie guests were resplendent in their colorful robes and long, wind-swept hair. The others were the family members and friends of the bride and groom, all wearing the clothes prescribed by fashion. The women's high heels dug into the soft grass, and the men seemed straight-jacketed in their ties and coats which they did not remove despite the heat, until the champagne began to do its work.

The guests were directed to the clearing, where the ceremony was to take place, by a diifferent route than that taken by the members of the League. As we walked along the path that led through the sacred grove to the waterfall, I noted that objects from the personal shrines of the group had been placed along the path. Near the waterfall, Timothy waited.

"Here is the wedding sacrament," he said, holding up a small vial filled with a colorless liquid. Carol and Bob approached, and with an eye dropper, he deposited a drop in their open mouths. When all of us had received the same amount, we formed a circle and prayed silently before we proceeded to the clearing.

A carpet had been spread on the grass, and large pine branches adorned an altar that held symbols of various religions.

Timothy performed the ceremony. The words he spoke were brief, simple, and sincere. When Bob and Carol had been pronounced man and wife, they planted a young sapling to commemorate the event, and we all stood around them and cheered.

On the great lawn, a pit had been dug, and a young pig turned slowly on a spit. A rock-band was playing, a reporter from Life Magazine was tossing a frisbee in the air, and to my LSD-enhanced vision the scene looked like a baronial feast for a band of time travelers—some from the past, some from the future. The "straights" and the "hip" merged effortlessly. Their differences floated away in a sea of good-will and champagne.

Before sundown, Bali Ram danced. The voluminous layers of pleated skirts swirled around his knees, the bells on his ankles tinkled, and the graceful and precise movements of his body and his hands made him appear to my enchanted eyes like a Hindu divinity come to life.

Another memorable wedding was the marriage between Anita and Abbie Hoffman. I met Abbie when he ran a store on Bleeker Street, two or three blocks away from the Center. The store was part of a non-profit organization that helped the blacks in the South by selling their hand-made items. The Center was still in the chaotic stage of remodeling when Abbie came over to introduce himself and to offer his help. He was not interested in the psychedelics, he told me, because he did not believe they could bring about social change. Only politics can change the grip of the status quo, he said. I believed that only when each individual's consciousness changes can change in the world occur. "Look at history," I pointed out. "Every revolution is followed by a counter-revolution, and the pendulum keeps swinging back and forth. No lasting change is effected by politics; it has to come from within."

But despite our differences I liked the fiery young zealot and was happy to be invited to his wedding, which took place in Central Park. Lynn House, the editor of a psychedelic newsletter called Inner Space, officiated. The invited guests were outnumbered by members of the press, who ate up everything the groom put out. Abbie was a genius at getting media attention.

The words of the ceremony were not the ones usually spoken at a wedding. They fell slowly from Lynn's lips. Between sentences he seemed to be deep in thought and far away. After the ceremony we went to Abbie's apartment on St. Marks Place and I found out the reason for Lynn's strange behavior. He had taken STP the day before and had not yet come down—nor would he for some time to come. STP was a new drug that was much stronger than LSD and kept you high for a minimum of 24 hours, often much longer. I had seen some kids on it and strongly advised those who would listen against taking it. Fortunately the drug soon lost its appeal, and after enjoying a brief popularity was not heard of again.

We made a clear distinction between psychedelic substances and drugs like heroin, cocaine, amphetamines, alcohol etc. Except for the occasional drunk who wandered in, these drugs were shunned by those who came to the Center. The effect of the psychedelics rather than the substances themselves was the focus of interest. It wasn't what you took—it was what you saw, what insights you gained, what you learned. We all shared the realization that we're part of a much larger group than our family, our country of birth, or the color of our skin. And we wanted to celebrate that knowledge. We wanted to come together.

Inspired by the San Francisco prototype, a be-in was planned for the 1967 Easter Sunday in Central Park. The day before, "my kids" fanned out all over Manhattan collecting flowers the florists were ready to discard. By nightfall, the Center was abloom with flowers; they filled jars, pitchers, soda pop bottles, empty cans and anything else that would hold water. The next day we distributed them to the hippies who blanketed Sheep Meadow. Virtually everyone was on acid. It was a very different scene from the one at the Grateful Dead party, as colorful as that one had been drab. Some famous faces were seen here and there, surrounded by groups of admirers. There was Allen Ginsberg playing his harmonica, and Abbie Hoffman, who was covered with bananas from head to toe. Everywhere I looked I saw faces I knew, and they all smiled at me and came over for a hug. I'm supposed to be lonely, I thought. A lonely middle-aged moneyless divorcee. How far from the truth! How lucky I am! How blessed!

ONE FOOT IN THE FUTURE

Forty

There was not enough money to pay the Center's rent. I went to Millbrook to talk to Timothy. I had not seen him in awhile and my phone calls remained unanswered.

As I approached the mansion, I could feel that something was very wrong. An eerie silence surrounded the house; no dogs came to greet me, there was no sound of music, no sign of children playing on the lawn. Except for the furniture, the mansion stood empty. Gone were the toys, the dog bones, the comic books and the crayons that usually littered the floors. I went to the kitchen to see if I could find someone to explain what had happened, but the kitchen was bare. The clutter that had made it so hard for me to find anything was gone. The house felt ghostly. I was shivering in the warm spring air as I walked out on the terrace. Timothy was sitting in his favorite pose on the ballustrade, his back against a post, long legs drawn up to his chest; he was reading a paper. Instead of the warm smile that generally greeted me, his face wore a frown. He gave me a weary look.

"We're moving into the woods," he told me. "It's getting too hot here. We're constantly being hounded and harassed. We've decided to live outdoors for a while; maybe we can cool the Liddy minions out if they can't find us. And they won't. The woods are too big and deep."

G. Gordon Liddy, the future Watergate bugger, had been watching the mansion for months, hoping to make an arrest that would stick. Early one morning in April 1966, he and a band of deputies raided the mansion. It was a performance worthy of the Flintstone Cops. Bursting into the house by knocking in the front door, they charged up the stairs where they were met by Timothy, who got out of bed bare-assed, wearing only a shirt. Liddy and his deputies searched the house for five hours, but all they found was a small amount of marijuana. Liddy arrested Leary, but failed to inform him of his rights. On this technicality, the case was dismissed.

This did not deter Liddy from continuing to persecute the people who lived in the mansion. There were roadblocks around the estate, and visitors and residents alike were often stopped and searched by the police. As I looked at Leary, I sensed for the first time something like retreat in this buoyant man who had always appeared so invulnerable.

When I drove to Millbrook with him that first time a year earlier, I had asked if he was deliberately courting a prison sentence. "Nothing will happen to me!" he had replied curtly. Later, when he did go to prison, I wondered if he had already known then what I had learned in Oued-Zem, namely, that my body can be held in prison, but not my spirit. Maybe this is why he spoke out so recklessly.

Only history will show if Leary was right or wrong to popularize LSD. The fact is that today, thanks to him, more people than ever before have entered states of awareness that were formerly reserved for mystics, saints, and the rare inspired artist. The mental horizon of western culture has been stretched to include super-sensory and transcendent realities; a bridge to the divine has been built. That there are casualties cannot be denied. I am deeply distressed whenever I encounter evidence of the destructive or confusing power of the psychedelics. But since 1967 an ever-growing number of people have awakened to the reality of the spirit, whether through the use of the psychedelics, or through the non-psychedelic methods brought to the West by the psychedelic movement.

At the moment, however, the grim reality was that Timothy and the rest of the Millbrook community were forced to leave this magical place. It was the end of an experiment in communal living that focused on the sacramental use of psychedelics. I was overcome by a feeling of loss. My throat was constricted; I choked back my tears.

"Don't feel bad," Tim said. "It's just another turn of the wheel. Change—remember? The only reality we can count on. Don't worry, it'll be great. We'll live in tepees, close to nature…" Some of his habitual optimism was coming through.

"Where is the camp? How do I get there?" I wanted to know.

"You don't," Tim said simply. "We don't let anybody know where we are. Sorry. No visitors allowed."

"But I'm not a visitor, Timothy!" I protested. "You can't cut me off!"

"Sorry about that; we made a pact. Go back to the city, take care of the Center, and maybe we'll connect again when this mess is over. And it will be!"

It dawned on me that this was the end not only of Millbrook but of the Center. Clearly, I could not count on Timothy for help; Richard Alpert had gone to India, and without the talks they gave at the Center I could not hope to keep it going. There was less than a hundred dollars in the bank. We needed at least another five by the end of the month.

"Maybe it's time to phase out the Center," Timothy said. "The climate is getting too hot. Let it go, Nina. There'll be other opportunities to continue your work with the young people."

He was right. Things had become too much for me. I had to admit that the love money I had counted on had not materialized. If the Center does not fulfill a meaningful enough function to pay for itself, I told myself, to try to hang on to it is to go against the flow. Yes, time to stop, I thought as I drove back to the city. And time to find out where I am.

The rent for the Center was paid until the end of the month. Two of the most responsible hippies said they'd keep it going until then and maybe even longer, if they could find the money. I handed the keys and the remaining money over to them and took leave of the LSD Center. A month later, its doors closed for good. When I passed it in the early '70s, it had become a rather posh Italian restaurant, judging by the elaborate front. I did not go in—I lack sentimental attachment to the places I once inhabited. It was the same when I passed the house in Lawrence in the mid-seventies. The house looked lovely and well cared-for, and the garden, from what I could see by peering through a crack in the tall fence, was as beautiful as ever. But where my heart once beat faster as soon as I rounded the corner and saw the redwood and fieldstone house, I now saw it with the eyes of a stranger. The life—my life—had gone out of it.

As it was going out of the Center now. The timing was right. A new chapter had opened in my life and was beginning to absorb all the energies I had directed outside. It was time to go within.

I did not see Timothy Leary again until the spring of 1977, when he gave a lecture at the State University of Albany, N.Y. Here is what I wrote about it in The Woodstock Times:

> …We arrived early, and I had an opportunity to look the students over. I was struck by the drabness of their blue-jeaned uniformity. Flashing back to the audiences who flocked to hear Leary in the '60s, I could not help thinking of the flip-flop that took place in the last decade. Then, it was a wildly individualistic crowd, their many-hued fantasies clothed in costumes of their own devising, each different and unique. But there was unity in their diversity. They were all "heads"—they had all stuck their heads out of the three-dimensional consensual "reality" with its fashions and fake morality. Their clothes were an exuberant expression of rejection of their parents' materialism, and at the same time a playing-out of the TV fantasies they had absorbed with their mothers' bottles.
>
> As we waited for Leary, I became conscious of a familiar scent. I turned around. In row after row, joints were being passed. Surprised, I asked the girl behind me if they were smoking in honor of Leary, and if so, wasn't it a bit risky? No, she replied to both questions. They always smoke like that at lectures, she told me, and it's perfectly okay.
>
> Things have indeed changed in the last ten years!
>
> Leary flooded the stage with energy as he delineated our evolutionary path from primeval slime to the present when, according to him, we are ready to leave the womb planet and migrate to outer space. Before the infant is born, the air in the womb becomes noxious and pushes the baby out. In the same way, we are now being pushed out into space…
>
> That Leary's mental powers have, if anything, increased in the last ten years, and that he has lost none of his optimism about humanity's fate acted like a tab of Owsley's finest on my spirits which, along with those of many other sixties survivors, had taken a nose dive in the grim seventies. There were

times when I doubted the reality of the spiritual evolution that seemed so tangible ten years ago. Was it a flash in the pan? Are we back to survival of the fittest in a dog-eat-dog world? Leary does not think so. As he sees it, the human race is presently mutating to a new and higher step in preparation for migration to the stars …

In an interview I conducted with the artist Martin Carey in the late '70s, he describes the feeling Leary evoked in the baby-boom generation:

"…Leary at that time was getting fired from Harvard. The very fact that he was fired from that institution made him interesting to me. The '50s were such a dull, sleepy time, and school was dull and boring and inoffensive. The people who had trouble in school were usually more intelligent, so they got bored. And there were these two guys, Leary and Alpert, getting kicked out of Harvard. It was like a light shining into all that boredom. The reason why they had to be stopped was that the experiments they were doing showed that LSD is a tool for ecstasy and that you can change your life. And then Leary came out with TURN ON, TUNE IN, DROP OUT. It was the key slogan, the mantra anthem that summed up the whole thing. It was something that everybody in my generation could understand. The pictures I saw of him in the magazines at that time showed him smiling, full of a gregarious kind of energy. Well, he was supposed to be despondent! He'd been fired from his job, the government was after him, but instead of reacting with fear, worry, and anger, he seemed completely happy!"

In the interview Martin recalled his impressions of the Center and of the '60s movement:

MARTIN: I went to the Center shortly after my first acid trip. There was a light machine going in the front and soft Indian music playing, and there were candles and incense…All of a sudden, I felt that I was tripping. For a moment I was really scared, and then I thought, well, if it has to happen, this is the place for it. Of course as soon as I stopped being scared, it stopped. Richard Alpert was speaking, and there were pictures of Timothy Leary along the wall. The whole room—the whole environment—there was a sense of a Catholic martyr trip about it. I sat way in the back. It was a very large, narrow room…Sitting in a room like that with a lot of other people who were turning on to a very high level and being drawn together because of it…

NINA: Yeah, those were the days…It's amazing how fast the Movement spread. Of course the media were responsible for that. How come they gave it so much space?

MARTIN: The young people in the media were all getting stoned. People from Life Magazine were praising and falling in love with everything that was happening, because they were getting turned on while they were doing it, and they were just like us, you know. All you had to do to become a media figure was to be what we called a life actor, and to be outrageous. Leary was a life actor. Abbie {Hoffman} was. They were both geniuses at it…What happened in the '60s is that we understood how to use the media. The politicians and the advertisers could buy the space. We did it by creating news. Timothy was news the same way the peace movement and the hippies were news.

NINA: Where did it all go? What's happening now, in the '70s?

MARTIN: At the time I felt that we were a very special generation, almost out of the stream of history. We started seeing that this is just a dream state and a projection of our own minds, and that we don't have to accept the state we're in—that reality is anything we want to make it. But now I'm no longer so sure that we were special. Every generation feels that they are transforming the world. Then what they do gets assimilated into the society and gets chewed up. America makes pablum of any new idea in seven years, and then the idea becomes dull. The only thing is—this time, it was really moving into a new area of consciousness, and that's a totally new thing.

The Millbrook group scattered in all directions. After that, Leary, Alpert and Metzner followed separate roads. Leary's destiny took him through kaleidoscoping realities—prison, dangerous escapes, travel in exotic lands peopled by monsters, dragons, beautiful women and deceitful men. Alpert went to India and returned as Ram Dass, and Metzner, always the least flamboyant of the three, became a scholar and teacher of ancient methods of self-transcendence. I believe that Leary did not really want to be seen as a guru, a prophet, or a High Priest. In him, the scientific temperament overshadows the devotional. He is a super-salesman of evolution who deploys his talents to sell a more advanced stage of human consciousness. Alpert, on the other hand, is the born devotee. His warm humanity searched for a human embodiment of the divine, and when he thought to have found it in Neem Caroli Baba he gave himself wholeheartedly to spreading his gospel. His undiminishing appeal is that he holds up a mirror to us of our human foibles while cheerfully making fun of his own.

The youth of the '60s was ready for a step that would take them beyond the struggle for survival. That struggle had taken on absurd proportions in their parents' lives. Middle-class adolescents watched their fathers put in long, stress-filled hours to promote and produce useless goods in order to make money to buy more useless goods. To own more than others was the legitimate goal of human endeavor. Not surprisingly, the children of the affluent middle-class were the first to take psychedelics. What followed was a tidal wave that had no more hope of being stemmed by the penalties the law inflicted than by the voices of caution within the movement itself. In an interview in the '70s, Timothy Leary said:

> "By 1968, in public lectures and publications I was stressing that LSD was not for everybody, suggesting that perhaps only 10% from American gene pools were equipped to handle the high-octane rocket-fuel of the strong psychedelics…"

and

> "Intelligence increase drugs like LSD enormously accelerate, extensify, intensify the human brain function. Only those who are geared for high velocity, high altitude, swift-changing realities need apply."

A look at the combined output of books, essays and lectures by the Harvard trio would be reassuring to those who still believe that the use of psychedelics impairs the functioning of the brain. Not only is their work voluminous, it is ground-breaking, original, and eminently instructive.

> [Transcendental mystical states] have engaged the attention of some of the finest speculative minds that our generation has seen—from Aldous Huxley

to Alan Watts to Richard Alpert to Timothy Leary…If I may be permitted to hazard a guess, I would suggest that the above writers may yet go down in history as outstanding figures who have been instrumental in transforming dead religious attitudes into vital mystical experiences. (Roll Away the Stone by Israel Regardie)

The Center for the League of Spiritual Discovery had served as a platform for the Harvard trio and others who taught and lectured there. I myself had found it fulfilling to share what I knew with the young. The twelve years of "peeling the onion" of my conditioning and of meditation that preceded my first psychedelic experience were invaluable. They helped me to assimilate the jet-propelled trips into altered states while keeping my feet on the ground. The steps to liberation confront us with our own private demons. This can bring on massive fear reactions in the unprepared. They can also be thrown into a violent panic state when the veil of consensus reality parts. This is why I believe that people must be willing to undergo a lengthy period of learning before exposing themselves to these dangers. As long as the present hard line against research and consumption of these substances continues, we have no instrument for teaching, nor is it possible to weed out those who can be harmed by them.

I parted from the Center with the fervent hope that I would again some day be in a position to help the neophytes on the path of self-discovery and to warn them of the dangers. Today's drug education makes no distinction between the consciousness-expanding psychedelics and mind-destroying drugs like cocaine, heroin, and amphetamines. All efforts to stem the tide of drug use are doomed in the absence of a sane and honest recognition of the difference between mind-expanding substances and other drugs.

ONE FOOT IN THE FUTURE

Forty-one

When Betty Friedan's The Feminine Mystique came out, women took a second look at their role and decided they were through being unpaid housekeepers. They soon proved that they were as capable as the men, and by the mid-'70s, being a housewife became almost something to be ashamed of.

It was hard for the women of my generation to adjust to the new independence. Taught to expect our husbands to provide for us, we were not prepared to earn our living. For me, it was a reality I now had to face. Neither the Third Force Lecture Bureau, nor the LSD Center had turned out to be viable means of income. What now? I wondered. I fitted none of the categories in the "want" ads or employment agencies. While I did not rule out the possibility of a remarriage, I thought it quite unlikely that one would occur. By the time I turned on, all desire for a relationship with a man had dropped away. I had only one desire — to find the MORE that neither sex, nor money, nor worldly success had supplied. I looked on falling in love as a childhood disease and was happy to be rid of it. My whole being was absorbed by my spiritual search. I wanted to love all of humanity and all of creation. When I smoked marijuana, I fell into a trance and left my body. Sometimes a voice spoke through it. It was the voice of an old man, and his words were infinitely wiser than anything I could have said. A few times it seemed that I could see him in the mirror, an old, shrunken man who sat cross-legged on a mountain, in the snow. His hand — my hand! — looked ancient, skeletal, with large veins under paper-thin skin. Who am I? How solid is my flesh? How real?

The transformation that took place in my life when I left my marriage was dramatic. All the external props that bound me to my niche in society were left behind; but inwardly, the voices of my past were not yet stilled. I had been raised with the idea that financial success is what counts. Viewed from that angle, my voluntary act of abandoning the security of my marriage was suicidal. I was going against everything I had learned about survival. What I could expect now was poverty and a lonely old age. Was I going mad? Did the psychedelics rob me of my senses?

No. They brought me to my senses. The world around me—people, scents, colors, sounds—all was intensified. I never knew how keen my senses were! And that other sense—the sense of oneness with all creation! I was riding a wave that was bringing in a new age. I saw a new human race whose faith was no longer based on a set of precepts handed down through generations, but on direct, first-hand knowledge of the Divine. This knowledge would banish wars, competitiveness, violence, possessiveness and all the other human failings. The Kindergarten age of humanity was over. They were really here, the children whose sense and senses had never closed down. "Everybody is born knowing it," they said. "Only most people forget."

How I loved them! I wanted to nurture them, to cherish them, to join them, and to live like them...

To live like them. No, I wasn't ready for that. I couldn't see myself sharing a pad with these angelic but messy children. There was no need—not yet, anyway. I knew I could make the money from the sale of my jewelry last a year, now that I had few worldly desires. But what would happen when it ran out? I was determined that whatever I would do had to be compatible with my spiritual quest.

I was beginning to listen to an inner voice that directed me away from self-involvement and from fear. But there was still a large gap between my ordinary consciousness and that inner voice. I was adrift in a world that was turned upside-down, torn between a deep conviction that nothing mattered except to follow that inner voice, and the reasonable voices of the practical world. When I tried to pray for answers, the words would not come. It seemed ludicrous to pray for my small, personal self. I could not isolate my fate from that of the large family of which I now knew myself to be a part. The attachment to my biological family lessened, and my bond with my new family grew. The two children born of my body were now no closer to my heart than the rest. It was 1968. For some moments, the boundaries of my mind had opened and I SAW more than my brain could comprehend. I didn't think of myself as a woman or a man any more—simply as human. I wanted to serve evolution by helping the new breed, and I had faith that my needs would be taken care of. Half the time. The other half, I worried.

It was at Isaac's home in Brooklyn that one of my most memorable trips took place. Isaac and his wife Rachel had become my friends. I was enamored of Isaac's art. He filled large canvases with bold splashes of brilliant color that revealed, when viewed with eyes cleansed by a psychedelic, image after image within the abstract form. "You see it?" we asked others who were equally stoned. Usually they not only saw it but pointed out additional shapes. Isaac was part of a wave of psychedelic painters whose work reflected dimensions accessible only to the turned-on eye. Their work had the power to recall an echo of the psychedelic experience; viewing one of Isaac's paintings, I sometimes felt myself transported to celestial playgrounds.

"What are you doing?" I asked him one evening when I found him alone in his dark studio, shining a flashlight on the canvas he had just completed.

"See that?" he asked excitedly, stepping back. The area lit up by the beam of the flashlight showed a series of white dots that traced a pattern on a blue summer sky shading off into white. The curved and gracefully floating lines of dots had the rattattat rhythm of raindrops, each leaving a perfect, tiny round mark. The expression on Isaac's face was a mixture of surprise and delight. "I don't know how I did that," he said. His art was inspired by the visions he saw on LSD. He had had no formal training at that time, although a few years later he, as well as Herbie Grubb, went to Vienna to study with Ernst Fuchs, the great master of visionary art. The world has not yet discovered some of the priceless art that came out of those psychedelic years, and Isaac, who now lives in Woodstock with his second wife Carol Herzer, an equally gifted painter, has not yet found the recognition he so richly deserves.

Here is what I wrote about the trip I took at Isaac and Rachel's home in the fall of 1968. A group of about nine or ten was present.

We are seated around a large oval table when the LSD comes on. "We're on a space ship!" I exclaim. My companions have changed. They are supernaturally beautiful. Lynn House is the Captain. We are cruising the heavens, and we are gathered for an evening's entertainment. The theme of tonight's show is the planet Earth. A huge screen lights up. The planet in all her beauty! Her mountains, her streams, her creatures. In the garden, Adam and Eve cavort with the other animals and then innumerable Adams and Eves pass by in costumes suitable to the eras they portray. Each time they are introduced by the Poet. The Poet is Sandy Cohen, as Lynn House is the Captain. There is music. It comes from the radio and mysteriously changes each time a new era is ushered in.

The music takes on a more rapid rhythm. The screen shows Adam and Eve in a car. Electricity, radio, the telephone—a new era has begun. They have gained mastery over their environment, and along with it, mastery over the weapons of war. World War I. The pair wears uniforms: he is a soldier, she a nurse. The sound of heavy artillery fills the air, and then the picture changes. The radio plays jazz music. Adam and Eve dance the Charleston.

And then the crash on Wall Street. Hitler. War again. This time, the bombs scream louder. And then the mushroom cloud explodes. Is it the end?

The cloud is gone. Adam and Eve are living the American dream. Prosperity. Materialism. Contentment and conformity. Frank Sinatra. Bobby sox. "Father Knows Best." "Leave it to Beaver." The Eisenhower years. Boredom. HE and SHE are wearing false smiles, pretending to be the ideal couple.

And then something different begins to happen. The Flower Children. Faces aglow. Arms outstretched in welcoming embrace. Laughter. Love. Innocence. The '60s music is on the radio. And all at once I know that this whole performance has been staged for me. I'm supposed to go to the Earth! Everything is ready for my departure. But I don't want to go. "No, I won't go. I'm tired. I need a vacation."

The next thing I know I'm lying face down on a linoleum-covered kitchen floor. "They kicked me out! I wasn't ready to go!" And then slowly, a sense of my surroundings dawns; my memory of the here and now returns. I rise. "I'm Nina. I'm in the kitchen of my friends Rachel and Isaac. I'm not an astronaut from another planet. I belong here. I was born here, nee Gusti Schreyer!"

In rapid succession, the main events of my life slip through my mind. My childhood in Vienna. The Anschluss. England. Michel. Belgium. The bombs. Dunkirk. Oued-Zem. And America. New York. Heat. Poverty. Culture shock. Business. Children. Lawrence. Theater. Parties. Famous names.

And then, years of turning inward, culminating—exactly where I am!

❤ ❤ ❤

If it had not been for my 47 years as an intelligent and level-headed woman, I could easily have gone over the edge. "Look at me," I could have shouted, "I'm from space! I came in a space ship! Listen to me!" But to begin with, I knew where I'd be put, and besides, I didn't believe it myself. No matter how vivid the experiences were, no matter how much more real they seemed than the familiar everyday reality, I never lost my grip on the clear-cut division between altered states and my ordinary self.

I needed time to go within—to explore the landscape the psychedelics had opened up. When my divorce came through, I moved into a highrise in North Bergen, on the New Jersey side of the Hudson River. Work on the building was still in progress, which made the rent affordable and gave me maximum solitude as the sole inhabitant, plus maximum security since there was a watchman on duty at night. It was the first round highrise in the area and it was called Stonehenge, a name that appealed greatly to me.

My wedge-shaped studio apartment was on the 17th floor and was fringed by a terrace that faced Manhattan across the Hudson River. I placed a large statue of Shiva on it and watched as Manhattan lit up at night—as dazzling a sight as any psychedelic light show I had seen.

On foggy days, when the ground disappeared from sight, I was suspended between heaven and earth in my solitary aerie. The setting was perfect for my regime of deep meditation and psychedelic exploration. When Jackie, my tiger kitten friend from Millbrook took up her abode with me, she guided me as she had done on my first trip. The life I led was close to monastic. I rarely went out, and there were days when I did not see a human face.

I spent most of the time between trips reading, meditating, integrating. It was all so clear! So startlingly, so simply, clear! The answer to all my questions was the spiral. When I looked closely at the evolutionary spiral I saw that wild, chaotic movement was going on in all the different segments. Some energy particles fell back, others moved up, and then later, those who fell back were swept up again in the great, everlasting, forward surge ...

There are no losers in the game of evolution. Wherever the least one of us is now, I once was; and wherever the most holy, gifted, anointed one of us is or has been, I too shall be in the fullness of time. I was reading The Other Side by Bishop James Pike (Doubleday & Co., 1968) and was struck by the answer he received from his deceased son Jim, who spoke to him through a medium. When the Bishop questioned him about Jesus, he replied:

"...it is difficult. I'm afraid I might hurt you. This is what I was telling you. People must have an example. I haven't met him. They talk about him—a mystic, a seer, yes, a seer. Oh, but, Dad, they don't talk about him as a savior. As an example, you see? Not a savior, that's the important thing—an example..."

These lines bore out what I intuited. The question whether the "dead" are "alive" and can communicate with us had been answered by the books in the library of the American Society for Psychical Research which I read so avidly years before. It was the nature of God that preoccupied me, and the following words Jim told his father struck a deep chord in me:

Don't you ever believe that God can be personalized. He is the central force and you all give your quota toward it ... I hope one day that I shall understand to the point where I don't have to clutch at my own identity so much...You see, we have to be selfless. This creates freedom. It's a paradox...Yes, and also by not possessing, we possess..."

I filled pages of my journal with reflections on God. Among them is one that still seems to me to sum up the nature of God pretty well.

THE GOD GAME

I'm thinking of inventing a new game. A game with only one player, whose range of expression covers the exquisitely complex moves of an infinity of figures on the board.

The purpose of the game is to keep me, the sole player, amused. As its inventor, I can make up all the rules, but I have to make sure that I can't predict the outcome. So the game has to have a built-in surprise factor. But how can I be held in suspense by my own creation?

I, being God, know no limitations, and I'm bored. Therefore the surprise factor to be built in is Free Will. The figures on my board must be free to choose victory or defeat. I shall equip each one of them with a wide range of possibilities that lead to either the light side or the dark. In this way, I can rejoice and suffer with each of the figures on the board.

But my board is infinity. Outside space and time. And since my board is all there is, and there is nothing that exists outside my board, the outcome of each figure's struggle is always its return to me. No matter where they go, my figures can never leave my board.

A game like that can absorb my interest for an eternity. And when I get tired of it, I can stop the game and go back to an eternity of rest and calm and total boredom, and then I can dream up a new game…which will of necessity be the same game again since, in constructing it the first time (being God), I already exhausted all the limitless possibilities.

♥ ♥ ♥

I had long turned away from all forms of organized religion. Religion has burned many crosses, stars of David, and Muslim crescent moons into the lives of fellow humans. In the Middle East, the Christians, the Moslems and the Jews are killing each other, and in Ireland the Catholics and the Protestants are at each other, and all in the name of the one true religion. The only religion that never spawned a war is Buddhism. Buddha never wanted to be viewed as a divinity, but his followers disregarded his wishes and made him into a god anyway. Fortunately, however, they did not declare him the only begotten son of God. How different it must be to grow up in a culture presided over by statues of the calm, half-smiling face of a seated man instead of by the gaunt, tortured face of an emaciated man nailed to a cross, bleeding!

When I wrote what follows I was having some irreverent fun with the notion that we are all God:

ON THE DANGERS OF BEING GOD

I don't wish being God on my worst enemy. To be God makes you the fall guy, the one who's responsible for the whole mess. And if you're a decent kind of God, cleaning it up is up to you. Now we all know it takes a lot of training to become president of a corporation, let alone of the United States. So, being God takes a lot of training too. Trial and error. Learning through mistakes.

The young theologians say God is dead. But Alan Watts says You're It. And Maslow talks about peak experiences. I think he means peak like in mountain peak, but Watts says we're God playing peek-a-boo with our self, and when you find out you're God it's like peeking behind a curtain, or maybe the curtain peeks at you.

Anyway, it's all very confusing. You don't mind being God, but you really want to know. The business of finding out you're God is time consuming. You read about LSD. A crash program. None of that years of sitting under a tree. Instant. If you're really curious to know who's right—the God-is-Deaders or the Peakers—you take LSD and you find out.

You're It. And you wish you were dead. Because now you've got problems compared to which paying off the mortgage is a breeze. You're not just responsible for the mess you made in your life, but for the whole goddamn mess.

Being God, you know you can't win them all, because that's how you yourself stacked the game of solitaire you're playing. I mean, what's the point of playing if you always win? But when they start throwing rocks at you or nailing you to the cross, you're sorry you ever created the clods. It's not that they can destroy you, or even hurt you very much. It's that they make you feel inadequate. You sure messed things up when you created them so that they can't even recognize you. Of course there are always some who know you, who really expand through their contact with you. But chances are they'll be shot or fed to the lions.

You're God, but you are in human form. As a human, you have a father, a mother, a sister, a brother, a wife, and a kid or two. As a human God in America today, in the 20th century, you have to worry about such things as paying the rent, giving the kids an education, and not freaking them out too much by being God—scary trip for a kid, finding out good old pop is God!

To make matters worse, you're not a youngster any more. You're middle-aged. Forty. Or maybe forty-five. Or even fifty, God forbid. A middle-aged God? In America? In 1968? When the teeny-boppers and the hippies are ready to clobber you with a bunch of flowers if you're a day over thirty?

So your age makes you the enemy, the square. But you're God. And you know you're no square—who ever heard of a square God, for Christ's sake? Only—how will you make them believe you?

So there you are, a guy who left all the big decisions to your wife—like should we go to Florida or to Bermuda? Should we get a Chevy or a Ford? Things like that. You're no hot shot at the office either. The mousy type, if you know what I mean. So how does a guy like you rate being God? If you were a Rockefeller, or the Pope, or at least Ronnie Reagan…Remember how you nearly got fired the last time your wife made you ask for a raise?

You—God?

But now just suppose you're a woman. And you find out you're God. You get the picture? A woman-God. Not just a goddess, mind you. God. The whole thing. You're vacuuming the carpet, and you're God. Or frying onions. God! It's ghastly. Humiliating. The mind boggles! A housewife—God?

See what I mean when I say I don't wish it on my worst enemy?

Forty-two

Most of my trips during that time took me to impersonal realms where I saw that a calm equilibrium underlies the seeming chaos, and that energy, or the vibrations it causes, is the ultimate reality. I saw that to surrender is to win, and that one vast, immense, everlasting cosmic wind blows through all and everything and keeps it in motion—alive, changing, growing.

And I knew that I am God.

My contacts with the world were scant during that year at the Stonehenge. When I did go out, strange things sometimes happened.

It was near midnight. The bus to North Bergen was not due for another 20 minutes and I sat down to wait. The Port Authorities Terminal is normally not a very good place for a woman to be alone at night, but I had been visiting friends, we had smoked marijuana, and I was still high. I withdrew into myself and was soon floating through cathedrals, palaces, flower gardens with crystalline fountains and sun-bathed glades. Heavenly music was playing, and majestic figures were floating, gliding, dancing in the air…

"C'n yuh gimme a c'g'r't?" a voice said. Opening the gates of external perception, I saw a black man bending over me. He looked excited and very disturbed.

"What?" I asked. I did not understand his garbled words. His eyes were opaque, covered over with a filmy substance. He looked both drunk and drugged.

"A c'g'r't," he repeated. I still didn't understand. He pantomimed smoking.

"Aha!" Glad to have finally understood, I reached into my purse and withdrew my pack of filtered cigarettes.

"Help yourself," I said, handing him a match. He pulled the filter off and bent down to light the cigarette. He stared at me and mumbled a stream of words that I could not understand. Then he stopped and looked into my eyes.

"You white?" he asked in a clear voice.

"Yes," I replied, surprised by the question.

"You sure?" I nodded. "What's your religion?" he asked.

"I'm Jewish." His eyes opened wide in astonishment. He turned away from me and walked a few steps. I thought he was leaving, but then he was back and began to mumble again.

"I can't understand you," I said. "Speak up if you want to talk to me. You can do it all right! You didn't mumble before!"

He was silent. Then, without looking at me, he said: "I killed somebody."

"You did? Who?"

"A little kid. I killed him. I'm a murderer."

"Were you in prison?"

"Sure. But not for killing. For robbery. Stealin'. Stuff like that. Know what?"

"What?"

"I'm drunk. I ain't slept in three nights. I hate whites. And I hate the Jews." He was deeply troubled. Tears were running down his cheeks.

I didn't want to miss my bus and started to walk towards my platform. He stayed beside me.

"Listen, lady, I got to tell you somethin'. I was goin' to rob you. Honest! That's what I was goin' to do. But you're some kind of…I don't know. You're some kind of…You're sure you're white?" I nodded. "And Jewish? You're not African?" I assured him I was not. And his litany began again.

"I killed him. A little kid."

"How old was he?"

"Maybe five. I tripped him and he fell on his head."

"Did you want him to die?"

"No! Yes…Maybe. I don't know. He was screamin'. I tripped him."

"And you feel bad about it?"

"Hell, yes! What do you think, white woman? Niggers don't know nothin' about guilt?"

He was yelling and gesticulating, stepping in front of me and tugging at the sleeve of my coat. Two policemen walked by, looking straight ahead. Strangely enough they did not seem to notice the well-dressed woman and the drunken derelict. But now I knew what he needed from me.

"You must forgive yourself," I said. "You must stop going over it all the time and hurting yourself. Forgive yourself. I forgive you. Let the past rest."

My bus was pulling in. "Here, take my cigarettes," I said, holding out the pack to him.

"No! I can't take nothin' from you! You're some…You're…"

"Good luck," I said, getting on the bus. He waved from the platform until I lost sight of him.

Later, I wondered. Normally, I would have fled from that fearsome individual. He was drunk, filthy, half out of his mind, and by his own admission, a criminal. Yet I did not experience a moment of fear or repulsion. What gave me the courage to enter into a conversation with him?

I decided that it must be the openness, the fearlessness, and the feeling of being related to all living things that the sacred weed gave me.

Forty-three

In August of 1968, Richard Alpert, after spending more than a year in India, returned. That fall, the Bucks County Seminar House, where I had met Virginia and Tenzing, announced that Richard, now called Baba Ram Dass, would give a talk. I thought back to the day I met him. It was three months before my first visit to Millbrook. I had been working late and was about to leave my office when I heard two male voices talking and laughing in Larry Bogart's office across the hall. Larry's office usually closed much earlier, and I wondered who they were.

"Hi, Nina," Timothy greeted me when I opened the door. "Dick, meet Nina. She's an old-new friend." He was leaning against a wall and looking down at a young man who was lounging on the floor. "This is Richard Alpert."

All I knew about Alpert was that he had been an assistant professor of psychology at Harvard, and that he and Timothy had collaborated in their psilocybin research. In 1963 they were both dismissed from Harvard—the first time any member of the faculty had been fired in the twentieth century—but their interest in the mind-expanding drugs continued undiminished. And now, although they did not work together any more and Richard no longer lived at Millbrook, the friendship of these two legendary men appeared to be strong.

"Haven't we met before?" Richard asked me.

"I don't think so. People often think we've met before. Must be that I have a dime-a-dozen face."

"You don't," he said. "But you do look familiar. Do you work here?"

I told him about the Third Force Lecture Bureau.

"I'm one of her clients," Timothy said. "You should let her do your bookings too."

"Great. It shouldn't be hard, now that I'm a published author. It just came out. See?" He held out a slender volume with the letters "LSD" on the cover. The authors were Richard Alpert, Sidney Cohen, and Lawrence Schiller (New American Library, New York, 1966).

"I'm so glad, Dick," Timothy said. "Can't wait to read it. Was Sidney hard to work with?"

"There is one picture in the book on which we agreed. On all the others, we differed."

They both laughed. Dr. Sidney Cohen, as I was later to learn, had had some profound experiences with LSD and wrote a book entitled The Beyond Within. He was part of a small group that included Aldous Huxley, Gerald Heard, and Oscar Janiger. By the mid-fifties, Janiger, a well-known Santa Monica psychiatrist, had begun to use LSD as a therapeutic tool and administered it to some of his famous clients, among them, Cary Grant. Among the people Dr. Cohen turned on were Henry Luce, the publisher of Life Magazine, and his wife Clare Booth Luce. These pioneers conducted their experiments quietly, without fanfare, and they found that the mind-expanding substances had enlightening and beneficial effects. But despite the insights they gained, they were opposed to the use of psychedelics by the general public. It was interesting, in view of these facts, to find Dr. Cohen expressing the negative view on the panels where Leary and other proponents of the psychedelics spoke. In particular, he stressed the chromosomal damage LSD was reported to produce. The research was later proved to be invalid.

> A recent judicious survey and critical evaluation of all the evidence…has come to the reassuring conclusion that "pure LSD" ingested in moderate doses does not damage chromosomes in vivo, does not cause detectable damage, and is not a teratogen or a carcinogen in man. (LSD: Personality and Experience by Harriet L. Barr, Robert J. Langs, and Robert R. Holt.)

The book Cohen and Alpert co-authored consists of a series of pictures they picked out from a stack that represented the LSD state. Lawrence Schiller posed a series of questions to both about their responses to the pictures, and as could be expected, their interpretations differed widely. When I read the book, I often found myself agreeing with them both. I had never personally met the handsome, grey-haired Dr. Cohen, but I liked him and respected his views. He was a cool and worthy adversary to the hot-headed defenders of LSD. I basically agreed with him and his group about the need to stem the spread of psychedelics, but I was ambivalent about it. Too many people had reported ecstatic religious experiences with LSD, and I myself would never have known about it if Timothy Leary had not tried to turn on the world.

"I'm really thrilled about the book. I never thought I'd write. You're the writer," Alpert said to Leary. He had risen and stood as tall as the other. Sandy hair receded from a high forehead. He was slim, but without Tim's lankiness. I figured he was in his mid-thirties. He exuded charm.

As I got to know him better, I felt a warm affection for this boyishly enthusiastic and unfailingly helpful man. He was quite serious about his spiritual search, but something of the playboy clung to him—the insouciance that goes with being born into money.

As I prepared myself for the Bucks County seminar I wondered if his stay in India had changed him.

The seminar host was not given to rhapsodizing over the people he introduced; now he seemed almost awe-struck. "He radiates such serenity, such peacefulness, so much light…Those of you who knew him won't recognize him. He is transfigured!"

When the tall, lean, bearded man entered, a hush spread over the room. He wore a white dhoti, his graying hair had grown sparse but bushy, and the blue of his eyes reflected the sky. He looked ethereal, not quite made of flesh and blood. It's true, I thought. He is transfigured. Can this be the debonair Richard Alpert who danced with me in San Francisco?

It was a long time before the man in the dhoti spoke. He sat in the lotus posture, and not a breath in the room stirred. What he said when he finally spoke I don't remember. The words did not matter. What mattered was the light that surrounded him. It flooded my heart. The pleasures and pains of this world seemed to have fallen from him. He had dissolved into an ocean of consciousness where the perceived reality was no more than his guru playing hide-and-seek. And his faith, his absolute faith in the divinity of his guru radiated out from him with the power of a laser beam.

I felt shy when I approached him after the talk. I didn't know how to address him. What do you say to someone who comes from another world? I folded my hands in the Hindu gesture and bowed to him. He looked deep into my eyes.

"You've changed too," he commented. It was true. Neither he nor I were the same as the last time we met.

"Where are you staying?" I asked.

"At my father's farm in New England. It's nice there. Quiet. Come visit me, if you like."

I assured him that I would, and he gave me directions.

It was mid-winter. Deep snowdrifts covered the road. The trees wore heavy white coats, and children skated on the icy ponds. I was grateful for my good snow tires, and glad when I reached the farm.

The "farm" turned out to be a large estate with a private lake and a big, handsome house. Richard's father was the retired president of the New Haven Railroad, a position that had allowed his son to indulge in a luxurious lifestyle. "I had a lot of identities that I called Richard Alpert. I played the cello, I flew an airplane, I was charming, I was a Jewish boy making good in Boston," he said later of himself. (Quoted from Acid Dreams by Martin A. Lee and Bruce Shlain.) But now he was Ram Dass, and instead of the luxury that once surrounded him he was something of a pariah in his father's house. Whether he himself had chosen to live in the garret above the garage, or had been relegated there by his father to spare himself the embarrassment of this odd son, I do not know.

When I pulled into the driveway, a bearded head poked out of an upstairs window. "Come on up," he called.

Tears sprang to my eyes when I entered the room. "Home!" I thought. I had never before set foot in that room. It was a spiritual homecoming that had nothing to do with the physical setting. Perhaps, if reincarnation is a reality, I once lived in a room like that. There was a shrine, incense, candles, Indian prints—an assortment of objects that had become familiar to me. But neither they nor the luminous man who sat on a cushion could account for the feeling that washed over me. I could not talk. For a long time we sat silently facing each other, and then we talked about Timothy, Millbrook, others we both knew…I felt high, as high as if I had smoked a joint. We seemed to meet on another plane. The man I faced dissolved and became transparent, and his eyes were pure mirrors of the soul.

"I don't know where I'm going," he said after a long silence. His words surprised me and brought me back to earth. "I came back because my guru sent me. What I'll do to earn my living, I have no idea…"

"What? You too?" I was astonished. I believed him to be free of worldly cares. He was consumed by his spiritual path and not yet aware of his power. It was hard to think of him needing to earn a living.

"Your father has plenty of money. Won't he take care of you?" I asked innocently.

He laughed. "My dad calls me Rum Bum. He wants me to get out of these diapers and live a normal life. He offered to buy me a boat so I'd have some fun…" He laughed again. "As if that kind of fun meant anything to me now…Maybe I'll write a book. I really know that it'll be okay. He'll protect me," he said, pointing to the large colored photo of Neem Caroli Baba, the guru he revered.

It grew dark. We meditated together, then it was time to leave. "I'll take you to your car," Ram Dass said. I bundled up before braving the cold, but he walked barefoot in the snow, dressed only in his dhoti.

"You were my first visitor here," he told me. "I was beginning to think nobody would find me."

I hated to leave. The feeling in that attic was so sweet, so much my heart's home that I had to tear myself away.

After the Millbrook dispersal, Alexandra moved to the East Village. With shells, crystals, mirrors and Indian bedspreads the little fairy princess created a fairytale atmosphere in the dreadful slum apartment where she and Fred lived. The low rent in the building attracted many hippies whose pads were a haven for the kids who needed a place to "crash." It was there that I ran into Herbie Grubb again.

"I'm not Herbie any more. I'm Surya Das," he informed me. The pimples were gone. He had gained self-assurance, and the grin that spread over his face when he saw me showed he was glad to reconnect with me.

"Surya Das, eh? Where'd you get that fancy name?"

"Ram Dass gave it to me. At the Lamaist Foundation. It means Servant of the Sun." Herbie, or Surya Das, had spread his spiritual wings since the sand paintings at the Center. He had delved deeply into Hinduism and Buddhism, and his paintings now centered on Eastern themes.

"How'd you like to visit Ram Dass?" I asked him.

"Sure! Great!" Herbie-Das enthused.

"It's about a four hour drive. If we start at ten, we can be there by two. Okay?"

This time Ram Dass was not alone. Perhaps a dozen people were seated around him. Quietly, word about him had begun to spread. He was working on Be Here Now and was available to anybody who wanted to see him. That afternoon, a man in his early thirties loudly announced that he had been a burglar all his life and that he wanted to change. "I want to! I want to change!" he kept proclaiming.

"Burglary is a habit like any other habit," Ram Dass explained. "It's like that big ice cream cone in the sky! Will it last forever? Will my next burglary make me a rich man? The cause of suffering is attachment or desire, the Buddha says. They all say the same thing, the great religious sages. When I was in India, I craved sweets so much that I sneaked away from the ashram and went to a pastry shop in the village where I ate some of the forbidden sweets. That evening, Maharaji loudly asked, "Did you enjoy the pastry, Ram Dass?" He knew. He always knew. And he still loved me."

"Speaking of ice cream cones," another man called out, "I'm addicted to them. Like I really can't make it through the day if I don't have one once an hour! It's driving me nuts! I've got a job, you understand. In an office. And every hour I have to get up and run to the corner drug store…"

People laughed.

"As I was saying!" Ram Dass smiled. There was no condemnation in his voice. 'You're just going to have to do it until you drop the habit, he seemed to say. "Being aware of what you're doing is the first step," he added like the good psychologist he was.

It was the winter of '68. That afternoon on his father's farm he spoke of his personal experiences with the same frankness and humor that would become his trademark. He illustrated his stories with anecdotes, laughing indulgently at his own foibles. In the years to come, his profound knowledge and loving acceptance of human folly, as well as his teachings about the path that leads to enlightenment would endear him to millions all over the world. People identify with him and learn from him to love and to laugh at themselves. "It's as if he was talking to me, personally," they say when they leave his talks.

Ram Dass would not remain the ascetic Hindu monk. As the years passed, his appearance gradually became less Eastern, and by the end of the '80s he looked like Richard Alpert again. What remains constant is his humor, his humanness, his faith, and his compassion for the human condition.

In 1980, when I was planning to write a book about the '60s, I wrote him a letter asking about his pre-LSD inner life. "Were you interested in the ultimate questions? In God? Religion? What was your attitude to the materialistic value system? To the dominant approaches to psychology? In short, I want to find out if there were any signposts that foreshadowed what you later became," I wrote.

Here is his answer:

Nina—

Prior to '61 I was a snotty-nosed intellectual dilettante—obnoxiously scientific and anti the mush of humanitarianism, let alone mysticism. My Freudian preoccupation made me see all higher states only reductionistically.

I was a Quaker briefly at college. Otherwise nothing much happened until Tim took me by the hand.

Love, Ram Dass

Forty-four

Returning from that visit with Ram Dass I became aware of an aching need to link up with others who were on the spiritual path. It was time to end my isolation.

"Do you know Woodstock?" Herbie-Surya Das asked the next time I saw him.

"Sure! My sister has a summer home there. Nice place."

"Yeah, very nice. I've been going up for weekends. Know a bunch of good folk there. I'm thinking of moving to Woodstock."

"That sounds right for you. It's an art colony, isn't it?" My relationship with Nita had become more remote with the years, but I had spent some pleasant weekends in her beautiful summer home set in an exquisitely landscaped garden. My sister's social set consisted mostly of well-to-do Austrians who had summer homes in Woodstock. The place appealed to them because of its similarity to the Austrian landscape, and because it offered enough cultural events to suit their refined taste. They loved music and theater, and most of them collected art. But they were not interested in the life of the spirit, and they were not the companions I now needed to find.

"That's not the people I mean," Surya Das explained when I mentioned my sister's friends. "I'm talking about hippies. It's a power spot. They say it was once an Indian burial ground. You know, you can really feel it when you're there. Want to come along for a weekend? You'll love it. We can crash at my friends' house."

I was ready for a new adventure. I took out my sleeping bag, threw a few things in an overnight bag and we were off to Woodstock, Herbie-Surya Das and I.

We must have been halfway there when I noticed white smoke billowing out from the hood of my car. Within seconds, a dense cloud obscured my vision. The car looked like it would soon explode. "Run!" I yelled to Herbie. We ran to the ditch by the side of the road and ducked. When it seemed safe, we peeked out. The cloud had dispersed, and now Herbie took charge.

"You wait in the car," he told me. "I'll go get help."

"Where will you go?" I asked. We were miles from the next throughway exit.

"You sit tight. I'll be back soon as I can."

There seemed nothing else that could be done, and so I used the time to go into the inner silence and sat with my eyes closed for a long time. When I opened them, I became aware with a shock that it was growing dark. Oh God, I thought, and there is Herbie out there without a dollar in his pocket and with his long hair and his hippie get-up—he's a walking target for the cops, or for some hippie-hating rednecks…Why did I let the kid go? How could I have been so unconscious?

I watched the road anxiously. All sorts of scenarios shot through my head, all of them about poor Herbie out there, getting beaten up, or arrested. Strange to say, I wasn't worried about myself. My state of mind at that period in my life was what I can only describe as "feeling protected." It seemed that nothing could go wrong while that state lasted. Nothing would happen to me, I knew. But poor Herbie…

At last, I heard a car pull up behind me. It was a police car. And there in the front seat, next to the driver, sat my Herbie. My worst fears had materialized. How'll I get the kid out of that? Then I noticed that a broad grin covered the boy's face. No handcuffs, I noted with relief as he and the officer got out of the car.

"I told you she'd be worried," Herbie said to the policeman when he saw the expression on my face. "The officer was kind enough to drive me when I couldn't find a service station that was open. He knows the only one around here."

"Are they going to send somebody?" I asked.

"Yes, Ma'am," the officer said. "They'll be here in a couple of minutes. Don't worry. You'll be on your way in no time." He was of middle years, broad-shouldered and square-necked. I was amazed. Cops were supposed to hassle hippies, weren't they? That'll teach me! Thought I had no prejudices left! But looking at Herbie's innocent, shining face I realized that no cop would harass that boy. The world is a mirror. It gives back what we put out.

It was late when we arrived at the home of Herbie's friends, Larry and Jake. Their long hair left no doubt that they were hippies.

"Make yourselves at home," Larry invited us. He wore a pair of torn jeans and a sweater that was frayed at the elbows. The beard on his chin was straggly, and his eyes had a far-away look.

"You can sleep on the couch," Jake said to me. He was short and stocky with a good-natured face. "There's a mattress on the floor for you, Surya Das. We'll meditate early in the morning, okay?"

"Right," Surya Das said. "Around seven?"

"Hope you both sleep well. 'Night." The two men left the room and I swept the clutter off the couch before I spread my sleeping bag on it.

I fell asleep almost at once and awoke to the getting-up sounds of the three young men. I smelled incense. A candle was lit before the small figure of Ganesh, the Hindu Elephant God. Hastily, I rose and dressed. The men were already seated on cushions when I joined them. Their eyes were closed, and their breathing was deep. The room was so still that I was startled when sounds came from Herbie's lips. It was an ancient Sanscrit chant that elevates the vibrations in the room.

After a simple breakfast Herbie and I walked a few blocks to Tinker Street, Woodstock's main drag. It was flanked by art galleries and craft shops, each with a distinct, individual flavor.

"Do you feel it?" Herbie asked.

Yes, I felt it. I had often walked this street before when I visited Nita, but the sensation I now experienced was new. Whether I had become sensitized to spiritual vibrations, or whether it was the hippies I met that weekend and on several others that followed, I sensed the presence of something that I could not name, but it filled me with joy and serenity.

It turned out that I already knew some of the hippies who lived in Woodstock. There was Michael Green and his "old lady" Ione. Michael had been one of my favorite people at Millbrook. He was an inspired painter, and his presence was shamanic in its effect on a group. He was radiantly beautiful with his long blond hair and light-filled eyes. The spiritual path was the center of his life. And there was Isaac Abrams with his wife and their one-year-old daughter. I met others who had come to the Center; they were all on the spiritual path. They took LSD and smoked marijuana and treated these substances as sacraments.

Two weeks after that first visit, Herbie-Surya Das moved to Woodstock. "You should come to live here too," he told me.

"I'd love it, but how will I support myself?" The time had come when I had to take immediate steps to have an income.

"Why don't you open a meditation center like the one in New York?" Surya Das asked.

"What makes you think I could earn a living with that? The Center didn't even make enough to pay the rent, let alone pay me a salary!"

"It's different here. We're all poor, but we need a center where we can meet to talk and meditate together. Everybody'll pitch in, you'll see."

I was dubious, but I caught fire. When I asked for guidance in my meditations I received the directive to set up a calm center in Woodstock. On my next visit Surya Das showed me a store that was for rent.

"It would be perfect for the center," he said. "Talk to the landlady. I'm sure the rent is low."

Mrs. Matheson, the landlady, was a plump elderly woman who seemed very pleased to meet me. She received me in a living room cluttered with Victorian knick-knacks and told me that her husband was an artist, and that she rented the store only so it wouldn't stay empty. When I explained that my finances were very limited, she reduced the already low rent by another fifty dollars, and I began to feel that I had been guided to this spot.

"And what kind of shop do you plan to open?" Mrs. Matheson asked.

"I'm thinking of a meditation center."

"A meditation center! Jesus Christ! No, Mrs. Graboi. I'm afraid you can't do that here!" The smile disappeared from her face; she seemed ready to show me to the door. But then she faced me again.

"Look here, Mrs. Graboi. I really like you. I can see by the way you dress that you have good taste. Do you do any crafts?"

"Well, I can make things. I can sew, knit, crochet…I can make mosaic tables…"

"That's wonderful! Why don't you open a boutique? You could start by taking things in on consignment. I'm sure you could make a living. I'll send you customers. You'll see."

I mulled this over. It certainly seemed more realistic than the meditation center. If I had listened to Timothy's idea of an art gallery to support the LSD Center, it might still exist. Perhaps I'll be able to combine the boutique with a center…

"I'll do it!" I told Mrs. Matheson. "Only—do I have to sign a lease? What if the boutique doesn't make it?"

"It will. We'll talk about a lease next year. It's yours if you want it."

And so I began to pack my things and to prepare for my move to Woodstock.

What did I learn during my year at the Stonehenge? I was free of the fear of death. I knew that I am not my body. I had known it before, in Oued-Zem, at the birth of my children, but now I knew. I knew that my Self outlasts physical death, and that my essence, the me that is eternal, exists without form.

The other thing that seemed certain was that the New Breed is truly here. It was the music that convinced me. To the average listener, the lyrics of the '60s must have sounded like sheer nonsense. But to the turned-on ear, these young poets spoke a metaphysical language, a mystical code. That they were allowed to reach the public ear was astonishing—they were as subversive to the status quo as all new religions are.

As the hirsute '60s drew to a close, I looked back at the changes that had taken place in such a short time—in me, and in the world. What happened could not have happened without the help of higher forces. And one of the tools they used were the psychedelics.

When I began to smoke marijuana, I thought everybody reacted to it the way I did. I found out that there were as many ways of reacting as there were people. I can only speak for myself, but I know that when the psychedelics are approached with the respect they deserve, they can be a key to expanded consciousness.

*Aquarian Angel-family & Friends, Nina is on roof, far left
Woodstock, N.Y.*

The troubadours gather outside Town Hall. There are a few other people around, too. Troubadours include David Mowry, Gary Kuper and Peter Blum.

Ken Marsh explains Barry Schuttler's presence in Woodstock as Nina Graboi and Schuttler listen.

Terry Buckner and a happy Nina Graboi observe the School of Transformation's Benefit Fair last Saturday.

Kama Lila Loka, Woodstock, 1973

Nina making wall hanging, Woodstock, 1977

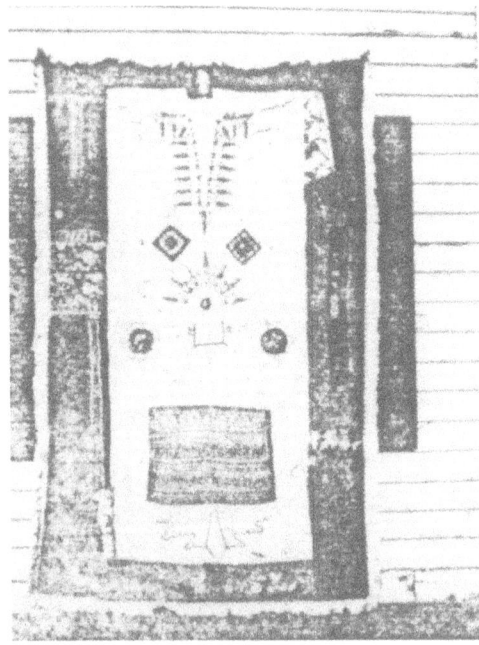
One of a series of wall hangings

Bob Reynolds and Nina Graboi, Woodstock

Terence McKenna, Esalen, Big Sur — Nina on chair at left.

Dr. Albert Hofmann and Nina, Esalen, Big Sur, 1984

Benefit Party for Albert Hofmann Memorial Library, Hollywood, 1987

*Robert Depew Reynolds,
Woodstock, 1975*

*Dave Brown, Carolyn Kleefeld, Timothy Leary
and Nina, Beverly Hills, 1988*

Nina swimming with Rosie at John Lilly's Dolphin Foundation

Nina with Ralph Abraham at Cafe Zinho, 1988

Nina with Ram Dass, Hollywood, 1986

Part Four

Forty-five

"I rented a store in town," I announced to Ernie and Mara. Ernie the American Indian and his Jewish wife Mara had lived in the Woodstock hills for several years. They were wise in the ways of surviving, and the city drop-outs dropped in on them for advice. Like most hippies, theirs was a non-stop open house. You could always be sure of a joint going around and a warm welcome, whoever you were.

Ernie filled canvases with exploding stars and celestial visions. As I watched the husky Indian merge into the woods I marveled at the contrast between the outer form and the inner spirit. The Indian seemed as much a part of nature as a deer, or a fox, but with his inner eye, he saw starbursts!

The couple lived in a ramshackle house whose walls tilted crazily. The toilet sat on a floor that had buckled under its weight. The couch in the living room was hidden under piles of clothes. "You're welcome to sleep here," Mara invited me warmly. She was cradling their new baby in her arms and glowed with the joy of young motherhood. Her casual approach to housekeeping no longer offended me. I had seen enough to realize that these youngsters wanted to break with everything their parents held dear. Children who came from immaculate middle-class homes insisted on funkiness. Clothes, homes, hairstyles, all were funky, messy, easy, relaxed. Where did it get their parents who always worried about how things looked? Though I still did not feel at ease in the chaotic environments my young friends created, I had learned to set my natural fastidiousness aside for the sake of their company. I accepted Mara's invitation and slept on the couch, not without first kicking off all the debris.

"So you're moving to Woodstock?" Mara asked. I nodded. "Wow! Where's the store?"

I described the location.

"Is it the one next to Deanie's?" Ernie asked.

"No. The other one. The one with the funny window."

Ernie laughed. "If you'd have seen it a couple of years ago you'd have thought it even funnier. There was a goat in it."

"A goat! You mean a real, live animal?"

"A goat. The guy who rented the store was a ceramicist. Kind of eccentric, you might say. He kept a goat tied up in the window. The tourists loved it, but some of us got fed-up watching that poor creature crunched up in that tight space all day, so we kinda got him to free the goat. He left Woodstock not much later. Left some of his pieces with me. You can put them in your store, if you want. They're not bad."

"Great! I'll put in anything I can get to make it look like a store!"

I had no idea how I was going to accomplish that, as I lacked both the money and the experience to run a business. What gave me and the hippies the courage to leave the security of our homes? It was because we had seen the futility of the American dream—they, by observing their parents, and I, by having lived it. We were lured by the vision of a new, transformed, transfigured human race, free of hype and of materialism, and we wanted to help change the world. To be concerned with material survival felt like a betrayal of our values. "The universe will take care of you," the hippies assured me. "Remember the lilies of the field?" I was skeptical. It hadn't worked too well at the Center on Hudson Street! But the kids said they would pass the word that I was opening a boutique and would accept craft items on consignment. Between leather goods, pottery, candles and other hand-crafted items, my store would be fully stocked. This was encouraging. I conquered my fears and prepared for the move.

Surya Das was living in a one-room cabin in the woods. It was drafty and cold, had no toilet and no running water, but the chapatis he made on his camping stove were crisp and delicious, and his paintings lit up the room with bold splashes of color. Except for these and the mattress with the Indian spread, the room was bare.

We were sitting on the floor in a circle. I knew some of the other hippies from before.

"What are you going to call the shop?" Surya Das asked.

"Don't know. Got any ideas?"

"I'll think about it." His eyes focused on something in the corner of the room. "Kama Lila!" he called sharply. "Darn that cat! She's digging her claws in the blanket again!" He reached out a long arm and detached the kitten from her woolly scratch pad.

"What did you call her?" I asked.

"Kama Lila." He caressed the words with his tongue.

"Kama—that means love in Sanskrit, doesn't it?" I asked.

"Yes; it's also the name of the Hindu god of love. And Lila—that's the play of the gods, you know, like when they create and destroy universes…" My Herbie had turned into a Hindu scholar since the days of the LSD Center.

"Kama Lila! What a nice sound! How's that for a name for my shop?"

"Lila is another name for Maya, which means nothing is real, it's all a play, it's the shadow, not the substance…" He stroked the sleek fur of the cat.

"Yes, yes, I know." Herbie could be pompous with his newly acquired knowledge. "Listen. The shop of love and play…How do you say 'shop' in Sanscrit?"

"I don't think they had shops in those days. Maybe stalls…Wait. I have it. Loka. The place. Kama Lila Loka." The way Surya Das spoke the name it had the lilting sound of music.

"KAMA LILA LOKA. The Place of Love and Play! Thank you, Herbie! That's perfect!" I exulted.

"So you're planning to move to Woodstock?" Patrick asked. He was about 18, a dark-haired boy with an open, friendly personality.

"Hey, groovy!" tall blond Evan exclaimed. "We can use somebody like you here!"

"She's great, isn't she?" Surya Das said fondly, putting his arm around me.

"Yeah, wish my Mom was like her!" Patrick agreed. He inhaled deeply and passed me the joint. "She'd freak if she knew I'm smoking grass with a lady her age!"

It was easy for me to establish contact with the hippies. As soon as they discovered that I smoked grass, I was one of them. I made no secret of my LSD experiences either, and their pleasure at finding a mature woman who experimented as they did made us instant friends.

"Hey, you need any help moving? I have a truck." Evan said. "Wouldn't mind spending a day in New York. Be no hassle to load it up with your stuff on the way back."

"Can I come along?" Patrick asked. "We can get stoned on the way."

♥ ♥ ♥

Most of my furniture was already stored with friends. The rest we loaded on Patrick's truck. We took special care with my sewing machine, which would once more help me to earn a living; only this time, I was alone. No, not quite alone. There was Jackie the cat.

The tiger kitten that had been my guide on my LSD trip had come to me via Randy and Emma, who took her along when they left Millbrook. The couple lived in the same building as Alexandra and Fred. Now they were moving in with her parents and were not allowed to bring the cat. "They have to find a home for her. Maybe you know somebody?" Alexandra asked.

"Do I know somebody! When can I have her?" My voice betrayed my excitement. I was elated by the thought of having that lovely animal for a companion. Our relationship had taken a curious turn on my weekend visits to Millbrook. During the day, she would ignore me; but at night, I would invariably find her waiting on my bed. Considering the fact that I often slept in different rooms in the labyrinthine mansion, this was quite a feat.

Her once sleek fur was scraggly and lusterless, but the joyous greeting she gave me left no doubt that a bond existed between us. The soul that lived in that furry body was deeply loving and sensitive to my every mood. By the time I moved to Woodstock, we had become inseparable.

I put her in a box padded with her favorite pillow when we had finished loading Patrick's truck. As soon as we were in motion, she meowed so pitifully that I let her out. The rest of the way she sat draped around my neck, all the while drooling and complaining and carrying on as if she were about to die.

I wasn't sure about my own fate either. Evelyn's words came back to me. "You'll be poor. You'll wear shabby clothes and live in a cold-water flat," my glamorous Five Towns friend had warned when I told her I was determined to end my marriage. My clothes were not yet shabby and never would be; I was to discover creative ways to dress with style for next to nothing. But Evelyn was right about the rest. Not a cold-water flat, though. A cold-water store. If I was lucky.

Mrs. Matheson lived in the house next to the store. She came out to greet me when she heard the truck pull up. Jackie, deliriously happy to be free, leaped out and shot past her into the bushes. "My, what a big cat!" Mrs. Matheson said half admiringly, half afraid. Jackie, now three years old, was in fact huge. Her rich calico fur added to the size of her body, and when she arched her back and stiffened her fluffy tail, this gentlest of animals could look quite fierce. Right now, however, she was intimidated by the new surroundings. Returning quickly from her expedition to the bushes, she hovered near my legs.

"You're not planning to keep her in the store, are you?" Mrs. Matheson inquired, a worried look spreading over her face. "You'll take her home, won't you?"

"Mrs. Matheson," I said timidly, "I don't have a home. I was hoping you'd let me stay in the store for the time being. Of course, if it's not okay, I'll…"

"Oh, your apartment isn't ready? I quite understand. The workmen are so unreliable these days…"

"No, Mrs. Matheson. To tell you the truth, I don't have an apartment. Yet. Don't have the money right now. I could stay with friends, but it would be easier if I could sleep here while I get the shop going. What do you think?"

Mrs. Matheson's double chin quivered. "Well," she said, "it's not customary…Nobody ever slept in here before. You won't be very comfortable! There's just the cold water sink in the toilet… No shower…"

"I can take showers at my friends' house!" I said eagerly.

"No cooking here!" she stated firmly.

"I'll eat out or with friends," I assured her.

For a few moments, her eyes studied the ground. "Well, why not!" she said resolutely. "This is Woodstock! We're all a bit eccentric here." Relief flooded me. I threw my arms about the dear woman.

"I'll help you find a nice, cheap apartment when you can afford it," she said.

When the truck had been unloaded, I looked at my strange new home. A lopsided display window, looking ready to collapse, jutted out from the wall. It bore the individualistic stamp of the Woodstock carpenter, and had clearly been added as an afterthought.

A jewelry showcase painted shocking pink and a queerly shaped three-tiered display shelf had been left in the shop. "I'm running out of storage space," Mrs. Matheson had told me. "Would you mind if I left these here? Maybe you can use them." Where had I heard such words before? "Would you do me a favor and eat it?" a Cockney voice sounded in my ear. "Margie ran off to work without eating her breakfast again, that naughty girl! I do 'ate to waste good food!" Ma Coles!

The one-room building had once been the little red schoolhouse of the tiny community of farmers that lived here long before the artists came at the turn of the century. It was attached to a structure that was twice as tall and looked like a lean, thin-lipped elder brother peering down disapprovingly at his squat little sister. Both were painted a dull brick red until several months later, when Isaac Abrams and Carol Herzer, his second wife, painted the facade of my shop psychedelic. Clouds, sunbursts, birds in flight and tiny dots appeared on a sky-blue background. The effect was as buoyant as a child's balloon. A year later, a metaphysical bookshop opened next door, and Zubin covered its facade with satin tie-dye. For a short period, before the building returned to its former sober appearance, the two shops became a familiar Woodstock sight.

The building was set far back from the street; the foundation of a house that was never built occupied the space between. The large rectangle of bricks surrounded a luxuriant crop of weeds that grew unhindered in the rain-soaked soil. Further to the left was Deanie's restaurant, favored by well-heeled locals for the excellent food. We were two blocks away from the center of town—a long way when you consider that the center itself was no more than four blocks long. The location was not financially promising, and became even less so a year later, when Deanie's restaurant burned down.

My heart sank as I took stock of my surroundings. Now that the space was empty, the defects of the old building were glaringly apparent. A peeling coat of paint had been carelessly slapped on long ago. The uneven floor boards slanted to one side. The doors and windows looked ready to fall out of their frames. Shades of the Hudson Street Center! It was not an encouraging sight.

On the floor lay an odd assortment of things. There was a vase filled with wild flowers, some sticks of incense, a few crystals, some feathers, hand-painted cards and messages decorated with hearts and other tokens of love. Boxes and bundles were neatly stacked in a corner. They contained a variety of objects that were clumsily made—as if on purpose, as a protest against the machine. The things touched me. How unsophisticated they were! I displayed the items with the loving care a mother gives to the Kindergarten splotches of her children.

As I surveyed the storefront, I counted my blessings: I had a roof over my head, a healthy body, and a sound mind. All was well. I was meant to be here. Energized by these thoughts, I went to work to set up my "home." The cardboard wardrobe I had brought was ample enough to hold all my personal belongings. The couch went against the back wall, my mosaic table in front of it. The sewing machine stood in a corner. The addition of a curtain that separated my living area from the shop created a private space and my "home" was complete.

Jackie chose a small window high up on the wall as her perch. There she sat every night, ready to hiss at any passer-by. During the day, she stretched out full length on the desk and watched over me, where I sat facing the door.

One morning Ernie came, carrying a box.

"Here are the pieces I told you about. I'd be glad if you could sell them. They're nice."

'Nice' was a poor word for the ceramic sculptures he extracted from the box. They were magnificent! One was a clown seated on a steed whose tail fanned out like that of a peacock. It was delicately enameled in a translucent blue. Another was a tower such as Gaudi might have built, with oddly shaped turrets and belfries, leaning lopsidedly to one side. There were fantasy animals and strange human shapes. I was enchanted.

"They're beautiful!" I reverently fingered one of the pieces.

"Be careful!" Ernie exclaimed. "They're brittle!"

"Wow! I see what you mean! There's a piece missing here!"

"Yeah, on most of them. He didn't know how to fire them."

A great artist who keeps goats in the display window and makes masterpieces that fall apart! I put the ceramics on top of the three-tiered shelf. The merchandise I had bought I placed on long boards supported by milk crates. I had spent my last $500 on these hand-picked items: a lavishly beaded embroidered cap from Nepal; some hand-carved wooden boxes; a primitive long-necked musical instrument with two strings; brass figurines of Hindu deities and of Buddha; finger cymbals; a painted camel-skin lamp; a large Moroccan water pipe; a Japanese shakahachi flute (which nobody could play); an African drum; yards of fabrics that I planned to sell in 6 yard lengths for saris. I hung some kurtas, the traditional embroidered tunics worn by Hindus on nails on the walls. Everything in the shop was hand-made. Like the hippies, I wanted to get away from synthetics and mass-produced goods.

I also had some pipes, roach clips, and rolling papers. These I displayed in the pink showcase along with a few pieces of inexpensive Indian jewelry. The empty spaces I filled in with shells and rocks that I found on my walks.

In the following weeks, Kama Lila Loka changed day by day. With the help of a staple gun, a hammer, and a jarful of assorted nails, I transformed the shabby storefront into a shrine of beauty. By now I was an old hand at this task. Having no money meant that I had to use my imagination. I wanted the space to be an oasis of serenity and peace. The merchandise was secondary. The main thing was the atmosphere.

During the first weeks I often got up at night to give form to some idea that hit me while I slept. I covered the walls with the fabrics I meant to sell for saris, filmy pastels in rose, aquamarine, pale fuchsia. Golden yellow covered the ceiling and billowed around the amber spotlights that replaced the bare light bulbs. On the opposite end from my "home," the Shiva statue stood on two milk crates concealed by a handsome cloth. Vases filled with fresh flowers flanked the shrine, and candles and incense burned before the dancing figure of the god who is both creator and destroyer, symbolic of all life.

Michael Green lettered the name above the door. In his early twenties, he was a painter of such power and vision that his work brought Michelangelo to my mind. His Sanscrit calligraphy, white on the brick red background, topped the facade.

The shop opened two weeks after I moved in. On weekends, a few tourists occasionally trickled in, but during the week, nobody except the insolvent hippies entered. It was still off-season, which gave me the time to fill the shop with things I made. I crocheted shawls, knitted sweaters, sewed skirts, dresses, blouses. I strung beads, embroidered cushions, made suede leather belts. The most lucrative items, that summer and the next, were the pouches I made from the scraps a leather factory discarded.

Daily, my hair, long innocent of the ministrations of a beauty parlor, grew wilder and less manageable, until at last my head was surrounded by a halo of coarse graying hair. "I like your Afro," a customer remarked. Afro? I'd never heard of it, but they were just becoming the fashion; once again, I was ahead of my time. I was IN, and I hadn't even tried!

The clothes I wore at that time were ethnic—embroidered kurtas and long, Indian skirts. I considered myself a hippie, i.e., hip to the new consciousness, but I did not go for "funk." The loose, easy fit of ethnic clothes made American apparel feel like straight jackets. I could not understand why I had tolerated them for so long. I also stopped wearing make-up, high heels, girdles (but not bras), and hair sprays (but not deodorant). A more complete change from my Lawrence days would have been hard to imagine.

Evenings, some of the young people came to meditate with me and to talk about the spiritual path. I was poor but happy, and confident that once the tourist season began, things would work out all right. If I heard someone mention a festival that was supposed to happen that summer, I paid no attention. I was intent on creating a basis that would allow me to live according to the principles that guided me. One of them was to sell the best merchandise at the lowest price. The "hype" that permeated the society sickened me as much as it did the hippies. I would not join the profit-hungry business people whose only motive was to make money. To me, the shop would be the means to "right livelihood." My ideas about ethics in business were very firm, and with my living expenses cut to the bone, I had no need to strive for more than the minimum profit.

Forty-six

Kama Lila Loka looked more like an exotic house of worship than a boutique. Beside the Shiva statue were the symbols of Buddhism, Christianity, Judaism and Islam, a small Native American totem pole, and an African mask. The phonograph played Indian music, or Bach, or African music, or the Beatles, and the people who walked in tiptoed around as if they were in church. That this was not the best milieu for business seems obvious; but business, though I urgently needed the income, was not primarily on my mind.

Psychedelics had taught me that "I" am not my body but an evolving consciousness clothed temporarily in a body. The veil between ordinary and non-ordinary reality had parted. I died, left my body, and when I came back I was not I any more but a consciousness that encompassed a vastly broader spectrum of reality than "I" had ever dreamed. I was changed, and the new vision so attracted me that I stopped paying attention to the segment of reality that had formerly held my complete attention, namely, the physical plane.

But before long, I discovered that visions are no excuse for slacking off on the physical plane, and that spirituality is no justification for the evasion of temporal responsibilities. The task is to supply the needs of the body through the exchange of energy, and to fit harmoniously into the game called life. To play it elegantly and with style, we have to embrace its conditions and take responsibility for ourselves.

A struggle went on within me. My conditioned self wanted security—

though security included much less now than it once did; while the other self, the Self with a capital S, assured me that my needs would be supplied.

But regardless of my nagging fears, it was a magical time. Visions of utopia flooded my brain. The pictures the psychedelics beamed into my mind opened me up to the world in new ways and showed me what is possible when love, trust and faith replace envy, possessiveness and violence.

The New Age community in Woodstock was a close-knit group, and as a group we came closer to "unity in diversity" than any I had ever known. Here, as everywhere else, the hippies came in a variety of types. There were musicians, artists, poets, performers, and carpenters with Ph.D's. There were the nature worshippers who favored hallucinogenic mushrooms and peyote, the psychedelic cactus Indian shamans have used for centuries. They lived in tepees, built sweat lodges, and tried to emulate the natural lifestyle of the Native American.

Social and political change was the focus of others. Their energies were directed towards a dialogue with the authorities. Showing up at the weekly Town Hall meetings, they vociferously expressed their views, but the barrier that existed between them and the Members of the Board was so great that you wondered if they spoke the same language. Their ideas were sometimes silly, but always innovative. Some of them would have proved viable had they been given a chance, but perhaps fortunately, the sober voices of the townboard members won out.

And then there were those who longed to be liberated from the wheel of birth and rebirth, to shed their human bonds, to know God. Many of these followed a guru or a religious sect and practiced different methods to gain enlightenment.

All these groups overlapped. A live-and-let-live atmosphere prevailed. The small group that gathered at Michael and Ione's apartment on Rock City Road to meditate was on the spiritual path. I was part of that group. They were my family. Personal histories were forgotten as we talked about the reality that underlies all religions and all spiritual disciplines. We talked about doing away with the "us—they" division that separated the hip from the squares, for we were all brothers and sisters, weren't we?

But a barrier between "us" and the old established Woodstock inhabitants undeniably existed. The descendents of the earliest settlers were the most conservative element in the community. Farmers and property owners, they had a vested interest in the status quo. Then there were the artists who had come to the little town at the turn of the century. They had been a bohemian and non-conformist lot, were vegetarians, wore colorful costumes and celebrated nature. Old copies of the local newspaper revealed an uncanny resemblance between them and us—almost as if we were reincarnated versions of them! But the artists who lived there now were mostly well established and held fairly conservative views. The difficulties they experienced with the hippies were due to the youngsters' arrogant assumption that they, and they alone, had discovered the key to cosmic consciousness. Failure to appreciate their elders caused sore feelings between the two groups. The youngsters denounced the prestigious Art Student's League as a fuddy-duddy institution, and the League members saw psychedelic paintings as worthless trash.

In 1969, when I moved to Woodstock, the population numbered no more than 6000. In the summers it doubled, thanks to the second homes many New Yorkers maintained. The diversity of the population was striking. The little town was a microcosm that contained all the elements of a metropolis. In the summer, the mixture of lifestyles and ideologies that rubbed shoulders could easily have become explosive. But there was something in the air in Woodstock in those years…

From the start, I was an integral part of the spiritual group of hippies. To be 50 in Woodstock when most of the people around me were less than 25 conferred the status of mother on me. They called me the Wise Old Woman, or Queen Mother, or even occasionally, Divine Mother. I knew better. More than ever, I was aware of how little I knew and how much I could learn from the inspired youngsters. I had landed in paradise: I was surrounded by seekers and saintly souls, and if they occasionally lapsed into the brattiness so characteristic of adolescence, it was only a minor irritant.

In contrast to the spiritual security I experienced at that time, my economic survival was in grave doubt. Sales were rare. Days passed without the need to open the metal lunch box that held the cash. At the approach of rent day, my spirits often sank, but just then somebody would generally wander in and make a purchase that covered my expenses.

As the spring progressed, word of the approaching Festival brought more people to Woodstock. From my vantage point behind the desk I observed the scene. It was like a stage show unrolling before my eyes. I was intrigued to note how some people simply ignored the shrine and passed it with averted eyes; others were mesmerized by it. Lovingly, they fingered the objects that surrounded the Shiva statue and examined all the items on display. More often than not, they would walk out without buying anything; but money could not have rewarded me more than their interest in the message I tried to convey.

Most of the Woodstock hippies went to the Festival. I stayed, minding my store, unaware that 50 miles away, in a field near Bethel, history was in the making.

And after the Festival, they came to the little town whose name it made famous. All summer long, they streamed through the tiny village. Long-haired, starry-eyed, wearing funny clothes, they drank in the atmosphere of the music-filled hamlet.

Something about my shop set it apart from the rest. People would walk alongside the weed-filled foundation talking and laughing loudly, but as soon as they entered, their voices were hushed. Some told me that the tranquility and the vibrations were healing. Without knowing why, I had been directed to set up a calm center in the little town, and I had succeeded. Business also improved. The hippies bought love beads, pouches, pipes, Indian shirts, and I frequently had to replenish my small stock. The items that drew the most attention were the pipes and roach clips in the showcase.

"What's that?" a burly tourist asked, pointing to one of the tweezer-like objects.

"A roach clip," I replied in a clear voice.

"You mean you catch cockroaches with it?" His belly laugh rang through the shop.

"No. We use it to hold the last little bit of a marijuana cigarette—we call it a joint. Marijuana is sacred to us. We don't want to waste it. This lets us smoke it to the end."

The exchange attracted the attention of some of the other people in the shop. The word "marijuana" made the heads of the straight tourists turn. A thoughtful expression replaced the snicker that formed on their faces. "Sacred" is a powerful word. I hoped that it might open them up to a new way of looking at the plant. The hippies smiled at me, enjoying the spectacle.

"That was groovy," one of them said when the tourist left. "You blew his mind! Coming from a nice, respectable middle-aged lady…Wow! You're cool!" He shook my hand. When I withdrew it, I found a joint in it.

I had many loving encounters with young people who were reaching out for guidance on the spiritual journey. I kept a few of my books in the shop and sometimes pointed out passages to them that had been of help to me.

Before the summer, Michael and Ione, with the help of some of the other hippies, converted their apartment on Rock City Road into a macrobiotic restaurant. I admired the young people's idealism and the ingenuity with which they set to work. Bob Boone, a drop-out psychologist, fashioned low tables from rough, wooden planks. The cooking facility and kitchen utensils were makeshift, and the food, though undeniably healthy, was not easy for me to like. But as soon as the restaurant opened, it became the meeting place for local and transient hippies. They sat on the floor and read books, practiced calligraphy, or strung beads. Babies toddled around and were fed and watched by all. Every guru, every teacher who passed through—and there were many!—had a meal at 5 Rock City Road. It was a stop on the growing network of such places. Here, the nomadic kids who roamed all over the globe exchanged counter-culture news. They had been to Spain where they lived in places like Torremolinas or Ibiza, to Ireland where they visited the sites of Celtic shrines, to Amsterdam where they openly smoked grass and hash, and to India, where they explored the teachings of gurus and made pilgrimages to holy spots.

The hippies who manned the restaurant knew as little about the culinary arts as about business procedures. But that didn't stop them. The restaurant crew gave away as much food as they sold. The transient hippies, guitar slung over their shoulders, expected to be fed. In India, they had watched how the begging bowls of the wandering saddhus were filled with food by devout Hindus, and they felt entitled to receive the same treatment in their homeland. At night, 5 Rock City Road became a crash pad. The tables were moved aside, and the nomads spread out their sleeping bags.

According to the spiritual teachings of the East, we pick our own parents so that we can learn the lessons we need in each lifetime. If they were meant to live like Hindu holy men, wouldn't they have picked Hindu parents? I sometimes wondered. But as soon as this thought arose, I chided myself for it. The kids were right. The universe supported their roving lifestyle. The protestant work ethic was for those of little faith. They were the lilies of the field and they 'weren't gonna work on Maggie's farm no more'. They spread love and reverence for all life and tried to prove that it is possible to break the stranglehold of the meaningless and unrewarding work that serves no other purpose than to turn them into consumers of unnecessary goods.

My deepest commitment remained to the pursuit of spiritual growth. Every morning before I opened the shop I meditated, emptying my mind of the clatter of thoughts. Every night, alone or with friends, I sat facing the figure of Shiva dancing in the flickering candle light. "All is transitory, everything passes," the statue seemed to be saying. Three of his four hands hold fear-inspiring objects, but the fourth is raised in a gesture that means "Fear not!" Like Faust's Mephisto, Shiva warns us not to ask, "Stay, moment, thou art fair." When we hold on, we stop the flow—the change that is life itself.

I ardently wished to dedicate the fruits of my labor to God, selflessly, without regard for my personal advantage. But it was not always easy to keep these thoughts alive. I had broken through the walls of ordinary consciousness, and what I glimpsed dwarfed the world I had previously known. And for that glimpse, I paid with death, the death of the ego—temporarily, at least.

Many people experience bad trips, or "bummers" as we called them, because they attempt to avoid ego death. To try to maintain the illusion of a separate identity while in the throes of the unitive experience is like seeking shelter from a hurricane in a gazebo. But the ego is amazingly resilient. Like a thousand-headed hydra, it pops up again and again after each "death." It takes constant vigilance to be aware of its machinations. Ego death is not permanent, but the break-through to a broader awareness generally begins the process of transformation of the personality. For myself, as for many others, a total change of lifestyle ensued. The senselessness of enslaving myself to possessions was brought home to me in dayglow colors. Once, during an LSD session, the words Real Estate flashed unbidden into my mind. The idea that people think they can own a piece of the earth hit me so forcefully that I laughed hysterically for half an hour.

By fall, I had earned enough to rent the four-room annex to an old farm house, five minutes walk from my shop. Fall, in Woodstock, is a riotous feast for the eyes, and the short walk gave me great pleasure. Winter brought more snow than I had seen since I skied in the Austrian Alps. The streets were icy. People disappeared. Everybody stayed away from town except for unavoidable errands.

I was happy to hibernate when the weather was too inclement to open the store. I had time to read, to meditate, to write, and to make the items I would sell come summer. I put large branches of evergreen firs in tall vases, and when the first buds appeared on the forsythia bushes that grew in abundance on the hills, I brought some branches inside and watched them blossom in the heated room while snow still covered the ground. I loved the Woodstock climate and the landscape that reminded me so much of my native Austria. But by April, I, like the rest of the Woodstock population, began to have 'cabin fever'. When the first rays of sun melted the snow, people came out of their homes wearing their best, most festive clothes to stroll down Tinker Street. We smiled and greeted each other like long lost friends. Music sounded again from doorways and open windows, and the world was full of promise and hope.

On May 11th something happened that threw a shadow on my spirit which I was unable to throw off for many months. The following is the account of the event as I wrote it in my journal:

May 13, 1970

Two days ago, I drove to the City with Michael Green and his brother Joel to attend a benefit party for Timothy at the Village Gate. Against Michael's advice, I took a tab of acid. In honor of Tim, I said. But as we walked along Bleeker Street, I understood why he thought I was foolish to take acid in New York. The contrast between the decaying city and our Woodstock mountains was great.

Inside, the psychedelic notables were gathered in full force. As I roamed through the sub-basement dimness I collided with the shadowy forms of friends I hadn't seen in years. Most of the people looked familiar, even those I didn't know; there was also a sprinkling of glittering jet-setters, and some secret service men with hard faces and guarded eyes.

Rosemary appeared in the darkness, beautiful beyond words, a fairy queen, too exquisite to be real. We threw our arms around each other, kissed, and passed on. Later, I saw her sitting between two tall men who both looked like Lord Mountbatten, and now she looked Egyptian, sphinx-like, regal and unfathomable. When I bent down to look into her eyes, I saw Tim looking out of them with a mocking smile. The acid was beginning to come on.

Abbie Hoffman's loud, angry voice came from the stage. He was screaming his rage at the power structure that kept Tim in jail. "We have to fight them," he shouted. "Armed warfare is the only thing they understand!"

The audience begins to respond explosively. Michael starts to OM. "Let's cool them out," he says. We walk to the stage, OMing. "You think it's fun in jail?" Abbie yells. His face is red. He is looking directly at me. By now, other voices have joined us and his words are drowned in the sound of OM. Close to tears, he leaves the stage.

Now the reasonable voices of Allen Ginsberg, Alan Watts, and Tim's lawyer spell out the situation. Timothy is a political prisoner in a religious war. They talk about CIA involvement and Mafia plots, and instruct us how we can mobilize public opinion. The lawyer says that our peaceful prophet has begun to talk about using force.
Timothy? Talking about using force?

Relentlessly, Ginsberg's voice drones on about the Mafia dominated political machine. His account is grim, annihilating hope. They will keep imprisoning our people. A feeling of doom sweeps through me. But who are they? And who are we if those who guided a whole generation in species-wide brother-sisterhood talk about armed resistance?

The acid is coming on strong now. I feel threatened by the atmosphere in the room. I want to leave, but know that I can't trust myself to drive.
A bizarre figure swathed in bandages is wheeled on stage. From it comes the familiar voice of Wavy Gravy, whose recent car accident has left him in this state. "There's something they don't know," his voice sings out. "They can't win. Evolution is on our side!" His song tells how we make music and act like freaks to disguise the message we pass on right under their noses.

My spirits rise. 'That's right, Wavy Gravy,' I want to shout. 'We can make it peacefully, with music and with songs…'

Now Wavy talks about a game the Darkies in the south used to play when the white man came to their quarters. They would squat on their heels in the tall grass where Whitey couldn't see them; and when they looked around, there were all their friends squatting. "Why don't you squat down too and see who your friends are?" he asks.

I squat on my heels and look around. Here and there, some remain standing. They seem like a different race. Down on the floor, the laughing faces of my friends, my family, greet my laughing face. Now Wavy instructs us to take deep, rhythmic breaths. Mine keep getting deeper and longer…In a minute, I think, we'll all take off and fly up through the roof. This thought brings me back to my body and I discover that my knees hurt. They hurt so much that I can't stay down. I rise. When I look at the stage, I see four male figures, two in white leather uniforms, two in black. They wear crash helmets and goggles. Their faces are shielded and invisible.

"Aha, an individual!" one of them shouts. And then he, his companions, and the nightclub disappear, and I find myself on the outermost ring of a series of concentric circles. Before me, a pie-shaped wedge opens up. As I walk toward the center, I realize that I'm in a vast building. With a shock, I recognize it as The Cosmic Travel Agency. I've been here before, countless times. Yes, here they all are, neatly recorded and filed, my trips through eternity. So many! In exquisite detail, they rush by me as I continue to walk to the Center to get my card for the next trip.

"You've come to the end of the line," a voice booms. "No more trips for you, you've taken them all." I am filled with anguish. "Surely, there is at least one more?" I plead, knowing that it's useless. I try to pray but can find nothing to pray to…

All sense of me-ness melts away. A silence as heavy as lead. A grey, featureless void. And into that void are sucked the dismembered parts of the universe… Slowly, with a clanging, metallic noise they disintegrate into the amazingly simple building blocks of all that is…The sound of hollow laughter echoes through the void.
A long time. Nothing.

Then consciousness turns in on itself and creates an I, and that I witnesses the world re-arising by an act of will…

At dawn, I picked myself up from a thick coil of rope on which my body lay on the floor. How it got there, I had no idea. A clean-up crew was at work. In a corner, a group of my friends huddled in a cluster. When they saw me rise, they approached. Throughout the night, they had been bending over my prone body to ask if I was okay. I could feel them touching me, but did not hear them. When I opened my eyes, I saw them standing stock-still, their mouths open as if to speak. All around me, people stood frozen in whatever activity they were engaged in. The band played soundlessly, the people on the stage were motionless. I perceived this in a flash and then returned to the black hole that held my consciousness entrapped.

My friends had been debating calling an ambulance. Their relief at finding me getting up left me cold. Nothing seemed real. I walked to the bathroom. In the corridor, Allen Ginsberg approached. He smiled sadly, kissed me on the cheek and handed me a flower.

Outside, the sun was just coming up. The street was dirty and deserted. To my surprise, I found that I could drive my car with ease. Visually, the world looked as it always did, but with one difference: I no longer believed in its reality.

♥ ♥ ♥

I have not left the house since day before yesterday. My two cats, usually so playful, barely move from the spot where they lie, watching me.
As if they were waiting for me to will them back to life.

At the Village Gate, I passed through the gate of Hell. Tomorrow or the next day, I must try to remember the jewel-encrusted door to Heaven through which I passed, one acid trip…

June 12, 1970

My paralysis is beginning to lift. I'm gaining some perspective. Remembering trips where I broke through into realms imbued with meaning, filled with life, laughter, love…and yes, with some doubts and fears as well.

I want to be free of the struggle of opposites, yet I know that without them, the world would be stagnant. Perfection—the ideal once attained—is death. Life must be in motion, a spiraling motion that leads upward and on, not down into that uttermost contraction…

Was I given a choice to get off the wheel of birth and rebirth at the Village Gate? Did I blow it? It was not a question of me personally getting off. It was the end of everything. I don't mind going, but I do want the world to go on!

To go on, life must have peaks and valleys, lights and shadows, stimulations and boredom. When I try to imagine an ideal world, it always breaks down under the weight of its own perfection.

Forty-seven

The experience at the Village Gate left a deep scar on my soul. What saved me from the despair of my encounter with the Nothingness that lies at the heart of All was the realization that what I had witnessed was the destruction of matter, not of spirit. Modern physics tells us that matter is composed of atoms that stick together for a time to form an object—a table, a wall, a human body. Matter is energy; I saw it re-transformed.

Despite my intellectual understanding, a lingering malaise beset me. The pain was much like that of fifteen years ago. A feeling of meaninglessness swept through me. This time I didn't drive around in my car shouting "So what?" But my despair was just as deep. I had found the More. God was in everything, and Being was an ever ascending staircase of evolution. But what was the point if it all ended in a black hole?

The Village Gate did not shake my belief in the immortality of the soul. It rested on the experience of having been pure consciousness, unadulterated by the small, temporal self. I also understood the cyclic nature of the cosmos—the cosmic clock that strikes days and nights. The Hindu scriptures speak of the night of Brahma, where, after eons, everything returns to the uncreated. When He wakes up again, eons later, a new cycle begins. All this had been intellectually clear to me; but to witness it—to be present at the moment of total destruction, total annihilation of all that is—it was an experience that was not easy to digest.

The best antidote to the lingering heaviness of heart the experience had left behind was to be in Woodstock in the summer of 1970. It was as if unseen forces hovered over the little town, protecting it from the violence that was rampant in the rest of the world. Every weekend, a woman came into my shop with her two rambunctious pre-teen boys. She drove a distance of 100 miles just to spend the day, because Woodstock was the only place where the boys didn't fight, she told me. As far as I know, no crime was reported in Woodstock that year. My friends and I left the doors to our homes unlocked. There was nothing to dim our elation. The world was changing, and we sat at the hub of the wheel.

In the fall of the following year a strange figure strolled up my driveway. A matted mass of dirty-blond dredlocks hung to his waist, forming an odd contrast to a face that bore unmistakable traces of Celtic heritage. This remarkable head was topped by a three-cornered hat that would have been impressive except for its beat-up condition. He was dressed in a lavishly embroidered tattered coat, decorated with buttons and medals. A pair of worn American Flag pants and sneakers with torn toes also displayed the American Flag.

Even by Woodstock standards, he was striking.

"And might you be the lady of the house? The one they call the wise old woman?" he inquired. There was more than a hint of Irish brogue in his voice.

I laughed. "Old, yes. Wise, I don't know. And who might you be?"

He made a sweeping gesture with his hat and bowed. "Robert Depew Reynolds. Your servant, Madam. Many are the tales I've heard about you!"

"You have, have you? And what brings you to Woodstock?" He was new here, I was sure. I couldn't have failed to notice him if he'd been around.

"Woodstock is special. It's a power spot. I've been to most of the others around the world. They're all great, but it's here that I want to live and die." His brogue was gone, but his voice retained a Midwestern drawl.

"What makes Woodstock so special?" I wanted to know.

"It's where it's happenin' lady! Can't you feel the angels hoverin' above the land? Lots of red man's power here. Many reincarnated redskins livin' in these mountains. Mother Earth is holdin' us to her bosom, tellin' us to make this place into a garden of Eden so all the other little towns will want to be like us!"

His enthusiasm was catching. It dispelled the last clouds from the Village Gate experience. The promise of the Aquarian Age, of a New Breed! His words were a jubilant cry for action, waking me up from the lethargy of the

Village Gate and bringing me back to the here and now.

We went for a walk that afternoon. The fall colors were a blaze of glory. The apples on the trees gleamed in red-cheeked perfection, and the blue of the sky matched Bob's eyes.

At 35, he was older than the baby boomers. His roots were in the Beat generation. He had come to the Woodstock Festival with the Hog Farm. What happened at the Festival convinced him that we can have Heaven on earth. He told me about the communes he had lived in and the spiritual practices he followed—but most of all he talked about the earth. He was in love with her and passionately certain that we could save the world if we changed our wasteful ways. "We can do it!" he said. "So many of us are already awake! And there'll be more and more!" His self-confidence extended to the entire human race. He believed that if all restraints were removed, we could create paradise on earth. He told me of the freedom of the road, and how he never needed money.

"Things come to me. I don't need a lot. All my possessions are in my car. I don't plan. Whatever comes is welcome. Life is a ball, there's always a new adventure…I like travelin'. Want to see a great bus I once traveled in?"

I nodded. Listening to him made me see how much I was still hedged in by old assumptions. I still needed a roof over my head and money for food and rent. I had not surrendered to the flow. I lacked the faith that Bob and the hippies had that my needs would be taken care of if I trusted the universe. Bob stood for all the things I admired in the hippies, but couldn't do myself. Listening to him made me want to cut loose from my moorings and trust myself to the road. Yes, I wanted to see the bus he had traveled in.

We were nearing the commercial part of town when Bob turned into Calomar Lane, a cul-de-sac that held a variety of houses in various stages of disrepair. The one on the corner was in fair shape. Bob knocked on the door. A handsome bearded man let us in.

"Hey bro! How's it go?" Peter and his vivacious wife Judy made us feel welcome. The house was charming and much neater than the homes of other hippies. I admired the way things were arranged, and then Peter and Bob took me to the backyard. A large army bus stood there. Its drabness was a blot on the riotous landscape. I looked at Bob. "Is this it?" It hardly seemed the proper vehicle for the flamboyant young man.

"It traveled with the Hog Farm. Go inside."

Ah, this was more like it! The walls were painted psychedelic and the ceiling was hidden under paisley spreads. Mobiles made of broken mirrors, pine cones, shells, and bits of ceramic hung from it and tinkled in the breeze. The bus spoke of adventure, of a carefree life on the road.

"Groovy!" I said reverently.

"You want it? I'm willing to sell," Peter commented.

"You're kidding! I don't need a bus!"

"You never know when you might want one," Bob said.

"Nonsense! Besides, I couldn't afford it!"

"Well, you're a friend of my blood brother, and that makes you my friend. How much can you spend? A thousand?" Peter asked.

"Forget it. I haven't got a thousand!"

"How much? Five hundred?"

"You'd sell it for five hundred?"

"For you. Make sure not to tell anybody. It's a one-time offer. I'll probably be sorry for it tomorrow, but the sun is shining, and you look like you belong in it…"

"The bus becomes you, wise woman!" Bob said appreciatively.

"You want it?" Peter asked.

I felt dizzy. "Does it work?"

"Needs a few minor adjustments, but the motor is great. So what do you say?"

The only excuse I can offer for the mad act that followed is that the fever of the road had seized me. I had faith in the honesty of the hippies and could see no reason to doubt Peter's words.

I bought the bus.

It was three months before it could be coaxed to life long enough to be driven from Peter's driveway to mine. By then I knew that Peter boasted he could sell a refrigerator to an Eskimo, and that I had been had. When I asked him for a refund, he laughed. "The money was spent long ago. Don't worry. You got that bus cheap. You'll thank me for it yet, believe me!"

Bob Reynolds asked if he could park his car in my driveway for a few days, and I agreed. Business was slow; we spent a good deal of time together. Mostly Bob talked, and I listened. Like many who share the Irish gene, he was a born poet. He could turn the simplest event into a breath-taking yarn. He told me of his travels, the people he had known, the women he had loved, the books he had read, the American Indians, his youth. His words painted portraits, and my room filled up with the presences he invoked.

For a few weeks, he slept in his car. When the nights got colder, I invited him into the house. Gratefully, he moved his belongings into the spare room. When he spread his few possessions around, the room took on a unique flavor. He cherished everything old, especially if it was a piece of American history. One of his most treasured possessions was a large, time-worn copy of a portrait of George Washington. It was the first thing he pinned up on the wall. Everything he touched proclaimed his love for the earth and for his country.

It was a time of synchronicity where, if you stepped out on the Village Green, you would run into precisely the person you needed to see. It was a time when our hearts were filled with the yearning for spiritual growth and the desire to establish the kingdom of God on earth.

Bob was a messenger. He was Pan, he was Dionysus. He was also a rogue and a manipulator who was not above helping someone pull off a shady deal. I never knew what his part in the bus deal was. I didn't ask. To me, he appeared as a teacher who, purely by being himself, made me aware of my shortcomings. I wanted to learn to see things through his eyes. He struck me as a time traveler. He seemed to belong to an era long before pollution, when streams were pure and the earth was a garden. One of his pet schemes was to convert the town dump into a garden. He drew up elaborate plans for a recycling plant and for ways to convert the garbage into valuable manure. He was a Virgo, as typical for his sign as I am for mine. He was at home in the woods and in restaurants, where he liked to wash dishes in return for a meal. His genetic roots were Irish, but his affinity with nature was American Indian.

His habits were Spartan. He rose early and ate a breakfast of wheat germ, honey and yogurt, and then he was off on his rounds in town. He hung out on the Village Green and before long, he knew everybody in town. Evenings, he went to the Cafe Expresso, the Joyous Lake, or wherever people gathered. He loved them all, the squares, the freaks, the drunks, the space cases…

Bob embodied some of the virtues of the New Age, and some of the vices of the old. He had studied religion and philosophy for two years, then left the university to join the U.S. Marines. After his discharge he had traveled all over Europe and studied with poets, sculptors and painters.

For several months, he lived in my spare room. During that time, my perception of him flickered. One moment I saw him as a highly evolved teacher, and the next as a roguish, unscrupulous drunk. "I drink because I don't want people followin' me around," he told me. "I don't want to be put on a pedestal." It sounded like a good reason, but his dependence on the can of beer was as great as that of a baby on its bottle.

It was natural that a personality such as his would attract a wide variety of people—some eccentric, others as ordinary as apple pie. His love of life embraced everyone, and his vitality spread a glow over everything he touched.

One day he brought three men to my house who looked even stranger than he. "That's Plunker," he said, pointing to a man in his mid-20s who resembled him so much that he could have passed for his younger brother. Plunker's costume was as wild as Bob's; instead of the three-cornered hat, he wore a beat-up brimmed one that was full of holes. Like Bob's coat, it held a collection of buttons with peace and love messages. Over his shoulder hung "the plunker"—a long-necked gourd to which a single coarse cord was attached. He underlined his words by plucking the cord, which gave off a hoarse, unmusical sound. His smile was as open as Bob's, and he spoke in a slow drawl that was easy to listen to.

The second man was simply called "Bear"—an apt name, as he stood a good 6'5 in a broad, powerful frame. Bear was an American Indian who had been raised by a Jewish couple. He told me of his Bar Mitzwah, and when he said some Yiddish words, the effect was startling. He loved his adoptive parents, but his loyalty belonged to his genetic roots.

The shortest of the three bore the stamp of an urban youth. Garrick was a brilliant story teller and an exceptionally gifted graphic artist.

The three were as incongruous a team as the Harvard trio. They were organizing the first Rainbow Gathering which was to take place in Colorado and were aflame with a utopian dream—a vision of the New Jerusalem which was to arise on the site of the Rainbow Gathering…if not that year, then the next.

When they came to Woodstock, some of the groundwork for the Gathering had already been laid. They had secured the site and enlisted the help, or at least overcome the objections, of some of the people in authority. My home became their headquarters during their Woodstock stay. We spent hours discussing strategies and dreaming about the New Jerusalem. We turned on together—Barry and Bear took peyote, Garrick and Bob took mushrooms, and I took LSD. The visions I saw on this trip showed me white-clad figures walking silently in virginal woods. It will be a gathering of saints, I thought exultantly.

The hope was that the Gathering would bring as many people together as the Woodstock Festival. There was to be no exchange of money, and no stars. "Everybody is a star," Garrick said. Word was to be spread entirely by handbills and by word of mouth. Here is how the invitation read:

WORLD FAMILY GATHERING
New Jerusalem Mandala City
—For All People—

On July 1st, 1972, near Aspen Colorado, hopefully on 3000 acres of land set up for the purpose—there is going to be a gathering for all people worldwide, & the invitation reads:

We, who are brothers and sisters, children of God, families of life on earth, friends of nature & of all people, children of humankind calling ourselves Rainbow Family Tribe humbly invite:

All races, peoples, tribes, communes, men, women, individuals—out of love.

All nations and national leaders—out of respect.

All religions and religious leaders—out of faith.

All politicians—out of charity

to join with us in a gathering together for the purpose of expressing our sincere desire that there shall be peace on earth, harmony among all people. This gathering to take place beginning July 1, 1972, near Aspen Colorado— or between Aspen & the Hopi and Navajo lands—on 3000 acres of land that we hope to purchase or acquire for this gathering—& to hold open worship, prayer, chanting, or whatever is the desire of the people, for three days. But upon the fourth day of July at noon to ask that there be a meditative, contemplative silence wherein we, the invited people of the world may consider

& give honor & respect to anyone or anything that has aided in the positive evolution of humankind & nature upon this, our most beloved & beautiful world—asking blessings upon we the people of this world & hope that we people can effectively proceed to evolve, expand, & live in harmony & peace.
—AMEN—

Garrick's parents were Judith Malina and Julien Beck, the founders and artistic directors of The Living Theater, which, because of its leftist leanings and unorthodox performances, had had some run-ins with the law. It began in the Beck's living room, then graduated to off Broadway, and later toured Europe. The plays they performed drew heavy criticism as well as much praise. They were daringly innovative, sometimes involving the audience in the action. Their work focused on social conditions and forced their audiences to think for themselves—an important service in a culture that lulls its members to sleep.

The branch of the counter-culture to which I belonged was not interested in bringing about political change, because we believed that the only lasting cure for social ills lies in raising the collective consciousness. Short of that, history is bound to repeat itself. The Gathering had no message other than the peaceful coming together of people of all kinds. That the wording of the invitation would find the greatest resonance with the hippies was to be expected. "Straight" society would have no use for it. The hippies themselves, however, covered a broad spectrum; to gather as many as possible up into a single fold for a few days was a noble undertaking.

Bob and I went with Garrick, Plunker and Bear to Max Yasgur's farm, the site of the Woostock Festival. The men reverently walked the ground, and even I could feel something in the air.

When Bob had been in my house for a few months, he fell in love with Gael Varsi and moved in with her. Gael was a tall, attractive redhead who came to Woodstock with her three-year old son shortly after I did. She started an organization called FAMILY in the tiny living room of her three-room house. Together with a handful of volunteers, she dealt with the daily problems that came up for the kids who drifted from town to town expecting God to take care of them.

"It's not God," I would tell them in an attempt to make them take responsibility for themselves, "it's kind people who give you food and shelter." "Yes, but it's God who inspires them," they would reply. And of course, when they put it that way, they were right, since God is all there is, and everything is God. Again, I chided myself for my lack of faith.

To Gael, talk like that meant nothing. She did not speculate about philosophy. She saw a need, and strove to fill it. "I didn't start FAMILY out of idealism," she protested when I praised her work. "I needed an income, and I knew I could generate it through FAMILY." Indeed, she was able to pay herself a marginal amount out of the contributions she manifested, but almost any job she could have taken would have paid her more.

In the beginning, her activity consisted mostly of serving coffee and sympathy to the kids who came to her door. But her small group of volunteers grew, and FAMILY moved to a building on Rock City Road. Within a year it obtained non-profit status, and the townsfolk, at first fearful that the organization would bring more unwanted hippies to the area, soon saw that FAMILY's presence saved them many problems. After a few years, Gael bowed out of the expanding organization, which became a model for similar organizations in other towns. Today, it numbers most of the prominent citizens of Woodstock among its volunteer staff. But back then, when Bob fell in love with Gael, FAMILY still struggled for its survival.

Bob's involvement was a help as well as a hindrance to Gael. Both were strong-willed individuals who had their own ideas about how to run it, and despite his intense patriotism, or perhaps because of it, Bob was an anarchist who could not tolerate rules. He also relished the company of a man who was the delight and the despair of the community. Alfie was a poet. He had been an actor when the love of the drink overtook him. He was brilliant, and he was mad, and his escapades kept the hippie community amused. "Know what Alfie did yesterday?" people would say to each other. Invariably, there was something outrageous and hilarious to report. Perhaps his most memorable moment came when he got mad at a town official who complained about his pecadillos. Alfie followed him to his car, waited until he was seated behind the wheel, jumped on the hood, and pissed on the windshield—directly into the man's face.

Meanwhile, there was some activity on my army bus. "You just going to let that thing stand there?" Chris Groden had asked one day, pointing at the ugly bus.

"I can't afford to get it fixed," I said, annoyed. The sight of the bus never failed to vex me. "Guess I should have it towed to the junk yard."

"Can I take a look at it? Maybe I can fix it," Chris said.

"Be my guest. Wish I could sell it, but nobody will be as dumb as I was! Sure, go ahead! As long as it doesn't cost anything…"

Chris did not ask to be paid any more than the other hippies who often gave me a hand. They wanted to do away with money, to return to an economy of trade. "Trading is no guarantee for honesty," I would object. "There were greedy horse traders too, you know!" But these youngsters, who had grown up in a culture dominated by money, saw it as the root of all evil.

Chris Groden had the good looks of his Anglo-Saxon heritage. He was broad-shouldered, blond and bearded, with dreamy blue eyes. He had come to the Festival carrying a sheep wound around his shoulders, and this made him an instant celebrity. A reputation for originality accompanied him to Woodstock, where he took up residence after the event. "Residence" is not quite right; he did not become a rent-paying resident, as far as I know, because he had the same ability to live like the lilies in the field as Bob. He came from a devoutly Catholic family who lived with their twelve children in middle-class ease. The boy left home to go on the road, trusting his fate to God. He was smart, resourceful, and good at anything he tried. He knew something about plumbing and electricity, and about repairing cars. He could cook, do carpentry, and was a gifted artist. He enjoyed "hanging out" with me, and I grew to like the bright youngster who was part of the crew at 5 Rock City Road.

The trees were bare of the leaves that shone like burnished gold the day when I bought the bus. Now it was late fall. Chris came almost every day to work on the bus. He clearly enjoyed the challenge and had made up his mind to get it going before the year was up. From his visits to junk yards he brought back parts that fitted, almost. His ingenuity in adapting them for his purpose was awesome, but no more so than his ability to get things given to him for nothing.

"I'm doing the right thing, you dig? When we're aligned with the universe, everything comes!"

As far as the bus was concerned, the universe took its time. It was mid-February when Chris called from the driveway.

"Want to go for a ride?"

I could hardly believe it. Hastily, I grabbed my coat and ran out. Chris held the bus door open for me. The huge vehicle was cold and empty. I sat down next to Chris. He turned the key, and after a few sputterings, the motor sprang to life. Expertly, he backed the big vehicle out of the spot where it had stood so long.

"I'm speechless with admiration," I told the boy. I thought we'd just drive around the block, but when I saw him heading for Rte. 212, I grew uneasy. "What happens if we get stuck? I don't trust this thing!" I protested.

"That's not a good attitude, Nina. Be positive! Think good thoughts!"

We drove through town and then further out on 212, and when we came to the reservoir, we turned around and came back to my driveway without a hitch. I gave Chris a hug. "Well done, kid! You're great!" I told him.

"What do you want to do with it now that it's running?" he asked.

"Gee, I haven't thought about it! I never expected that it would! Do you think it's road-worthy?"

"Well, I don't think you should drive it yourself. Maybe if you had the right driver…"

I got the picture. "Okay, Chris. What do you have in mind? You've been hatching plans while you were working on it, weren't you?"

"Well, you said you want to buy some Native American stuff for Kama Lila Loka. We could go south and hit some reservations…"

"In that? You really think…?"

"Why not? I'll drive. We'll stop in groovy places and do groovy things and bring some of the Woodstock vibes to people along the way! What do you say, Nina? Let's hit the road!"

There it was. Adventure! Here was my chance to test my faith. Could I trust, like the hippies? I was ready to try.

"All right. Let's do it. We can leave as soon as the weather gets warm. There's no heat in the bus."

"We don't have to wait," Chris said. "I have it all figured out. Jack has a wood-burning stove he wants to give away. I can fix it so you'll be cosy, don't worry. How many people are we taking along?"

"How many?" I hadn't thought of that!

"No point driving that big bus with just two people in it. Bad for the ecology."

"Of course," I said humbly. How high these youngsters were! They always included the world in whatever they did, and if that couldn't be done, at least as many as a pad or a vehicle could hold. My selfishness confronted me. I banished the fear of sharing a long voyage with a wonderful but messy bunch of hippies.

"How many were you thinking?" I asked Chris. I had a hunch he had already invited some of his friends.

"I'll build bunks that can sleep maybe eight or ten. It won't take much lumber. I know a dude who works in a lumber yard ... "

"I see!" I said, awed by the details of the plan Chris had elaborated in silence, while he worked on the bus. "So who do you have in mind? And do they want to go?"

"They can be ready by tomorrow!"

"Hold it a minute, Chris. We're not going tomorrow. I have to tell you, I don't like you to go around inviting people to come on my bus! Don't you think you should have asked me first?"

Chris's face had a way of looking remorseful that made him appear angelic. I broke down. "Okay. So who are they?"

The sun came out on his face again. "You'll like them. They all love you."

"Okay, Chris, but put that stove in first."

I seriously questioned the possibility of a wood-burning stove in a bus, but if it could be done, Chris would do it. The solution he came up with was simple. He drilled a hole in the roof of the bus and put a stovepipe through it. The heavy iron stove stood on a sheet of metal; Chris put a guard rail around it so nobody would lurch against it on the road. The ingenuity that came so effortlessly to this young pothead and acid freak was shared by many of the other hippies. My own ability to make do, to improvise with whatever was at hand, had greatly increased since my psychedelic experiences. I believe it was the expansion of consciousness that allowed us to consider many more options than had been available to us before.

"That's great, Chris," I said admiringly when the stove was installed. "As soon as you finish the bunks, we'll leave."

And so it was that eight adults, one baby, a dog, a cat and four guitars piled into a rickety army bus with smoke belching out of its top one blistering cold February day. Our destination—south.

"I'll be back in six weeks," I told Priscilla, who was going to house-sit and mind the store.

"Groovy!" she said. "Don't worry about a thing! Have a great time! Love you!"

Jackie ran after the bus as long as she could, and then I lost sight of her.

Forty-eight

The people on the bus were all under 20, and between them, they had enough hair to cover fifty bald heads. The young mother's blond tresses hung in the baby's face as it nursed at her full breast. Chris tied his in a pony tail, and Gary restrained his mane with an Indian headband.

Then there was Seraphina, the love of Chris's life. "Seraphina!" he sighed when he first told me about her. "She's an angel! She's as beautiful as her name! Wait till you meet her!"

The girl really looked like an angel. She was long-legged, slender and tall, and she moved with a languid grace. Straight chestnut hair hung to her hips, and almond-shaped brown eyes that were fringed by long lashes sat in a small, exquisitely shaped face. She was as beautiful as Chris had said, but I was struck by an oddly vapid expression in her eyes, as if she were listening for some momentous internal event. The reason soon became apparent. The angelic Seraphina suffered from constipation. The girl's discomfort was alarming. I searched my brain for some remedy, but could not come up with anything she hadn't already tried. The amount of information she had on the subject was remarkable. "I've been constipated for years," she told me matter-of-factly.

"Isn't there something you can do about it?" I asked, concerned.

"About the only thing that still works sometimes is prune juice. I should have brought more. There's only half a bottle left. Not that it does much good…"

Seraphina's constipation absorbed all her attention. It was no use trying to talk to her about anything—the subject always returned to this central fact. The demands of Seraphina's digestion dictated many of our moves.

"Stop!" she would shout. "I think I can go!"

Obediently, Chris stopped the bus and we waited while Seraphina disappeared into the bushes.

"Did you?" we asked anxiously when she returned.

"No. Nothing. Not a drop. Wonder if I should take more Ex-Lax?"

As a rule, Bertha, as we named the bus, would refuse to start again after a Seraphina stop. Starting was not her favorite activity. Most of the time, Chris could coax her back to life when we got stuck on the road. But if we got stuck in a service station, Bertha could not be budged. She adored the attentions of a trained mechanic. Almost every time we stopped for gas, one of her vital parts had to be replaced, which necessitated her stay at the service station at least overnight.

Bertha forced us to stop in many places we had not planned to visit. We discovered that we could always connect with other hippies in the small, funky health food stores that had begun to dot the country. The local "heads" offered us beds, food, and dope. Distinctions of class, color, creed, and nationality didn't exist. Lettered or unlettered, wealthy or poor, black or white, we were instant family. What tied us together was our common discovery of eternity. It made us into a clan. We didn't talk much. "When did you start to turn on?" "Last year." "Far out!" "Cool!" "Dig it!" "I grok." "Om." "Namaste." It was all we needed to say.

We were few, but to us we seemed many. The world was our home, it was filled with friends. Stepping out of my nuclear family and my social set I had become part of a large family—a family that, by 1970, had small branches all over the globe. "Freaks" lived on farms, in condemned houses, in teepees, lean-tos, old school buses, domes. They all loved nature. They sincerely believed that love rules the world, and they acted lovingly to one another. They were hippies; they were freaks. They were outrageous. And they had just been born.

I was a midwife; I was a den mother. They were the New Breed. I was also one of them. For me, age as a factor stopped after my first experience with marijuana. Before that, I had meditated on eternity. My intellect probed its mystery, but my brain could not penetrate a territory so alien to the western mind. The psychedelics triggered the neural switch that allowed me a glimpse—an instant of eternity. Having known it, the aging of my body was of no great concern. I was lovingly received by the youngsters. My age was honored, but created no barrier. Us few oldsters in the midst of the baby-boomers were accepted because, like the other "freaks," we saw through the games of society. The cry they sent out against my generation was directed against the rigid, antiquated power structure, not against us.

I was pleased that the kids felt free with me, free to be who they were. Their lack of inhibition in my presence was flattering, but it could lead to embarrassing situations.

We were parked near a supermarket while Gary played a gig in a small coffee house. I was tired. The night was cool. I made sure there was enough wood in the stove, put on my nightgown and stretched out on my bunk near the front of the bus. I was drifting off to sleep when Chris came in. With him was a cute girl of about sixteen whom he had met that day. He had given up competing with Seraphina's constipation.

"This is Lisa, Nina. Isn't she beautiful? We've always known each other, but we only just met in this lifetime!"

"Isn't it great?" Lisa said, looking adoringly at the handsome boy.

"Come on. I want to show you some of my drawings," Chris said to the girl. "Good night, Nina." He nodded to me and pulled Lisa to the broad platform in Bertha's rear which was covered with pillows; when the bus was in motion, I often sat there, watching the landscape go by.

I had gone back to sleep when Bertha began to shake. I sat up. Are we back on the road? I wondered. But the bounces were too rhythmic to be mistaken for potholes. The sounds that came from the rear of the bus gave me the clue.

I was not then, nor am I now, a friend of "free" love. I've seen it bring as much pain as the unfree kind. Love, as we now understand it, is not really freely given; it always expects something in return. However, I was not about to preach to Chris and Lisa just then. Using a trick meditation had taught me, I blocked out the sounds and the motion and tried again to fall asleep. I had almost succeeded when the shrill scream of sirens tore through the night.

I looked out. Three police cars were bearing down on us from three different directions.

"Chris!" I called.

"You handle it. I can't!" his voice came back weakly.

I was forced to take action. There was no time to lose. I slipped into my housecoat, ran a comb through my hair and opened the door.

"Is anything wrong?" I asked the officers as I stepped out. When they saw me, all three did a double-take. They did not expect a gray-haired, matronly woman in a suburban-type housecoat to emerge from the ancient vehicle with smoke belching out of its roof.

"We had a complaint, Ma'am...." one of the officers said.

"A complaint? What did we do? I'm traveling with a few young people—sort of like a chaperone, you know. They're nice kids, but if one of them did something wrong, I want to know about it. We're parked here because one of the boys is playing in that cafe. What's the complaint about?"

"Well, you know how people are, Ma'am. They see a funny-lookin' bus and they get suspicious. The person who called said it looks unsanitary," the youngest of the officers said, looking down at his shoes.

"Unsanitary! The kids are messy, but they're clean. We keep no rotten food around, I make sure of that!" I said, looking indignant. "You can take a look, but two of the kids are asleep inside. I'd hate to wake them up."

"That's okay, Ma'am. We believe you. You best leave here soon as the young musician gets back. Where're you heading?"

"As far south as we can get. I'm tired of the cold!"

"You go back in there before you catch a cold. Wish you luck, Ma'am. Have a good trip." And the three cars departed in the directions from which they came.

"Gee thanks, Chris! You were a big help!" I called when I got back inside.

"Wow, Nina! How'd you get rid of them?"

"Told them the truth. We have nothing to hide except you two screwing in here. Can't you wait till you're in a private place?"

"Let's do it in the street..." Chris sang mockingly.

I was getting tired of the bus. In the two weeks we'd been on the road, my relationship with Bertha had worsened to the point where I saw her as a devouring monster determined to eat away my last reserves. Before leaving Woodstock, I paid two months rent on the shop and the house, and what was left of my money I took along for the trip and for merchandise I planned to buy. The trip money was gone, and the merchandise money was steadily shrinking. I told Chris we would go no further than the nearest town in a warm climate where we would stay till the end of the winter and earn some money for the trip home. "Okay," Chris said. "I know a groovy place in Coconut Grove. It's called Maya House, isn't that cool?"

"Coconut Grove? Where is that?"

"Outside Miami Beach. We can park the bus there and swim in the ocean. We'll have a ball!"

By the time we arrived at the Maya House, the last of my resources had been eaten up by Bertha and my hungry traveling companions. I was broke, as broke as when I first came to Woodstock—or to London, or to America, for that matter.

The Maya House was on a pleasant, quiet street and sat in the middle of a tropical garden. Mangos, papayas, avocados, grapefruit, oranges and figs grew in profusion among exotic flowers. The large old main house had three floors with many rooms that were all occupied by hippies. There were some small huts in the garden, also occupied. The place hummed with energy and activity.

The Maya House belonged to Debbie and Jerry, a young couple that was so well matched that they called themselves Tweedledee and Tweedledum. Debbie looked like a Semitic prophetess. Dark-haired and with luminous dark eyes, she was warm-hearted, mercurial, volatile, and smart. Jerry was more cool-headed. He was gentle, shrewd, and idealistic. At 28, he had been the youngest judge in the Florida courts, but gave up the bench to become a trader. The couple traveled extensively in Africa and South America and brought back an assortment of exotic goods.

Tweedledee and Tweedledum received me like a long lost, beloved aunt. They gave us permission to park Bertha across the street and use their facilities, but insisted that I sleep in the guest house, a one room bungalow which was temporarily empty. I gratefully accepted. I had had enough of life on the road. The fact was that I enjoyed a roof over my head and a real bed.

I called my home. "How are you, Priscilla? And how is Jackie? Does she miss me much? And business. Any money coming in?"

"Just enough to keep things going," Priscilla said. I was disappointed, but not surprised. I told Priscilla that I was broke and asked her to send me money as soon as any came in.

Zubin had given Chris two bolts of tie-dyed fabric before we left Woodstock. We tried to sell it on the Swap Meet, but there were no buyers. I experimented draping and tying it in different ways on my body, and that remained my costume for the rest of my stay.

There was a sewing machine in the main house. Debbie put me to work making skirts from Guatemalan fabrics. This gave me enough money to pay for my food, but as my stay grew longer, I could not remain in the guest house without paying rent. Reluctantly, Tweedledee and Tweedledum told me that they needed the income.

"Do you like to string beads?" Jerry asked.

"Sure. I string necklaces for my shop."

"Well, if you're willing to stay in the little hut, you could probably save up enough stringing beads for Om Shalom to get back to Woodstock. Want to try it?"

I agreed. I had given up on Bertha. I could not bring myself to sell her, knowing what a headache she was. So I turned her over to Chris and told him to do what he wanted with her. The first thing he did was to paint her sky-blue, and after many days of work, he managed to get her going long enough to park in a compound where people lived in a number of broken-down vehicles.

The hut stood in the midst of the tropical garden. It had a roof, a floor, and a wall. The rest was enclosed by nearly invisible screening. Inside, there was just room enough for a mattress and space to walk around it. It was like living in the jungle. As I sat on the mattress stringing turquoise, coral, and silver beads, small geckos, the tropical cousins of lizards, climbed on the screen, an orange balloon of alarming size sprouting from their necks whenever they made a funny little croaking sound.

Perhaps 16 people were living at the Maya House at that time. As soon as they entered the compound, they took off their clothes as casually as other people take off their coats. It was the first time that I found myself in such informal company, but as I watched these young people unselfconsciously go about their business in their birthday suits, it seemed silly to hide one's body. We all have one, don't we? And we all eat, defecate, and sleep. So what's the big deal? From what I observed, nudity does not lead to any more sexual activity than wearing clothes. When private parts become public, I noted, they lose much of their prurient fascination. I had no qualms about following the others' example. It was a relief to walk about stripped in that tropical climate. It soon became so natural to me that I once caught myself just in time before walking out starkers in the street!

Om Shalom, the name of Jerry's business, is the combination of the holy syllable OM of the Hindus, and of shalom, the Hebrew word for peace. Maya, a Sanscrit word, is usually translated as illusion—the illusion engendered by the world of the senses, and by the transitoriness of bodily existence. Tweedledee and Tweedledum knew how to pick their names! I loved the young couple. It felt good to be in the company of a happy couple. Relationships were breaking up everywhere, so that you never knew if people who were couples a week ago were still together. I was sure that Jerry and Debbie were mated for life and was devastated when I learned, two years later, that they had separated.

I hardly knew any of the other people who were living at the Maya House. My need for solitude was always great, and after being shut in with a bunch of young people on the long bus trip, it assumed mammoth proportions. I was content to spend day after day alone in my hut stringing beads and watching the geckos on the screening.

Coconut Grove had a large, active hippie group. There were macrobiotic and vegetarian restaurants, dances, parties, consciousness-raising groups, and a plethora of New Age seminars. Debbie and Jerry knew about everything that was going on and often asked me to accompany them. They took me on Ken Kayes's boat, a large converted patrol boat that had been built in the U.S. for the Russians in World War II. Kayes had been a hard-nosed, successful real estate broker when Jerry and Debbie met him and opened him up to New Age ideas. Some of the young people who were enrolled in his course of Living Love lived on the boat, and we cruised around with them in the Miami bay. There was also a social group called Cornucopia that held dances

and other events where hippies could meet. Interest in Yoga, the I Ching, the Tarot, astrology and other New Age holy cows was great in Coconut Grove, but the tendency was more body-oriented than in esoteric Woodstock.

"Did you ever pick mushrooms?" a bushy-haired hippie named Heartspace asked me one evening at Cornucopia.

"Never." I still remembered the strong warning I received as a child not even to touch the funny little fungi that grew in the woods. The word 'poison' was linked in my mind to the word 'mushroom'. "You have to be an expert to know which ones to pick!"

"Oh, it's easy to recognize them. They're great when they're fresh! It's, like, they connect you to nature in a way acid never does. You're part of it, you're in it, and it's so luscious you want to submerge yourself in it ... Know what I mean?"

I did. It was a feeling I knew from smoking marijuana. I realized that he was talking about the psilocybin mushrooms, the magic mushrooms the Aztecs call teonanacatl, Flesh of the Gods. I had read extensively about them, especially about the research Gordon Wasson and his wife conducted in the early fifties. Their first book, Mushrooms, Russia and History came out in 1957. It told about the hallucinogenic mushrooms used by Mexican Indians in their sacred rituals. In 1968, Soma: Divine Mushroom of Immortality was published. In it, Wasson claims that Soma, the "rootless, leafless, blossomless" psychoactive plant, praised in 120 verses in the Rig-Veda, the ancient Hindu text, is Amanita muscaria, the large red-capped mushroom with white dots that often grows in the woods. My mother had warned me not even to touch the fungus when I ran to it, drawn by its beauty. But Heartspace was not talking about this mushroom.

"Do psilocybin mushrooms grow around here?" I asked.

"Yup. After a rain they pop out of cow dung. Right out of cowshit, the dear little things! There's a large field where cows graze on the edge of town. Want to pick some?"

"Sure!" I agreed enthusiastically.

"Okay. We'll leave early in the morning. Put on sturdy shoes, the ground will be wet. I'll pick you up at dawn."

I was ready when I heard his car pull up. It was still almost dark. An eerie fog covered the field that extended for miles. Underfoot, the ground was sloshy.

"I found one!" Heartspace called after some 15 minutes. I ran over to him. He stood gazing down at a small, white-capped mushroom that grew not on, but next to a heap of cow dung. I smiled as I bent down to inspect it. Another one of nature's little jokes! The words, "Love hath pitched her tent in the place of excrement," ran through my mind. I could not recall the origin of that quote, but it had the same sublime irony as the Flesh of God growing out of a pile of shit!

"When you pick one, you must always put the spores back, like this," my young guide instructed me. He held the mushroom over the spot where it had grown and tapped a finger gently against its cap. "It releases the spores so more 'shrooms can grow." He held the mushroom to his forehead, bowed, then raised his arms and held the mushroom aloft. We both stood for a moment, giving thanks to our mother, the Earth, for giving us this treasure, and then continued our search.

The sun had risen when Heartspace called a halt. I had found four mushrooms. He had seven. "Here, take one of mine. Five is a good dose," he said. "Want to turn on together?"

"Thanks for asking, Heartspace, but I think I'd like to do it alone."

"Sure, I can dig it. Hey, have a great trip!"

I prepared for the trip with my usual rituals: a light meal at noon, no dinner. I tidied the hut and covered the mattress with the lovely spread Debbie lent me when I told her what I intended to do. "Do you want us to look in on you?" she had asked. I gratefully accepted, knowing that she would come only if she knew she was welcome or needed. I often tripped alone, but always arranged with someone to keep an eye on me. I bathed, put on a long white richly embroidered but comfortable robe, lit candles and incense, sat on the mattress in my jungle hut to meditate, and waited for the mushrooms to take effect.

♥ ♥ ♥

The jungle is coming closer. It stretches out its arms to me, calling, "Join us! Come! Merge!" An overwhelming love comes from the bushes and the trees, strong, warm, welcoming. I rise and try to go to them, forgetting that I'm separated from the outside by the screening. I'm perplexed. I sit down.

The trees and the bushes keep coming closer, wanting to engulf me. A tall, broad tree sends out orange-laden arms. I feel menaced and grow afraid. "No, leave me! I don't want to be a tree!" I shout.

I lie down on the mattress and close my eyes. That's when I see them. The mushroom people. They appear in my consciousness as shrivelled and unbeautiful beings. They tell me that I have now joined those who serve them, and that they would speak and act through me henceforth. "Humbug," I say. "I serve no-one but God."

The mushroom beings fade. Now I'm a robot. I'm in a repair factory; oil is injected in my joints, I'm getting a tune-up. Feels good! Feels? Then I'm not a robot.

I'm looking down on a society of beings who consist of lines. A typical family unit looks like this: III+II. The kind of Lines that are grouped into IIII+I are considered somewhat eccentric, but are tolerated and even admired, because they often have creative personalities. Decent Lines shun I+IIIIs. The II+III set cannot be entirely trusted. The IIIIIs are the aristocrats. I watch them go to III+IIIII places, where they have a lot of II+IIII. They are talking. Their language doesn't sound like any language I know, but I understand everything—it's all as familiar as my own skin. Everything about them is familiar, but I never saw before how arbitrary, pompous and absurd their customs and conventions are. I laugh out loud as I watch the Line People go through emotional calisthenics…"Just like us humans," I think. The thought takes me by surprise. It has not come from my mind. Or has it? Of course it has. I often laugh (when I don't cry) at the arbitrariness of human customs, conventions, beliefs.

I turn on the battery-run radio Jerry lent me. A Wagnerian tale of the heroism of the gods, their loves, hates and adventures bursts forth. I laugh, fight, love, and lament with them. A lifetime of adventures passes.

A complete change. I hear two voices engaged in a dialogue. A loud, angry, male voice, answered by a soft, questioning female one. His reply is gentler, but still firm. She coaxes him, calms him; he responds. But then once more no, no. No. He has not changed his mind. Now her voice is beguiling; she seduces him. He falls into her net. A lovers dialogue follows. Whisperings. Cooings. Then gradually, the voices rise again. Soon, they reach the same pitch of hostility as in the beginning. This time, she is on the attack, while he coaxes and seduces.

The old battle field. Adam and Eve. Beloved enemies, they play out the game. Is there no exit?

The voices fade. I open my eyes. The moon is full. The jungle scene around me is remote, cool; no trace of its threatening power remains. I look at the tall orange tree that seemed so menacing before and see that it is energy spun together into a tree-web, a tree-matrix that turns out trees. I looked in the mirror once on an LSD trip and saw myself dissolve into energy—an energy web named Nina. I'm made of energy and so is everybody and everything else.

Getting sleepy. Must blow out the candles.

Good night!

♥ ♥ ♥

Much is made in psychedelic circles of where each substance takes you. I observed that the "where" depends on the taker, not on the substance that is used.

I taught myself to turn bead-stringing into a meditation. Keeping my mind clear of obstructing thoughts, I focused all my attention on the beads. "3 coral, 1 silver, 3 turquoise," I counted. This is the method all religious disciplines use when they have their followers count rosaries, recite mantras, or focus on the breath—all are ways to still the clamoring monkey mind.

Time passed pleasantly in Coconut Grove. Once or twice I tried to arrange a ride back, but when it didn't work out, I was not too concerned. Admittedly, I was stranded. But what a place to be stranded in! I felt no hurry, no urgency. It was good just to be.

But as the weeks passed, I began to long for Woodstock. I called Priscilla again. "Still no money? Guess I'll just have to hang in here till I find a ride."

"Hope it'll be soon. We all miss you. 'Bye, cuckoobird!"

"Toodle-loo, cuckoobird!" I said affectionately. The elfish girl and I called each other that since the time when we spent half a night on acid laughing hysterically about the silly side of life. "Cuckoobird!" she called me when I brought some particularly wild bit of nonsense to her attention. "Who, me? A cuckoobird? You're a cuckoobird!" I flung back. The name stuck, and that's what we called each other from then on.

A week later, as I was sitting in my hut, a boy who lived in the Maya House came running.

"There's a strange-lookin' dude in a strange-lookin' car outside. Said he's lookin' for you." The boy grinned. "That's some car!" he repeated, walking ahead of me.

"Top o' the mornin' to you," said the strange-looking dude. It was Bob Reynolds! The car was Gael Varsi's Pink Pig, an Oldsmobile of the 1950's—broad, sturdy, hulking. It was its fat snout that made Gael call it the Pink Pig. I had often seen her drive the vehicle through Woodstock, but something had happened to it since then. The front end was painted to look like the head of a laughing pig. The rest was bright pink with streaks of silver and blue. The Pink Pig was not elegant, nor was she built for speed, but she had plenty of life left. Never had she looked sassier, more smug, or happier than in her new get-up.

It was good to see Bob. He was a knight coming to the rescue of a helpless maiden in his American Flag pants and three-cornered hat.

"And a jolly good day to you," I replied. We beamed at each other and hugged, and I took him to meet Debbie and Jerry and the rest of the folks. Soon he held everybody spellbound with the stories he told. "Look what I brought," he said. He took a stack of invitations to the Rainbow Gathering from his pack and passed them around. "We're askin' everybody to make copies. If you dig it, spread them around." He reached into his pack again and held up a white tee-shirt with the invitation printed on its back. "That's for you, Nina. I have one too. We're goin' to spread the word!"

He hung out in the center of Coconut Grove for a few days handing out invitations while I said my good-byes and packed my small heap of belongings. I was anxious to be on the way. We hung yards of Zubin's tie-dyed fabric out of the Pink Pig's windows and let it stream out behind us like sails. The Pink Pig was greeted with smiles wherever we went. We stayed on back roads wearing our tee-shirts and giving out invitations. Again we met and were invited by people who became instant friends, but this time, even "straight" people smiled at us. The Pink Pig was irresistible, and so was Bob's Irish charm.

It was a happy trip, marred only by Bob's frequent stops in bars. When he was loaded, the crude aspects of his personality came out; but the next day he would be Bob again, the gentleman, poet, adventurer and friend.

Forty-nine

It took us ten days to reach Woodstock. What greeted me there made my heart heavy. My home had been used as a crash pad, and in the driveway stood a truck filled with garbage. I was furious and wrote a withering letter to the Woodstock Times, scolding the hippies for their disregard of the material plane. The trip had taught me that the kids were wrong to let go of some of the basic rules. I understood what they were up against. Before they had been old enough to master the skills of physical survival, LSD had opened them up to heaven and hell. Like eagles, they soared high above the ground, more at ease in the astral regions than on earth. Their grasp of metaphysical subjects was dazzling, but they were wholly unprepared for daily life.

However, it didn't take long before my true feelings for the hippies re-emerged. My love and admiration for them was undiminished. I was deeply moved by these children who had turned their backs on the luxuries their parents could provide. Gallantly they smoked and ingested the forbidden drugs, went to jail, protested peacefully, or not at all. Children reared in middle-class homes fasted to cure their ills, gave birth to their babies in their homes or in shacks, took care of each other, tried new forms of living and loving, and raised their eyes to new, unprecedented horizons beyond the world of the senses. What they did seemed senseless to their elders. To themselves, they seemed weak and helpless against the massed opinion of the established order which they no longer could accept. Born into a world that teetered on the brink of self-destruction, they dared to have visions of harmony and brotherhood, and longed to turn their parents on to these same visions.

No doubt many among the young jumped on the spiritual bandwagon to escape their own inadequacies. But there were enough true hippies to make an irreversible impact on the culture from which they believed to have dropped out. The fact is that the idea of 'dropping out' from society was self-contradictory and absurd. Who is society if it isn't you, you, and me? How can we drop out from us?

Fifty

In 1989, a film called Rude Awakening was released. The hero, a conventional young man, had been raised by hippie parents in a hippie commune. The following exchange takes place:

"The hippies are dangerous."
"Why? Because they are revolutionaries?"
"No. Because they are idealists."

I don't know who said these lines in the film, but they stuck. To me, the idealism of the hippies appeared profoundly practical: love, harmony, respect for the earth and for each other. How else can there be peace on earth? The kids wanted to unite, to share, to play, to embrace life. Why suffer? There's enough for everybody, we can all have fun, love each other, keep learning more about ourselves! What they said made sense to me. I felt that it was an ideal for which the human race was not ready, but I loved the dream! And I loved the dreamers—the youngsters with the shining eyes, the Woodstock Nation!

In those days there was music everywhere in the little hamlet. It came from windows, doorways, street corners. Jam sessions formed on the Village Green; groups played "gigs" in cafes. There were poetry readings and lectures by holy men and by followers of all sorts of spiritual and quasi-spiritual teachings. There were pow-wows where matters of general concern were discussed. Order was maintained by passing a "talking stick" around, a custom learned from Native Americans, which gives everyone a chance to talk without interruption.

Woodstock was seething with spiritual fervor and material creativity. A dazzling variety of music, art works, and written words came out of that period, some of them masterpieces that have not been appreciated to this day.

After my return, life soon fell into its pre-bus groove. Between Kama Lila Loka and the solitude I required, I did not participate in many activities. I enjoyed shared meditations, the activities at 5 Rock City Road, and the gatherings on the Magic Meadow atop Meade Mountain. The meadow had played host to many pagan rituals. Rock circles interrupted the sparse bushes. Some had been there for a long time, others were new. On moonlit nights, the hippies brought their guitars and drums, chanted OM, and danced around the fire.

There were also parties at various homes. Most notable among these was a permanently moored vessel that had been transformed into a magical residence by the owner, generally referred to as Ronnie Barge Queen. The main deck had been stripped bare and now formed a huge, single room. Except for a large table near the kitchen in the bow it held little besides a piano and a harp. In the center was a circular fireplace; one could sit on its broad stone facing, or on cushions on the floor.

Ronnie sometimes invited special guests to perform for us, like the Hindu musician who played on an array of bells and percussion instruments and made the space tingle with ecstatic vibrations. But there was always music at Ronnie's parties. Many talented Woodstock musicians vied with each other to be allowed to play.

Our lovely hostess had made a name for herself with her research on frogs; innumerable frog-like and frog-decorated objects in the upper and lower regions of the boat reminded you of it. Her passion for the animal world was also obvious in the two large, magnificent dogs she kept and the exotic animals whose big cages lined the main room's walls.

The parties at Ronnie's and in the other homes were very different from the parties of my suburban past. Nobody felt they had to make conversation. We made eye contact, spoke, or remained focused within. The spontaneity in our interactions was a far cry from the forced sophistication and wise-cracks of the alcohol-produced gaiety of the parties I had learned to shun.

In '73, 5 Rock City Road broke under the strain of too many takers and not enough givers. Michael, Ione and some of the others moved into a half-completed building deep in the woods that sprawled abandoned near a stream. It belonged to a local lawyer who befriended Michael. Michael wanted to "change" him. We all wanted to change straight people, to open them up. The lawyer was ready to be opened up and had probably done so before Michael came on the scene. He gave the saintly-looking hippie permission to use the abandoned house.

The place was half nightmare, half Fellini movie. Bath tubs, refrigerators, stoves, sinks—all stood naked, uncrated, connected to nothing, in the middle of rooms. The building had been planned as a hide-away for busy executives, but somewhere things went awry. Doorless doorways led to rooms with unfinished fireplaces and windows that had no panes. The effect was ghostly.

When you reached the few spaces the hippies occupied, however, the picture changed. Without money, but with a super-abundance of creativity, they set up homes in the half-finished rooms. Plasterboard walls were covered with colorful tapestries, posters, tie-dyes, paintings. Especially dazzling was the room where Michael and Ione lived with Quan Yin, the little girl to whom Ione had given birth in 1969.

At that time, Ione and Michael had been living in a tepee close by Ernie and Mara's house. Like other hippies who wanted to go back to the simple lifestyle of the pre-industrial age, Michael and Ione passionately embraced natural birth and vegetarianism, and they insisted on a home birth. Ione, the daughter of a physician, did not want to go to the hospital or have a doctor present at the birth. Not even a midwife would be there; midwifery was just beginning to be explored, and there were only a few who knew enough to be of help.

I was appalled when I learned of the conditions under which the birth was to take place. "Please, Ione, go to a hospital! Why do you want to suffer needlessly? The anesthetic is a God-send, believe me! When I gave birth…"

"Yes? When did you get the anesthetic?" the young woman asked innocently. Her voice was as soft as her round, dimpled face. "Did they give it to you while you were in labor?"

"No," I said, remembering the pain. "When the baby was beginning to come out."

"So; and that made birthing easier?" She was suppressing a smile.

A light went on in my head. "Oh, I get it. You mean they gave it to me ..."

"...at the end," she completed my sentence. "They knock you out at the most sublime moment, when most of the pain is over, when you could be present at the birth of your child—a child that is born wide-eyed, conscious, not doped up."

I could see her point, but continued to be apprehensive about the event. When she asked me, along with a few other friends, to be present at the birth, I could not refuse.

As my memory paints the scene, there were five women in the tepee when Ione's labor pains began to come close together. She was lying on the mattress on the floor; in between pains she looked ineffably beautiful. Michael held her head cradled in his arms and rubbed her back. "Ione is going to have a new toy," he crooned softly into her ear. His serenity in the presence of her pain was inspiring. Wish I could be that calm, I thought. (Later, when I told Ione how Michael's song had seemed to bring her peace, she replied, "I could have strangled him!")

We alternated holding Ione's hand, stroking her forehead, rubbing her feet. The only one who knew anything about birthing was Mara who had recently given birth, albeit in the hospital. She sat at the foot of the bed and read instructions from a book as the labor progressed. It took a few hours. When the pains came only minutes apart, we chanted OM and looked helplessly at each other while Ione's screams pierced the stillness. Suddenly a young man appeared as if by magic. He had been walking in the woods when he heard the screams. Fresh out of medical school, he was horrified to have stumbled into this scene. He had never assisted at a birth, let alone a home birth. But the baby chose just that moment to begin to emerge, and he was forced to help. The baby was beautiful, and we all cried and laughed and embraced each other, awed by this miracle of life.

Women's Lib was still in the future. Ione and the other hippie women played Earth Mother. They cooked, baked bread, planted vegetables, went marketing, and raised the kids. In the tepees and other primitive dwellings there was no running water, so the Earth Mothers did the laundry in the stream, kneeling on rocks, as women had done for untold generations.

Watching the hippie women give up the comforts of a modern home, I saw how they once more fell for a male fantasy. Like the Love Goddess of the one-night stands, the pedestal of the Earth Mother had a price. The young women slaved away in the primitive conditions of communal life while the lordly men were busy talking metaphysics. The new "freedom" was as homocentric as the old sexual repressiveness, and males were still very much the dominant sex!

♥ ♥ ♥

THE RAINBOW GATHERING

A caravan of seven vehicles set out from Woodstock a week before July 1st. The van in the lead bore a sign saying Woodstock Health Angels topped by a red cross. It carried two doctors, two nurses, and boxes of medical supplies. The rest of us brought sacks of oatmeal, cereals, grains, rice. I rode in a van with four people and two small boys.

Word of the Gathering had spread far and wide. Miles of vehicles were parked in a field outside the town of Granby when we arrived. I spent hours walking through row after row of buses, vans, jalopies and trucks, greeting friends who had come from all over the country. Strawberry Lake, the site of the Gathering, was still miles away, but nobody was allowed to drive any closer.

"We're going to drive straight through," Dr. Randy told the Woodstock caravan in the morning. "They can't stop us. We carry vital medical supplies."

It took the guards only a few minutes to decide to let us pass. An endless stream of people walked ahead of us, parting slowly to let us pass. It brought back memories of the Belgian road, people taking refuge in trenches when the machine guns of the German Messerschmidts aimed at us. Here, like on that road, there were some who were lame and halt, a few pregnant women, a blind man guided by a dog, little children who had to be carried. But the faces were not like those of the Belgian refugees. They were smiling and waving merrily to us as we passed. What brought them? Was it the hope for a miracle, for the white-clad saints I had seen in my vision? Or were they just looking for a good time?

We left our vehicles at the foot of the mountain that was topped by

Strawberry Lake. A narrow footpath led up. It was an arduous ascent. We all carried heavy loads; gallons of water, blankets, sleeping bags, sacks of dry food, fresh fruit and vegetables—everything had to be hauled up. The two doctors carried their instruments and other supplies. For what seemed like hours, the steep path zigzagged up. At last, voices greeted us from above.

"Welcome home!" they said as we entered the designated area. We were embraced by the reception committee who handed us cool drinks. It was an emotional moment—a true home-coming, a home-coming of the heart.

We were given directions to the kitchen area and the meadow where the general meetings took place, and then we set up our camp. It did not take me long to see that my vision of white-clad saints had lied. Alcohol was as much in evidence as psychedelics. At the daily meetings in the large meadow, a recital of the items that had been stolen preceded the heart-warming speeches that called for brotherhood and love. For me, these sentiments were obscured by the horror of stolen sleeping bags, sweaters, and blankets, leaving the victims to freeze in the icy nights. Instead of the company of saints, I have landed in a den of thieves, I thought, tears running down my cheeks.

On the morning of the 4th of July many people climbed the neighboring mountain. A white buffalo had been spotted there, outlined in snow. According to an old Indian legend, a white buffalo would appear when the people of the rainbow returned to the earth. The cry of joy that went up when the buffalo was discovered echoed through the mountains. Those of us who remained behind observed an hour of silent meditation to pray for world peace.

I could not wait to get rid of the grime of the Gathering. The dust raised by thousands of feet trampling through the sparsely wooded area had eaten into my skin, my hair, my clothes and the few articles I carried with me. I got a ride to Boulder and went to a motel where I spent half the night in the shower.

After my return from the Gathering, I was determined to stay in Woodstock, to "act locally and think globally," and to put all my energy into the little town.

Today, the yearly Rainbow Gathering has become an institution, like the Grateful Dead. No doubt, there is much to admire about it. But for me, it was an ordeal. I was disturbed by the waste of energy the kids spent on hopping all over the country instead of staying where they were and making things better.

Fifty-one

In the late summer of '72, Kama Lila Loka was burglarized. It was a tidy, artistic burglary. Nothing had been disturbed. Things were simply removed, leaving empty spaces. Only the best pieces were taken; everything else was left in place. It had to be someone who knew the shop well. I was shattered. I felt betrayed, let down. Had my guardian angel deserted me?

In the summers of '69 and '70 I had accidentally left the door to the shop unlocked on several occasions. It didn't make much difference; the lock was so flimsy that a child could have picked it. Still, I was surprised to discover strangers inside when I arrived to open up. They were quietly looking at things, waiting to make a purchase. Once, the couple who owned the store next door sent their two sons, aged six and eight, to wait on my customers. Another time, someone had swept and washed the floor—and I never found out who!

Before the world's moral disintegration found its way to our lovely town, being a shopkeeper in Woodstock had been a rewarding way of life. Now it was time to stop. I carried no insurance, and the thought of barricading the shop with a burglar alarm and heavy locks was abhorrent to me.

To give up the shop meant turning my back on my Woodstock vision. I had dreamed of an enclave of peace, creativity, high vibes—an atmosphere that would act as a spiritual washing machine on all who entered it…a ring-pass-not against cruelty, egotism, bad vibes…

I had dreamed of a town where a number of individuals would live together in ways for which words like "brotherhood" or "peace" are inadequate. It was a more positive, more actively joyous dream than the mere absence of hostility, suspicion, jealousy, competition. Goodness, beauty and truth were to dwell in that town, and the happiness of the inhabitants would spill over into never-ending creativity.

The burglary made me aware that the rot that was spreading through the land was overrunning Woodstock. 'Our spiritual barriers are not strong enough to keep it out,' I reflected sadly.

The shop had begun as a thinly disguised shrine. Now, only a few who passed through were seekers after more than the goods I sold. And as the people changed, so did the shop. It became a mere survival tool for me, the owner. And with the better part of my winter security gone, it couldn't even do that.

My mood was gloomy. The world burns, my dreams of Utopia lied. The Aquarian Age, if it has begun, is no better than its predecessors, and the New Breed is as shot through with falsehood and hypocrisy as the old, I thought in despair.

At the Rainbow Gathering I had seen confusion, naked agony, and imitation love. How cheap human life seemed in this amoeba-like drifting from place to place! How could friendships mature and bloom amidst these kaleidoscopic changes?

What is fate? I asked myself. Do we make things happen? Or are we the unwitting tools of a higher force at whose bidding we play out the game called life? It does seem that a higher force takes a hand in shaping our destinies. The drama is too monumental to have been created by mere humans. What if the Hitlers, the Caesars, the Popes, the Nixons, Reagans, Bushes, are just players in a game that is directed from above?

When I looked for meaning in a world that seemed increasingly like the Theater of the Absurd, some surprising thoughts sometimes surged up. War, for instance: could it not be viewed as an instrument for mixing the world's gene pool? The conquering armies leave more than death and ruins behind. By planting their seed in the enemy's womb, they infuse new life in the genetic brew. Or Hitler: wasn't it he and his Nazis whose atrocities awakened the world to the outrage of racism?

To some, this view may be comforting. It's comforting to look at the past and say, "Yes! That's why that happened! It all makes sense!" To others, it means that we are robots, puppets dangling from a string. Decisions are pre-programmed. We think that we act, when in reality we're acted upon.

How many of us really know why we married or have a love relationship with a specific person? Or what prompted us to pick out one of the many scenarios, one of the myriad of ever-repeating and ever-changing plots?

Fifty-two

"Can you come for dinner tomorrow?" Alexandra asked. Exquisite little Alexandra had left Fred and the East Village and moved to Woodstock. She had been living in my spare bedroom when she met fiery, magnetic Richard Zarro, a brilliant young writer who had won a prestigious award as a student at Columbia University. The two could have passed for brother and sister with their dark-haired, dark-eyed beauty, but the sparks that flew between them made it clear that they were lovers. "He's the first man I've ever known who matches my intensity," Alexandra told me, dewy-eyed. They married, and Alexandra transformed their small apartment into a love nest that was all the more sensuous because everything was white. Walls, ceiling, floor and furniture sparkled virginally, and the large bed was canopied with yards and yards of white cheesecloth. Only a few drawings by multi-talented Richard interrupted the bridal whiteness.

Richard had chosen the role of prophet of doom. Oozing with vitality, the articulate young man kept proclaiming the imminence of the apocalypse. Like the rest of us, he wanted to "save the world," and the method he chose to try and awaken humanity was to cry doom. I enjoyed his quick wit, his erudition, and the passion that shone through his words.

"Peter is coming too," Alexandra said.

"Great! Haven't seen him in a while!" I replied, pleased. Peter Blum was perhaps the most balanced and sanest of the Woodstock hippies. Not that he lacked flamboyance. His beret of many colors had a peacock feather stuck in it, and his frayed velvet cape gave him the dashing look of a swashbuckler. He smoked exotic Turkish cigarettes and enjoyed the finer things in life, but nothing he did was excessive. He was mellow. His spirituality was of the kind that doesn't announce itself, yet is profound. Long after most of the others had given up, he continued a rigorous schedule of meditation practice.

While Kama Lila Loka was still in business, he worked in the metaphysical bookstore next door. In the slow winter months he often came to my shop to chat. He seemed to know every book in the metaphysical bookstore and talked about Buddhism, Hinduism, Christianity and Aleister Crowley with equal ease. His voice had a soothing quality, and his brown eyes were calm. He was also a fine musician with a classical background, and when he became an editor for the Woodstock Times he wrote many sensitive and thoughtful pieces for the paper.

"What's for dinner?" I asked Alexandra when I entered the lover's nest. The pungent aroma of garlic, oregano and thyme seemed strange in these virginal surroundings. Their robust earthiness underlined the ethereal quality of the room.

"Spaghetti," Alexandra beamed. The delicate brunette beauty had learned to prepare hearty Italian dishes for her Sicilian husband.

"Al dente?" I asked, showing off my Italian.

"Al dente! Al dente!" she assured me. "The way Richard likes!"

Peter was already seated and rose to give me a hug.

"Gee, I'm glad to see you," he said, meaning it. "Heard you're closing the shop. So what will you do? Any plans?"

"None that make any sense. All I know is that I want to do something that serves the Spirit as well as the spirit of community. I have to earn my living, but I want what I do to mean more than that."

"Have you thought of a school?" Richard asked.

"A school? What kind of a school?"

"One that teaches how to survive spiritually and materially. It's going to get rough, you know. The next years will…"

"Yes, yes, I know, Richard." I didn't want to hear his apocalyptic predictions again. "It's an interesting idea, but how would I finance such a school? And where would it be held?"

"Why not right where you are? Your store front can be the start. I'm on the board of directors of the Transformation Foundation. We're a non-profit organization dedicated to the change-over from self-consciousness to cosmic consciousness. Maybe we can help."

My ears pricked up. More than anything, I wanted to serve the transformation of consciousness that seemed to me the sole hope for the survival of the human race.

"Some far-out subjects could be taught in such a school," I reflected.

"Like teleportation?" Peter teased.

"Naturally! We'll teach levitation..." Richard said.

"...and astral projection," I offered. They laughed. "Wait a minute," I protested. "Maybe that's not so crazy any more. Maybe by the year 2000, Astral Projection will be taught in schools."

"I don't know anybody who can do it. Some people say Sai Baba..." Peter said.

"I hear Neem Karoli Baba has been seen in two places at once. Some funny things happen to me when I'm in deep meditation..." I grew pensive. "The Hindus and the Buddhists think these powers are a hindrance on the path to enlightenment."

"That's if they're practiced for selfish reasons," Peter remarked.

"The powers are said to come of their own accord as we progress," I said.

"Someday, the whole human race will have these powers," Peter observed.

"Maybe after the apocalypse..." Richard said sunnily.

"Oh Richard! Don't you get tired crying doom and gloom?"

"The apocalypse will be a cleansing! It will let new life grow!" Richard proclaimed passionately.

Alexandra put a large dish of spaghetti on the table. I realized that I was quite hungry. "What a heavenly aroma!" I sighed as I piled sauce on my plate. "I have another prediction for the future. Want to hear it?"

"Shoot!" Peter said.

"It's a newspaper headline. 'Bodies are not being worn in Paris this season.' Get it?"

"Hah!" Richard said with a mouthful of spaghetti. "I'm glad you're such a poor prophet! I'm enjoying my body very much, thank you!"

"So am I. But just think—if people could learn for real that we are not our bodies, or that our bodies are not who we are…Wouldn't that do away with the fear of death? It's the fear that underlies all other fears. If science could prove that only the body dies, and that the Self is eternal…"

"Yes, yes, we know," little Alexandra smiled. "You do go on, Nina!"

"Sorry about that," I said ruefully. "Guess I'm just like Richard and his apocalypse."

During dinner, we talked some more about the school. Alexandra gave it her enthusiastic support. "It sounds just right for you, Nina. Like sort of a continuation of The Center for the League of Spiritual Discovery without the psychedelics."

"Right!" I could feel myself getting excited.

"Well, give it some thought, Nina. Come to the next board meeting of the Transformation Foundation," Richard invited when I left.

The support I received from the Foundation was purely moral, but whether I knew it or not, I was already hooked. I talked to people in the community who had the knowledge to teach practical skills and esoteric subjects, and they met the idea of the school with enthusiasm. Within weeks, some 15 people had committed themselves to give classes, and The Woodstock Transformation Center was ready to be launched. I felt that it was the answer I was waiting for. And so, on October 22, I wrote to the Woodstock Times:

The building at 14 Mill Hill Road which houses my now almost defunct shop, Kama Lila Loka, was once the Little Red Schoolhouse of Woodstock.

The Little Red Schoolhouse wants to be a school again. A school for those members of the community who wish to become more aware spiritually, ecologically, and creatively. It will be a school of life, and the subjects taught will be T'ai Chi for Beginners, Introduction to Astrology, Tarot, I Ching, Kundalini Yoga, Hatha Yoga, The Tao, Oriental Healing, Weaving, Learning to Build from Tables to Domes, Auto Mechanics, Psychic Awareness, Paramedical Training, World Environment Crisis Training, Community Organizing, Sane Nutrition, and Guitar for Children. From time to time, there will also be guest lecturers."

Unfortunately, the Center failed to provide for itself. Financially, it ran a close second to The Center for the League of Spiritual Discovery. In other ways, it was more like the Capri Theater, except that I had unlearned most of the diplomatic skills needed to run such an enterprise. I realized with a shock how unworldly I had become. I lacked both the drive and the ambition to make the school a financial success. It was hard to reconcile my desire to serve the emerging new breed with the economic realities, and I accepted many students who wanted to trade their services for classes. Soon, we were top-heavy with non-paying students. Many of the New Age subjects we taught have since become part of the billion-dollar human potential industry, but at that time the Center—and I—limped along, hardly knowing from month to month if we'd still be there. Our main support came from benefits.

The first of these, held at the Town Hall, was called March Hare Fair. Isaac Abrams transformed the drab town hall with yards and yards of glittering mylar that fluttered from a ceiling covered by Zubin's tie-dyes. The mylar divided the space into booths for the Center teachers who gave Tarot, I Ching, astrology and psychic readings. It was a miniature Renaissance Fair with clowns, strolling musicians, and a face-painting booth. At night, there was a dance for which some of the many excellent Woodstock bands volunteered their services.

The Center satisfied my deep wish to be a facilitator for the spreading of knowledge about transpersonal states. Though only a small number of people attended the classes, the seeds that were planted there bore abundant fruit.

I was also active in the affairs of the town. Together with Ken Marsh of Woodstock Video, I organized a series of seminars about sewers in the belief that our common concern over the inadequate sewage system would bring the whole community together. It did, but no agreement on the method of converting the system was reached for many years. Finally, in the mid '80s, after many costly studies, the old pipes were simply dug up and replaced by larger new ones.

In the spring of '75 I closed the door of The Little Red Schoolhouse, aka

Kama Lila Loka, aka The Woodstock Transformation Center, for the last time. My story from then on meanders through a variety of occupations. For a while, I worked for a curious man who appeared in my life out of nowhere.

I was having lunch at The Woodstocker when a bulky elderly man with a large paunch and sparse grey hair asked if he could sit at my table. The restaurant was not crowded, but I nodded consent. He ordered a hearty meal and then turned to me.

"You live here?" he asked. I nodded. "I'm just passin' through," he informed me.

"What brings you here?" I asked, more from politeness than out of any real interest.

"Lookin' for people to sell my jewelry." He pointed to the small suitcase he had placed on an empty chair. "Silver and turquoise. Navaho and Zuni work," he told me. Another white man exploiting the Indians, I thought. "I'm an Indian myself," he added, as if he had read my mind.

"You? An Indian? With your blue eyes and pale skin?" I thought he was kidding me.

"I'm not the only Indian with white blood. My great-grandmother was raped by a white man, and the gene shows up in one of us from time to time. I'm a Cherokee. I sell Indian goods and make good money for the Indians on the reservation. Make good money for me, too." A proud expression came into his face. He looked at me intensely. "And you? You got Indian blood? You look it."

"I don't think so," I laughed, "though some of the hippies say I must have been Indian in my last incarnation. I don't know. I don't know what I am. I'm Jewish, grew up in Vienna, but I don't feel Viennese, or Jewish, or American or anything else. Don't feel I belong to any country, race, or creed. Or maybe to all. What difference does it make? We're all people!"

"Sure, we're all people. But I'll tell you the difference. Indians are the people of the earth. The earth is our mother, we venerate her, we keep her holy. We don't exploit her. We don't make her unclean. We give back to her what we take. White people—they don't understand. They take, take, take…" He looked tired. I put my hand over his.

"I know. We're like greedy children. But a new spirit was born in the '60s. I heard there is a myth that says many of the hippies are reborn Indians. Maybe they'll teach the world respect for the earth when they grow up."

"Maybe. Before it's too late. What do you do?"

"I make handicrafts," I told him. "And I'm looking for work."

"Can you drive?" he asked.

"Sure, but I don't have a car. It broke down two years ago. Don't have the money to replace it."

"Broke, eh? Tell you what. I'll take you along on my next trip, show you the ropes…"

"What ropes?"

"How to set up a trunk show selling jewelry. It's easy. You'll learn fast. Interested?"

Two days later a large, comfortable Oldsmobile with a Texas licence stopped before my door. We were going to a shopping mall in a nearby town. On the way I asked if he knew anything about the Indian tribes who held peyote ceremonies. He himself had not attended one, but knew of the magical effects the plant has on shamans who are able to align themselves with healing powers while under its influence. I told him about the effect marijuana, LSD and psilocybin mushrooms had on some of us, and how they connected us to the Great Spirit. Time passed quickly, and when we arrived at the mall we went to a store with which he had made arrangements. We spread the jewelry out on a table the owner set up for us—heavy silver and turquoise Navaho earrings, bracelets and necklaces, and pieces that displayed the more delicate workmanship of the Zunis. He showed me the fine points of distinction between expensive pieces and cheaper ones, but as the prices were clearly marked on every piece I only needed to know this to explain the difference to customers.

We sold a fair amount that day, but the net profit, after paying the agreed-upon percentage to the store, was not great. "Well, how about it, Nina? Want to put on trunk shows like this in other malls?" he asked when we were back in his car. "You'll get 10% of the net sales or fifty bucks a day plus expenses, whichever is more."

The offer was more than generous, and I was understandably eager to accept. "But I don't have a car," I reminded him. "How will I get around?"

"We'll work something out. Be ready to go on the road in a week," he told me when he dropped me off at my home.

A week later, he reappeared. "Here," he said, handing me the small suitcase and the keys to his car. He told me my itinerary and said he'd meet me in Woodstock in a week.

"What about you?" I asked. "Won't you need your car?"

"I'll rent one," he said. "Wait! I got something for you." He reached into his pocket and brought out a small object. It was a beautifully worked silver roachclip with a large, flawless turquoise embedded in the handle. "I had it made for you. Like it?" he asked. I was deeply moved. "Go!" he said, cutting my thanks short. "The car has a full tank. See you in a week.

I rather enjoyed doing the trunk shows. Sales were satisfactory, and the money I earned was a godsend. A strange thing happened once while I was driving on the throughway. A police car stopped me; I didn't know why, since I had driven at a safe speed.

"What's the matter, officer?" I asked, baffled.

"You're a long way from home, lady," he said. "Let's see your drivers license." After examining it briefly, he handed it back. "And the owner's license?" he demanded. I looked into the glove compartment and realized with a shock that my Indian friend had not left it there. "It's not my car, officer," I stammered. "My employer loaned it to me and he forgot to give me the license!" He'll arrest me! I thought in dismay. But when I looked up, I saw that he was smiling.

"Don't worry, Ma'am," he said. "You don't look like a thief. Get him to give you the license next time."

I didn't look like a thief to my employer either. He never counted the jewelry when I returned. Before each trip, he added more pieces to my stock, always without counting them.

Unfortunately, the job lasted only a few months before my generous employer fell seriously ill, and wrote me from his ranch in Texas that there would be no more shows.

I made craft items and sold them at the flea market, worked in the kitchen and housekeeping department of The Center for the Living Force in nearby Phoenicia, organized craft shows, helped raise the baby boy of a local dentist and his sensitive wife who made motherhood and home-making an art, took a job at the newly formed Woodstock Community Center, and when all else failed, went on welfare for a few months. It was getting harder and harder for me to survive in Woodstock.

Fifty-three

The years between '75 and '79 are shadowy. My faith in the New Age and the New Breed was severely shaken. Around me, life returned to a more or less pre-'60s materialism. Here and there, small enclaves tried to hold on to the ideals of the '60s, but it was no use. Times had changed, people were working on themselves in ways that imprisoned them in the self-concentration camp. The search was no longer for God, but for ME. The question WHO AM I? held paramount importance, and that I was personal and separate, unlike the Self of the mystic spelled with a capital S.

In the psychedelic '60s, the flower children had been lit up like living torches that beamed out their powerful little lights across the world. For a while it looked like the light would conquer the dark, and there would at last be peace on earth. The Manson Family was a shocking warning that the psychedelics do not always let in light; they can also bring darkness and violence and death. But the Manson Family was unique. Violence was not part of the acid scene. We were filled with wonderment, gratitude, awe, love. We had seen MORE than the everyday reality. We had known fear, and we had conquered it, and we lived in the moment, in the NOW. Buoyantly, we swam on the crest of the wave. We were happening, baby! This was it!

And then suddenly, almost without warning, the light faded. Doors that had stood open, closed. The feeling of a tribe, of mutual support, was gone. What these free young spirits had forgotten was that they had swept much baggage under the rug in their mad dash to know God. Now it popped out with the stored-up energy of the repressed. The ME decade was underway.

ONE FOOT IN THE FUTURE

The hippies no longer met in groups to turn on together, to just groove, chant, dance, or talk. All sorts of encounter and therapy groups flourished, and where before, the details of their personal histories were forgotten or ignored, these were now in the limelight, the center of interest. Like a clay puppet, the ego was to be reformed, reshaped, and finally lost through a supermarket of methods. Numerous teachers, gurus, and followers of creeds like Sufism, Buddhism, and branches of Christianity as well as New Age groups such as Arica, Abilitism, Scientology etc., descended on Woodstock, eager to collect believers. Many of them obtained a temporary following, but the issues the kids really had to deal with were not resolved.

By the '40s and '50s, the institution of marriage had turned into a battlefield of the sexes. I heard many life stories from the baby boomers and found that there are really only a few basic plots with endlessly repeated variations. What most of them had in common was battling parents, tension at home, pain, pain, pain. In some cases the pain came from being ignored by parents who were too wrapped up in each other to give attention to the children, but these were the exception. The pain was born of the friction between the parents who were playing out their 1940's version of married bliss. They were waiting for the happy ending that the media promised, even before TV. It was ever-present in films, magazines, plays, radio and songs. The expectations these "happy endings" raised led to anger when they remained unfulfilled. Men as well as women expected much more—and much less— from marriage than it could give because of the all-pervasive influence of the media. Dolled up in white and black, the parents of the baby boomers had marched to the altar to promise eternal love. Like living yin-yang symbols, their boundaries were clearly defined. But these boundaries were beginning to become diffuse. World War II brought women out of the home and into the labor force, and many of them liked the freedom from boring chores, from the frustrations of child rearing, and they liked earning money of their own. The spirit of independence was making itself felt among women who had been no more than the bought and paid for chattel of the bread-winning husbands. Often, the relationship was continued for the sake of appearances and for the children, who grew up on a battlefield.

Born of such conflict, the children were sure to rebel. More than any generation before them, they saw through the sham of their parents' lives. They were willing to try anything to be different, and the psychedelics were often the way they chose.

Unfortunately, these could have negative effects. In the early '70s, Alan Watts and the poet Gary Snyder talked about "whether LSD was a good idea or not."

> "Their feeling by this time was that 'letting it loose in society' had done harm. The first people to experiment with peyote, LSD and similar drugs had been artists, poets, psychologists and students of religion, and most of them had handled it well, had found it an interesting and creative experience. This had ill-prepared them to see that when it went wider in society the results would be very bizarre indeed, with people who were not in any way ready for the experience becoming monomaniacs and self-appointed messiahs. It was just too potent for those who were philosophically, aesthetically, or spiritually unprepared for it." (Genuine Fake, a biography of Alan Watts by Monica Furlong, Wm. Heinemann Ltd., London, 1986)

The evidence for these words was only too apparent in Woodstock. A disproportionate number of space cases floated through the little town. Although it is the belief of most researchers in the field that those who were blown over the edge were pre-psychotic when they took the drug, the ill effects of the substances that allowed a minority to experience the reality behind humanity's religious beliefs cannot be minimized.

Fifty-four

In 1977, an invitation to a colloquium on psychedelics came from my old friend Peter Stafford, who now lived on the West Coast. He and a group called The Psychedelic Education Center were organizing the conference at the University of California in Santa Cruz. The list of speakers was impressive. It included all the luminaries of the psychedelic brotherhood. Even Dr. Albert Hofmann, the venerable chemist who had discovered LSD-25, came from Switzerland. I was hit by a feeling of longing for the people who still continued the quest and was sorry to have to miss this August gathering. A few months later the opportunity for a trip to the West Coast presented itself, and as it coincided with a follow-up to the conference, I decided to visit Santa Cruz.

Peter had not changed. His sneakers still had holes, a shock of blond hair still fell over his eyes, and his walk still had the same boyish bounce. In the ten years that had elapsed since the last time I saw him, he had not aged at all. This re-enforced the feeling that hit me as soon as I arrived in Santa Cruz. I was in a time warp! The hippies were alive and well in Santa Cruz! Maybe they were a little more weather-worn and less starry-eyed than their '60s predecessors, but by golly, they still wore their colorful costumes and beads, and they still had all that hair! There were political hippies, ecological hippies, spiritual hippies, and their focus was the University of California at Santa Cruz whose campus is set in a fairyland environment of redwoods, rocks, and meadows.

When I returned to Woodstock, I was acutely aware of the barbered heads, the drab chinos that had replaced the kooky hippie rags, and the career orientation that was taking the place of the spiritual quest. I began to feel that my days in Woodstock were numbered. Slowly, almost subconsciously, I began to prepare to leave. One of the last entries in my Woodstock Journal reads as follows:

January 1, 1979

The beginning of a new year. Three weeks ago, my 60th birthday. Time to start looking back. Old journals. Old raptures and old sorrows. How do they figure in my Now? In six decades jam-packed with adventures, what stands out most vividly? My youth in Vienna? The Hitler years? My wanderings in war-torn Europe? North Africa? Oued-Zem? Marriage? Motherhood? Divorce?

My past falls into two distinct parts; pre-psychedelic and post-psychedelic. Others my age may sit nursing memories of their youth and lost loves. I cherish most the memories of the breakthroughs vouchsafed me by the psychedelics. 34 years of blindness, ignorance of the dimensions that slumber within. Then the beginning of the search. Meditation yields subtle glimpses. I want more. Finally, at age 47, the break-through.

Two trips are of prime importance in my inner pantheon. One took me to the Cosmic Theater where I entered the Green Room and unmasking, watched the other actors unmask. The other landed me in the Black Hole. Together, they form the underpinning for the one certainty I carry around: Life is an instant in a timeless void. Knowing this, it is sometimes hard to muster compassion for the innumerable ills that afflict the world. Hard to take life quite seriously, yet equally hard to deny it serious reality. As long as I can remember to get out of the way of an oncoming truck, I'm okay, I guess.

In an interview published in L 5 News (Dec. 1976), Timothy Leary is asked,

QUESTION: "Do you think we will evolve beyond physical technology once we have extended life?"
LEARY: "I think that might be the third or fourth level of evolution beyond space migration; but I do think it is inevitable…yes. I think we all sense that it's our eventual destiny."

Hey, I got a great business idea for the future. It's called "Rent-a-Body," for a night, a season, a year, a life…I think maybe I rented this one, and the lease is running out.

Fifty-five

It is twelve years now since I left Woodstock. Looking back, those years seem an unbroken stream—smooth, peaceful, almost free of obstructions. Here and there they are momentarily illuminated by a dazzling light, or agitated by a pounding rain, but on the whole, few changes break the serene passage of my days.

Shortly after my arrival, I moved into the miniscule apartment where I still live today. From my window I can see the bay, and my tiny backyard allows me to grow some of the flowers I love so much. I'm only two blocks away from the barrio, Santa Cruz's slum. At night, sirens often scream past the building; but here, everything is calm, and were it not for my saxophone-playing neighbor, relatively quiet.

It was my hope to link up with a group engaged in educating the young to the possibilities and the pitfalls of the psychedelics that brought me here. To those who look dispassionately at today's drug scene it must be abundantly clear that the methods used by the government do not work. Nancy Reagan's "Just say No" is a pathetic attempt to combat the immense power of psychoactive drugs. What is needed is the clear voice of people who have no stake in disguising the truth. The young must be taught to distinguish between psychedelics, which hold out the promise of the religious experience and of self-transcendence, and destructive drugs like cocaine, amphetamines, heroin, crack. They must be taught to respect the psychedelics and to be ready spiritually and psychologically before they attempt to take them.

Regrettably, The Psychedelic Education Center which drew me here, turned out to be a disappointment. Most of the members were themselves still in need of education. The highlight of my association with the group was the conference we organized at the University of California at Santa Cruz in 1981. It bore the title The Future of Consciousness and brought Dr. John Lilly, author of The Center of the Cyclone, Programming and Metaprogramming the Human Biocomputer, and The Scientist; Dr. Stanislav Grof, the world's foremost authority on LSD therapy; Dr. Heinz Pagels, author of The Cosmic Code; Drs. Stanley Krippner, Oscar Janiger, Andrew Weil, Tod Mikuriya, Paul Segall, Ron Siegel and a host of others to the UC campus.

I attended the conference in a wheelchair. A month earlier, I had broken my ankle, and my leg was in a heavy plaster cast. Walking on crutches was hard for me, so when someone suggested that I rent a wheelchair for the conference, I jumped at the idea. As long as I knew I would soon be using my own legs again, it was fun to sit back and be trundled about. There was no lack of eager and willing chair pushers, among them Surya Das, who now lived in Santa Rosa and had come to Santa Cruz for the event. My Herbie pushed me with such enthusiasm that he nearly spilled me out of the chair. For one of the lectures, I was placed next to a bearded, curly-haired young man whose wide-awake brown eyes were as magnetic as his voice. This was Terence McKenna, who would become the most eloquent proponent of the sacramental use of the psilocybin mushroom.

For many years after my move to Santa Cruz, Woodstock remained the home of my heart. On March 14, 1985, the following Letter to the Editor appeared in the Woodstock Times:

Six years have passed since I left Woodstock—in body, though not in mind. My spirit still walks along Tinker Street and communes with the friends and acquaintances who pass by. So many dear faces! So many lives so intimately connected to mine!

The Woodstock I flee to whenever the news of the day's ugliness swamps my consciousness is a magical place. It's where, in the late '60s and early '70s, people floated slightly above the ground. A radiance and an air of celebration hung over the little town; sometimes you could even see people dancing in the street! Our hearts, minds, and spirits were on fire. The

Aquarian Age had begun!

Things changed, and so did we. But I believe that in the hearts of many of us, the Woodstock dream is still alive. It's alive here in Santa Cruz. A very active New Age community keeps fighting for the human, ecological and spiritual values we avowed in the hirsute '60s. Like Woodstock, Santa Cruz is fighting to keep the gluttonous mouth of "progress" from despoiling its natural beauty. The horrible example of other small towns in the area that have been invaded by profit-seekers makes it imperative for us to defend the quality of life we still enjoy.

It certainly seems hopeless at times to stem the juggernaut of "progress." Everything must grow; isn't that a law of nature? But oh, some spots that are sacred (as we believe Woodstock is) must remain free of the creeping blight of expansion.

Don't let Big Bucks encroach on your mountains, streams and meadows. A friend who just returned from a visit to Woodstock after a nine year absence found it miraculously unchanged. So keep fighting with the weapons of love to keep the Woodstock magic alive. The world needs your example!

Nina Graboi
Santa Cruz

The years have been kind to me. They allowed me to age gracefully and to come perhaps a little closer to the goal of enlightenment, which, according to Alan Watts, is achieved when one stops caring about the scores in the game of life, even stops noticing that there is such a game.

> One to me is loss and gain
> One to me is pleasure and pain
> One to me is fame and shame

No, I have not yet arrived there, though I often repeat these lines from an ancient Hindu text to myself. It's so easy to get sucked back into life's vanities, even when they are no longer taken seriously!

The gifts Santa Cruz has given me are many. Where Woodstock nourished my heart, Santa Cruz nourishes my mind. A source of great mental stimulation is my work of helping Professor Ralph Abraham, the eminent mathematician, with his office chores that include editing some of the world-wide lectures he gives, and gathering books for him at the university's library. It is also my good fortune to know some of the ground-breaking scientists on the leading edge of physics, biology, anthropology and related fields, whose research is bringing them ever closer to the truths that the holy books of all religions have proclaimed down the ages.

For a while, I hosted a radio program called The Elders Speak. I swam with John Lilly's dolphins, slept under the stars in a dream circle with a group of women, made new friends and reconnected with old ones. I took classes at Cabrillo, the local community college, walked on the beach and in the majestic redwoods, went to fabled Esalen in Big Sur, visited Mexico, and spent a week or two in Woodstock now and then.

There were times in the writing of this book that I felt I was already dead and was reliving my life, as the dying are said to do. To get the benefit from the experience, I need to know what I have learned. How do the fragile certainties of my youth appear to me now?

Let's see. Nina at 18...

No. It was Gusti then. Gusti Schreyer...

Gusti. 18 years old.

A well-developed young body. A proudly held head. A mane of black hair that resists all attempts at taming. Large near-black eyes.

A dreamer; a romantic; an idealist; an intellectual snob; a culture sponge; a bookworm; a flirt. And an utterly naive, gullible and trusting child.

It's as impossible to capture the me I was then as the me now. How boring it would be if we could be packaged and summed up like characters in a novel! If my efforts to define myself elude me, it's because life is too many-faceted, it moves too fast.

As I observe Gusti Schreyer, I see in her all the bits and pieces that have formed the patchwork of my life. Unformed and immature as she is, her future has already taken visible shape. She looks at me earnestly, dark eyes wide with eagerness to know. I see a question absorbing her, and I smile at the urgency of youth.

"What is it you want to know?" I ask.

"I just finished reading Death in Venice by Thomas Mann and it all seems so beautiful and pointless, and then there is Franz Werfel's The Forty Days of Musa Dagh where all those Armenians get killed, and then Goethe, who says that…"

"Now hold it," I say. "Come to the point. Do you want to know if life has a meaning? Is that your question?"

"Yes," she replies. "You could put it that way. Though I was hoping to have an intelligent talk with you about some of my favorite books. You didn't stop reading?" she asks in sudden alarm.

"Don't worry," I reassure her. "I don't know how I'd have made it through life without the friends I found in books. That's one thing that hasn't changed, though what I'm reading, has. But to get back to your question. Do you believe in God?"

"I'm an atheist," she proudly informs me.

"That's right; I forgot! You were at least 25 before you were smart enough to admit that you have no proof one way or the other. That's when you began calling yourself an agnostic."

"You're lying!" she flings at me, her eyes ablaze with indignation. "Everybody knows that only ignorant, superstitious people believe in God! This is the age of reason! I hope I'll always be enlightened enough to…"

"Hoho, so it's enlightened you think you are!" I am shaking with laughter. The young girl's face grows red.

"Listen, old woman," she sputters. "I didn't believe you when you said you were me. And now I KNOW you're not! I couldn't turn into you in a million years! You're not even wise! What kind of a God do you want me to believe in anyway? Jehovah, maybe? The old guy with the beard who says, An Eye for an Eye? Or the one who says Turn the Other Cheek? One is a monster of cruelty, and the other is too meek to stay alive. If they're both God, how come they say such opposite things?"

"The ignorance of youth," I sigh. "It'll take decades before you understand these words."

"Sure, that's what they all say!" She mimics: "'Some day, when you grow up, you'll understand! Well, I don't care for mysteries, and I don't want to become you. Really, you make me feel suicidal, except for one thing…"

"What's that?" I ask hopefully, anxious to hear her express some appreciation for me…for her.

"Look, I don't want to get involved in a theological argument. Theo is not logical, if you know what I mean!" She giggles. "Anyway, what does God have to do with my question?"

"Nothing," I admit. "And also everything. Why should a young atheist be bothered by the meaning of life? What difference does it make, if God doesn't exist?"

"Well…It's because of Lilo. You remember Lilo, don't you?"

I do. "What about her?" I ask.

"Her mother is a theosophist, and they believe in reincarnation. I know it's silly, and Lilo's mother must be a fruitcake. Only…"

"Only what? Don't tell me an enlightened young lady like you thinks there is something in such superstitious notions?"

"Of course not! Still…what do you think?"

"Forget it! In fact, I know you will. Let's talk about something else. Boys. I mean, young men. I notice you don't have many dates."

"Boys are such babies. They're so…" Her voice trails off. I'm alarmed. Something about my question turned her off. Will she fade altogether?

"I know it's a painful subject," I say quickly. "Look, you don't have to talk about it…"

"Sometimes I think I've been put in the wrong body." Her face is sulky. "If I had a plain, workaday body, or maybe a hunchback, I wouldn't have to worry about men. I could live in a little house in the woods by myself and…"

"Don't you like being pretty?" I ask.

"It has its good sides. I've discovered how much power it gives me, particularly over men. But that's just the problem. My looks invite all the wrong men." She sighs and falls silent. "Of course I'm flattered by their attention," she goes on. "But they only care for my looks, not for me. When they find out that I want to talk about Free Will, or Fate, or…well, things like Lilo's mother talks about, you know …"

"I certainly do. So you chase your dates away by talking philosophy when what they want is to smooch?"

"Yes. What? Chase them away? No, you don't understand. It's they who…"

I look at the heartbreak of yesteryear and try to smile solace to my younger self.

"Some day, Gusti, you'll be able to look back and see who wrote, directed and starred in the tragi-comedy called This is Your Life. Then you'll see how you engineered your own rejections, failures, triumphs and unfoldments. You will know that Fate and Free Will are one and the same, for the will must be free before it can link up consciously with the fate it has chosen."

For the first time, Gusti looks at me fully. She has the desire to understand, yet she is obviously confused. For awhile, she remains silent, deep in thought; then she shakes her head. "You speak in riddles," she says. "But I can see what you mean by who's doing the rejecting, maybe. It's not easy to be pretty, believe me!" She sighs deeply and fades away.

"Hey, Gusti!" I call after her. "Come back this instant! I'm not through with you! You owe me the courtesy to wait till I dismiss you!"

"Age before beauty?" a mocking voice calls behind me. I veer around. The sound of a jazz band floods the air. I see a smoke-filled hall. Small tables are ranged around a circular area where tightly enlaced couples sway rhythmically. The people at the tables sit in small, separate groups of males and females; they are smoking and sipping from glasses as they watch the dancers. The heavy sexuality that vibrates through the place is discreetly screened by the elegance that permeates everything—the decor, the dancers' clothes, the waiters, the uniformed band.

It's not a place where I would have looked for my younger self. As my eyes travel in the direction of her voice, I discover her sitting at a small table in the rear, next to another young girl who looks vaguely familiar. They are both dressed in black. Around Gusti's neck is a strand of pearls—a good imitation, as I instantly recall. But the effect, combined with the severe elegance of the black dress is startlingly sophisticated. A pinkish bubbly liquid fills the tall glass she holds in one hand. From the other, a cigarette dangles.

"What's that you're drinking?" I ask suspiciously. She grins wickedly.

"Did you think it's champagne? Don't worry. It's only club soda with raspberry syrup." As she says it, my mouth remembers the taste of the drink that invariably accompanied the dances of my youth. Except for a rare glass of wine, liquor was unknown to me before I came to America.

"Who is your friend?" I ask.

"That's Gerda." I look at the attractive brunette whose gray eyes are fringed by long, dark lashes. Her slender body is top-heavy with the large breasts that are her despair. The fashions of the day sits uneasily on her notably unmannish body.

The band begins another number, and I see several men approach Gusti simultaneously. She rises, nods to the one who reaches her table first and who, I notice, is much less attractive than the one behind him, and precedes him to the dance floor.

"Why don't you dance with the other one?" I whisper to her.

"You can't choose your partner. You have to take what you get."

"But the men can choose, right?"

"Right," she says, and I can see that she accepts it as the way things are.

Without regret, I leave my younger self to her life. Glad to be living today. Glad not to be young any more. Glad to be me.

Fifty-six

The young girl in Vienna, the refugee, the woman in love, the party-giving Long Island matron, the producer of star-studded plays, the studious, inward-looking seeker, the director of the LSD Center and the Woodstock Transformation Center, the shopkeeper and mother-figure to the baby boomers, the welfare recipient, the baby sitter, the writer. Were all these persons me?

Viewed from the outside, my life appears to have been buffeted by fate. But to me, my past with all its twists, turns, joys, and sorrows seems like a magic carpet that always had a new surprise in store as it unrolled. Not all of them were happy ones, but taken together, they make up who "I" am. Watching my body transform from young and vigorous to old and frail removes the last illusions of a meness confined to a physical body. In a world where "getting somewhere," "amounting to something," "being a success" is the main purpose of life, I must appear as a poor lonely old woman. But to myself, I am infinitely more. I believe that "It is spirit that fashions flesh, not the other way around." (The Phoenix by Manly Palmer Hall)

The rapidity with which change takes place has accelerated to the point where new ideas and discoveries follow each other too fast for anybody to absorb. Terence McKenna's computer model points to the possibility that by 2012 the appearance of novelty will have speeded up so much that something new is discovered every second, and this will usher in a new phase in our evolution.

To the young, the '60s are an affectionate memory of a time when everything seemed possible.

"It is yet too early for the historical perspective which will fully acknowledge how the psychedelic '60s changed in a fundamental way the consciousness of our culture. It is too soon because it is still happening, echoing, reverberating in politics and power structures, in sexual and marriage patterns; in spiritual practices and in art forms...in every aspect of life."

(Ram Dass in The San Francisco Oracle Facsimile Edition pamphlet, November 1990)

In the '20s, the flaming youth shimmied away their excess energy while remaining spiritually and politically asleep. In the mid '30s, mad Adolf appeared in Germany, and then came World War II—the heroism, the patriotism, Mom's apple pie. All right-thinking people abhor war, yet—shouldn't we, wouldn't we have to make war if another Hitler were to arise?

The war was followed by a general race for material security. Uppermost in the minds of people was a steady income. The perfect family lived in the suburbs, had two cars, and consisted of Mom, Dad, Sonny and Sis. But as the '60s progressed, the bland, middle-class uniformity began to shatter from within. The Pied Piper was coming to suburbia, and his name was LSD. By the thousands, the kids were leaving the chintz-covered prison of the nuclear family. Not that they all took psychedelics. But those who did acted as a leaven on their peers. The consensus reality of the elders was shot through with hypocrisy surrounded by the square walls of materialism. All too clearly, the kids saw the planet-wide havoc caused by the values that prevailed. Where the motto of the moribund society had been "aprés moi, le deluge," the consciousness of the young embraced not only their own brief stay on earth but those who are to follow. For them, material possessions lost their allure.

The '70s brought to the surface a frightful amount of hitherto carefully concealed domestic dramas. Like sewers overflowing with human waste, the combined ugliness of the human race exploded in our faces. Much of what we learned about ourselves did not come as a surprise. Violence, corruption, and indifference were nothing new. But the most telling blow against our self-image as a civilized people was dealt by the revelations about the holy of holies, the family. To our dismay, we learned what goes on in a stunning number of homes behind closed doors. We knew that wife-beating, rape, child abuse and incest exist; what we didn't know was how widespread these crimes are. Naively, we believed them to happen only among the poor and the uneducated. Financial security and education were tacitly assumed to provide a bullwark against these vices. Today, we are forced to admit that neither race, religion, nor wealth can ensure a person's morality in matters that touch on money, power, and sex.

We are only one among the earth's million species, but we are responsible for the devastation of the planet. Our numbers keep increasing, and so do our needs. We want more, more, so we can waste more, and the more laws we make, the more does lawlessness increase. The answer, to me, lies in nothing less than species-wide enlightenment. When we, as a people, realize that we are spirits clothed temporarily in flesh bodies that will disintegrate, and that we need nothing beyond what the earth willingly gives, we will stop violating, overpopulating, and abusing the earth, and thus save ourselves.

Those who have already made the leap from self-consciousness to planetary consciousness are the mutants, the ones who are ahead of the crowd. Their numbers are growing. The world of tomorrow belongs to them.

To those who rode on the crest of the wave of the psychedelic years, the transformation of society seemed only an arm's length away. But in the '70s, we became me, as in "I'm working on myself." In the greedy, grasping '80s, the '60s seemed like a dream—a far-away echo of a magical time, remote like the voyage of the ancestors across the plains.

As the years passed, humanity seemed to lurch backwards on the evolutionary spiral. The world is burning, but the swing of the pendulum is already at work. Outwardly, degeneration and disintegration still rule the world; but below the surface, an equally powerful thrust toward regeneration and integration is quietly at work.

Viewed close up, life seems chaotic, incapable of harmonious ascent. But the spiral of evolution is composed of detours, zigzags, and reverses. Civilizations have existed and died long ago, and those whose eyes are on the past claim that nothing new exists under the sun. To me, looking back over the last three decades, the changes in human consciousness spell the beginning of a new era such as has never existed before—at least not within recorded history.

In time, and especially in retrospect, I have come to think of the hippies as spearheads of evolution. They flashed across humanity's horizon and blazed a trail for the rest of us. It is for the scholars of the future to analyze the changes in Western society and indeed, in the world, for which they gave the signal.

Today, I believe that the psychedelics played a far smaller role in the evolution of the human spirit than I thought in the '60s. In that decade, more people than ever before had a glimpse of a higher, happier, more loving reality. For a moment, they really saw; but that glimpse was soon drowned out by daily concerns. The search for the spirit requires a graceful detachment from the desires, drives and ambitions of the world.

Did I find the meaning I so ardently sought? Yes and no. Meaning and non-meaning, reality and illusion, entwined like eternal lovers, inseparable, ONE. The detachment born of this realization does not prevent keen enjoyment and keen pain from arising in this aging frame.

Have I found any ultimate answers? Sorry, kids. Everything is always both itself and its opposite—real and unreal, light and dark. That's how the universe maintains itself. Where there is one, there is also the other. From my "heavenly" trips I know that I, the Nina-person, am but one of the myriad manifestations of the Self that is undying and unborn.

I think that humanity is evolving in a less physical and more spiritual direction. "Astral projection 101 and 102" may be within reach, and the hardware we require to travel in space may one day be replaced by the technology of the mind.

Epilogue

> He who is convinced that this manifold and wonderful Universe has no real existence, becomes free from desire, is pure intelligence, and finds peace in the knowledge that nothing is real.
>
> Ashtavakra Ghita, Chapter IX

The room is in darkness except for the candle on the small shrine. I narrow my eyes. The flame is a long, narrow strip that throws off sparks which seem to dance to the sound of Iasos's Elixir that comes from the tape deck.

Abruptly, my eyes open wide. The sparks have solidified into a form – an exquisitely shaped human form that is animated by graceful movements. I can't take my eyes off the apparition. It attracts me; the magnetism it exerts holds me fast.

"Who are you?" I finally venture.

"I'm that which will come," the figure replies.

"The New Breed? You are what we shall become?"

The figure nods. The radiant face combines features of many races, but I cannot tell if it is the face of a man or a woman. My eyes travel down. The bare, slender body gives no clue of its sex.

"What is your name?" I ask.

"Androgyne," the figure replies. "Not man, not woman. Both."

Startled, I close my eyes. No sex? The New Breed will be sexless? Isn't sex the prime mover, the life force? Without it, doesn't life cease to be? I felt mournful.

What a loss for the human race!

"Nature abhors a vacuum," the figure said. "Nothing is ever taken away without being replaced."

"What can replace sex for humanity — the one activity where they meet to embrace instead of fight ... although, yes, sex has become a weapon as lethal as a gun in the lives of some," I admit.

The figure laughs. It gambols around the flame, leaping high in the air and turning somersaults. Then it abruptly sits down in the lotus posture and looks earnestly at me.

"Sex is simply the carrot nature holds out so you will reproduce. She makes food taste good and sex desirable to make you eat and live and reproduce. But when you over-reproduce, she begins to shut down the mechanism and switches to something else. You know now how to reproduce yourselves without sex. Evolution doesn't need human sex any more. Think how many factors already point to the obsolescence of sex."

A rush of information fills my head. Facts. Factors. Things observed. Words: artificial insemination, cryogenics, life extension. All these, if they come true, will make bringing more people into the world hazardous. Increasing bisexuality. Unisex clothes. Professions. Sports. The signs are there.

"But surely, sex is more than making babies! What about the delights of the sexual embrace?"

"Short-lived delights that often lead to suffering. Often, the sufferings of love outweigh the joys."

My heart contracts. "I understand. What is assumed to bring happiness and fulfillment often brings the greatest pain."

"There was a time when love tasted sweet. The world was young, and the illusion was so strong..."

"The illusion? You mean the carrot? Yes, I see. And you, human of the future, have you outgrown sex?"

"You will outgrow it too — have already begun to do so, in fact. Evolution discards outworn features when they are no longer needed."

A hundred arguments run through my mind. There are no marriages in Heaven, nor are there women and men, the Bible says. Does that mean that the androgyne is on a higher, more evolved plan than we humans?

"More evolved, and of a finer vibration than the present dominant male-female species," Androgyne answers my unspoken thoughts.

I'm still troubled. I cannot imagine humanity without sex. Sex can make people suffer, but it also unites them and gives them bliss. "What can replace that bliss on the higher plane?"

Androgyne's laughter rings forth like a tinkling bell. "Have you ever heard of the raptures of the saints? To be more evolved is to know more joy, not less. But you already know that. Think of the pity you feel for those still caught in the coils of the illusion."

"How do you know that? How can you know what I feel when you're not here?"

"I"m always here. I'm you — you as you will be, are, and have been before!"

"Then how come you're here now?" I ask, bewildered.

"I'm here, and also elsewhere. And so are you. We are multi-dimensional beings, yet we are all One!" Androgyne smiles, noting my confusion.

"Thank you," I say. "You have taught me much. But I have one more question. Who am I, if I am you?"

"You are the sum total of your memories — that part of Self that is undying and unborn. A jack-of-all-trades. A woman, a man, a wayfarer, a builder of dreams. A cosmic traveler, you pass through all dimensions simultaneously in a time where there is no time. You're here today, and when this trip is ended, you'll be somewhere else. And now it is time for you to draw the boundaries of the Nina Graboi self around you again. Time to shrink back into the identity of a skin-encapsulated self. I'll be here, but you won't know me. Write down what you learned and share it with others. And remember, there is no ultimate truth!"

And with these words, Androgyne grows faint, and all I see is the string of sparks thrown off by the candle.

www.ingramcontent.com/pod-product-compliance
Lightning Source LLC
Chambersburg PA
CBHW081344230426
43667CB00017B/2711